That God May Be All in All

That God May Be All in All

A Paterology Demonstrating That the Father
Is the Initiator of All Divine Activity

RYAN L. RIPPEE

FOREWORD BY
BRUCE A. WARE

☙PICKWICK *Publications* • Eugene, Oregon

THAT GOD MAY BE ALL IN ALL
A Paterology Demonstrating That the Father Is the Initiator of All Divine Activity

Copyright © 2018 Ryan L. Rippee. All rights reserved. Except for brief quotations in critical publications or reviews, no part of this book may be reproduced in any manner without prior written permission from the publisher. Write: Permissions, Wipf and Stock Publishers, 199 W. 8th Ave., Suite 3, Eugene, OR 97401.

Pickwick Publications
An Imprint of Wipf and Stock Publishers
199 W. 8th Ave., Suite 3
Eugene, OR 97401

www.wipfandstock.com

PAPERBACK ISBN: 978-1-5326-1967-0
HARDCOVER ISBN: 978-1-4982-4615-6
EBOOK ISBN: 978-1-4982-4614-9

Cataloguing-in-Publication data:

Names: Rippee, Ryan L. | Ware, Bruce A. (foreword)

Title: That God may be all in all : a paterology demonstrating that the Father is the initiator of all divine activity / Ryan L. Rippee, with a foreword by Bruce A. Ware

Description: Eugene, OR: Pickwick Publications, 2018 | Includes bibliographical references and index.

Identifiers: ISBN 978-1-5326-1967-0 (paperback) | ISBN 978-1-4982-4615-6 (hardcover) | ISBN 978-1-4982-4614-9 (ebook)

Subjects: LCSH: God—Fatherhood—Biblical teaching | Trinity | God (Christianity) | Theology

Classification: BS544 R46 2018 (print) | BS544 (ebook)

Scripture quotations are from the ESV® Bible (The Holy Bible, English Standard Version®), copyright © 2001 by Crossway, a publishing ministry of Good News Publishers. Used by permission. All rights reserved.

Manufactured in the U.S.A.   02/27/18

I dedicate this work to my family: my parents, Chris and Joni Rippee; my in-laws John and Pam Fernandez; my siblings and in-laws; my nephews and nieces (all twenty-one of them!); and especially my wife, Jennafer, and our children, Gavin, Delaney, Liam, Caedmon, and Ainsley. I love you all very much and am most grateful for your support and patience during these four years. I also want to dedicate this work to the memory of my brother-in-law, Yuri Trebotich, who went home to be with the Lord Jesus in 2016, and whose Spirit-empowered life and example still reflect and point to our Father in heaven.

Contents

Foreword by Bruce A. Ware | ix
Preface | xiii
Abbreviations | xv

1. Introduction | 1
2. The Father's Existence from Eternity Past | 21
3. The Father's Work of Planning All Things from Eternity Past | 59
4. The Father's Work of Creating and Preserving the Heavens and the Earth | 84
5. The Father's Work of Providing Salvation in Redemptive History through the Sending of the Son | 110
6. The Father's Work of Producing Salvation in His Elect and Conviction in the World through the Pouring Out of the Holy Spirit | 133
7. The Father's Work, through the Son and Spirit, of Perfecting Creation and Salvation through Judgment and the Restoration of All Things | 152
8. Worship as a Response to the Father's Work through the Son and Spirit | 174
9. Conclusion | 200

Bibliography | 203
Author Index | 231
Subject Index | 235
Scripture Index | 237

Foreword

HAVE YOU LEARNED TO notice, as you read your Bible, how many Trinitarian indicators there are? That is, do you pay attention to and incorporate into your understanding of Scripture how often divine pronouns and other references to God come in the form of references to one or another Trinitarian Person? Of course, there are several references to the one God who alone is God (e.g., "You believe that God is one. You do well; the demons also believe and shudder" James 2:19). But far more often, if you look carefully, you'll see that most divine pronouns and other divine references (particularly in the New Testament) are not to the one God, *per se*, but rather they refer specifically to one or another Trinitarian person. They are references to God the Father, or to God the Son, or to God the Holy Spirit. Seeing this opens up a vast world of awe and wonder, not to mention deepened theological understanding, than if you had failed to notice these many and frequent Trinitarian indicators.

Think for example of Paul's statement, "In all wisdom and insight He made known to us the mystery of His will, according to His kind intention which He purposed in Him" (Eph 1:8-9). Stop and consider: who are the He's, the Him's and the His's? If you answer that God is the one who had such wisdom and who has made known to us his will and purpose, you would not be wrong, but you would be imprecise. Paul is more specific than this answer would indicate. The clue in this particular text comes for us at the end of v. 9, where Paul speaks of this purpose and intention and will being accomplished "in Him." Who would the "in Him" be here at the end of v. 9? Well, if you look back at the context, you see that Paul has just spoken of redemption that has been accomplished for us through the shed blood of Christ (1:7), and earlier we read that every blessing brought to us comes only "in Christ" (1:3). So, it seems pretty clear that the "in Him" at the end of v. 9 should be understood of as "in Christ." What, then, does this make of the previous He's, and Him's, and His's? Amazingly, these all refer specifically, then, to the Father, whose wisdom, insight, will, intention, and purpose are manifest in the plan he designed for Christ, that through the work of Christ His Son, Christ might have the preeminence in all things (Eph 1:10). So, allow me to offer Eph 1:8-9 again, this time suggesting the Trinitarian specificity that we should understand this passage to be stating: "In all wisdom and insight He [the Father] made known to us the mystery of His [the Father's] will, according to His [the Father's] kind intention which He [the Father] purposed in Him [the Son]" (Eph 1:8-9). Amazing, isn't it. And not only amazing, but glorious, wondrous, and awe-inspiring, that the Father would love and honor his Son so much that he would plan, before the creation of the world (see Eph 1:4) that all of history would unfold, and all of creation participate, in the exalting of his Son above all things.

Yes, Trinitarian specificity matters.

In light of this, it would seem appropriate that special attention would be given in various biblical and theological studies to what the Bible tells us specifically about the person and work of the Father, the person and work of the Son, and the person and work of the Holy Spirit. And sure enough, some of this work has been done and continues to be done. We have, for example, many works through the history of the church on "Christology" where the Bible's teaching on the person and work of the Son as taught in Scripture is unfolded. And at least from the beginning of the twentieth century, many "Pneumatology" studies have been done from Scripture on the doctrine of the person and work of the Holy Spirit.

But what of the Father? What work has been done on biblical and theological teaching from Scripture on the specific person and work of the Father? Although this answer may seem implausible, the answer here is that very little direct attention has been paid to this area of study. Of course, the Father is discussed much through the history of the development of Trinitarian theology, and the special importance of the Father within the Trinity has been well-established. But still, when we ask, what specialized studies have been done to focus our attention on the specific biblical teaching on the person and work of the Father, there is very little available to us throughout all of church history.

In light of this, we owe to Dr. Ryan Rippee a deep expression of gratitude that he has undertaken to provide here a careful and thorough study of the Bible's teaching on the person and work of the Father. This "Paterology" offers to readers a vantage point from which to marvel at the grandeur and glory of the Father, and to see more clearly how the Father's purposes always are to work through the agency of his Son and the Holy Spirit. Not only does the Father's work unite with the Son and Spirit, but his goal always is to see his Son lifted high through the accomplishment of the work given him to do, as assisted always through the power of the Holy Spirit.

Readers of this volume will encounter a feast of glorious truth and wisdom, which cannot help but translate into richer and more precise theological understanding as well as more vibrant worship. Beholding here the glory of the Father, whose person and work are united with the Son and Spirit, is a foretaste of what we will behold in greater splendor in the age to come. But don't wait until then! See now something of that unsurpassable glory through a study of the Father's own self-revelation to us of who he is as the Father who is always with his Son and Spirit. Here then is an invitation to contemplate, worship, pray, and live in renewed ways—to the glory of the Father, through the accomplishment of the Son, and in the power of the Spirit. *Soli Deo Gloria.*

Bruce A. Ware

T. Rupert and Lucille Coleman Professor of Christian Theology
The Southern Baptist Theological Seminary, Louisville, Kentucky

Preface

MY PERSONAL INTEREST IN Paterology began as a research assignment given by my dear friend and mentor, Frank Griffith, while I was taking theology proper in 2005 at The Cornerstone Seminary. He identified a lack of academic studies directed specifically at the first person of the Trinity. As a result of that assignment, my interest steadily increased so that both my pastoral sermon preparation as well as my academic studies often turned in the direction of God the Father. I took the opportunity at the culmination of my M.Div. to devote my Theology in Research class to the subject of Paterology. As a result, it seemed natural to begin my doctoral studies with this topic in mind, and under the guidance of Bruce Ware and Michael Haykin, I have labored to pursue the subject in both a historical and exegetical manner.

I am deeply grateful for those who made this work possible. First and foremost, our triune God ought to receive all of the glory and praise. I thank the Father through our Lord Jesus that by his Spirit I was able to finish this work as well as the doctoral program.

I am also thankful to my family: to my parents, my siblings, my in-laws and especially my beloved wife and children. Each of you is a precious gift from God. I particularly want to thank my dad, Chris Rippee, who read and edited every chapter and who has been one of my biggest encouragers to persevere. My wife, Jennafer, has helped edit and given her gracious feedback through the whole process, as well as praying for me and with me, and has kept me fed and sane!

I am grateful for Calvary Community Church, who have lovingly and financially supported me throughout this entire endeavor, and who I pray has received the firstfruits of my labors in my service to them. I am also grateful for my fellow elders, Frank Griffith, Chris Hunt, and Ryan Pedersen, kindred co-laborers in Christ. My dear brother Mike Moore has also read through my dissertation and given constructive input that has sharpened my thinking improved this book. I must also mention Pastor Wes Wade, a former student and dear friend, who reviewed the extensive footnotes of chapter 2, making sure I made no mistakes with the references to Hebrew names and their combinations.

I finally want to thank each member of my dissertation committee—chair Bruce Ware, James Hamilton, Stephen Wellum, and my external reader John Frame, all of whom have given of their expertise and time to polish my thinking and writing.

Soli Deo Gloria.

Ryan Rippee
Brentwood, California
April 2017

Abbreviations

ANF   *Ante-Nicene Fathers: Translations of the Writings of the Early Fathers Down to A.D. 32.* Edited by Alexander Roberts and James Donaldson. Grand Rapids: Eerdmans, 1974.

BDAG   Walter Bauer, Frederick W. Danker, W. F. Arndt, and F. W. Gingrich. *Greek- English Lexicon of the New Testament and Other Early Christian Literature.* 3rd ed. Chicago: University of Chicago Press, 2000.

CD   Barth, Karl. *Church Dogmatics.* Translated by Geoffrey William Bromiley and Thomas Forsyth Torrance. London: T. & T. Clark, 2004.

EDNT   *Exegetical Dictionary of the New Testament.* Edited by Horst Robert Balz and Gerhard Schneider. Grand Rapids: Eerdmans, 1990.

HALOT   *The Hebrew and Aramaic Lexicon of the Old Testament.* Edited by Ludwig Köhler, Walter Baumgartner, et. al. Leiden: Brill, 1999.

NPNF1   *A Select Library of the Nicene and Post-Nicene Fathers.* Edited by Philip Schaff, Series 1. Grand Rapids: Eerdmans, 1978.

NPNF2   *A Select Library of the Nicene and Post-Nicene Fathers.* Edited by Philip Schaff, Series 2. Grand Rapids: Eerdmans, 1978.

TDNT   *Theological Dictionary of the New Testament.* 10 vols. Edited by Gerhard Kittel and Gerhard Friedrich. Translated by Geoffrey W. Bromiley. Grand Rapids: Eerdmans, 1964–76.

TDOT		*Theological Dictionary of the Old Testament.* 14 vols. Edited by G. Johannes Botterweck and Helmer Ringgren. Translated by Geoffrey W. Bromiley et al. Grand Rapids: Eerdmans, 1974–2004.
TLOT		*Theological Lexicon of the Old Testament.* 3 vols. Edited by Ernst Jenni and Claus Westermann. Translated by Mark Biddle. Peabody, MA: Hendrickson, 1997.
TWOT		*Theological Wordbook of the Old Testament.* Edited by R. Laird Harris, Gleason L. Archer, and Bruce K. Waltke. Chicago: Moody Press, 1980.
WTT		*Westminster Leningrad Codex.* Philadelphia: Westminster Theological Seminary, n.d.

1

Introduction

SINCE 1975, WHEN NILS Dahl asserted that God is the "neglected factor" in New Testament studies,[1] there has been a resurgence of writing on God the Father, particularly in the Johannine literature.[2] However, most give attention to the *metaphor* of God as Father, rather than directly address the subject of Paterology;[3] that is, the study of the person and work of God the Father. Instead, Paterology has been historically subsumed under Theology Proper, and as such, neglected in favor of studies on the Trinity. Thomas Smail, in his book *The Forgotten Father*, has argued that the neglect of God the Father is also true at the church level:

---

1. Dahl, "Neglected Factor," 5–8. For a more recent argument, see Kim, "Necessity of Rediscovering Patrology," 14–29. Kim rightly identifies a lacuna in past studies, but Kim's reasons for the gap are too simplistic in the reading of church history so as to be compelling. It is a more fruitful study to look at the *biblical reasons* for which Christ-centered theology and Spirit-empowered theology are more common. As I hope to demonstrate in this book, it is because the Father has ordained in this age that the Son be the direct object of the Christian's response to salvation, and that the Spirit be the empowering agent of the Christian's response to salvation.

2. For example, see Meyer, "The Father," 255–73, where he forcefully argues that "everything in the Gospel's presentation of Christ is also a 'presentation' of God." Meyer, "The Father," 256. See also Tolmie, "Characterization of God," 57–75, where, using a narrative approach, Tolmie presents God as the Father, first of Jesus, and then through him, of believers. Finally, see Stibbe, "Telling the Father's Story," 170–93. Stibbe writes that the Gospel of John is not so much about the "life" of Jesus as it is a "life" of God the Father. Köstenberger and Swain have devoted two chapters to the Father in Köstenberger and Swain, *Father, Son, and Spirit*, and Matthew Fisher has written his immensely helpful dissertation on the Gospel of John. First, he examines the Father in an expositional commentary format, and then, synthesizes the material into a Paterology. See Fisher, "God the Father."

3. I have checked numerous academic dictionaries and encyclopedias for the use Paterology versus Patrology for the study of the first person of the Trinity. I have only found one systematic theology that uses the term "Paterology." See Barackman, *Christian Theology*. Therefore, I prefer the term "Paterology" over "Patrology," since academic sources use "Patrology" or "Patriology" as the older term for patristics (the study of the church fathers).

> Indeed when one widens the scope and looks at vital modern Christian movements of any kind, one has to admit that emphasis upon and devotion to the Father has not been a main characteristic of many of them. Evangelicals have been concerned chiefly with Christ the Son, his divine person, his adequate atonement, his real resurrection and have of course not denied, but not made much of the fact that the Son is only the Son because he comes from the Father.
>
> Charismatics on the other hand have often switched the emphasis from the Son to the Spirit as the sovereign source of renewal, power, and spiritual gifts and fruit.[4]

In addition to Smail, John Koessler's work, *God Our Father*, is one of the only other published words devoted completely to the first person of the Trinity.[5] Koessler divides his work evenly between a systematic study of the role, nature, attributes, names, and work of the Father, and the believer's relationship with and response to the Father; however, he limits the Father's works to the broad categories of Creation, Redemption, and Providence.

Recently, Gerald Bray laments,

> If the history of Christian theology had ended in the third century, there would be no doubt that the person and work of the Father would be regarded as its most fundamental feature....
>
> Yet from the standpoint of the modern world, and indeed for many centuries now, the picture looks very different. Books on the work of Christ and the work of the Holy Spirit are easy to find, but who has written anything on the work of the Father, considered as one of the Trinity and not just as a personification of the divine?[6]

Thus, the development of Paterology as a discipline is greatly needed.

---

4. Smail, *Forgotten Father*, 19. Smail gives his purpose in writing: "This book is an attempt to explore the fatherhood of God *theologically* from its place in the gospel, *existentially* in relation to the current renewal in the church and *personally* from the point of view of one whose human need has specially oriented him towards this search for the Father and his family." Ibid., 20. He later explains his thesis: "The thesis of this book is that Christian maturity and holiness are not to be found in a narrow pursuit of charismatic experiences and manifestations in and for themselves, but in the existential rediscovery of Abba Father." Ibid., 45.

5. Koessler, *God Our Father*.

6. Bray, *God Has Spoken*, 206.

Thesis

Through a biblical and exegetical study of the Father's roles and works, this book will argue that within the inseparable operations of the Triune God, the Father is the initiator of all divine activity. This does not mean that God the Son or God the Holy Spirit are inferior, for initiation is a question of order, not rank. Scripture repeatedly affirms that there is one and only one God; that God exists eternally in three distinct persons (Father, Son, and Holy Spirit), and that these persons fully possess the divine essence and attributes.[7] Furthermore, the initiating role of the Father is consistent with inseparable operations. Again, Scripture teaches that there are real distinctions, without ultimate separation, in regard to how the three persons of the Trinity operate. As such, this book will quite often shift the lens from their unity to their uniqueness. Thus, what this book will demonstrate is that within the undivided work of the Triune God, the distinct appropriation of the Father is to be the initiator. In the context of a loving eternal relationship with the Son and Spirit, the Father has planned and purposed all things, creating through the Son and by the Spirit, promising and accomplishing redemption through the sending of the Son and the Spirit, and perfecting salvation by bringing about a new heavens and new earth through his Son and Spirit. Finally, I believe that the role and works of the Father are best discovered through an exegetical study of all the relevant biblical texts rather than beginning with historical, philosophical or theological systems. Nevertheless, because those studies are useful in the formation of theology, I will engage them throughout the discussion.

Background

The Unbegotten God and the Father as the "Fountainhead of Divinity"

The rise of the term "unbegotten" by the church fathers is, by far, the earliest and most significant development in paterological doctrine. Justin Martyr (ca. 100–165) first uses the term in his *Apologia*:

> But to the Father of all, who is unbegotten, a name is not given. For by whatever name He is called, He has as his Elder, the one who gives Him the name. But these words Father, and God, and

---

7. Historically, the teaching that the Son is "consubstantial" (*homoousios*) with the Father was used at the Council of Nicaea and later by Athanasius to defend against the teachings of the Arianism. See Athanasius, *De decretis* V.18–24, and *De synodis* 40–55.

Creator, and Lord and Master, are not names but appellations derived from His good deeds and works.[8]

Gerald Bray argues that what may have begun as a way to distinguish the Father from the Son later became applied to the being of God as a whole under the influence of the word's Platonic origins.[9] Thus Bray concludes, "It took longer for 'unbegotten' to develop to the point where it almost became a title of the Father, but by the fourth century it was being used as the standard designation of his particularity within the Godhead."[10]

The first heresy to arise in connection with the Father came from the modalistic monarchians. Essentially, in saying that the persons of the Godhead were simply modes of the one God, they denied that the Son and Spirit were distinct persons from the Father.[11] In doing so, they believed they were guarding against tritheism. Tertullian (160–220), in his work *Against Praxeas*, articulates their doctrine: "[This position] thinks it impossible to believe in one God unless it says that both Father and Son and Holy Spirit are one and the same."[12] Refuting this position, Tertullian coined the term "Trinity (*trinitas*)" to demonstrate that the way in which God is one (*substantia*) and the way in which God is three (*persona*) belonged in different categories of thinking:

> That they are all of the one, namely by unity of substance, while none the less is guarded the mystery of that economy which disposes the unity into trinity, setting forth Father and Son and Spirit as three, three however not in quality but in sequence, not in substance but in aspect, not in power but in [its] manifestation, yet of one substance and one quality and one power, seeing it is one God from whom those sequences and aspects and manifestations are reckoned out in the name of the Father and the Son and the Holy Spirit.[13]

Thus, by establishing a clear yet inseparable distinction between the one divine substance and the three divine persons, Tertullian demonstrated

---

8. Justin Martyr, *Apologia*, II.6.
9. Bray, *God Has Spoken*, 116.
10. Ibid.
11. Apparently Sabellius identified the Father not merely as the name of the one *hypostasis*, but as equal to the *hypostasis*. The Roman modalists, exemplified by Callistus, taught that the "spirit" made flesh in the womb of Mary was the Father (based on John 14:10). For a thorough discussion of the nuances among modalists, see Heine, "Christology of Callistus," 56–91.
12. Tertullien, *Against Praxeas*, CAP 2, 132.
13. Ibid.

that the Father was a person, as was the Son and Spirit, not merely a personification of the divine essence.[14]

Origen (184/185–253/254) is important for two more related developments in the doctrine of God the Father. First, he identified the Father as the "fountain of deity,"[15] connecting the Father with the divine substance in a way different than the Son or Spirit, for in Origen's thinking, they derived their substance from the Father.[16] Because of this, Origen argued that only the Father is *autotheos* (God of himself).[17] According to Peter Widdicombe, Origen's motive was to balance the truth of the Son's real existence as a distinct person as well as his full participation in the divine nature.[18] The second development is brought out by Robert Letham:

> Confusion reigned [in Origen's day] about the meanings of created (*genetos*) and uncreated (*agenetos*), and begotten (*gennetos*) and unbegotten (*agennetos*). In this linguistic and conceptual mire, Origen makes a crucial distinction between God uncreated (*agenetos*), applicable to all three persons, and God unbegotten (*agennetos*), only to be said of the Father.... Origen ... distinguishes them, enabling the Son's begottenness to be understood in the sphere of deity, so paving the way for greater clarity in the next century through Athanasius.[19]

Thus, Origen lays the foundation for the priority of the Father in the Godhead as "fountain" and "unbegotten," while maintaining the full equality of the Trinitarian person as "uncreated."

The Father's Eternal Generation of the Son

Though the Arian heresy of the fourth century was not a direct attack on the person of God the Father, it forced the church fathers like Athanasius (ca. 296–373) to clarify that the Son is everything that the Father is with

---

14. For a further discussion of these issues, see Holmes, *Quest for the Trinity*, 69–73.
15. Origen, *On First Principles*, 1.3.7 and *John*, 2.3.20.
16. Origen, *On First Principles*, 1.2.13.
17. Origen, *John*, 2.2.17. Bray highlights Origen's exegetical reasons from John 17:3: "To support this interpretation Origen relied on two arguments. First, he said that John made a clear distinction between 'God' with the definite article (*ho theos*), which he used to refer to the God of the Old Testament, and 'God' without the article (*theos*), which he used of the Word (*logos*) or Son. Second, Origen quoted the words of Jesus, which he believed supported his interpretation." Bray, *God Has Spoken*, 119.
18. Widdicombe, *Fatherhood of God*, 85–86.
19. Letham, *Holy Trinity*, 107.

one exception; he is not the Father.[20] For Athanasius, eternal generation is not only the notion that the Father gives life to the Son, but also one of relational participation among the persons of the Trinity,[21] strengthening the belief that the Father has always been the Father and the Son has always been the Son.[22] Further, for Athanasius, and the later Pro-Nicene church fathers, eternal generation had no correspondence to human generation (the misunderstanding of Arius and his followers); rather, eternal generation expressed the unity of the divine nature. Thus, eternal generation answered two important questions: (1) What is the *origin* of the persons? The unbegotten Father. (2) What is the *distinction* between the persons? The irreversible Father/Son relation marked by the Son's eternal relation of subsistence from the Father.

The Procession of the Spirit from the Father

Among other important contributions, the Cappadocians were instrumental in the defense of the Holy Spirit's full deity. Basil the Great (330–379), on the Spirit's relation to the Father, writes, "He is moreover said to be 'of God;' not indeed in the sense in which 'all things are of God,' but in the sense of proceeding out of God, not by generation, like the Son, but as Breath of His mouth."[23] Elaborating upon this distinction, Basil's brother Gregory of Nyssa (ca. 335/340–394/400) emphasized the irreversible taxis within the Godhead "from the Father, through the Son to the Holy Spirit,"[24] which, nonetheless, maintained full equality between the three persons of the Trinity who coeternally and mutually indwell one another.[25]

---

20. Athanasius, *Statement of Faith*, 2. "Neither is the Father the Son, nor the Son the Father. For the Father is the Father of the Son, and the Son, Son of the Father." See also *Four Discourses*, 1:20–21. For studies that deal with the theological development of the fourth century, see Ayres, *Nicaea and Its Legacy*, and Hanson, *The Search for the Christian Doctrine of God*.

21. Athanasius, *Four Discourses*, 5:14. See Widdicombe, *Fatherhood of God*, 3, and Kovach and Schemm, "A Defense of the Doctrine of the Eternal Subordination of the Son," 466.

22. Athanasius, *Letters to Serapion*, 4.6.
23. Basil of Caesarea, *On the Spirit*, 18.46.
24. Gregory of Nyssa, *Against Eunomius*, 1.36.
25. Ibid.

The Divine Monarchy

Interestingly, for Gregory of Nazianzus (ca. 329–390), though the monarchy of God is a fundamental component of his theology, balances the tension between the Father's primacy as the causal source of the Son and Spirit:

> How then are They not alike unoriginate, if They are coeternal? Because They are from Him, though not after Him. For that which is unoriginate is eternal, but that which is eternal is not necessarily unoriginate, so long as it may be referred to the Father as its origin. Therefore in respect of Cause They are not unoriginate; but it is evident that the Cause is not necessarily prior to its effects, for the sun is not prior to its light. And yet They are in some sense unoriginate, in respect of time, even though you would scare simple minds with your quibbles, for the Sources of Time are not subject to time.[26]

Yet, for Gregory, the divine monarchy belongs not to the Father alone, but to the entire Godhead:

> When then we look at the Godhead, or the First Cause, or the Monarchia, that which we conceive is One; but when we look at the Persons in Whom the Godhead dwells, and at Those Who timelessly and with equal glory have their Being from the First Cause—there are Three Whom we worship.[27]

From this Thomas Noble has argued that Gregory wants the monarchy to be the whole Trinity, but also among the persons, Gregory wants to preserve the priority of the Father.[28] Furthermore, Christopher Beeley contends, "The monarchy of God the Father—his unique identity as the 'only source' and 'sole principle' of the Trinity—figures prominently in each of Gregory's major doctrinal statements and proves to be the most fundamental element of his theological system."[29] Because of this, Beeley concludes,

> For Gregory, as for any Nicene theologian, there is no unity and equality in the Trinity—and there is no Trinity—if the Father does not convey his Divinity to the Son and the Spirit by generating them; and there is no sense of causality and ordered hierarchy in the Trinity except the one by which the Father produces the Son and the Spirit as full partakers in his Divinity and thus

---

26. Gregory Nazianzen, "Oration 29.3."
27. Gregory Nazianzen, "Oration 31.14."
28. Noble, "Paradox in Gregory," 97.
29. Beeley, "Divine Causality," 206–7.

ontological equals. Gregory would firmly reject the suggestion that the Father set the Trinity in motion (as if previously), and now that it is up and running, the ordered structure of the relations of origin somehow fades into the background, leaving a purely reciprocal, "perichoretic" exchange of Divinity.[30]

Thus, the divine monarchy rightly understood upholds monotheism, balancing the full equality of the persons while upholding the one divine rule with the Father the "first cause."

Filioque and Inseparable Operations

Augustine (354–430) made two important contributions to paterological studies. First, he taught that the Holy Spirit proceeds jointly from the Father *and the Son*:

> And as to be the gift of God in respect to the Holy Spirit, means to proceed from the Father; so to be sent, is to be known to proceed from the Father. Neither can we say that the Holy Spirit does not also proceed from the Son, for the same Spirit is not without reason said to be the Spirit both of the Father and of the Son.[31]

Yet, Augustine clarifies the proper order of this dual procession:

> Yet He [Jesus] did not say [in John 15:26], Whom the Father will send from me, as He said, "Whom *I* will send unto you from the Father,"—showing, namely, that the Father is the beginning (*principium*) of the whole divinity, or if it is better so expressed, deity. He, therefore, who proceeds from the Father and from the Son, is referred back to Him from whom the Son was born (*natus*).[32]

Thus, Ayres concludes, "The Father's *monarchia*, his status as *principium* and *fons*, is central to Augustine's trinitarian theology. . . . For Augustine, the Father's status as *principium* is eternally exercised through his giving the fullness of divinity to the Son and Spirit such that the unity of God will be eternally found in the mysterious unity of the *homoousion*."[33]

---

30. Ibid., 212–13.
31. Augustine, *On the Trinity*, 4.29.
32. Ibid., 3:85.
33. Ayres, *Augustine and the Trinity*, 248.

Augustine's second contribution is found in his articulation of the doctrine of inseparable operations: "although the Father, and the Son, and the Holy Spirit, as they are indivisible, so work indivisibly. This is also my faith, since it is the Catholic faith."[34] Keith Johnson, remarking on Augustine's statements, says, "That the divine persons act inseparably *ad extra* according to their relative properties *ad intra* is an assumption Augustine shares not only with the entire Latin pro-Nicene tradition, but also with the Greek-speaking theologians of the East (e.g., the Cappadocians)."[35] Augustine's concern was to make sure that the Son and the Spirit are not seen as inferior to the Father, for though the Father is *principium*, the power that is exerted in the working of either the Father, Son or Spirit is done from the indivisible divine nature.

Perhaps this is why studies on the Father's works are absent throughout church history. If the Father always initiates, then, for some, there is an implication that the Son and Spirit are essentially inferior, or that the Father is God in a way that the Son and Spirit are not. Nonetheless, Bray summarizes the paterological developments in the early church:

> To this day, the classical creeds begin, "I believe in God the Father, the Almighty, Maker of heaven and earth (and of all things visible and invisible)." And despite more than seventeen centuries of theological development, that remains all that most Christians ever confess about the Father as a person in his own right![36]

"Relation" as the Principle of Difference

Throughout the Middle Ages, not one single written work is devoted to the person and work of God the Father. In fact, by the time of Thomas Aquinas (1225–74), his *Summa Theologia* emerges as a pattern for the systematic study of God in theological textbooks.[37] As a result, it is impossible to

---

34. Augustine, *On the Trinity*, 1.7.

35. Johnson, "Trinitarian Agency," 121. See also Claunch, "What God Hath Done Together," 781–800,

36. Bray, *God Has Spoken*, 163. In n. 50, Bray reflects, "It cannot really be said, for example, that the Reformation confessions or the decrees of the Roman Catholic 'ecumenical' councils have got much beyond this."

37. Letham, *Holy Trinity*, 4. Letham describes the pattern: "In part 1 of *Summa Theologia*, he discusses the existence and attributes of God in questions 1–25, turning to the Trinity only in questions 27–43." Only one question is devoted to God the Father (Part 1, q.33).

separate Aquinas's theology of God the Father from his Trinitarian theology.[38] Aquinas is perhaps best known in Trinitarian discussions for advancing the idea of "relation" as the primary principle of difference between the divine persons. He wrote,

> Some, then, considering that relation follows upon act have said that the divine hypostases are distinguished by origin, so that we may say that the Father is distinguished from the Son, inasmuch as the former begets and the latter is begotten. . . .
> This opinion, however, cannot stand—for two reasons. Firstly, because, in order that two things be understood as distinct, their distinction must be understood as resulting from something intrinsic to both. . . . Now origin of a thing does not designate anything intrinsic, but means the way from something, or to something; as generation signifies the way to a thing generated, and as proceeding from the generator. . . . Whence, since the persons agree in essence, it only remains to be said that the persons are distinguished from each other by the relations. Secondly, because the distinction of the divine persons is not to be so understood as if what is common to them all is divided, because the common essence remains undivided; but the distinguishing principles themselves must constitute the things which are distinct. . . .
> It is therefore better to say that the persons or hypostases are distinguished rather by relation than by origin. For, although in both ways they are distinguished, nevertheless in our mode of understanding they are distinguished chiefly and firstly by relations; whence this name *Father* signifies not only a property, but also the hypostasis; whereas this term *Begetter* or *begetting* signifies property only; forasmuch as this name *Father* signifies the relation which is distinctive and constitutive of the hypostasis; and this term *Begetter* or *Begotten* signifies the origin which is not distinctive and constitutive of the hypostasis.[39]

Contrary to Origen, then, Aquinas denies that the Son and Spirit are dependent upon the Father for their being. In doing so, he is concerned to demonstrate that the Son and Spirit are not subordinate to the Father in their essence. For Aquinas, because procession does not require dependence

---

38. John Ku attempts to do exactly this in Ku, *God the Father*. He uses q.33 as an organizing structure for his work, using Aquinas's three "notions," or identifying characteristics of the Father: (1) innascibility (the Father has no origin), (2) paternity (the Father's relation to the Son), and (3) spiration (the Father's relation with the Son to the Holy Spirit).

39. Aquinas, *Summa Theologica*, I, q. 40, a. 2 corp.

or subordination, the essence does not beget another essence, but rather, the Father eternally begets the Son. Thus, Aquinas undermines Origen's belief that only the Father is *autotheos*.[40]

The Advancement of Exegetical Studies Typified by Calvin and Owen

Throughout his ministerial life, John Calvin (1509-64) faced a number of Trinitarian controversies. He was forced to defend and define his doctrine due to a number of men in and around Geneva, who either accused him of heresy or promoted their own anti-Trinitarian views.[41] The disputes were mainly focused on the issue of the "eternal generation of the Son,"[42] and therefore led Calvin to emphasize the unity of the Godhead in his ministry and writing.[43] For Calvin, this was simply continuity with the pro-Nicene Fathers[44] and their doctrine of inseparable operations.[45] Calvin's approach, however, was vastly different. Rather than beginning with philosophical

---

40. See Durand's discussion in Durand, "Theology of God the Father," 375-76.

41. Most notable were the controversies with Pierre Caroli in 1537, Michael Servetus in 1546, Giovanni Valentino Gentile in 1556-57, and Giorgio Blandrata in 1558. For a summary of the theological issues and responses, see Helm, *John Calvin's Ideas*, 40-44; Greef and Bierman, *Writings of John Calvin*, 159-67; Barth and Bromiley, *Theology of John Calvin*, 341-42; and Van den Belt, *Restoration Through Redemption*, 17-22.

42. For a history of various interpretations of Calvin's position, see Swinburnson, "John Calvin," 26-49. See also Richardson, "Calvin on the Trinity," 32-42; Ellis, *Calvin*, and Barth and Bromiley, *Theology of John Calvin*.

43. Karl Barth argued that emphasis on the *unity* of the Godhead was true of all the reformers: "The reformers undoubtedly tended to stress the unity rather than the distinction in God, as we see plainly in Calvin." Barth and Bromily, *Theology of John Calvin*, 327.

44. There has been recent discussion on the main influence of Calvin's Trinitarian theology, particularly whether it was Augustinian or Cappadocian. The writings of Warfield and Helm argue that the main influence is Augustine, while Torrance argues for Gregory of Nazianzus. For an in-depth investigation, see Slotemaker, "John Calvin's Trinitarian Theology," 781-810. For Calvin's consistency with the Nicene and Constantinople creeds, see Owen, "Calvin and Catholic Trinitarianism," 262-81.

45. Colin Gunton, a critic of inseparable operations and Augustinian Trinitarianism, pits the Eastern emphasis on the three persons of the Trinity against the Western emphasis on the unity of the Trinity. See Gunton, *The One, the Three, and the Many*. Arie Baars, building on Gunton's premise, believes that Calvin modified Augustine's doctrine. See Baars, "Opera Trinitatis Ad Extra Sunt Indivisa," 131-41. Kyle Claunch, on the other hand, holds that pro-Nicene Fathers from both East and West embraced the Nicene Creed and Gunton's East vs. West paradigm is to be rejected. Claunch also concludes, contra Baars, that Calvin embraced Augustine's doctrine of inseparable operations. See Claunch, "What God Hath Done Together," 781-800.

discussion of terminology, his *Institutes* begin with biblical exposition. In doing so, Calvin maintained the earlier teaching that the united work of the Trinity also included particular actions in the economy of salvation[46] that could be distinctly appropriated to a particular person of the Godhead.[47] Thus, Calvin argued that the appropriation attributed to the Father is one of initiation and beginning of activity:

> It is not fitting to suppress the distinction that we observe to be expressed in Scripture. It is this: to the Father is attributed the beginning of activity, and the fountain and wellspring of all things; to the Son, wisdom, counsel, and the ordered disposition of all things; but to the Spirit is assigned the power and efficacy of that activity. Indeed, although the eternity of the Father is also the eternity of the Son and the Spirit, since God could never exist apart from his wisdom and power, and we must not seek in eternity a before and after, nevertheless the observance of an order is not meaningless or superfluous, when the Father is thought of first, then from him the Son, and finally from both the Spirit.[48]

Likewise, Robert Letham argues that John Owen's (1616–83) Trinitarianism "is classic and orthodox in the Western sense but he avoids some of its problems. One of the ways he achieves this is by his overwhelmingly Biblical approach; there is a remarkable absence of philosophical terminology, a profusion of Biblical exegesis."[49] Whereas John Calvin highlighted the unity of the Godhead in his ministry and writing, Owen distinguished himself by continually meditating on the diversity of persons within the

---

46. For a thorough discussion of the relationship between the immanent and economic Trinity in Calvin's thought, see Helm, *John Calvin's Ideas*, 46–50, and also Ngien, *Gifted Response*, 137–38.

47. Sometimes called "distinct personal appropriations." For example, even though all three persons of the Trinity were at work in the incarnation, only the person of the Son became incarnate. For a discussion on Calvin's nuance of inseparable operations and distinct personal appropriations, see Doyle, "Basic Expectations," 151–74. Baars does seem to have read Calvin rightly when he says, "In Calvin's opinion the external works of the triune God are only undivided *intrinsically*. When we consider these works *extrinsically*—i.e. as God reveals himself in these works to *us*—it is quite possible for us to distinguish between the special activity of the Father, the Son, and the Holy Spirit. Nevertheless, these distinct operations of the three persons remain the work of the one and only triune God!" Baars, "Opera Trinitatis," 134.

48. Calvin, *Institutes*, 1:13.18.

49. Letham, "John Owen's Doctrine of the Trinity," 190.

Godhead,[50] with the contrast being one of emphasis, not difference, and never at the expense of divine unity.

An example of this pattern can be seen in *Communion with God*. Owen outlines the book using the Trinity, and in chapter 3 writes about each person in the Godhead's respective works:

> There is a concurrence of the *actings* and operations of the whole Deity in that *dispensation*, wherein each person concurs to the work of our salvation, unto every *act* of our communion with each singular person. ... [For example], suppose it to be the act of faith:—It is bestowed on us by the Father: "It is not of yourselves: it is the gift of God." Eph. 2:8. It is the Father that revealeth the gospel, and Christ therein, Matt. 11:25. And it is purchased for us by the Son: "Unto you it is given in the behalf of Christ, to believe on him," Phil. 1:29. ... And it is wrought in us by the Spirit; he administers that "exceeding greatness of his power" which he exerciseth towards them who believe, "according to the working of his mighty power, which he wrought in Christ, when he raised him from the dead." Eph. 1:19, 20; Rom. 8:11 [emphasis original].[51]

---

50. Letham writes, "[Owen's] focus on the three persons was and is missing from the West in general." Letham, "John Owen's Doctrine of the Trinity," 196. According to Dale Stover, Owen's emphasis went too far and was a danger to the theology of a unified Triune God. Stover, "The Pneumatology of John Owen," 304. Kapic, however, argues against Stover's conclusion and writes, "Against the charge of Stover, Owen's Trinitarian emphasis on the distinct roles of the three divine persons does not weaken his Christology, but actually may be understood as strengthening it. This will quickly become apparent in the emphasis he gives to communion with the Son in his book *Communion with God*. Christ is the mediator between God and humanity, and only through him are relations between the divine and human secure." Kapic, *Communion with God*, 32–33.

51. Owen, *Works*, 2:18. Likewise in his *Discourse Concerning the Holy Spirit* he writes, "The beginning of divine operations is assigned unto the Father, as he is *fons et origo Deitatis*,—'the fountain of the Deity itself:' 'Of him, and through him, and to him, are all things,' Rom. 11:36. The subsisting, establishing, and 'upholding of all things,' is ascribed unto the Son: 'He is before all things, and by him all things consist,' Col. 1:17. As he made all things with the Father, so he gives them a consistency, a permanency, in a peculiar manner, as he is the power and wisdom of the Father. He 'upholdeth all things by the word of his power,' Heb. 1:3. And the finishing and perfecting of all these works is ascribed to the Holy Spirit, as we shall see. I say not this as though one person succeeded unto another in their operation, or as though where one ceased and gave over a work, the other took it up and carried it on; for every divine work, and every part of every divine work, is the work of God, that is, of the whole Trinity, inseparably and undividedly: but on those divine works which outwardly are of God there is an especial impression of the order of the operation of each person, with respect unto their natural and necessary subsistence, as also with regard unto their internal characteristical properties, whereby we are distinctly taught to know them and adore them." Owen, *Works*, 3:94–95.

For Owen then, the beginning of any divine work is assigned to the Father, which he accomplishes through the agency of the Son, and the completion of any divine work is accomplished by the Spirit, who is the power and wisdom of the Father. Owen does not mean that each person of the Trinity takes turns in their part, but rather, that there exist true inseparable operations with distinct appropriations fitting to the Trinitarian *taxis*.

The General Neglect of the Father in the Modern Period

Unfortunately, the rise of systematic theology after Aquinas and Calvin has not produced any works devoted to the first person of the Trinity. In the nineteenth century, not one theology contains a separate discussion of God the Father.[52] Up to the present day, Berkhof limits the entirety of his discussion to a paragraph:

> *The opera ad extra ascribed more particularly to the Father.* All the *opera ad extra* of God are works of the triune God, but in some of these works the Father is evidently in the foreground, such as: (1) Designing the work of redemption, including election, of which the Son was Himself an object, Ps. 2:7–9; 40:6–9; Isa. 53:10; Matt. 12:32; Eph. 1:3–6. (2) The works of creation and providence, especially in their initial stages, I Cor. 8:6; Eph. 2:9. (3) The work of representing the Trinity in the Counsel of Redemption, as the holy and righteous Being, whose right was violated, Ps. 2:7–9; 40:6–9; John 6:37, 38; 17:4–7) [emphasis original].[53]

The vast majority of theologies do not dedicate a separate chapter or section on God the Father,[54] with the only notable exception being Floyd Barackman's *Practical Christian Theology*. Barackman has a separate chapter (11 pages) entitled "Paterology," in which he covers (1) the Father's nature, (2) the Father's relationship with the other persons of the Trinity, the

---

52. For example, see Dabney, *Systematic Theology*; A. A. Hodge, *Outlines of Theology*; Charles Hodge, *Systematic Theology*; Shedd, *Dogmatic Theology*; and Strong, *Systematic Theology*.

53. Berkhof, *Systematic Theology*, 91.

54. For example, see Bancroft, *Elemental Theology*; Bavinck, *Reformed Dogmatics*, vol. 2; Barth, *CD* 2/1–2; Bloesch, *God, the Almighty*; Boice, *Foundations of the Christian Faith*; Bray, *Doctrine of God* and Bray, *God Has Spoken*; Brunner, *Dogmatics*; Buswell, *Systematic Theology*; Chafer, *Systematic Theology*—though he does have a chapter devoted to the metaphor of Father; Erickson, *Christian Theology*; Grudem, *Systematic Theology*; Horton, *Christian Faith*; McGrath, *Christian Theology*; Oden, *Systematic Theology*, vol. 1; Reymond, *Systematic Theology*; and Thiessen, *Systematic Theology*.

universe, and his people, (3) the Father's works (creation and governance are covered elsewhere, so Barackman devotes this section to the salvation of the elect, and the Father's role in the Messianic works), (4) the Father's location, (5) the Father's names, and (6) our interaction with God the Father as his children-sons (contains the largest section of material in the chapter).[55] Finally, one dissertation stands out. Matthew Fisher has written his immensely helpful dissertation at Southeastern Baptist Theological Seminary on the Gospel of John; first, examining the Father in an expositional commentary format, and then, synthesizing the material into a Paterology.[56]

The Modern Subordination Controversy

In the last four decades, most monographs dedicated to God the Father are concerned with the metaphor of Father, rather than his person and work.[57] However, a debate has emerged among evangelicals concerning the Father's role among the Trinity, particularly regarding the nature of his authority over the Son and Spirit; that is, how the Father relates to God the Son and God the Holy Spirit. Some (e.g., Gilbert Bilezikian, Millard Erickson, Kevin Giles, Tom McCall) would limit the Father's role to the economy of salvation, while others (e.g., Wayne Grudem, Bruce Ware, Robert Letham, J. Scott Horrell, Andreas Köstenberger) would affirm that the submission of the Son and Spirit to the Father have their basis in the eternal relationships of the immanent Trinity. Several articles have been written on both sides of the debate, very often in connection with the egalitarian vs. complementarian dispute,[58] along with a number of monographs dedicated to the issue.

55. Barackman, *Christian Theology*, 129–40.
56. See Fisher, "God the Father."
57. Smail devotes the beginning of his book to the metaphor of God as Father in Smail, *Forgotten Father*. For recent academic treatments of the metaphor of Father, see Marianne Meye Thompson, *Promise of the Father*; chap. 2 in Witherington and Ice, *Shadow of the Almighty*; Chen, *God as Father in Luke-Acts*; and Mengestu, *God as Father*. For a historical study, see Widdicombe, *Fatherhood of God*.
58. For those advocating a temporary authority/submission relationship, see Bilezikian, "Hermeneutical Bungee-Jumping," 57–68, Giles, "Doctrine of the Trinity," 19–24, Giles, "The Evangelical Theological Society," 323–38, Giles, "Response to Michael Bird and Robert Shillaker," 237–56, and most recently Geis, "The Trinity and the Eternal Subordination," 23–28. For those advocating an eternal authority/submission relationship, see Letham, "The Man-Woman Debate," 65–78, Kovach and Schemm, "A Defense of Eternal Subordination," 461–76, Ware, "Tampering with the Trinity," 1–17, Letham and Giles, "Is the Son Eternally Submissive," 11–21, Bird and Shillaker, "Subordination in the Trinity," 267–83, Ware, "Christian Worship," 28–42, and Ware and Starke, *One God in Three Persons*.

In 2002, Kevin Giles wrote *The Trinity and Subordinationism: The Doctrine of God and the Contemporary Gender Debate* in order to refute the conservative evangelical case for permanent subordination of women, devoting a third of the book to the denunciation of the eternal subordination of the Son in role and authority to the Father. He primarily argues his case from church history.

In 2005, Bruce Ware authored *Father, Son and Holy Spirit: Relationships, Roles and Relevance*. In it, he argues that what distinguishes the Father from the Son and Spirit is his particular role within the Trinity and the relationships he has with the other persons of the Godhead.[59] Ware then examines "four distinguishing aspects of the Father's role and relationships,"[60] including (1) The Father as supreme among the persons of the Godhead, (2) the Father as the architect and designer of creation, redemption, and consummation, (3) The Father as the giver of every good and perfect gift, and (4) The Father often providing and working through the Son and Spirit. In his chapter on the Son, he briefly mentions the authority/submission debate in his section entitled, "The Son's submission to the Father in eternity past."[61]

Kevin Giles wrote another work dedicated specifically to the subordination debate in 2006. Titling the work *Jesus and the Father: Modern Evangelicals Reinvent the Doctrine of the Trinity*, Giles wrote it as a warning to fellow evangelicals whom he is convinced teach Trinitarian doctrine that is "contrary to the most fundamental teaching of the New Testament and to what the best theologians of the past and present tell us is orthodoxy."[62] After an overview of the current situation and church history, Giles devotes an entire chapter to the scriptural statements about the Trinity (chp. 3), dedicating the remainder of the work to the historical arguments for his position.

In 2009, Millard J. Erickson presented his analysis of the disagreement in *Who's Tampering with the Trinity? An Assessment of the Subordination Debate*. He says, "My aim here has been to investigate as thoroughly and fairly as possible the alternative positions on the subject before attempting to decide which is the more adequate theory."[63] Defining those who hold to an eternal hierarchy as the "gradational view" and those who hold to a temporary hierarchy as the "equivalence view," he ultimately argues that the

---

59. See chap. 3 in Ware, *Father, Son, and Spirit*.
60. Ibid., 46.
61. Ibid., 76.
62. Giles, *Jesus and the Father*, 9.
63. Erickson, *Who's Tampering with the Trinity*, 11.

equivalence view is the more plausible view based upon biblical, historical, philosophical, theological, and practical considerations.

In 2010, Thomas McCall wrote *Which Trinity? Whose Monotheism? Philosophical and Systematic Theologians on the Metaphysics of Trinitarian Theology*, in which he devotes chapter 6 to the philosophical critique of "eternal functional subordination." Believing that this view should be resisted by everyone who upholds orthodoxy, McCall argues that those who assert an eternal functional submission of the Son to the Father have denied the *homoousion* of Nicene orthodoxy, granting to the Father and Son different essences.[64]

In 2012, Dennis W. Jowers and H. Wayne House edited a collection of papers from both sides of the debate into the book, *The New Evangelical Subordinationism? Perspectives on the Equality of God the Father and God the Son*. The goal was to "propose a multitude of arguments for and against the notion that the Son *qua* divine eternally submits to the authority of his Father."[65]

In 2015, Bruce Ware and John Starke edited a collection of essays in the book, *One God in Three Persons: Unity of Essence, Distinction of Persons, Implications for Life*. In it, the contributors address the eternal relationships of authority and submission within the Godhead from biblical, historical, theological, and philosophical disciplines.

Finally, in 2016, Michael Ovey wrote *Your Will be Done: Exploring Eternal Subordination, Divine Monarchy and Divine Humility*. As a response to the charge of Arianism, as well as broader discussions in Trinitarian theology, Ovey argues that eternal subordination in relations (but not in being) preserves the divine monarchy and monotheism, meaning that within the Trinity there are asymmetrical personal relationships concerning the divine attributes of power and love. Consequently, Ovey also responds to the charge of monothelitism, arguing that an orthodox understanding of dyothelitism in the incarnate Son does not conflict with the Son's eternal subordination of relation to his Father.

The Present Work

My contribution to the doctrine of Paterology is a thorough biblical and exegetical study of role and works of God the Father from eternity past to eternity future. Not only will I demonstrate that the Father is the initiator of every divine action, but I also will contribute to the present subordination debate by suggesting that the authority of the Father is *initiating* authority

---

64. McCall, *Which Trinity*, 179.
65. Jowers and House, *New Evangelical Subordinationism*, xxi.

complementary to the divine *taxis*, rather than *superior* authority, which would make the Son and Spirit inferior. Furthermore, I do not want to lose sight of the fact that this book on God the Father is not so much an intellectual exercise as it is an exposition of the character of a person. Because theology ought to be put into practice, piety is the only proper response to the study of God the Father, and this Paterology ought to be written for the benefit of the church.

Method

In order to determine the relevant biblical passages for study, chapter 2 will examine every use of θεός, κύριος, and πατήρ in the New Testament to determine when they identify the first person of the Godhead, as well as every nominal (personal pronoun, relative pronoun, article, and divine passive) that refers to God the Father as its antecedent. Since pronouns inherently refer to persons and not the divine nature as such, identifying their use was immensely helpful to establish the use of θεός and κύριος in a given context.

In the biblical quotations, I have in many places, added the words, "the Father," "the Son," "the Spirit," next to "God" or "Lord" in order to clarify which person of the Godhead is being mentioned. By this, I do not intend to convey that "God" and "Father" are identical, nor do I intend to blur the semantic distinctions. Rather, I am identifying from the biblical context which person of the Trinity is referred to by the divine name. Further, I will employ the New Testament's quotations of the Old Testament as a starting point for the examination of the Old Testament names and nominals that indicate God the Father. In doing so, I understand the Old Testament author would not think in categories of "first person," "second person," or "third person." Nor would they think in categories of "Trinity." However, just as it is helpful in Christology to see uses of *Yahweh*, *Elohim*, or *Adonai* in reference to God the Son (e.g., Ps 45:6 quoted in Heb 1:8 or Ps 102:25–27 quoted in Heb 1:10–12), it is helpful to identify uses of *Yahweh*, *Elohim*, and *Adonai* in reference to the Father where possible.

Chapter Summaries

In chapter 2, I argue that within the unity of the Godhead, the Father eternally holds the first place in order among the persons of the Godhead: (1) Within the divine name, the Father possesses the first place within the operational ordering of the personal names (e.g., Father-Son-Spirit), (2) Within the divine nature, the Father occupies the first position of relational order among the divine persons (e.g., unbegotten, eternal generation, eternal procession), (3) Within the divine action, the Father's distinct personal appropriations are always as the initiator, planner and originator.

In chapter 3, I argue that the consistent testimony of Scripture is that the divine decree is designed and planned by God the Father because it is initiated by him. This is based upon three evidences: (1) Scripture defines the decree as the *Father's* wise, eternal, all-inclusive, sovereign plan, (2) the decree is rooted in the Father's love and good pleasure, and (3) specific determinations and allowances in the decree are always attributed to the Father. Nevertheless, the Father planned all things in the context of his eternal, loving Triune relationship with the Son and the Spirit (John 10:38; 14:10, 20; 17:21).

In chapter 4, I argue that the Father sets the stage for the display of the Triune God's glory by creating the heavens and the earth through the agency of his Son (Gen 1:1; John 1:3; 1 Cor 8:6; Col 1:16; Rev 4:11) empowered by the Holy Spirit (Gen 1:2; 2:7; Job 33:4; Pss 33:6; 104:30). Furthermore, the Father preserves and governs his creation through his Son and by his Spirit so that Triune Godhead will receive glory in a Christocentric manner (Eph 1:9–10; Phil 2:10–11). This divine work accomplishes the Father's purposes (Neh 9:6; Heb 1:3; Col 1:17; Rom 8:28). In doing so, I will argue that the Father is the initiator of both creation and providence, which is consistent with the Trinitarian *taxis*. The Father works through the agency of the Son and Spirit, but never vice versa. Furthermore, it is just as glorious for the Son and Spirit to be the divine agents of creation and providence as it is for the Father to begin creation and providence, directing the Son and the Spirit.

In chapter 5, I move on to redemptive history, arguing that after the fall, the Father did not abandon his creation, or his people, but rather, unfolds his plan of redemption by manifesting his presence in the temple and promising a Savior through his prophets (John 5:46; 12:41; Gal 3:8, 17–21; Rom 1:2; 16:26; Titus 2:10). In due time, the Father sent his Son to be a substitutionary sacrifice for sin and the sole focal point for the display of his glory (John 3:16–17; 2 Cor 5:21; Gal 4:4; 1 Tim 2:5). Thus, the Father raised up the Son, and exalted him to his right hand, setting him over all things (Eph 1:22; Phil 2:9; Col 3:1; Rev 1:5).

In chapter 6, I argue that the Father continues his work of salvation by seeking worshipers and drawing his elect to himself through the proclamation of the gospel and the giving of his Holy Spirit (John 6:44, 65). Through the Spirit, the Father unites believers to his Son, causing them to be born again and thus, giving them new life through a new status and a new nature (John 1:12–13; 17:21; Col 1:27; Rom 8:9). The Father will sanctify his children completely through his word and through the Spirit (John 17:17–18; 1 Thess 5:23), conforming them into the image of his Son (1 John 3:2). Furthermore, they are sealed and kept by the Father, and no one will ever snatch them out of his hand or the Son's hand (John 10:28–29), and because of their union with Christ, the Father places them into a new community (1 Cor 12:18, 24) and relates to them as his children in a radically new way (Gal 4:9; Rom 8:14–18; 2 Cor 5:11). On the other hand, those who refuse to believe the gospel and to love the Father are under his wrath and will never know him or eternal life (John 3:36).

In chapter 7, I argue that the Father completes his plan of salvation by sending his Son a second time to gather his elect and raise the dead, bringing them before his judgment seat (1 Thess 4:14; 2 Thess 1:6–7; 2 Cor 4:14; 13:4). There, through the agency of the Son, the Father will righteously judge, giving eternal rewards to his children and eternal punishment to the lost (Rom 14:10, 12). By the Spirit, the Father will make all things new and will dwell on earth to reign, giving his children the consummation of their adoption (Rev 21:1–3). It is then that the Son himself will then hand over all things to the Father, so that the Father will be all in all (1 Cor 15:24–28). Finally, for all eternity, the Father will be continually revealing the incomparable riches of all that he graciously accomplished for his children in and through Christ (Eph 2:7). Thus, they will always be with him and they will worship the triune God (Rev 22:1–3).

In chapter 8, I develop a Trinitarian shaped definition of worship:

> Worship is the Spirit-illumined calling of the saints to *remember* the greatness and goodness of God the Father in the face of Jesus Christ so that they will cultivate Spirit-wrought *submission* in their hearts that draws near to the Father through lordship of the Son and then in turn be commissioned to use their lives in Spirit-empowered *service* for the glory of Christ, to the praise of the Father.

Because the eternal Trinitarian *taxis* informs our worship, I argue that both in this life and for all eternity, everything Christians do should be informed by the Gospel as an explanation of the new covenant, and shaped by the reality of this Christocentric Trinitarianism: from the Father, through the Son, by the Spirit back to the Father, through the Son, by the Spirit.

2

The Father's Existence from Eternity Past

Introduction

GOD THE FATHER HAS existed from eternity past in a loving Triune relationship with the Son and the Spirit. Further, Scripture witnesses to their unity in the divine name, the divine nature, and divine action. In keeping with this truth, William David Spencer has recently argued, "The Persons of the Godhead indwell each other (John 17:21), expressing perfect love and mutual glorification (John 17:1; 23–24), each sharing cooperatively in humanity's creation, redemption, and sanctification."[1] In doing so, Spencer also aims to prove that no person of the Godhead has eternal primacy over the others, and so clarifies his statement with a footnote:

> Even the order in which the Persons of the Trinity are mentioned can be changed according to emphasis in the Bible, as can be seen in 2 Cor 13:13 [most translations have this as 2 Cor 13:14] . . . so no strict protocol of mentioning the Father first as having superior precedence is rigidly maintained.[2]

But does this assertion hold up to the whole testimony of Scripture? In this chapter, contra Spencer, I argue that within the unity of the Godhead, the Father eternally holds the first place of order among the persons of the Godhead: (1) Within the divine name, the Father possesses the first place within the operational ordering of the personal names (e.g., Father-Son-Spirit), (2) Within the divine nature, the Father occupies the first position of relational order among the divine persons (e.g., unbegotten, eternal generation, eternal procession), (3) Within the divine action, the Father's distinct

---

1. Spencer, "Evangelical Statement," 218–19.
2. Ibid., 219n8.

personal appropriations are always as the initiator, planner and originator of all that takes place in creation and redemption.

Thus, the Father's relationships within the Godhead demonstrate that a fixed order exists within the Trinity, such that the Father is always the initiator of divine action.

The Divine Name and the Father's Position

God's name is a means by which he makes himself known. Following Bavinck[3] and Berkhof,[4] I distinguish between the proper names (*nomina propria*) of God and the personal names (*nomina personalia*) of God.[5] The proper names are those revealed by God that designate the divine identity (who God is), that make known the virtues and excellencies of his nature and that can be used of any person among the Godhead. The personal names, on the other hand, are those that distinguish between the persons of the Godhead and are not interchangeable between the persons of the Trinity. God's proper names then are אֱלֹהִים (*Elohim*), יהוה (*Yahweh*), אֲדֹנָי (*Adonai*), θεός, and κύριος, while the personal names are πατήρ (αββα), υἱός, Ἰησοῦς, and τὸ πνεῦμα τὸ ἅγιον.

Starting with the Old Testament, I will consider the proper names *Elohim*, *Yahweh*, and *Adonai*. I then turn to the New Testament use of these Old Testament divine names and confirm that they can be used by any person of the Trinity. From there, I will investigate the New Testament use of the proper names θεός and κύριος, as well as the personal name πατήρ, concluding with an analysis of the Trinitarian *taxis* within the personal names, demonstrating that a fixed order exists among the persons of the Godhead.

---

3. Bavinck, *Doctrine of God*, 88–110.

4. Berkhof, *Systematic Theology*, 47–51.

5. Soulen's recent study on the divine names must be mentioned. In his thorough work, he argues that there are three ways to understand the doctrine of the Trinity through the divine names corresponding to each person of the Trinity. For Soulen, a proper understanding how the divine "name" *Yahweh* relates to the other "names" of God requires restoring *Yahweh* to its "proper place in the infinite economy of trinitarian names." Soulen, *Divine Name*, ix. Soulen discerns three patterns for naming the persons: (1) the *theological pattern* identifies the persons in terms of giving, receiving, and glorification of the divine Name, the unspoken Tetragrammaton, (2) A *christological pattern* of naming that identifies the three persons as the Father, the Son, and the Holy Spirit, and (3) A *pneumatological pattern* of naming that identifies the three persons by using an open-ended variety of ternaries, such as "Love, Lover, Beloved," "God, Word, Breathe." Ultimately, I found Soulen's paradigm (theological, christological, pneumatological) of "divine name and divine names" to be unhelpful for my own categorization of proper and personal names.

Divine Names in the Old Testament

Elohim

"In the beginning, God created the heavens and the earth." With this first line of Scripture and with אֱלֹהִים (*Elohim*)[6] as the first subject, Moses compels his Israelite audience to contemplate the question, "Who is God?" Moses asserts that the God who delivered them out of the hands of the Egyptians and brought them to the foot of Mount Sinai is the one who is the sovereign creator of the whole universe. Although *Elohim* may be used as a general designation for any deity, throughout the rest of Scripture, *Elohim* is often used as a proper name for God. For example, in Psalm 68, David uses *Elohim* no fewer than twenty-six times as the righteous "exult before God" (v. 3), and "sing praises to his name" (v. 4), and as David calls on the kingdoms of the earth to "sing to God" (v. 32) and "ascribe power to God" (v. 34), for he is not just the "God of Israel" (vv. 8, 35), but also the one who "rides the heavens, the ancient heavens" (v. 33). In Isaiah, God calls himself *Elohim* when he says, "For your Maker is your husband, the Lord of hosts is his name; and the Holy One of Israel is your Redeemer, the God [*Elohim*] of the whole earth he is called"[7] (Isa 54:5).

Yahweh

In Genesis 2, Moses reveals another divine name to his audience: יהוה (*Yahweh*).[8] "These are the generations of the heavens and the earth when they were created, in the day that the Lord [*Yahweh*] God [*Elohim*][9] made

---

6. Though it is plural in form, and as such, can refer to foreign deities, when referring to the one supreme deity, it can be treated as a common word for God, which is plural in form but singular in meaning. For an examination of *Elohim*, including its possible origin, see "God, Names of," in *Baker Encyclopedia*, 881–82, and Schmidt, "אֱלֹהִים *'elōhîm* God," in *TLOT*, 115–26.

7. On the origin of *Elohim*, see "God (I)," in *Dictionary of Deities and Demons*, 352–53. If the origin of *Elohim* is from אֵל (*El*), then a notable example of its use as a proper name is seen in Gen 17:1, "When Abram was ninety-nine years old the Lord appeared to Abram and said to him, 'I am God [*El*] Almighty; walk before me, and be blameless.' If the origin of *Elohim* is from אֱלוֹהַּ (*Eloah*), then an example can be seen in Deut 32:15, But Jeshurun grew fat, and kicked; you grew fat, stout, and sleek; then he forsook God [*Eloah*] who made him and scoffed at the Rock of his salvation."

8. For an excellent discussion of the apparent contradiction between the revelation of *Yahweh* for the first time in Exod 6:3 and calling on the "name of the Lord" in Gen 4:26, see Ross, "Did the Patriarchs Know," 323–39.

9. For the *Elohim-Yahweh* combination's use in various phrases beginning with "The Lord [Yahweh], the God [Elohim] of . . . ," see Gen 9:26; 24:3, 7, 12, 27, 42, 48; 28:13;

Exod 3:15, 16, 18; 4:5; 5:1; 7:16; 9:1, 13; 10:3; Num 27:16; Deut 1:11, 21; 4:1; 6:3; 26:5; 29:25 (29:24 in WTT), Josh 7:13, ;19, 20; 8:30; 9:18, 19; 10:40, 42; 13:14, 33; 14:14; 18:3; 22:24; 24:2, 23; Judg 2:12; 4:6; 5:3; 6:8; 11:21, 23; 21:3; Ruth 2:12; 1 Sam 2:30; 10:18; 14:41; 17:45; 20:12; 23:10, 11; 25:32, 34; 2 Sam 5:10; 12:7; 1 Kgs 1:30, 36, 48; 8:15, 17, 20, 23, 25; 11:9, 31; 14:7, 13; 15:30; 16:13, 26, 33; 17:1, 14; 18:36; 19:10, 14; 22:53 [WTT 22:54]; 2 Kgs 2:14; 9:6; 10:31; 14:25; 18:5; 19:15, 20; 20:5; 21:12, 22; 22:15, 18; 1 Chr 15:12, 14; 16:4, 36; 17:24; 22:6; 23:25; 28:4; 29:10, 18, 20; 2 Chr 2:12 [WTT 2:11]; 6:4, 7, 10, 14, 16, 17; 7:22; 11:16; 13:5, 12, 18; 14:4 [WTT 14:3]; 15:4, 12, 13; 19:4; 20:6, 19; 21:10, 12; 24:18, 24; 28:6, 9, 25; 29:5, 10; 30:1, 5, 6, 7, 22; 32:17; 33:16, 18; 34:23, 26, 33; 36:13, 15, 23; Ezra 1:2, 3; 4:1, 3; 6:21; 7:6, 27; 8:28; 9:15; 10:11; Neh 1:5; 9:7; Pss 41:13; 59:5; 72:18; 80:4 [WTT 80:5], 19 [WTT 20]; 84:8 [WTT 84:9]; 88:1 [WTT 88:2]; 89:8 [WTT 89:9]; 106:48, Isa 17:6; 21:10, 17; 24:15; 37:16, 21; 38:5; 45:3; Jer 5:14; 7:3, 21; 9:15; 11:3; 13:12; 15:16; 16:9; 19:3, 15; 21:4; 23:2; 24:5; 25:15, 27; 27:4, 21; 28:2, 14; 29:4, 8, 21, 25; 30:2; 31:23; 32:14, 15;, 36; 33:4; 34:2, 13; 35:13, 17, 18, 19; 37:7; 38:17; 39:16; 42:9, 15, 18; 43:10; 44:2, 7, 11, 25; 45:2; 46:25; 48:1; 50:18; 51:5, 33; Ezek 44:2; Hos 12:5 [WTT 12:6]; Amos 4:13; 5:14, 15, 16, 27; 6:8, 14; Jonah 1:9; Zeph 2:9; Mal 2:16.

For various uses of *Elohim-Yahweh* in parallel or as synonyms, see Gen 7:16; 26:24; 28:21; 32:9 [WTT 32:10]; Exod 3:4; 6:2; 9:28; 18:1; 19:3; Lev 11:45; 18:21; 19:12, 14; 21:6, 8, 12, 21; 22:33; 26:45; Deut 4:35, 39; 26:17; 32:3, Josh 22:16, 22, 34; 24:18, 19, 27; Judg 10:10; 20:18; 1 Sam 2:2, 25; 3:3; 4:4; 6:20; 10:19; 14:45; 2 Sam 3:9; 6:2, 7; 7:24, 26, 27; 10:12; 22:7, 22, 32, 47; 1 Kgs 2:23; 3:5; 8:60; 18:21, 24, 37, 39; 2 Kgs 19:16, 19; 1 Chr 13:10; 14:10; 15:26; 17:20, 22, 26; 19:13; 21:15, 17; 28:2, 9, 12; 2 Chr 5:1; 10:15; 13:10; 18:13, 31; 20:15, 29; 22:7; 24:7, 9; 26:5; 28:24; 30:19; 31:20; 33:13; 34:27; 36:18; Ezra 1:5; 2:68; 3:8; 6:22; 8:35; Neh 5:13; 8:6, Job 1:8, 9; 2:3; Pss 3:7 [WTT 3:8]; 14:2; 18:6 [WTT 18:7], 21 [WTT 22], 31 [WTT 32], 46 [WTT 47]; 24:5; 31:14 [WTT 31:15]; 33:12; 38:15 [WTT 38:16], 21 [WTT 22]; 40:3 [WTT 40:4]; 46:7 [WTT 46:8], 11 [WTT 12]; 47:5 [WTT 47:6]; 48:1 [WTT 48:2], 8 [WTT 9]; 55:16 [WTT 55:17]; 56:10 [WTT 56:11]; 58:6 [WTT 58:7]; 68:16 [WTT 68:17], 26 [WTT 27]; 69:13 [WTT 69:14]; 70:1 [WTT 70:2], 5 [WTT 6]; 84:3 [WTT 84:4], 8 [WTT 9]; 91:2; 92:13 [WTT 92:14]; 94:22; 100:3; 104:33; 116:5; 144:15; 146:2, 10; 147:7, 12; Prov 2:5, Isa 1:10; 25:1, 9; 35:2; 37:17; 40:3, 27, 28; 41:17; 45:5, 18; 48:1, 2; 49:4, 5; 50:10; 51:20; 52:10, 12; 54:5, 6; 55:7; 59:13; 60:19; 61:2, 6, 10; 62:3; 66:9; Jer 5:4, 5; 10:10; 23:36; 24:7; 31:1, 33; 32:27; 50:40; Ezek 34:24; Hos 4:1; 5:4; Joel 2:17; Amos 4:11; Mic 4:2; 6:6, 8; 7:7; Hab 3:18; Zeph 3:2; Hag 1:14; Zech 8:23; 12:5; 13:9; Mal 2:17; 3:14.

For the *Elohim-Yahweh* combination's use in the phrase, "Lord [Yahweh] God [Elohim]," or with a pronoun, e.g., "Lord [Yahweh] my God [Elohim]," see Gen 2:4, 5, 7, 8, 9, 15, 16, 18, 19, 21, 22; 3:1, 8, 9, 13, 14, 21, 22, 23; 27:20; Exod 3:18; 5:3; 6:7; 8:10 [WTT 8:6], 26 [WTT 22], 27 [WTT 23], 28 [WTT 24]; 9:30; 10:7, 8, 16, 17, 25, 26; 15:26; 16:12; 20:2, 5, 7, 10, 12; 23:19, 25; 29:46; 32:11, 27; 34:24, 26; Lev 4:22; 11:44; 18:2, 4, 30; 19:2, 3, 4, 10, 25, 31, 34, 36; 20:7, 24; 23:22, 28, 40, 43; 24:22; 25:17, 38, 55; 26:1, 13, 44; Num 10:9, 10; 15:41; 22:18; 23:21; Deut 1:6, 10, 19, 20, 21, 25, 26, 30, 31, 32, 41; 2:7, 29, 30, 33, 36, 37; 3:3, 18, 20, 21, 22; 4:2, 3, 4, 5, 7, 10, 19, 21, 23, 24, 25, 29, 30, 31, 34, 40; 5:2, 6, 9, 11, 12, 14, 15, 16, 24, 25, 27, 32, 33; 6:1, 2, 4, 5, 10, 13, 15, 16, 17, 20, 24, 25; 7:1, 2, 6, 9, 12, 16, 18, 19, 20, 21, 22, 23, 25; 8:2, 5, 6, 7, 10, 11, 14, 18, 19, 20; 9:3, 4, 5, 6, 7, 16, 23; 10:9, 12, 14, 20, 22; 11:1, 2, 12, 13, 22, 25, 27, 28, 29, 31; 12:1, 4, 5, 7, 9, 10, 11, 12, 15, 18, 20, 21, 27, 28, 29, 31; 13:3 [WTT 13:4], 4 [WTT 5], 5 [WTT 6], 10 [WTT 11], 12 [WTT 13], 16 [WTT 17], 18 [WTT 19]; 14:1, 2, 21, 23, 24, 25, 26, 29; 15:4, 5, 6, 7, 10, 14, 15, 18, 19, 20, 21; 16:1, 2, 5, 6, 7, 8, 10, 11, 15, 16, 17, 18, 20, 21, 22; 17:1, 2, 8, 12, 14, 15, 19; 18:5, 7, 9, 12, 13, 14, 15, 16; 19:1, 2, 3, 8, 9, 10, 14; 20:1, 4, 13, 14, 16, 17, 18; 21:1, 5, 10, 23; 22:5; 23:5 [WTT 23:6], 14 [WTT 15], 18 [WTT 19], 20

the earth and the heavens" (Gen 2:7).[10] Of course, *Yahweh* was known to Israel since he had revealed his name to Moses at the burning bush (Exod 3:14–15). Further, he delivered his chosen people out of the hand of Egypt (Exod 6:7), fed them in the wilderness (Exod 16:12), and dwelt in their midst (Exod 29:45–46) so that "they would know" that God is "*Yahweh*" their God. As such, *Yahweh*, becomes the name *par excellence*, and reveals most intimately who God is, especially to his covenant people, Israel. Thus, God declares, "I am the LORD [*Yahweh*]; that is my name; my glory I give to no other" (Isa 42:8) and will make it known, not only to Israel but also throughout the world:

> For from the rising of the sun to its setting my name will be great among the nations, and in every place incense will be offered to my name, and a pure offering. For my name will be great among the nations, says the LORD of hosts. (Mal 1:11)

Israel's response was to publicly sing, "O LORD [Yahweh], our Lord, how majestic is your name in all the earth" (Ps 8:1, 9), "Ascribe to the LORD the glory due his name" (Pss 29:2; 96:8), and "Your name, O LORD, endures forever, your renown, O LORD, throughout all ages" (Ps 135:13).

What, then, is the difference between the two names? Murray Harris articulates the nuance well:

[WTT 21], 23 [WTT 24]; 24:4, 9, 13, 18, 19; 25:15, 16, 19; 26:1, 2, 3, 4, 5, 10, 11, 13, 14, 16, 19; 27:2, 3, 5, 6, 7, 9, 10; 28:1, 2, 8, 13, 15, 45, 47, 52, 53, 58, 62; 29:6 [WTT 29:5], 10 [WTT 9], 12 [WTT 11], 15 [WTT 14], 18 [WTT 17], 29 [WTT 28]; 30:1, 2, 3, 4, 5, 6, 7, 9, 10, 16, 20; 31:3, 6, 11, 12, 13, 26, Josh 1:9, 11, 13, 15, 17; 2:11; 3:3, 9; 4:5, 23, 24; 8:7; 9:9, 24; 10:19; 14:8, 9; 18:6; 22:3, 4, 5, 19, 29; 23:3, 5, 8, 10, 11, 13, 14, 15, 16; 24:17, 24; Judg 3:7; 6:10, 26; 8:34; 11:24; 1 Sam 7:8; 12:9, 12, 14, 19; 13:13; 15:15, 21, 30; 25:29; 30:6; 2 Sam 7:25; 14:11, 17; 18:28; 24:3, 23, 24; 1 Kgs 1:17; 2:3; 3:7; 5:3 [WTT 5:17], 4 [WTT 18], 5 [WTT 19]; 8:28, 57, 59, 61, 65; 9:9; 10:9; 11:4; 13:6, 21; 15:3, 4; 17:12, 20, 21; 18:10; 2 Kgs 5:11; 16:2; 17:7, 9, 14, 16, 19, 39; 18:12, 22; 19:4, 19; 23:21; 1 Chr 11:2; 13:2; 15:13; 16:14; 17:16, 17; 21:17; 22:1, 7, 11, 12, 18, 19; 24:19; 28:8, 20; 29:1, 16, 20; 2 Chr 1:1, 9; 2:4 [WTT 2:3]; 6:19, 41, 42; 9:8; 13:11; 14:2, 7, 11; 15:9; 16:7; 19:7; 20:20; 26:16, 18; 27:6; 28:5, 10; 29:6; 30:8, 9; 31:6; 32:8, 11, 16; 33:12, 17; 34:8, 33; 35:3; 36:5, 12; Ezra 7:28; 9:5, 8; Neh 8:9; 9:3, 4, 5; 10:34 [WTT 10:35], Pss 7:1, 3; 13:3 [WTT 13:4]; 18:28 [WTT 18:29]; 20:7 [WTT 20:8]; 30:2 [WTT 30:3], 12 [WTT 13]; 35:24; 40:5 [WTT 40:6]; 50:1; 76:11 [WTT 76:12]; 81:10 [WTT 81:11]; 84:11 [WTT 84:12]; 94:23; 99:5, 8, 9; 104:1; 105:7; 106:47; 109:26; 113:5; 122:9; 123:2; 146:5, Isa 7:11; 26:13; 36:7; 37:4, 20; 41:13; 43:3; 48:17; 51:15; 55:5; 60:9; Jer 2:17; 3:13, 21, 22, 23, 25; 5:19, 24; 7:28; 8:14; 13:16; 14:22; 16:10; 22:9; 26:13, 16; 30:9; 31:6, 18; 37:3; 40:2; 42:3, 4, 5, 6, 13, 20,21; 43:1, 2; 50:4, 28; 51:10; Ezek 20:7, 19, 20; 28:26; 34:30; 39:22, 28; Dan 9:10, 13, 14, 20; Hos 1:7; 3:5; 7:10; 12:9; 13:4; 14:1 [WTT 14:2]; Joel 1:14; 2:13, 14, 23, 26, 27; 3:17 [WTT 4:17]; Amos 9:15; Jonah 2:1 [WTT 2:2], 6 [WTT 7]; 4:6; Mic 4:5; 5:4 [WTT 5:3]; 7:10, 17; Hab 1:12; Zeph 2:7; 3:17; Hag 1:12; Zech 6:15; 9:16; 10:6; 11:4; 14:5.

10. In Genesis, wherever the word שֵׁם (*shem*) is associated with God, his name is *Yahweh* (4:26; 12:8; 13:4; 16:13; 21:33; 26:25).

Even when אלהים stands as a virtual proper name equivalent to יהוה, it should not be regarded as identical in sense with יהוה. יהוה is more appropriately used to emphasize the direct and personal character of God's merciful loving relationship with his covenant people and his immediate lordship over nature and history, while אלהים highlights God's transcendence and power as the universal, majestic, eternal God who created the world and rules and judges it in righteousness.[11]

Adonai

In Genesis 15, אֲדֹנָי (*Adonai*) is used as a third proper name for God,[12] and is closely tied to both *Elohim*[13] and *Yahweh*.[14] Abraham uses *Adonai* (together

---

11. Harris, *Jesus as God*, 26.

12. To be sure, the singular form אָדוֹן (*adon*) is used more than 300 times for an earthly lord or master. See *HALOT*, 12.

13. For the *Elohim-Adonai* combination's use in various phrases beginning with "The Lord [*Adonai*], the God [*Elohim*] of . . ." see Gen 24:12, 27, 42, 48. For various uses of the *Elohim-Adonai* combination in parallel or as synonyms, see Pss 35:23; 40:17 [WTT 40:18]; 54:4 [WTT 54:6]; 68:17 [WTT 68:18], 32 [WTT 33]; Dan 9:17, 19. For the *Elohim-Adonai* combination's use in the phrase, "Lord [*Adonai*] God [*Elohim*]," or with a pronoun, e.g., "Lord [*Adonai*] my God [*Elohim*]," see Pss 86:12; 90:17; Dan 9:3, 9, 15.

14. For the *Adonai-Yahweh* combination's use in various phrases beginning with "The Lord [*Adonai*], the God [*Yahweh*] of . . ." see Isa 3:15; 10:16, 23, 24, 33; 19:4; 22:5, 12, 14, 15; 28:22; Jer 2:19; 46:10; 49:5; 50:25, 31; Amos 9:5. For various uses of the *Adonai-Yahweh* combination in parallel or as synonyms, see Exod 4:10; 5:22; 15:17; Josh 3:13; Judg 13:8; 16:28; Neh 8:10; Pss 16:2; 30:8 [WTT 30:9]; 35:22; 38:15 [WTT 38:16]; 71:5; 97:5; 135:5; Isa 1:24; 3:17; 49:14; Lam 2:7, 20; Amos 7:8; Mal 1:14; 3:1. For the *Adonai-Yahweh* combination's use in the phrase, "Lord [*Adonai*] God [*Yahweh*]," or with a pronoun, e.g., "Lord [*Adonai*] my God [*Yahweh*]," see Gen 15:2, 8; Exod 23:17; 34:23; Deut 3:24; 9:26; Josh 7:7; Judg 6:22; 16:28; 2 Sam 7:18, 19, 20, 29; 1 Kgs 2:26; 8:53; Pss 68:20 [WTT 68:21]; 71:16; 73:28; Isa 3:1; 7:7; 25:8; 28:16; 30:15; 40:10; 48:16; 49:22; 50:4, 5, 7, 9; 52:4; 56:8; 61:1, 11; 65:13, 15; Jer 1:6; 2:22; 4:10; 7:20; 14:13; 32:17, 25; 44:26; Ezek 2:4; 3:11, 27; 4:14; 5:5, 7, 8, 11; 6:3, 11; 7:2, 5; 8:1; 9:8; 11:7, 8, 13, 16, 17, 21; 12:10, 19, 23, 25, 28; 13:3, 8, 9, 13, 16, 18, 20; 14:4, 6, 11, 14, 16, 18, 20, 21, 23; 15:6, 8; 16:3, 8, 14, 19, 23, 30, 36, 43, 48, 59, 63; 17:3, 9, 16, 19, 22; 18:3, 9, 23, 30, 32; 20:3, 5, 27, 30, 31, 33, 36, 39, 40, 44, 47, 49; 21:7 [WTT 21:12], 13 [WTT 18], 24 [WTT 29], 26 [WTT 31], 28 [WTT 33]; 22:3, 12, 19, 28, 31; 23:22, 28, 32, 34, 35, 46, 49; 24:3, 6, 9, 14, 21, 24; 25:3, 6, 8, 12, 13, 14, 15, 16; 26:3, 5, 7, 14, 15, 19, 21; 27:3; 28:2, 6, 10, 12, 22, 24, 25; 29:3, 8, 13, 16, 19, 20; 30:2, 6, 10, 13, 22; 31:10, 15, 18; 32:3, 8, 11, 14, 16, 31, 32; 33:11, 25, 27; 34:2, 8, 10, 11, 15, 17, 20, 30, 31; 35:3, 6, 11, 14; 36:2, 3, 4, 5, 6, 7, 13, 14, 15, 22, 23, 32, 33, 37; 37:3, 5, 9, 12, 19, 21; 38:3, 10, 14, 17, 18, 21; 39:1, 5, 8, 10, 13, 17, 20, 25, 29; 43:18, 19, 27; 44:6, 9, 12, 15, 27; 45:9, 15, 18; 46:1, 16; 47:13, 23; 48:29; Amos 1:8; 3:7, 8, 11; 4:2, 5; 5:3; 7:1, 2, 4, 5, 6; 8:1, 3, 9, 11; 9:8; Obad 1; Mic 1:2; 4:13; Hab 3:19;

with *Yahweh*) to ask God about his promised heir (v. 2), and to ask about the promised land (v. 8). Similarly, Moses uses *Adonai* in combination with *Yahweh* in the context of giving the Sabbath law (Exod 23:17) and renewing the covenant (Exod 34:23).[15] As a proper name, Daniel's use of *Adonai* in Daniel 9 deserves mention. As Daniel turns to the "Lord [*Adonai*] God [*Elohim*]" in prayer (v. 3), he prays to the "LORD [*Yahweh*] God [*Elohim*]" and says, "O Lord [*Adonai*], the great and awesome God [*El*] . . ." (v. 4). Daniel declares that to the Lord (*Adonai*) belongs "righteousness" (v. 7), "mercy and forgiveness" (v. 9), while rebellious Israelites are full of shame as sinners deserving of punishment (v. 8). Daniel appeals to God's past faithfulness in the Exodus where *Adonai* made a "name for [himself]" (v. 15), and pleads, "O Lord [*Adonai*], hear; O Lord [*Adonai*], forgive. O Lord [*Adonai*], pay attention and act. Delay not, for your own sake, O my God [*Elohim*], because your city and your people are called by your name" (v. 17).

Summary

Throughout the remainder of the Old Testament, these three proper names serve to reveal who God is;[16] not only to Israel, but also through them to the rest of the world. As such, these names are an effort to express the fullness of God's being and character. Perhaps the greatest display of God's name is found in Moses's conversation with God in Exod 33:12—34:9. When Moses requests to see God's glory, God responds, "I will make all my goodness pass before you and will proclaim before you my name 'The LORD [*Yahweh*].' And I will be gracious to whom I will be gracious, and will show mercy on whom I will show mercy" (33:19). Of course, Moses cannot see the full, undiminished glory of God and live, so he is hidden in the cleft of the rock. As God descends in the cloud and reveals his backside glory, he proclaims his name:

> The LORD [*Yahweh*], the LORD [*Yahweh*], a God [*El*] merciful and gracious, slow to anger, and abounding in steadfast love and faithfulness, keeping steadfast love for thousands, forgiving iniquity and transgression and sin, but who will by no means clear

---

Zeph 1:7; Zech 9:14. For the *Adonai-Yahweh* combination's use in the phrase "the Lord [*Yahweh*] our Lord [*Adonai*]," see Neh 10:29 [WTT 10:30]; Pss 8:1 [WTT 8:2], 9 [WTT 10]; 109:21; 140:7 [WTT 140:8].

15. See Jenni, "אָדוֹן," in *TLOT*, 23–29.

16. For the *Elohim-Yahweh-Adonai* combination's use, see Exod 34:23; Deut 10:17; Judg 16:28; 2 Sam 7:22, 28; Neh 10:29 [WTT 10:30]; Pss 69:6 [WTT 69:7]; 73:28; Isa 51:22; Jer 2:19; Ezek 14:11; 20:5; 34:30, 31; Dan 9:4; Amos 3:13; 5:16; 6:8.

the guilty, visiting the iniquity of the fathers on the children and the children's children, to the third and the fourth generation. (Exod 34:6-7)

Thus, as the central expression of God's character in the Old Testament, God's name reveals his glory (33:18), his goodness (33:19), and answers the question, "Who is God?" He is the one who, out of his nature dispenses mercy as well as justice on whomever he wills as an act of his lordship and sovereignty.[17]

The New Testament Use of the Old Testament Divine Names

Turning to the New Testament, another question arises regarding the identity of God: in any given context, to which person of the Trinity do each of these proper names and their uses refer? Karl Rahner in *The Trinity* argues that the God of the Old Testament is the Father only.[18] Admittedly, his concern is with those who imply that there lies a "godhead" behind the three persons of the Trinity that creates a "quaternity" in God. Therefore, Rahner refers to the Father as the ungenerate *fontalis* to whom every use of God in the Old Testament refers.[19] Rahner ultimately displays historical and philosophical concerns that do not hold up to exegetical investigation.[20]

The New Testament authors consistently use the proper name θεός to translate the Old Testament *Elohim* and the proper name κύριος to translate the Old Testament *Adonai* and *Yahweh*,[21] and when the New Testament

---

17. Piper, "Prolegomena to Understanding Romans 9:14-15," 215.

18. Rahner, *Trinity*, 58-61.

19. It must be noted that Rahner is also quick to affirm "The Father, as the concrete God of the Old Testament, is known as Father only when the Son is known. Then we understand also that he acts and can act only in the unity with the Son and the Holy Spirit." Ibid., 60.

20. For a short refutation of Rahner's assertion, see Rowe, "Biblical Pressure and Trinitarian Hermeneutics," 303-6. Hofer also constructs a historical and philosophical refutation of Rahner's assertion using the teaching of Aquinas. See Hofer, "Who Is God in the Old Testament," 439-58.

21. Rowe writes, "A further crucial point to be made is that the Creator of the world and Redeemer of Israel had a proper name and had revealed this name to Israel. In Hebrew, the name is YHWH. How this name was conveyed in Greek is debated, but it is safe to say that the writers of the New Testament understood this name in Greek as kyrios. In almost every single instance where the New Testament cites the Greek Old Testament (LXX) as it corresponds to the Hebrew Old Testament YHWH, the New Testament authors wrote kyrios for the divine name." Rowe, "Biblical Pressure and Trinitarian Hermeneutics," 301.

authors use the proper names, they normally refer to the first person of the Trinity, while less often they refer to the second and third persons.²² The New Testament, then, demonstrates unity within the divine proper names, in that they are attributed to every person of the Godhead.

What about the possibility of the proper names referring to the entire Trinity? Murray Harris is worth quoting at length:

> A related question demands brief treatment. To whom did the NT writers attribute the divine action described in the OT? To answer "the Lord God" (אלהים יהוה = LXX κύριος ὁ θεός) is to beg the question, for the authors of the NT wrote of OT events in the light of their trinitarian understanding of God. A clear distinction must be drawn between what the OT text meant to its authors and readers and how it was understood by the early Christians who lived after the advent of the Messiah and the coming of the Spirit. Certainly the person who projects the trinitarian teaching of the NT back into the OT and reads the OT through the spectacles of the dynamic or trinitarian monotheism of the NT is thinking anachronistically. On the other hand, it does not seem illegitimate to pose a question such as this: To whom was the author of Hebrews referring when he said (1:1), "At many times and in various ways *God* spoke in the past to our forefathers through the prophets?" . . . Since the author is emphasizing the continuity of the two phases of divine speech (ὁ θεὸς λαλήσας . . . ἐλάλησεν), this reference to a Son shows that ὁ θεὸς was understood to be "God the Father." Similarly, the differentiation made between ὁ θεὸς as the one who speaks in both eras and υἱός as his final means of speaking shows that in the author's mind it was not the Triune God of Christian theology who spoke to the forefathers by the prophets. That is to say, for the author of Hebrews (as for all NT writers, one may suggest) 'the God of our fathers', Yahweh, was no other than 'the God and Father of our Lord Jesus Christ" (compare Acts 2:30 and 2:33; 3:13 and 3:18; 3:25 and 3:26; note also 5:30). Such a

---

22. In *Jesus and the God of Israel*, Richard Bauckham makes the same argument: "It is clear from our summary of the evidence that, more often than not, Paul took the referent of YHWH to be God and, less frequently, took it to be Christ. It is indeed noteworthy that Paul seems only very rarely, if at all to take 'God' (Heb. *el elohim*, Gk. *ho theos*) in the text to refer to Christ, and we shall return to this point. But it is equally significant that he clearly does not simply equate YHWH with Christ, but can take the divine name to designate either God or Christ, occasionally even in the same text cited on different occasions (Rom. 11:34; 1 Cor. 2:16; Isa. 40:13)." Bauckham, *Jesus and the God of Israel*, 191. See also Wright, *Knowing God the Father*, 15, and Toon, *Our Triune God*, 90.

conclusion is entirely consistent with the regular NT usage of ὁ θεὸς. It would be inappropriate for אלהים or יהוה ever to refer to the Trinity in the OT when in the NT θεὸς regularly refers to the Father alone and apparently never to the Trinity.[23]

Why is this important? Plainly, embedded within the normative use of proper divine names is an irreversible *taxis* of Trinitarian persons such that when the second and third persons are not explicitly identified, the Father ought to be the assumed referent because he holds the first position of order.

Elohim in the New Testament

In the creation account of Genesis 1–2, the New Testament author consistently identifies *Elohim* as the first person of the Trinity.[24] For example, Hebrews 1:2 speaks most clearly: "but in these last days [God] has spoken to us by his Son, whom he appointed the heir of all things, through whom also he created the world." God the Father is in distinction from his Son, and made the world "through him (cf. Heb 11:3)." Paul affirms the same thing in 1 Corinthians 8:6: "yet for us there is one God, the Father, from whom are all things and for whom we exist, and one Lord, Jesus Christ, through whom are all things and through whom we exist (cf. Col 1:16; John 1:3)."[25]

The New Testament's identification of *Elohim* as the Father in Genesis 1–2 is true not only of the big picture of creation, but also in many of the details as well: God the Father, as the initiator, though not apart from the Son and Spirit, created light (Gen 1:3 quoted in 2 Cor 4:6),[26] he formed the earth through water and out of water (Gen 1:6–9 alluded to in 2 Pet 3:5),[27] he gave a "body" to each kind of seed (Gen 1:11 alluded to in 1 Cor

---

23. Harris, *Jesus as God*, 47n112.

24. Only one other passage outside of Gen 1–2 is quoted in the New Testament with *Elohim* identified as the Father. See Job 5:13, quoted in 1 Cor 3:19. θεός in 1 Cor 3:16 is in distinction from the Spirit, and in 1 Cor 3:23 is in distinction from Christ. Thus, Paul intends θεός in 1 Cor 3:16 to be the Father.

25. In chap. 4, I will look at how the work of Creation argues for the Father's initiating role within the Trinity, but here I am concerned only with which person of the Trinity is referenced in any given Old Testament context.

26. In 2 Cor 4:6, God is clearly in reference to the Father, for in the near context he is distinguished from and revealed in the "face of Jesus Christ."

27. It is possible that "word of God" is a reference to the Son as the eternal Word (cf. John 1:3; Heb 1:2); however, it is more likely that Peter is simply stating that the world has existence only because God the Father commanded it. Thus, it is a reference to the phrase "God [*Elohim*] said . . . ." See Schreiner, *1, 2 Peter, Jude*, 376.

15:38),²⁸ and he rested on the seventh day (Gen 2:2 referenced in Heb 4:4 and 4:10).²⁹ Further, Genesis 1:26–27 is quoted or alluded to no fewer than eight times in various New Testament passages.³⁰ For instance, in Matthew 19:4 (cf. Mark 10:6), Jesus argues for the sanctity of marriage by appealing to God's creation of man and woman.³¹ Likewise, Acts 17:29; 1 Corinthians 11:7; Ephesians 4:24; Colossians 3:10 and James 3:9 all refer to man and woman being made in the image of God.³²

At first glance, then, Rahner's assertion that God in the Old Testament is always the Father seems to have some validity. However, according to the New Testament, *Elohim* is used of the Son in at least two Old Testament passages. The first is found in Psalm 45:6 (quoted in Heb 1:8). "Your throne, O God [*Elohim*], is forever and ever." The author of Hebrews uses this verse to demonstrate that the Son fully shares in the divine nature and identity while remaining distinct from the Father (Heb 1:9).³³

The second is found in Isaiah 9:6, "For to us a child is born, to us a son is given; and the government shall be upon his shoulder, and his name shall be called Wonderful Counselor, Mighty God [*El*], Everlasting Father, Prince of Peace."³⁴ Portions of the verse are alluded to in many NT passages: "The government shall be upon his shoulder" (Matt 11:27; 26:64; 28:18; John 5:22; 18:36); "wonderful counselor" (1 Cor 1:30); and "prince of peace" (John 14:27; 16:33; Acts 10:36; Rom 5:1). Further, the near context (Isa 9:2) is quoted in Matthew 4:13–16. Finally, Isaiah 7:14 (cf. Isa 8:8, 10) speaks of the son of Isaiah 9:6 as born to the virgin and named "Immanuel." Matthew quotes this passage to explain the incarnation (Matt

---

28. The context of θεός in every use in 1 Corinthians demonstrates that τοῦ θεοῦ is in distinction from the Son. Paul's point is that God is the one who chooses and determines a body for each kind of seed. See Grosheide, *First Corinthians*, 382.

29. The greater context of chaps. 1–4 demonstrates that ὁ θεός is in distinction from the Son, particularly where he is distinguished from the Holy Spirit in Heb 3:7, and from Christ in 3:14.

30. Paul alludes to Gen 1:26–27 in 1 Tim 2:13, but in that immediate context, he does not make clear who is the implied subject of the passive verb πλάσσω.

31. In Matt 19:6, the one who created them is ὁ θεός. Further, Jesus is speaking and is not likely referring to himself.

32. Interestingly, Gen 1:26 uses a plural verb, "Then God [*Elohim*] said, "Let *us* make man in our image, after *our* likeness [emphasis mine]." See Wenham, *Genesis*. *1–15*, 27–28 for all the possibilities of the plural verb. Contrary to Wenham, along with passages where God speaks in the plural (Gen 3:22; 11:7; Isa 6:8; 53:1), I take this use to denote a plurality within the Godhead. The Father is speaking to the Son (cf. Prov 8:22–31) and Spirit (Gen 1:2).

33. See Harris, *Jesus as God*, 205–27.

34. See Young, *Isaiah*, 1:329–42.

1:23). Thus, though *Elohim* is commonly used to refer to the Father, it is not his personal name, but rather a proper name that is used for at least two persons of the Godhead.

Yahweh in the New Testament

Like *Elohim*, the first use of *Yahweh* (found in Gen 2) refers to the Father: Genesis 2:7 (cf. 1 Cor 15:45, 47), 8 (cf. Rev 2:7), 9 (cf. Rev 2:7; 22:2, 14, 19), 18 (cf. 1 Cor 11:9), 21–23 (cf. 1 Cor 11:8). With *Yahweh*, however, the data in the New Testament is much more robust. At least ninety-seven quotations or allusions can be found in the New Testament where *Yahweh* can be identified with the first person of the Trinity.[35] In fact, it is why Christopher Wright can assert,

35. Gen 12:1–4 (cf. Acts 3:25; 7:3–4; Gal 3:8; Heb 11:8), 7–8 (cf. Acts 7:5; Gal 3:16); 15:1–10 (cf. Rom 4:3, 9, 18, 22; Gal 3:6; Heb 11:12; Jas 2:23), 13–14 (cf. Acts 7:6–7); 22:16–18 (cf. Luke 1:55, 73–74; Acts 3:25; Rom 4:13; Heb 6:13–14; 11:12); Ex 3:4–7 (cf. Matt 22:32; Mark 12:26; Luke 20:37; Acts 3:13; 7:30–35), 15 (cf. Matt 22:32; Mark 12:26; Acts 3:13); 9:16 (cf. Rom 9:17); 19:5–6 (cf. Titus 2:14; 1 Pet 2:5, 9; Rev 1:6; 5:10; 20:6); 23:20 (cf. Matt 11:10; Mark 1:2; Luke 7:27); 24:8 (cf. Heb 9:20); Lev 11:44–45 (cf. 1 Pet 1:16); 19:2 (cf. Matt 5:48; 1 Pet 1:16), 12 (cf. Matt 5:33); 20:7–8 (cf. 1 Pet 1:16); 20:26 (cf. 1 Pet 1:16); Deut 6:4–5 (cf. Matt 22:37; Mark 12:29–30, 32–33; Luke 10:27; Rom 3:30; 1 Cor 8:4), 13 (cf. Matt 4:10; Luke 4:8), 15–16 (cf. Matt 4:7; Luke 4:12); 8:3 (cf. Matt 4:4; Luke 4:4); 18:15–19 (cf. John 1:45; 6:14; Acts 3:22); 29:4 (cf. Rom 11:8); 31:6 (cf. Heb 13:5); 32:21 (cf. Rom 10:19; 11:11), 35 (cf. Rom 12:19; Heb 10:30), 43 (cf. Rom 15:10); 1 Sam 13:14 (cf. Acts 13:22); 2 Sam 7:12–16 (cf. Luke 1:32–33; Acts 2:30; 13:23); Pss 2:1–12 (cf. Matt 3:17; 17:5; Mark 1:11; 9:7; Luke 3:22; 9:35; Acts 4:25–26; 13:33; Heb 1:5; 5:5; Rev 19:5); 8:2 (cf. Matt 21:16), 4–6 (cf. 1 Cor 15:27; Eph 1:22; Heb 2:6–8); 14:1–7 (cf. Rom 3:10–12; 11:26–27); 16:8–11 (cf. Acts 2:25–28, 31; 1 Cor 15:4); 18:49 (cf. Rom 15:9); 22:1–8 (cf. Matt 27:39, 43, 46; Mark 9:12; 15:29, 34; Luke 23:35–36), 22 (cf. Heb 2:12); 24:1 (cf. 1 Cor 10:26); 31:5 (cf. Luke 23:46); 34:8 (cf. 1 Pet 2:3), 15–16 (cf. 1 Pet 3:10–12), 20 (cf. John 19:36); 36:1 (cf. Rom 3:18); 40:6–8 (cf. Heb 10:5–8); 44:22 (cf. Rom 8:36); 53:1–6 (cf. Rom 3:10–12); 69:9 (cf. John 2:17); 78:23–24 (cf. John 6:31); 82:6 (cf. John 10:34); 89:27–28 (cf. Heb 1:6); 91:11–12 (cf. Matt 4:6; Luke 4:10–11); 94:11 (cf. 1 Cor 3:20); 95:7–11 (cf. Heb 3:15; 4:3, 5); 104:4 (cf. Heb 1:7); 110:1–7 (cf. Matt 22:44; 26:64; Mark 12:36; 14:62; 16:19; Luke 20:42–43; Rom 8:34; 1 Cor 15:25; Eph 1:20; Col 3:1; Heb 1:3, 13; 5:6, 10; 6:20; 7:3, 17, 21; 8:1; 10:12–13; 12:2); 118:6 (cf. Heb 13:5); 118:22–23 (cf. Matt 21:42; Mark 12:10–11; Luke 20:17; Acts 4:11; 1 Pet 2:4, 7), 26 (cf. Mark 11:9; John 12:13); 132:11 (cf. Acts 2:30); Prov 3:34 (cf. Jas 4:6; 1 Pet 5:5); Isa 1:9 (cf. Rom 9:29); 8:17–18 (cf. Heb 2:13); 9:7 (cf. Luke 1:32–33); 10:22–23 (cf. Rom 9:27–28); 11:2–3 (cf. Eph 1:17); 28:11–12 (cf. 1 Cor 14:21), 16 (cf. Rom 9:33; 10:11; Eph 2:20; 1 Pet 2:4, 6); 40:8 (cf. 1 Pet 1:24–25), 13 (cf. Rom 11:34; 1 Cor 2:16); 42:1–9 (cf. Matt 12:18–21; Luke 2:32; Acts 26:18); 45:23 (cf. Rom 14:11; Phil 2:10–11); 49:6 (cf. Luke 2:32; John 8:12; Acts 13:47; 26:23); 52:13–53:12 (cf. John 12:38; Rom 10:16); 55:3 (cf. Acts 13:34); 56:7 (cf. Matt 21:13; Mark 11:17; Luke 19:46); 59:20–21 (cf. Rom 11:26–27); 61:1–3 (cf. Luke 4:18–19); 64:4 (cf. 1 Cor 2:9); 65:1–2 (cf. Rom 10:20–21); 66:1–2 (cf. Acts 7:49–50); Jer 7:11 (cf. Matt 21:13; Mark 11:17; Luke 19:46);

It is certainly true from a whole-Bible perspective, that the God Yahweh of the Old Testament "embodies" (if that is not too human a word), the Son and the Holy Spirit. But on the whole it is probably more appropriate in most cases that when we read about Yahweh, we should have God the Father in mind.[36]

It is also why the development of "divine identity" as a means of construing Christology (by theologians such as Richard Bauckham and Larry Hurtado)[37] has been so fruitful.[38] When *Yahweh* is used of Jesus or the Spirit, it identifies the Son and Spirit with the divine identity, consequently showing that they are fully divine and share in unity with the Father.[39]

It should be no surprise then, that like *Elohim*, the New Testament authors sometimes identify *Yahweh* as the Son: Paul uses the Song of Moses in Deuteronomy 32:4 (cf. 1 Cor 10:4) to conclude "the Rock was Christ"[40] and in Philippians 2:10 references Isaiah 45:23–24 to argue that, as *Yahweh*, Jesus is worthy of worship,[41] the author of Hebrews declares Jesus to be *Yahweh* of Psalm 102:25–27 (cf. Heb 1:10–12) that "laid the foundation of the

---

31:31–34 (cf. Matt 26:28; Luke 22:20; Rom 11:27; 1 Cor 11:25; 2 Cor 3:3, 6; Heb 8:8–12; 10:16–17; 1 John 2:27); Ezek 36:25–32 (cf. 2 Cor 3:3; Heb 10:22); 37:24–28 (cf. John 10:16; Heb 13:20; Rev 21:3); Dan 7:13–14 (cf. Matt 24:30; 26:64; 28:18; Mark 13:26; 14:62; Luke 21:27; Rev 1:7, 13; 11:15; 14:14; 19:6); Hos 1:10 (cf. Rom 9:26; 1 Pet 2:10); 2:23 (cf. Rom 9:25; 1 Pet 2:10); 6:6 (cf. Matt 9:13; 12:7; Mark 12:33); 11:1 (cf. Matt 2:15); Joel 2:28–30 (cf. Acts 2:17–21); Amos 5:25–27 (cf. Acts 7:42–43); Mic 5:2–5 (cf. Matt 2:6; John 7:42); Hab 1:5 (cf. Acts 13:41); Hag 2:6 (cf. Matt 24:29; Luke 21:26; Heb 12:26); Zech 4:6 (cf. 1 Cor 2:3–5); 13:7 (cf. Matt 26:31, 56; Mark 14:27, 50); Mal 1:2–3 (cf. Rom 9:13); 3:1 (cf. Matt 11:10; Mark 1:2; Luke 1:17, 76; 7:27)

36. Wright, *Knowing God the Father*, 15.

37. Bauckham, *Jesus and the God of Israel*. Also, Hurtado, *Lord Jesus Christ*.

38. As Gathercole writes, "Bauckham has emphasised as a third way (without pronouncing a plague on both the other houses) the category of 'identity' as a means of avoiding the Scylla of anachronistic philosophizing on the one hand and the Charybdis of low Christology on the other. . . . Jesus' sharing the name of YHWH is a good place to start because a name is so obviously concerned with identity." Gathercole, "Trinity in the Synoptic Gospels and Acts," 57–58.

39. Holmes argues in a similar manner: "The Son is named as God (John 1:1; 20:28; Rom. 9:5; Titus 2:13; Heb. 1:8-9); both Son and Spirit are given the title 'Lord' (for the Spirit, see 2 Cor. 3:17), the English translation of a Greek word, κύριος, used to translate the name of God revealed to Moses at the burning bush (YHWH). Similarly, both the Son and the Holy Spirit can be blasphemed against (Luke 12:10). If a divine title is properly applied to the Son or the Holy Spirit, then it is an indication that Son and Spirit somehow share in the divine identity or glory." Holmes, *Holy Trinity*, 53.

40. See Thiessen, "The Rock Was Christ," 103–26. In it, Thiessen forcefully argues for Deut 32; Pss 78 and 95 as the background of Paul's assertion.

41. See Beale and Carson, *New Testament Use of the Old Testament*, 837–38.

earth" and whose years will "have no end,"[42] and the apostle John writes in his Gospel (John 12:41) that Isaiah saw Christ's glory (Isa 6:1–12) and spoke of him.[43] Correspondingly, John ascribes the name *Yahweh* to the Son in the "I am" statements (John 6:35, 48, 51; 8:12, 58; 9:5, 28; 10:11, 14; 11:25; 14:6; 15:1, 5), and in the confession of Thomas, "My Lord [κύριός] and my God [θεὸς]" (John 20:28).

Further, Isaiah 40:3 is quoted in all four Gospels (cf. Matt 3:3; Mark 1:3; Luke 1:76; 3:4–6; John 1:23) in order to prove that John the Baptist prepares the way of the Lord (*Yahweh*) (who is Jesus).[44] Similarly, Paul tell the Corinthians in both of his letters to boast in the Lord Jesus (1 Cor 1:31; 2 Cor 10:17) who is *Yahweh* of Jeremiah 9:24.[45] Finally, John 1:18, lends weight to the evidence that some of the Old Testament theophanies were "*christophanies*," particularly when the "angel of the Lord" is mentioned (Gen 16:7–14; 21:17–19; 22:11–18; 31:11–13; 32:24–30; 48:15–16; Exod 3:2–6; 14:19–22; Josh 5:13–16; Judg 2:1–5; 6:11–14; 13:2–23; Ezek 40:1—47:12; Zech 1:1—6:8).[46]

Unlike *Elohim*, at least one passage uses *Yahweh* with regard to the Spirit, which is found in 2 Corinthians 3:16–18 (alluding to Exod 34:34). The passage is notorious for its difficulty, but is best understood as follows: "But when one turns to the Lord [Jesus], the veil is removed. Now the Lord [Spirit] is the Spirit, and where the Spirit of the Lord [the Father] is, there is freedom. . . . For this come from the Lord [Spirit] who is the Spirit." Duane Garrett's understanding is helpful:

---

42. See Bruce, *Hebrews*, 21–23.

43. See Carson, *John*, 449–50. Jesus makes a similar statement in John 8:56. Saville takes this to be a reference to Genesis 18, where *Yahweh* visits Abraham in the appearance of three men. He writes, "Since Jesus says that the cause of Abraham's rejoicing was meeting him, it must have been a conscious recognition of him as a divine person distinct from the Father." Saville, "Old Testament Is Explicitly Christian," 18.

44. Commentaries are divided on whether these passages refer to the Father or the Son. Stein's insight is helpful: "In Isaiah 'the way of the Lord' refers to 'the way of the LORD,' that is, 'YHWH,' but in Mark it refers to the 'Lord' Jesus (cf. 2:28; 5:19–20; 7:28; 11:3; 13:35; and esp. 12:35–37). . . . It is not surprising, therefore, that the followers of Jesus became known as the followers of 'the way' (Acts 9:2; 19:9, 23; 22:4; 24:14, 22; cf. also 13:10; 16:17; 18:25–26)." Stein, *Mark*, 43–44. The same can be said of the parallel passages.

45. That Jesus is called *Yahweh* is supported by the fact that in 1 Cor 1, Jesus is referred to every time as "Lord." So too every use of "Lord" in 2 Cor 10–11 refers to Jesus. By applying the OT reference of *Yahweh* to Jesus, no higher view can be held regarding the person of Christ.

46. For a recent defense of theophanies as christophanies, see Gieschen, "Real Presence of the Son," 105–26.

The term primarily refers to Moses' experience of YHWH but secondarily points toward the Christian experience of Jesus. It is striking that Paul would identify the revelation of YHWH to Moses as "the Spirit," but it is not surprising, since he views the Spirit as the agent of both revelation and life, and since he sees the work of the Spirit as the great benefit (the "glory") of the new covenant. The identification of YHWH (or Jesus) with the Spirit is functional rather than ontological (in other words, Paul does not imply that every mention of YHWH in the OT refers to the Spirit, nor is he suggesting that Jesus and the Spirit are one and the same). This functional identification shows that for Paul, universal access to the Spirit of God is the fundamental mark of the new covenant, and Christians receive the Spirit by turning toward Jesus, just as Moses did through his encounters with YHWH.[47]

Thus, like *Elohim*, *Yahweh* is commonly used to refer to the Father, yet is not his personal name.[48] Rather, *Yahweh* is a proper name that can be used for any person of the Godhead.

Adonai in the New Testament

Many of the quotes and allusions to *Adonai* in the New Testament are found in the combination *Adonai-Yahweh*: Abraham calls God the Father "Lord God" (Gen 15:2, 8), the one in whom he believed (Rom 4:3, 9, 18, 22),[49] the "Lord God" (Isa 28:16) who chooses Jesus to be the cornerstone (cf. Rom 9:33; 10:11; Eph 2:20; 1 Pet 2:4, 6) is the Father,[50] the Spirit of the

---

47. Garrett, "Veiled Hearts," 761.

48. A good example of this can be seen in the *Shema* of Deut 6:4–9 (cf. Deut 11:13–21; 15:37–41; Zech 14:9; Mal 2:10). Jesus uses the *Shema* to speak of the Father (Matt 22:37; Mark 12:28–34; cf. John 10:30). Likewise, New Testament authors refer to the Father in their use of the *Shema* (Jas 2:19; 1 Cor 8:4–6; Rom 3:29–30; also possibly Eph 4:4–6; Gal 3:20; 1 Tim 2:5). All of this argues for the *uniqueness* of the divine identity rather than *unity* of persons within the divine nature. For a list of all of the possible understanding of Deut 6:4, see Barrick, "Inspiration and Trinity," 194–97 and Block, "How Many Is God?," 193–212. For the use of the *Shema* in the New Testament, see Gerhardsson, *Shema in the New Testament*.

49. Commenting on Rom 4:24, Moo writes, "It is typical for Paul to designate God as the one who raised Jesus from the dead . . . but it is somewhat unusual for him to designate God himself as the object of Christian faith. Undoubtedly he does so here to bring Christian faith into the closest possible relationship to Abraham's faith. Not only is our faith of the same nature as Abraham's; it ultimately has as its object the same God, 'who gives life to the dead' (cf. v. 17b)." Moo, *Romans*, 287–88.

50. See Arnold, *Ephesians*, 170–71.

"Lord God" (Isa 61:1) that is upon Jesus (Luke 4:18–19) is the Spirit of God the Father,[51] and the "Lord God" who promised to give a new heart (Ezek 36:23–32) does so by the Spirit, because God the Father is the living God (2 Cor 3:3; cf. Heb 10:22).[52]

In contrast, the New Testament only alludes to one passage where *Adonai* stands by itself, which is found in Matthew 15:8–9 (cf. Mark 7:6–7). Quoting Isaiah 29:13, Jesus rebukes the Pharisees and scribes for giving lip service to God [the Father] when their hearts are far from him.[53] In the Isaiah context, the one speaking is *Adonai*: "This people . . . honor me [*Adonai*] with their lips, while their hearts are far from me [*Adonai*]."[54]

Although there are no uses of *Adonai* for the Spirit, there are three uses in reference to the Son. The first is found in Ephesians 4:8. In it, Paul quotes from Psalm 68:18 to speak of the incarnation and ascension. In the psalm, the one who ascended is *Adonai* (Ps 68:17, 19).[55] The second is found in Isaiah 6:1–12 (cf. John 12:41). When Isaiah saw the glory of the pre-incarnate Jesus, he said, "In the year that King Uzziah died I saw the Lord [*Adonai*]."[56]

The third is Psalm 110 (the most quoted Old Testament passage in the New Testament), which begins with the phrase "The LORD [*Yahweh*] says to my Lord [*Adonai*]." As such, it became a key text Jesus used to argue for his own deity (cf. Matt 22:44; 26:64; Mark 12:36; 14:62; 16:19; Luke 20:42–43; 22:34–35). The New Testament authors also used it to describe the Son's present ministry of ruling and reigning over the kingdom of God (Rom 8:34; 1 Cor 15:25; Eph 1:20; Col 3:1; Heb 1:3, 13; 5:6, 10; 6:20; 7:3, 17, 21; 8:1; 10:12–13; 12:2).[57]

Summary of the NT Use of the OT Divine Names

Nowhere does a New Testament author use one of the proper divine names *Elohim*, *Yahweh*, or *Adonai* as a reference to the Trinity (or Godhead). Sometimes a New Testament author uses a proper divine name to refer to the second or third person of the Trinity, demonstrating the unity of the

---

51. See Lenski, *Luke*, 248–50.

52. See Garland, *2 Corinthians*, 159–62.

53. In the context of Matt 15, Jesus refers to θεός as "my heavenly Father" (Matt 15:13).

54. See Motyer, *Isaiah*, 191.

55. See O'Brien, *Ephesians*, 288–93.

56. See Young, *Isaiah*, 237.

57. For a thorough discussion of Ps 110 as a Messianic Psalm, see Davis, "Is Psalm 110 a Messianic Psalm," 160–73.

divine persons. Most often the New Testament authors use *Elohim, Yahweh,* and *Adonai* (when it is a divine name) in Old Testament quotations to refer to God the Father. What does this pattern mean? Clearly, contra Rahner, the proper names of God cannot refer exclusively to the Father, for the Son and Spirit are identified with those same divine names. Furthermore, it requires the divine commentary of the New Testament authors to properly identify any Old Testament usage in order to maintain integrity regarding the progress of revelation.

Divine Names in the New Testament

θεός

θεός is the normal word for God in the New Testament.[58] Because of this usage, and in light of later Trinitarian developments, it is common for theological works to assume that (ὁ) θεός refers to the Triune God in general. For example, Henry Alford asserts, "[Johann] Hofmann remarks that where the Father is not expressly distinguished from the Son by the context, the Godhead, in its unity, is to be understood by ὁ θεός: and the same may be said of ὁ κύριος."[59]

In contrast, Murray Harris argues against Alford's position in the introduction to his book, *Jesus as God*.[60] After dialoging with Rahner, and substantially agreeing with him, Harris proposes the following, "Customarily, (ὁ) θεός denotes the Father, but exceptionally it refers to the Son."[61] Harris then gives three bases for his proposition: (1) The use of the compound appellative θεός πατήρ in various combinations, (2) when the Father, Jesus and the Spirit are mentioned in conjunction, the word θεός is used of the Father and never of the Son or Spirit, and (3) numerous passages where θεός is distinguished from κύριος.[62] After investigating the various categories of New Testament literature (Synoptic Gospels, Johannine Corpus, Acts, Pauline Corpus, Hebrews, James, Jude, and Petrine Epistles), Harris concludes,

---

58. For statistical analysis, classification and summaries of the use of θεός in the New Testament, see Harris, *Jesus as God*, 21–50.

59. Alford, *Greek Testament*, 4:277.

60. Harris, *Jesus as God*, 41.

61. Ibid., 42. He does clarify that concurrence with Rahner on the latter point, "exceptionally it refers to the Son," presupposes his discussion and conclusions in the rest of the book, Ibid., 42n92.

62. Ibid., 42.

The writers of the NT themselves supply the key by speaking not only of ὁ θεός and Ἰησοῦς but also of ὁ πατήρ and ὁ υἱός, of ὁ υἱός τοῦ θεοῦ and of ὁ θεὸς καὶ πατήρ κυρίου ἡμῶν Ἰησοῦ Χριστοῦ. God is the Father (in the trinitarian sense), Jesus is the Lord (1 Cor. 8:6). When (ὁ) θεός is used, we are to assume that the NT writers have ὁ πατήρ in mind unless the context makes this sense of (ὁ) θεός impossible.[63]

It is worthwhile to look at the exceptional uses of θεός. First, θεός can be used for the divine nature. John 1:1 states, "In the beginning, the Word was with God [the Father], and the Word was [as to his nature] God." Here, God the Father is in an eternal and intimate relationship with the Word, and though distinct from the Word, they both fully possess the very nature of God.[64] When John says, "the Word was God," his use of θεὸς is qualitative, meaning that their essence is identical.[65] Similarly, Paul writes in Philippians 2:6, "who, though he was in the form of God [as to his nature], did not count equality with God [the Father] a thing to be grasped." The use of μορφή means Christ possesses the very nature of God.[66]

Second, at least six passages use θεός in reference to the Son: (1) John 1:18, "the only God [the Son], who is at the Father's side, he has made him known,"[67] (2) John 20:28, "My Lord and my God (Jesus),"[68] (3) Romans 9:5, "is the Christ, who is God over all,"[69] (4) Titus 2:13, "our great God and Savior Jesus Christ,"[70] (5) Hebrews 1:8, "your throne, O God (the Son), is forever and ever,"[71] and (6) 2 Peter 1:1, "the righteousness of our God and Savior Jesus Christ."[72] Two other passages are possible but unlikely: (1) Acts

63. Ibid., 47.

64. In the verse, John assumes that the person God (ὁ θεὸς) possesses the divine nature, and works to explain that the person Word (ὁ λόγος) also possesses the divine nature (the second, anarthrous use of θεὸς).

65. Wallace, *Greek Grammar*, 269.

66. See discussion in Hawthorne, *Philippians*, 81–84.

67. θεὸς is in apposition to μονογενὴς. See Carson, *John*, 134, 139.

68. It is a vocative, addressed to Jesus. The vast majority of grammars and commentaries support this view. See Morris, *John*, 753n81.

69. This phrase highlights Christ's inherent, full divinity and equality with the Father. See Harris, *Jesus as God*, 166. For an exhaustive bibliography supporting this position, see ibid., 154n22.

70. The phrase θεοῦ καὶ σωτῆρος refers to one person. See Knight, *Pastoral Epistles*, 322–23.

71. ὁ θεὸς here is a vocative. See Lane, *Hebrews 1–8*, 21, 29.

72. The phrase τοῦ θεοῦ ἡμῶν καὶ σωτῆρος refers to one person and parallels later statements in 2 Pet 1:11 and 3:13. For an insightful discussion, see Bigg, *Epistles of Peter and Jude*, 250–52.

THE FATHER'S EXISTENCE FROM ETERNITY PAST   39

20:28, "the church of God, which he obtained with his own blood,"⁷³ and (2) 1 John 5:20, "he is the true God and eternal life."⁷⁴

Third, θεός refers to the Spirit in Acts 5:3-4. In it, Peter tells Ananias he has lied to the Holy Spirit (v. 3) and in doing so, has lied to God (v. 4). Polhill argues that a lie to the Spirit is ultimately a lie to God the Father.⁷⁵ Though possible, this view is ultimately unlikely because the parallelism of τὸ πνεῦμα τὸ ἅγιον (v. 3) with τῷ θεῷ (v. 4) indicates that Peter is calling the Holy Spirit God.⁷⁶ Lenski is insightful on this passage:

> Peter's word to Ananias undoubtedly identifies God and the Holy Ghost. This is often denied, and the claim advanced that the lie was made to God indirectly through the Holy Ghost, the latter serving only as the medium. But this virtually declares that the Holy Ghost was as ignorant of the fraud as men were. God is not behind the Holy Ghost as he is behind the apostles and the church so that whatever is done against them is done mediately also against God. The Holy Ghost is God; the sin was committed against him as God. The old dogmaticians and the church are right when they here find a clear expression of the deity and the personality of the Holy Spirit, the Third Person of the Godhead.⁷⁷

Finally, one passage may use θεός as a reference to the Triune God. In 1 Corinthians 15:28 Paul writes, "When all things are subjected to him [the Son], then the Son himself will also be subjected to him who [the Father] put all things in subjection under him [the Son], that God [θεός] may be all in all." Some have taken the phrase "that God may be all in all" to refer to the Godhead. For example, in a recent attempt to deny the eternal authority of the Father over the Son, Linda Belleville attempts to prove that it is the Davidic messiah handing over the kingdom to the Godhead.⁷⁸ After linking the context to the Davidic Psalms, and Jesus to the language of ἀνθρώπου

---

73. τοῦ ἰδίου here is being used substantively, thus, "the church of God [the Father], which he obtained with the blood of his own [Son]." Moulton mentions that ἴδιος was used in the papyri as a term of endearment and close relationship. See Moulton, *Grammar of New Testament Greek*, 1:90. Here, ἴδιος would be related to μονογενὴς.

74. Though the nearest antecedent to οὗτός is the Son, it is more likely a reference to the Father (τὸν ἀληθινόν). Further, John had previously referred to the Father as τὸν μόνον ἀληθινὸν θεὸν (the only true God) in his Gospel (John 17:3). See Dodd, *Johannine Epistles*, 140.

75. Polhill, *Acts*, 158.

76. See Bruce, *Acts*, 133.

77. Lenski, *Acts*, 200.

78. Belleville, "'Son' Christology," 69-70.

(vv. 21-22) and Χριστός (v. 23), she asserts, "ὁ υἱὸς ὑποταγήσεται τῷ ὑποτάξαντι αὐτῷ cannot refer to God the Son's subjection, for this would make his sovereignty temporary."⁷⁹ She concludes "the subjection of this 'son' results in ὁ θεὸς [τὰ] πάντα ἐν πᾶσιν—a statement of God's total supremacy which must include all members of the Trinity."⁸⁰

In response, if θεός here were a reference to the full Trinitarian God, it would be Paul's only usage in his entire corpus. Further, a careful examination of the implied personal and relative pronouns (in the masculine singular) most likely make the reference to θεός the Father: (1) the implied subject of the verb θῇ (v. 25) is identified as the implied subject of ὑπέταξεν (v. 27), both of which are taken from Psalm 110 where the Father puts the Messiah's enemies under his feet, (2) the subject of the verbless clause ἐκτὸς (v. 27) and the participle τοῦ ὑποτάξαντος is God the Father, for it is clear that the Father is not subject to Christ, (3) the implied subject of the participle τῷ ὑποτάξαντι (v. 28) is the Father, consistently arguing in these verses that the Father puts all things in subjection under the Son. Therefore, the referent to these pronouns is identified as θεός of v. 28.

Thus, θεός normally refers to the Father and exceptionally refers to the Son and Holy Spirit, while apparently never referring to the Trinity.

κύριος

κύριος, as a proper name for God, is often used in the Septuagint as a translation for *Adonai* and *Yahweh*.⁸¹ This is true for the New Testament as well, and in many places, it signifies the Father. First, and most often, the Father is called (ὁ) κύριος in Old Testament quotations and allusions.⁸² Similarly, the phrase ὁ ἄγγελος κυρίου (angel of the Lord) is used eleven times in the New Testament, and every reference is to the Father.⁸³

Second, Luke often uses κύριος in the narrative material of both Luke and Acts to describe what the Father is doing.⁸⁴ Other speakers in Luke's

---

79. Ibid., 70.
80. Ibid.
81. Foerster, "κύριος," in *TDNT*, 3:1058.
82. Matt 1:22; 2:15; 4:7, 10; 5:32; 21:9, 42; 22:37, 44; 23:39; 27:10; Mark 11:9; 12:11, 29-30, 36; Luke 2:23-24; 4:8, 12, 18-19; 10:27; 13:35; 19:38; 20:42; John 12:13, 38; Acts 2:20-21, 25, 34; 3:22; 4:26; 13:47; 15:17; Rom 4:8; 9:29; 10:16; 11:3, 34; 12:19; 15:11; 1 Cor 2:16; 3:20; 10:26; 14:21; 2 Cor 6:18; Heb 7:21; 8:8-11; 10:16; 12:5-6; 13:6; Jas 5:4, 10-11; 1 Pet 3:12; Jude 9; Rev 11:4, 15; 18:8; 21:22; 22:5, 6.
83. Matt 1:24; 2:13; 2:19; 28:2; Luke 1:11; Luke 2:9; Acts 5:19; 8:26; 12:7, 23; 2 Tim 2:19.
84. Luke 1:6, 9, 58, 66; 2:22, 26, 39; 5:17; Acts 2:47; 8:25; 8:39; 9:31; 12:17; 13:44,

account also use κύριος when referring to the Father: (1) angels (Luke 1:15–17, 28, 32), (2) Elizabeth (Luke 1:24, 45), (3) Mary (Luke 1:38, 46), (4) Zechariah (Luke 1:68, 76), (5) the shepherds at Jesus birth (Luke 2:15), 5) Peter (Acts 2:39; 3:20; 5:9; 8:22; 12:10), (6) Stephen (Acts 7:31, 33), (7) Simon Magus (Acts 8:24), and 8) Lydia (Acts 16:15). Likewise, in the Gospel of Mark, Jesus uses κύριος for the Father when talking to others (Mark 5:19; 13:20).

Third, κύριος is often an address to God the Father, whether in prayer or worship: (1) by Jesus (Matt 9:38; 11:25; Luke 10:2, 21), (2) by Mary (Luke 1:46), (3) by Zechariah (Luke 1:68), (4) by Simeon (Luke 2:29), (5) by disciples (Acts 1:24; 4:24, 29; Jas 1:7), and (6) by the hosts of heaven (Rev 4:8, 11; 6:10; 11:17; 15:3; 16:6; 19:6).

Finally, even the miscellaneous uses seem to be tied to the Jewish understanding of κύριος for *Yahweh*: (1) servants of the Lord (Rom 12:11; 1 Cor 3:5), (2) the commands of the Lord (1 Cor 14:37), (3) the Spirit of the Lord (2 Cor 3:17), (4) "only Sovereign, the King of kings and Lord of lords" (1 Tim 6:15), (5) tabernacle of the Lord (Heb 8:2), (6) and the application of Old Testament principles to the church (Heb 12:14; Jas 3:9; 4:9, 15; 2 Pet 2:9, 11; 3:8–10, 15).[85]

In stark contrast to all other proper names in the New Testament, κύριος is less often used of the Father and more often used of "the Lord Jesus Christ." Bauckham has ably shown that early Jewish Christians understood this to mean that Jesus was included in the divine identity. He writes,

> The exalted Jesus is given the divine name, the Tetragrammaton (YHWH), the name which names the unique identity of the one God, the name which is exclusive to the one God in a way that the sometimes ambiguous word "god" is not. . . . Connected with this naming of the exalted Jesus by the divine name is the early Christian use of the phrase "to call on the name of the Lord," as a reference to Christian confession and to baptism. . . . It means invoking Jesus as the divine Lord who exercises the divine sovereignty and bears the divine name.[86]

As shown in the section on *Yahweh*, one passage in the New Testament uses κύριος for the Spirit: "Now the Lord is the Spirit, and where the Spirit of the Lord [the Father] is, there is freedom. . . . For this comes from

---

48–49; 15:35–36, 40; 16:14, 32; 18:25; 19:10, 20.

85. Other disputed uses of κύριος in the commentaries (do they refer to the Father or Son?) include Acts 2:20–21; 5:14; 8:25 (cf. 11:16; 13:44, 48, 49; 15:35, 36; 16:32; 19:10, 20); 13:2; 1 Cor 1:31.

86. Bauckham, *Jesus and the God of Israel*, 24–25. On Jesus as Lord, see also Foerster, "κύριος," in *TDNT*, 3.1039–95 particularly the section "E. Κύριος in the New Testament," sub-section "3. Jesus as Lord."

the Lord who is the Spirit" (2 Cor 3:17–18). Thus, κύριος is a proper name and though normally used of the Son in the New Testament, can be used of any person of the Trinity. Mark Edwards summarizes the implications for Trinitarian theology:

> Christians, however, were required to hold, on the authority of Jesus and the prophets, that God is one (Deut. 6:4; Mk 12:29), while they were also required to acknowledge Jesus himself not only as Son of God but as Lord (Matt. 7:21–2 etc.), as creator of all (Jn 1:3–4; Heb. 1:2), and as the one on whom the name above all names had been conferred (Phil. 2:9). To us, declares Paul, there is one God and one Lord Jesus Christ (1 Cor. 8:6); the Church is thus required to make one of two, but, since the same apostle prayed that his correspondents might receive the fellowship of the Holy Spirit along with the grace of Jesus Christ and love of the Father (2 Cor. 13:13), and since the last injunction of Christ in the Gospel of Matthew is to baptize the nations in the name of the Father, the Son, and the Holy Spirit (Matt. 28:19), it would seem that where there are two there must be three.[87]

πατήρ

Scripture has two basic uses for πατήρ when used for God: (1) as a simile, metaphor, or analogy and (2) as a personal name. Most literature on the Father is concerned with the metaphor, "God *as* Father." Joachim Jeremias' lexical studies on ἀββά (and the many responses) are a notable exception.[88] Some studies on the metaphor of πατήρ want to deny that it is ever used as a name for the first person of the Trinity, usually originating from a concern for feminist theology.[89] A thorough response can be found in *Speaking the Christian God: The Holy Trinity and the Challenge of Feminism*, which is a collection of essays edited by Alvin Kimel.[90] In it, many of the authors emphasize the importance of Father, not only as a metaphor but also as a personal name. For example, T. F. Torrance writes,

---

87. Edwards, "Exegesis and the Early Doctrine of the Trinity," 80.

88. See vol. 1 of Jeremias, *Neutestamentliche Theologie*, as well as his *Abba*. For an English version, see Jeremias, *Central Message of the New Testament*. Recently Georg Schelbert has conducted an exhaustive analysis and critique of Jeremias in Schelbert, *Abba Vater*. For an English critique of Jeremias, see Barr, "Abba Isn't 'Daddy,'" 28–47.

89. For example, see Van Wijk-Bos, *Reimagining God*, and Thompson, *Promise of the Father*. Thompson's introduction provides a very helpful overview of the nuances in feminist theology.

90. Kimel, *Speaking the Christian God*.

When we turn to the Scriptures of the New Testament, we find a radical deepening of the Old Testament doctrine of God, for "Father" is now revealed to be more than an epithet—it is the personal name of God in which the form and content of his self-revelation as Father through Jesus Christ his Son are inseparable. "Father" is now the name of God that we are to hallow, as our Lord Jesus taught us: "Our Father who art in heaven, hallowed be your name."[91]

To be sure, studies on the Fatherhood of God are necessary and fruitful.[92] Furthermore, God *as* Father reveals the first person of the Trinity, God *the* Father. It is more appropriate to say that because the first person of the Trinity is named "Father," his character and actions in Scripture reveal him as a Father.[93] Therefore, a study of πατήρ for God cannot be limited to the metaphor.

The personal name "Father" is not arbitrary, nor is it temporary.[94] He is the eternal Father of the eternal Son.[95] John argues clearly in his Gospel that the "Word" who became flesh is the "only Son from the Father" (John 1:14), existing in a Father-Son relationship from the "beginning" (John 1:1). The Father is seen to be the initiator in their relationship, caring for and

---

91. Torrance, "Christian Apprehension of God the Father," 131.

92. Recent dissertations include James Harriman's study in Deuteronomy of Yahweh's paternity: Harriman, "Our Father in Heaven"; Diane Chen's argument that the Fatherhood of God is the hub of theology in Luke-Acts: Chen, *God as Father in Luke-Acts*; Abera Mengestu's study of the Pauline Epistles that asserts God's Fatherhood provides kinship language that forms the early Christian community: Mengestu, "God as Father in Paul"; and Amy Peeler's work in Hebrews investigating the theological, Christological, and ecclesiological implications of God's fatherhood: Peeler, "You Are My Son."

93. It is important to recognize that the name Father does not mean everything for God that it means when applied to human beings.

94. Millard Erickson objects that the names "Father" and "Son" might not be eternal names when he says, "The references to the names may be those used at the time of writing but may not indicate that the persons actually had those names at the time to which the writing." Erickson, *Who's Tampering with the Trinity*.

95. There is only one use of the Hebrew word אָב for the second person of the Godhead, found in Isa 9:6: "and his name shall be called Wonderful Counselor, Mighty God, Everlasting Father, Prince of Peace." Implicit in the title is argument that Messiah is God, but it cannot mean that the Messiah is God the Father, the first person of the Trinity. In fact, the context of v. 7 make it a reference to the Messiah's relationship as God with his people (rather than his relation with the other persons of the Godhead). Thus, it is most likely a metaphor referring to the benevolence of his eternal reign as the promised seed of David. See Meyers, "Meaning and Significance of the Messianic Epithets in Isaiah 9:6," 74–79. Less likely, it may be a genitive construction demonstrating that the Son as the "mighty God" fathered the ages (cf. Col 1:16; Heb 1:2). See Chambers, "The Everlasting Father," 169–71.

nurturing "the only God [the Son]," who is in his bosom.[96] The Son is the one who is from the Father,[97] who has seen the Father (John 6:46), and as such is the qualified to make the Father known (John 1:18). It is also why in John 17:1-5, Jesus prays to the "Father," and asks that he would "glorify [the Son (v. 1)] in [the Father's] own presence with the glory that [the Son] had with [the Father] before the world existed."

Horrell's insight is important:

> Although not by any means the only terms for deity in the New Testament, the designations, Father, Son, and Spirit carry us into the heart of God's internal relations. . . . Jesus seems always to distinguish his own relationship with God the Father from that of his followers ("*my* Father and *your* Father," 20:17). For this reason the words "Father" and "Son" have been understood in nearly all church history as those which best describe the deepest personal ontology of God [emphasis original].[98]

Further, the name Father cannot be understood apart from the Son and Spirit. Paul, in Galatians 4:4 gives Trinitarian shape to the personal names of God. He writes, "But when the fullness of time had come, God sent forth his Son, born of woman, born under the law, to redeem those who were under the law, so that we might receive adoption as sons. And because you are sons, God has sent the Spirit of his Son into our hearts, crying, 'Abba! Father!'" God here is identified in v. 6 as the Father, the one who has been in an eternal relationship with the Son and Spirit, and in the course of redemptive history, sends the Son and Spirit. Thomas Smail contends,

---

96. Fisher insightfully comments, "One is reminded of the 'separate but equal' status of both parties. However, just as the Logos is 'from the Father,' (1:14) implying some kind of gentle subordination, so also here, the concept of the Logos (= 'unique one' = God) is subsumed under the overshadowing presence of the Father." Fisher, "God the Father," 119.

97. The giving and sending language demonstrates that the second person of the Godhead was the Son before his incarnation (cf. John 3:16; 1 John 4:9-10). Likewise, the language of Heb 1:1-2 demonstrates that the second person of the Godhead was the Son when God created the world through him, and the foreknowledge and predestining of God into the Son's image was also before the incarnation. See Grudem, "Doctrinal Deviations," 28-32.

98. Horrell, "Complementarian Trinitarianism," 345. He later quotes Widdicombe's research on the Fatherhood of God in Athanasius. "There can be no speculation about the nature of God that does not take the two terms Father and Son as its starting point. . . . All thought about the nature of God ultimately is to be about the Father-Son relation; that relation is theology's beginning and end." Widdicombe, *Fatherhood of God*, 170, quoted in Horrell, "Complementarian Trinitarianism," 346.

> The function of the Father is to send the Son and the Spirit, so that he cannot be rightly understood or approached as Creator except through his Son and his Spirit. God the Father out of the context of the coming of Christ quickly ceases to be Father at all. He quickly becomes instead the remote and distant God of the philosophers, the anonymous and abstract ground of our being, who is in everything in general but never does anything in particular.[99]

Thus, as the eternal Father of the eternal Son (likewise the Spirit is the "Spirit of the Lord/Spirit of God" who is the Father as well as the Spirit of Christ), the Father's distinct appropriation is to initiate all divine activity, with an intrinsic initiating authority in carrying out the Triune God's work. Kevin Giles has objected to this claim, saying that the names "Father" and "Son" "are not used in the New Testament to suggest that the divine Father has authority over the Son. They speak rather of an "eternal correlated relationship" marked by "intimacy, unity, equality, and identical authority."[100] However, Cowan ably demonstrates that John's original readers would have understood authority as intrinsic to the name Father:

> The Son can do nothing on his own, but only what he sees the Father doing; as the Father does, so the Son does (John 5:19). The Father taught the Son (8:28), whose obedience is evident because he always does what pleases the Father (8:29) and speaks what he has heard from him (8:38). Jesus honors his Father (8:49; cf. Ex. 20:12) and keeps his word (John 8:55). When Jesus's hour draws near, he tells his disciples that he is going to the Father, "for the Father is greater than I" (14:28). Clearly, the language of "Father" and "Son" reflects an intimate, familial relationship: "the Father loves the Son" (3:35; 5:20). Yet a relationship of loving intimacy does not rule out a relational hierarchy—which the Father-Son terminology conveys in its original context.[101]

Thus, initiating authority to send the Son is part of what it means for the Father to possess the divine name, "Father."

---

99. Smail, *Forgotten Father*, 24.

100. Giles, *Jesus and the Father*, 127. Giles also objects that arguing for the Father's authority by analogy to human father-son relationships is "exactly like" the Arian error of speaking of the Son as "begotten," and therefore it is the same as arguing that the Son was created, just as human children are begotten by their fathers. Ibid., 66–67.

101. Cowan, "I Always Do What Pleases Him," 52–53. See also Grudem's extended discussion on the Father's authority and the Son's submission indicated by the names "Father" and "Son," in Grudem, "Biblical Evidence," 227–32.

Summary of the Divine Names and Their *Taxis*

This study has shown that though the proper names of God customarily refer to the Father, they do not exhaust the divine identity. They can also refer to the Son (especially in the case of κύριος) and Holy Spirit. Also, we have seen that the personal names of Father, Son, and Spirit are not arbitrary, nor are they temporary.[102] How then do the personal names within the Trinity relate to the proper names of God?

In Matthew 28:19, Jesus commands his disciples to baptize in the "name" (singular) of the Father, the Son and the Holy Spirit, demonstrating that a fixed, irreversible order exists among the personal names of God (Father-Son-Spirit) within the divine identity. After evaluating the rest of Scripture for Trinitarian passages (2 Cor 13:14; Rom 15:16, 30; 2 Cor 1:21–22; 3:3; Eph 2:18; 3:14–16; Gal 4:6), Gerald Bray concurs,

> It appears that every possible combination except one is represented, but in spite of this, the pattern of personal operation is remarkably stable. God the Father is the person who ordains, establishes, judges and appoints; he is also the person to whom worship is chiefly directed.[103]

Regarding the other persons of the Trinity, the early fathers believed that the Father's operations of sending the Son and Spirit (evident in the economy of creation, providence and redemption) was also true of the processions of Son and Spirit in their eternal relations to the Father.[104]

Finally, initiating authority for divine work is embedded in the personal name πατήρ. What this authority does not mean is that the Son or Spirit are somehow inferior to the Father, for they fully share the divine identity.[105]

---

102. Aquinas brings out this fixedness of names in his *Summa Theologica* when he argues that to understand the names as designations, without there being intrinsic characteristics that adhere to the name, is meaningless. See Aquinas, *Summa Theologica*, I, q.40, a. 2. Calvin in his *Institutes* says the same: "Indeed, the words 'Father,' 'Son,' and 'Spirit' imply a real distinction – let no one think that these titles, whereby God is variously designated from his works, are empty – but a distinction, not a division." Calvin, *Institutes*, 1.13.17. Calvin further explains in 1.13.18, "It [the distinction] is this: to the Father is attributed the beginning of activity, and the fountain and wellspring of all things; to the Son, wisdom, counsel, and the ordered disposition of all things; but to the Spirit is assigned the power and efficacy of that activity." Ibid., 142–43.

103. Bray, *Doctrine of God*, 146–47.

104. Letham, "Eternal Generation," 121.

105. Letham clarifies: "It [*taxis*] is a question of order, not rank. We recall that the orthodox and the Arians used the word taxis in different ways. The Arians used it to support their heretical idea that the Son was of lesser rank or status than the Father.

Revelation 22:1 gives a beautiful picture (one to which we will return in chap. 7) of the initiating role of the Father for all eternity future: "Then the angel showed me the river of the water of life [a reference to the Holy Spirit], bright as crystal, flowing from the throne of God [the Father] and the Lamb."[106] Thus, for all eternity, the persons of the Godhead will forever dwell among their people, manifesting their love and life to the saints and revealing themselves from the Father through the Son by the Spirit.

The Divine Nature and the Father's Distinction

Within the divine nature, the Father occupies the first position of relational order among the divine persons (e.g., unbegotten, eternal generation, eternal procession). Among the incomprehensibility and glory inherent in the divine nature, the Father's distinction is revealed in the economy, by which the Son and Spirit are known and make the Father known. Further, Scripture unanimously testifies that the Father, Son, and Spirit are ontologically "one" regarding the divine nature, and yet the Father is distinguished by his role among the persons as the one initiating all work from eternity past.

Incomprehensibility and the Knowledge of the Father

Although God's incomprehensibility is sometimes included in the list of divine attributes, it more properly describes our inability to fully understand the divine nature.[107] It is fascinating that every text acknowledging the incomprehensibility of God has the first person of the Trinity as its subject, whether *Yahweh* (Ps 145:3; Isa 40:28), θεός (Rom 11:33–36; 1 Cor 2:6–16; 1 Tim 6:16) or πατήρ (Matt 11:25–27; Luke 10:21–22). Paul writes that the Father is partly known in his Creation:

> For what can be known about God [the Father] is plain to them, because God has shown it to them. For his invisible attributes, namely, his eternal power and divine nature, have been clearly perceived, ever since the creation of the world, in the things that have been made. So they are without excuse. (Rom 1:19–20)[108]

The pro-Nicene used the word in the sense of a fitting and suitable disposition, not a hierarchy." Letham, *Holy Trinity*, 400.

106. See John 7:37–39 where the "living waters" are a reference to the Holy Spirit. See Beale, *Revelation*, 1103–4.

107. Durand, "Theology of God the Father," 373–74.

108. In Rom 1, θεός is in distinction from the Son: v. 1, "Christ Jesus . . . gospel of God;" v. 2–3, "he promised . . . concerning his Son;" v. 7 "God our Father and the Lord

However, the sendings of the Son and Spirit in redemptive history were intended to give a greater knowledge of the Father. Therefore, John writes, "No one has ever seen God [the Father]; the only God [the Son], who is at the Father's side, he [the Son] has made him [the Father] known" (John 1:18). Previously, in v. 14, John had identified what it was that the Son made known: the Father's glory.[109]

The Father, thus, sends the eternal Son to become the incarnate Son in order to reveal a true knowledge of himself (albeit along with the Son and Spirit) and thereby give eternal life to his adopted sons.[110] Jesus says in John 7:28 (cf. John 8:26–27), that he knows the Father because he comes from him and was sent by him. Jesus, as the true bread of God the Father "comes down from heaven and gives life to the world" (John 6:32–33), he is the one who has the words of eternal life (John 6:69), and he is the one who declares: "this is eternal life, that they know you the only true God, and Jesus Christ whom you have sent" (John 17:3; cf. 1 John 5:20).[111]

Jesus Christ;" v. 8, "God through Jesus Christ;" v. 9 "God . . . gospel of his Son."

109. Furthermore, by using the word "dwelt" (σκηνόω) for the incarnation, John is pointing back to the Old Testament tabernacle and is proclaiming that the manifest glory of *Yahweh* in the Old Testament tabernacle is the same glory revealed in the incarnate Son. Additionally, John chooses to highlight two attributes of the Father's glory: grace and truth (John 1:14, 17). John's choice is not arbitrary. Rather, in them John specifically refers to the revelation given to Moses in Exodus 33–34. There, the Father's glory (Exod 33:18) is equivalent to his name (Exod 33:19), and the Father reveals his name to Moses as "The Lord, the Lord, a God merciful and gracious, slow to anger, and abounding in *steadfast love* and *faithfulness*, keeping steadfast love for thousands, forgiving iniquity and transgression and sin, but who will by no means clear the guilty, visiting the iniquity of the fathers on the children and the children's children, to the third and the fourth generation" (Exod 34:6–7). When the Father tells Moses he abounds in steadfast love (*hesed*) and faithfulness (*emeth*), John translates it "grace and truth" (χάριτος καὶ ἀληθείας). Therefore, Jesus can proclaim, "I have come in my Father's *name*" (John 5:43) and the crowd on Palm Sunday can rightly declare, "Blessed is he who comes in the *name* of the Lord" (John 12:13). Jesus is the one on whom the Father has set his seal (John 6:27), and therefore, is the "Holy One" (John 6:69) God the Father has set apart to be the "Christ, the Son of God, who is coming into the world" (John 11:27).

110. During the life of Christ, this claim did not go unopposed. The Pharisees said, "This man is not from God" (John 9:16) and "we do not know where he comes from" (John 9:29). In doing so, they revealed they do not know the Father (John 17:25).

111. It is also why John writes, concerning Jesus, the following words at the beginning of his first epistle: "That which was from the beginning, which we have heard, which we have seen with our eyes, which we looked upon and have touched with our hands, concerning the word of life—the life was made manifest, and we have seen it, and testify to it and proclaim to you the eternal life, which was with the Father and was made manifest [by the Father] to us" (1 John 1:1–2).

Likewise, the Holy Spirit produces regeneration, bringing to the human mind and heart the true knowledge of God the Father (1 Cor 2:11–12) as he has revealed himself in the person and work of his Son.[112] The Spirit regenerates as part of his work of uniting the believer to Christ, and is why Paul declares, "For through him [Christ] we both have access in one Spirit to the Father" (Eph 2:18). Therefore, the Spirit enables the believer to draw near to the Father through a new and "living way" found in the Son (Heb 10:19).[113] Thus, as Durand articulates, "Knowledge of the person of the Father arises, therefore, from the economy, in which the Word and the Holy Spirit are like the two 'hands' of the Father, through whom he acts to our benefit."[114]

Glory and the Revelation of the Father

The glory inherent in the divine nature is the sum-total of God's attributes and perfections.[115] In Scripture, these are often ascribed to the Father (e.g., his being is "Spirit" John 4:24; "self-existence" Rev 1:8; "love" 1 John 4:8; "holiness" 1 Pet 1:15; "goodness" Matt 19:17; "omnipotence" Rev 19:6; "immutable" Jas 1:17; "sovereign" John 6:37–44). They are also ascribed to the

---

112. In Phil 3:3, Paul writes, "For we are the circumcision, who worship by the Spirit of God and glory in Christ Jesus and put no confidence in the flesh." Furthermore, Paul teaches that this circumcision is synonymous with regeneration: "And you, who were dead in your trespasses and the uncircumcision of your flesh, God made alive together with him, having forgiven us all our trespasses" (Col 2:13).

113. The author of Hebrews teaches that a believer's approach ought to be one of "confidence" and "boldness," which stand in stark contrast to the restrictions placed on the people of God in the earthly temple under the old covenant. Now, there is great confidence because the high priest has gone before and left the way open (Heb 10:20-21), and the Spirit has washed hearts clean (Heb 10:22), and is why the children of God are exhorted to "with confidence draw near to the throne of grace, that we may receive mercy and find grace to help in time of need" (Heb 4:16). Believers have a Father who has drawn near to them through his Son and made them to be his temple, the place where his glory dwells, and he invites them to draw near to him as a perfect Father.

114. Durand, "Theology of God the Father," 374.

115. Thomas McCall has argued that if "authority" is an attribute, and therefore eternal functional subordination is true, then the Father has an attribute (authority) that the Son does not possess, and thus the Son is *heteroousios* rather than *homoousios*. See McCall, *Which Trinity*, 179–80. Contra McCall, authority is not an attribute of the divine nature. Power relates to the *ability* to act, but authority relates to the *right* to act. Therefore, the Triune God exercises all authority over creation *and* the Father exercises initiating authority in all the works of the Triune God. For a full response, see Ware, "Does Affirming an Eternal Authority-Submission Relationship" 237–48. For a thorough examination of the words "power" and "authority," see House, "Eternal Relational Subordination, 151–53.

Son (e.g., Matt 20:19; John 1:1–3; 1:18; 5:22–29; 8:58; 14:6; 17:22–24; 20:28; Rom 1:4; 9:5; Phil 3:21; Col 1:15; 2:3; Titus 2:13; Heb 1:3; 13:8; 1 John 5:20; Rev 22:12, 13) and the Holy Spirit (e.g., Matt 28:19; Luke 1:35; John 14:16; 15:26; 16:7–14; Rom 8:9, 26; 1 Cor 12:11; 2 Cor 13:14). Furthermore, the description of the Son and Spirit's relationship to the attributes is always in the context of their relationship to the Father.[116] It is why Jesus can say, "No one is good except God [the Father] alone" (Mark 10:18; Luke 18:19; cf. Matt 19:17). Similar statements are seen in John's Gospel and epistles concerning love and life.

Regarding *love*, John considers it as a fundamental description of the Father when he says, "love is from God" (1 John 4:7)[117] and "God is love" (1 John 4:8, 16).[118] This love has been eternally and perfectly poured out on the Son (John 5:20; 15:9; 17:23, 26). Reciprocally, the Son loves the Father (John 14:21), and though no mention is made of the Father or Son's love for the Spirit or the Spirit's love for Father and Son, Köstenberger and Swain make a compelling argument that "while the Spirit is strictly speaking anonymous in the prayer of John 17, he is nonetheless the essential link in the prayer's great chain of gifting."[119] A fundamental part of that gifting is so that the "messianic community . . . might participate in the intra-trinitarian fellowship of love, glory, and *gifting* that existed 'before the creation of the world' ([John] 17:24)."[120]

---

116. Regarding glory, it is important to see the contrast between the intrinsic glory that the Triune God has possessed from all eternity and the ascribed glory that is due the Godhead for creation and redemption. This is clear in John 17:4–5 where in v. 4, all the works of Jesus bring ascribed glory to his Father, whereas in v. 5, Jesus desires to be glorified with the intrinsic glory he had with the Father before the world existed. It is the Father's intrinsic glory (along with the Son's) manifested by his presence that will give the New Jerusalem light forever: "And the city has no need of sun or moon to shine on it, for the glory of God gives it light, and its lamp is the Lamb" (Rev 21:23). The Spirit's intrinsic glory is not explicitly mentioned; however, in the book of Revelation, as the "seven spirits" (Rev 1:4), he is intimately tied to "the one who sits on the throne," and as the "seven horns and seven eyes" (Rev 5:6), he is intimately connected to "the Lamb." For a good discussion of this contrast, see Carson, *John*, 556–57.

117. The context makes clear that θεὸς is not in the generic or as Trinity because this same God "sent his Son into the world" (v. 9) "to be the propitiation for our sins" (v. 10). Furthermore, he has given "his Spirit" (v. 13).

118. Brown sees "love" here as God's action rather than merely an attribute (Brown, *Epistles of John*, 515). However, Yarbrough sees it as a primary attribute of God (Yarbrough, *1–3 John*, 235). Trinitarian thinking helps us here to see that this love has been manifested in the immanent Trinity from all eternity, and thus is a part of the Triune God's nature as well as an action between Father, Spirit, and Son.

119. Köstenberger and Swain, *Father, Son, and Spirit*, 177.

120. Ibid.

Regarding *life*, Jesus taught that it comes from the Father, for "the Father has life in himself" (John 5:26), and calls him "the living Father" (John 6:57).[121] The Father "has granted the Son also to have life in himself" (John 5:26) and the Son lives "because of the Father" (John 6:57).[122] Hence, John can call the Son "the eternal life" (1 John 1:2).[123] Likewise, it is the "living water" (John 4:14; 7:38–39) of the Spirit "who gives life" (John 6:63), so the Spirit also has life in himself. Moreover, closely tied to the concept of life are the phrases "God is Spirit" (John 4:24), and "God is light" (1 John 1:5). In both contexts θεὸς refers to the Father,[124] whose essential nature is morally excellent and pure spirit, and thus, the source of all true life.[125]

Michael Ovey draws out the implications for the Father's role as initiator:

> In this asymmetrical and co-relative relationship, there is deep but asymmetrical love between the Father and the Son. The Father's love is paternal in that he loves his Son and accordingly, as a father, is lavishly generous both in eternity and within time: in eternity he gives the Son the same kind of life that he has himself, life-in-himself (uncreated life); and within the framework of created space and time he gives his Son all things in creation as his to rule over. The Son's love is filial in that he loves the Father and reveals this by his obedience to his Father and his will.[126]

---

121. Every time the phrase "living God" is used in the New Testament (Matt 16:16; 26:63; Acts 14:15; Rom 9:26; 2 Cor 3:3; 6:16; 1 Tim 3:15; 4:10; Heb 3:12; 9:14; 10:31; 12:22; Rev 7:2), it is in reference to the Father.

122. Arguing for eternal submission of the Son to the Father, Randy Rheaume says in the thesis of his article, "A careful look at the Johannine theme of the Son's life, particularly, in 5:26 and 6:57, is pertinent to the question. . . . [I]n the Fourth Gospel, Jesus' sonship markedly connotes a unilateral dependence for his life upon the Father; second, that this life dependence is evident not only during Jesus' earthly mission, but is also characteristic of his eternal filial status; and third, that this life dependence is an indicative of an eternal, superlative relationship with his Father, who ever extends this fellowship to the Son." Rheaume, "John's Jesus on Life Support," 50. That Jesus is the "Son" not merely during his incarnation is evident. The one sent into the world was the Son (John 3:17). In addition, Carson argues that the "life-in-himself" which the Father granted to the Son must mean the same as the "life-in-himself" which the Father has in the same verse (5:26). The most natural understanding of the phrase is that it refers to the Father's self-existence. Thus, Carson interprets this as an "eternal grant" from Father to Son establishing the eternal nature of their Father-Son relationship. See Carson, *Difficult Doctrine of the Love of God*, 37–38.

123. Kruse, *John*, 57.

124. The personal pronouns used here by Jesus helpfully demonstrate that this is the person of the Father and not a broader reference to the Trinity.

125. See Morris, *John*, 240, Yarbrough, *1-3 John*, 48–49, and Brown, *John*, 194–95.

126. Ovey, *Your Will Be Done*, 77.

Reflecting on the Son's dependence upon the Father, Christopher Cowan agrees,

> Jesus's dependence on the Father reaches back into his preexistence in John 17:24. Here, Jesus prays to the Father that his disciples might be with him, so that they might behold his glory, "which you have given me because you loved me before the foundation of the world" (cf. 17:5: "the glory I had with you before the world existed"). The glory which the Father had given to the Son was a result of his love for him prior to creation. Thus, the Son's dependence on his Father for his glory reaches into eternity past before the incarnation.[127]

This priority of the Father is what the church fathers meant when they called him *fons* (fount), *principium* (beginning), and *aitia* (cause).

The Son and Spirit's Relation to the Father

One in nature

From the opening verses of John's Gospel (John 1:1, 2), God the Father is in an eternal and intimate relation with the Word, and though distinct from the Word, they both fully possess the very nature of God.[128] When John says, "the Word was God," his use of θεός is qualitative, meaning that their essence is identical.[129] And though not as explicit, John also ascribes the divine nature to the Spirit. The Spirit is the one "from heaven" (John 1:32),[130]

---

127. Cowan, "Father and Son," 63.

128. Again, in the verse, John assumes that the person God (ὁ θεὸς) possesses the divine nature, and works to explain that the person Word (ὁ λόγος) also possesses the divine nature (the second, anarthrous use of θεὸς).

129. Wallace, *Greek Grammar*, 269. For a thorough treatment of all possibilities see Harris, *Jesus as God*, 57–71.

130. Just as the Son was sent from heaven, so also is the Spirit sent from heaven, and thus, by implication, also possesses the divine nature. Therefore, the Spirit exerts the divine prerogative to give life (John 6:63), and is why Jesus will later call him "another Helper (ἄλλον παράκλητον)" (John 14:16), who will dwell in God the Father's children (John 14:17).

the one who is "before his [the Father's] throne" (Rev 1:4),[131] and the one who holds all things in common with the Father and Son (John 16:15).[132]

Likewise, Philippians 2:6, "though he [the Son] was in the form of God [the Father]," Colossians 1:15, "He [the Son] is the image of the invisible God [the Father]," Colossians 2:9, "For in him [the Son] the whole fullness of deity dwells bodily," and Hebrews 1:3, "He [the Son] is the radiance of the glory of God [the Father] and the exact imprint of his nature" speak to the divine unity of the Father and Son. Finally, in John 10:30 (cf. John 5:18; 17:11, 22), Jesus makes the statement, "I and the Father are one." The Father and Son's oneness emphasizes the unity of their works, and yet a unity of nature is also assumed,[133] which leads Meyer to conclude, "Jesus is the one who has been 'sent' by God. . . . Such language, while it maintains the evangelist's stress on unity in action, preserves also the distinction between Jesus and the Father—and is the principal reason why the evangelist's theology cannot be collapsed into his Christology."[134]

Differing Roles

In John 14:28, however, Jesus gives a contrasting testimony, "The Father is greater than I."[135] John 10:30 and 14:28 are reconciled by asserting that though the Son is not ontologically inferior to the Father, nevertheless, the Father is greater than the Son in reference to his authority,[136] for the Son's submission to the Father was not only manifested in his incarnate ministry but is rooted in his eternal sonship.[137] In the context, this submission was to bring the disciples great joy because the greater authority of the Father to

---

131. Although some take "seven spirits" here to be the angels of the seven churches or archangels, it is better considering Old Testament allusions (cf. Zech 4) to see "seven spirits" to be a reference to the Holy Spirit (cf. Rev 3:1; 4:5; 5:6). Importantly, the seven spirits are not just before the throne of the Father, they are also closely associated with the Lamb, Jesus Christ (Rev 1:5). See Osborne, *Revelation*, 61–62, 74.

132. A careful identification of pronouns is necessary for this conclusion. "All that the Father has is mine [Jesus']; therefore I [Jesus] said that he [the Spirit] will take what is mine [Jesus'] and declare it to you [the Apostles]." See Köstenberger, *John*, 474.

133. Carson, *John*, 394. See also discussion in Köstenberger, *John*, 312.

134. Meyer, "The Father," 261.

135. Cf. also John 10:29; 13:16, where Jesus says the "Father is greater than all" and "a messenger [is not] greater than the one who sent him."

136. Hoskyns and Davey, *Fourth Gospel*, 464.

137. Köstenberger, *John*, 445.

send both the Son and Spirit will provide the power for the disciples to do "greater works" (John 14:12).[138]

Further, the phrase "before the foundation of the world" often speaks of the Father's role as the initiator of redemption accomplished by his Son: the Father chose his elect in Christ before the foundation of the world (Eph 1:4), the Father's purposes and grace were planned for his elect in Christ Jesus before the ages began (2 Tim 1:9), the Father knew that the Son as "the Lamb" would be the one to shed his blood for sinners (1 Pet 1:19–20; Rev 13:8), and the Father placed the names of his elect in the Lamb's "book of life" before the foundation of the world (Rev 13:8; 17:8). All of this work is rooted in the Father's love and affection toward his Son, for Jesus asks, "Father, I desire that they also, whom you have given me, may be with me where I am, to see my glory that you have given me because you loved me before *the foundation of the world* [emphasis mine]" (John 17:24).[139]

Summary

This brief glimpse into the divine nature and the Father's distinct personhood demonstrates that the Father eternally holds the first place of order among the persons of the Godhead and is the initiator of divine action evident in (1) the sendings of the Son and Spirit for the purpose of revealing the Father, (2) the frequent assignment of attributes to the first person of the Godhead (e.g., God is love, God is light, God is spirit, God is holy), and (3) differing eternal roles for each person of the Trinity. Nevertheless, Scripture is abundantly clear that a difference in roles does not entail a difference in nature or an inferiority of persons. Father, Son, and Spirit are all fully God, fully possess the divine nature, and are equally and infinitely glorious. In wrestling with these very issues, the early fathers explained the Trinity *ad extra* (economic Trinity) as a reflection of the Trinity *ad intra* (immanent Trinity).

Just as the Son is "begotten" into the world (John 1:14, 18; 3:16; Ps 2:7 quoted in Acts 13:33 and Heb 1:5; 5:5) and the Spirit "proceeds" from the Father and Son (John 15:26) in the economy of redemption, so too, the early fathers argued, the Father, as the fountainhead of divinity, eternally generates the Son and eternally spirates (the eternal procession of) the Spirit.[140] Therefore, the doctrines of generation and procession are a necessary

---

138. Fisher, "God the Father," 291.

139. For the Father's role among the persons of the Trinity, see Ware, *Father, Son, and Spirit*.

140. The meaning of μονογενής (e.g., John 1:14, 18; 3:16) is under discussion. It

consequence derived from the reality of Father, Son and Spirit as persons in the Godhead. As Kevin Giles writes, "A father-son relationship presupposes begetting. Fathers beget children."[141] Thus, if the Son is the eternal Son, then he must be eternally generated, and if the Spirit is the eternal Spirit, he must proceed from the Father and Son.

Giles explains further:

> Designating the eternal Father-Son act of self-differentiation, "the begetting of the Son" is justified because Psalm 2:7 and Proverbs 8:25, which both use the term "beget" (*gennaō*) are interpreted christologically in the New Testament. Calling this *eternal* begetting is justified because these texts ultimately refer to Christ, who is God. What is created is temporal; what is divine is eternal.[142]

Because the Trinity *ad extra* is a reflection of the Trinity, *ad intra*, Scripture permits us to speak of the eternal generation of the Son and procession of the Spirit. As the Nicene-Constantinople Creed (381) declares: "And in one Lord Jesus Christ, the only-begotten Son of God, begotten from the Father before all ages.... And in the Holy Spirit, the Lord and life-giver, Who proceeds from the Father."[143]

The Triune God exists *a se*, and therefore (contrary to Origen) it is proper to speak of Son or Spirit as *autotheos*, along with the Father. Calvin argues, "whosoever says that the Son has been given his essence from

---

either comes from the root of γένος, meaning "class" or "kind," or from the root of γεννάω, meaning "generate" or "bring forth." For example, John Feinberg, arguing for γένος, concludes that the Nicaean idea of begottenness "seems to be a case of forcing metaphysical distinctions and doctrines into the text of Scripture where they don't belong." Feinberg, *No One Like Him,* 492. Others, however, would see wider implications in the term μονογενής than simply uniqueness. Malcolm Yarnell, in his recent work, writes "This [the Son's derivation described by the word γεννάω] is according to the descriptions of the Son as begotten in Psalm 2:7, which was repeated in Hebrews 1:5–6 and 5:5–6 (cf. 7:13, 17), and according to the description of Wisdom as begotten in Proverbs 8:25 (LXX). Generation or begetting is also implied in the Johannine contexts in which *monogenes* is used (cf. 1:13, 18; 3:3–8, 16)." Yarnell, *God the Trinity,* 124. See also Horrell, "Complementarian Trinitarianism," 347n13. Usage of the word is far more important than the etymology in determining meaning. See Dahms, "The Johannine Use of *Monoge[set macron over e]nes* Reconsidered," 222–32.

141. Giles, *Eternal Generation,* 69.

142. Ibid. Later, Giles usefully shows that John's wording in 1 John 5:18, "he who was born of God [the Son] protects him [the Christian born of God]," suggests the preexistence of the Son. He was "born" and existed before he came into the world. See Giles, *Eternal Generation,* 83.

143. Kelly, *Early Christian Creeds,* 297–98.

the Father denies that he has being from himself."¹⁴⁴ According to Calvin, what the Son receives from the Father is not his divine essence, but his personhood: "Therefore we say that deity in an absolute sense exists of itself; whence likewise we confess that the Son since he is God, exists of himself, but not in relation to his Person; indeed, since he is the Son, we say that he exists from the Father."¹⁴⁵

If this is true, the divine names of Father, Son, and Spirit are eternal and are to be confessed as true to the deepest realities of the Godhead. Further, the Father is the origin of the Father-Son relationship in some way that the Son is not (as well as the Father-Spirit relationship in some way that the Spirit is not). Likewise, that the Son, rather than the Father or Spirit, became incarnate, was not arbitrary. Nor was it some sort of arbitrary, divine choice that the Spirit is the one sent by both the Father and the Son. Thus, the language of unity, diversity and *taxis* is expressed with the words "begottenness" and "spiration."

Divine Action and the Father's Role

Opera trinitatis ad extra sunt indivisa (the external works of the Trinity are undivided). Historically articulated as the doctrine of inseparable operations, it is understood to be true because of divine unity and mutual indwelling.¹⁴⁶ The Gospel of John, more than any other New Testament book, teaches the mutual indwelling of Father, Son, and by implication, Holy Spirit. The first reference of the Father "in" the Son and the Son "in" the Father is found in John 10:38 (cf. 14:10, 20; 17:21): "believe the works, that you may know and understand that the Father is in me and I am in the Father." Therefore, the Father and Son are inseparably "one" (John 17:21). Furthermore, the many 'just as' statements give evidence to mutual indwelling (John 5:21, 23, 26; 6:57; 8:28; 10:15; 12:50).¹⁴⁷ Similarly, the Spirit's interpenetration of Father and Son is implied by John 14:20, for the knowledge of the Father and Son's mutual indwelling was made known by the Spirit at his coming.¹⁴⁸

144. Calvin, *Institutes*, 1.13.23.

145. Ibid., 1.13.25.

146. The terms *circumincessio, circumcessio, circumcession, perichoresis*, and *coinherence* are older technical terms that have been used for this idea of mutual indwelling. For a history of *perichoresis*, see Letham, *Holy Trinity*, 139–40, 178–83, 240–41.

147. I am indebted to Köstenberger and Swain, *Father, Son, and Spirit*, 74n41 for this line of research.

148. A more oblique reference is seen in the titles for the Spirit. He is the "Holy Spirit" (John 1:33; 14:26; 20:22), the "Spirit of God" (1 John 4:2; Rev 3:1; 4:5; 5:6) and "Spirit of Christ" (esp. Rom 8:9 where "Spirit of God" and "Spirit of Christ" are together;

Alongside, but not independent of, the doctrine of inseparable operations also stands the reality of actions called "distinct appropriations," that are ascribed to a particular person of the Godhead.[149] Therefore, for example, all of the persons of the Godhead worked in incarnation: the Father sending the Son (John 8:42), the Son becoming "flesh" (John 1:14; Phil 2:6–8), and the Spirit miraculously conceiving the human nature and by that the hypostatic union (Matt 1:20; Luke 1:34–35). However, it is only the Father who sent the Son to earth, only the Son took on a human nature and lived on earth, and only the Holy Spirit produced the hypostatic union of two natures in the person of the eternal Son. Most important for our discussion, the *taxis* of distinct appropriations within the doctrine of inseparable operations is never reversed. All actions and work initiate with the Father, who is the originator of all divine action.

In the Johannine literature, mutual indwelling necessarily leads to and is revealed through the unity of divine action, which is why Jesus says, "believe the works" (John 10:38) and "the Father who dwells in me does his works" (John 14:10). Furthermore, it is what leads Matthew Fisher to conclude, "Taken in harmony with 9:3–4 and 10:32, 37, this statement about the Father's working in 14:10 fits very well with the immediately preceding statement about the interpenetration of the Father and Son—the Son does the Father's works and the Father does his own work through the Son."[150] Therefore, Peter can preach in Acts 2:22, "Men of Israel, hear these words: Jesus of Nazareth, a man attested to you by God with mighty works and wonders and signs that God [the Father] did through him in your midst."

The remainder of this book is an examination of the Father's works (his distinct appropriations) from eternity past to eternity future, demonstrating the Father's priority (not hierarchy) in all that the Triune God is doing (inseparable operations). Even so, it will be good here to briefly note the Father's role in the broad categories of the decree, creation, redemption, and the consummation. In the decree, the Father is the one who planned everything according to his purposes, for he "works all things according to the counsel of his will (Eph 1:11)."

In creation, the Father is the architect and designer who created the universe through his Son (Heb 1:2; Col 1:16) in the power of the Holy Spirit (Gen 1:2). In redemption, the Father designed the perfect means of salvation that is his secret and hidden wisdom (1 Cor 2:7), which was promised

---

also 1 Pet 1:11; Gal 4:6; Phil 1:19).

149. Doyle brings out Calvin's nuance of inseparable operations and distinct personal appropriations. Doyle, "Basic Expectations," 151–74.

150. Fisher, "God the Father," 285. See also Morris, *John*, 572.

beforehand through his prophets (Rom 1:2), and is concerning his Son (Rom 1:3). Because of the Father, believers are placed in Christ (1 Cor 1:30; 2 Cor 1:21) through the ministry of his Spirit (2 Cor 1:22), the Father working in his children "both to will and to work for his good pleasure (Phil 2:13)." In the consummation, the Father, who put everything under the authority of his Son (1 Cor 15:27), will receive back the kingdom from Christ at the end of the age (1 Cor 15:24). Even the Son will be subject to the Father (1 Cor 15:28), so that the Father will be sovereign over all (1 Cor 15:28). As sovereign, the Father grants his kingdom to his children (Gal 5:21; 2 Thess 1:5; 1 Cor 6:9; 15:50; Eph 5:5), and will make known his glorious riches to them for all eternity (Rom 9:23; Eph 2:7). Thus, the saints will serve (Rev 7:15) and worship (Rev 22:3) the Father through the Son and by the Spirit day and night forever.

Conclusion

This chapter has shown that Scripture proves the equal glory and coeternal majesty of the Father, Son, and Holy Spirit, and that they share full unity regarding the divine name, the divine nature and divine action. Furthermore, embedded in the eternal *taxis* of Father, Son, and Holy Spirit, the Father holds the first place among the persons of the Godhead from all eternity. The Father is customarily the referent when the proper names of God are used (*Elohim, Yahweh, Adonai*, θεός, and κύριος), which is expected since the Father occupies the first place within the operational ordering of the personal names (e.g., Father-Son-Spirit) and is the initiator of all divine action.

As to the divine nature, the Father holds the first position of relational order among the divine persons (e.g., unbegotten, eternal generation, eternal procession). Furthermore, regarding the inseparable operations of the divine action, the distinct personal appropriation of the Father is always as the initiator, purposer, and planner of Trinitarian works. Thus, the Father's relationships within the Trinity confirm that an eternal, unchangeable *taxis* exists within the Godhead, such that the Father possesses operational and relational priority of order, not rank.

In the following chapters, I will biblically and exegetically consider the Father's works (his distinct appropriations) from eternity past to eternity future. Consequently, this Paterology will substantiate my claim that the Father is the initiator of all divine action.

3

The Father's Work of Planning All Things from Eternity Past

Introduction

IN THE PREVIOUS CHAPTER, I argued that the unity of the divine identity, divine nature, and divine action demonstrates the full and equal deity of the Father, Son, and Spirit. Furthermore, an eternal *taxis* exists among the persons of the Godhead, such that the Father holds the first place from all eternity and within the inseparable operations of the Godhead, the Father is the initiator, architect and designer of all Trinitarian works.

Millard Erickson disagrees,

> Although one person of the Trinity may occupy a more prominent part in a given divine action, the action is actually that of the entire Godhead, and the one person is acting on behalf of the three. This means that those passages that speak of the Father predestining, sending, commanding, and so on should not be taken as applying to the Father alone but to all persons of the Trinity. Thus they do not count as evidence in support of an eternal supremacy of the Father and an eternal subordination of the Son.[1]

However, as this chapter to show, Erickson confuses the ability to plan and act (based upon attributes of the divine nature like omnipotence, omniscience, etc.) with the actions attributed by Scripture to a specific person of the Godhead (in this case, the Father). Divine plans and actions do not merely emanate from the divine nature; rather, omnipotent persons of the Trinity work according to their eternal roles within the Godhead. Appropriately, before the Father acts, he designs and wills all that comes to pass.

---

1. Erickson, *Who's Tampering with the Trinity*, 138. For refutation, see Grudem, "Doctrinal Deviations," 20–22.

Therefore, in this chapter, I will summarize the works of the Father from eternity past in the theological term, "the decree." Rather than deciding some things in eternity past and some things later, the Father decreed all things at once in eternity past.[2]

Thus, in this chapter, I will argue for the Father's initiating role based upon three evidences: (1) Scripture defines the decree as the *Father's* wise, eternal, all-inclusive, sovereign plan, (2) the decree is rooted in the Father's love and good pleasure, and (3) specific determinations and allowances in the decree are always attributed to the Father.

The Definition of the Father's Decree

In question 12 of the Westminster Larger Catechism (1646), the writers explained,

> God's decrees are the wise, free, and holy acts of the counsel of his will, [Eph. 1:11, Rom. 11:33, Rom. 9:14–15,18] whereby, from all eternity, he hath, for his own glory, unchangeably foreordained whatsoever comes to pass in time, [Eph. 1:4,11, Rom. 9:22–23, Ps. 33:11] especially concerning angels and men.[3]

The expression, "divine decree,"[4] is a summary attempt to systematize all of the various terms used in the Scriptures that speak of God the Father's plan and purpose for all things: "counsel" (סוֹד, עֵצָה), "purpose" (יָצַר, זָמַם, βουλή/βούλομαι), "good pleasure" (חָפֵץ, εὐδοκία), "will" (θέλημα/θέλω), "predestine" (προορίζω), "determine" (ὁρίζω), "determine beforehand" (προτάσσω), "prepare beforehand" (προετοιμάζω), "plan" (πρόθεσις/προτίθημι), "promise" (ἐπαγγελία/ἐπαγγέλλομαι), "foreknow" (πρόγνωσις/προγινώσκω), and "election" (ἐκλεκτός, ἐκλέγομαι, ἐκλογή).[5] In fact, only seven verses (Matt 11:27; Luke 10:22; John 5:21; 15:16, 19; 17:24; 21:22) use these words in reference to Jesus, and only one verse (1 Cor 12:11) uses

---

2. This is in contrast with open theism (which asserts that God's sovereignty is general, but not specific). For an excellent critique, see Ware, *God's Lesser Glory*. For Ware's defense of theism, see Ware, *God's Greater Glory*.

3. *Westminster Confession of Faith*, 172–73.

4. Theologies since the Westminster have consistently used this expression; for example, *Second London Confession* (1689); Brakel, *Christian's Reasonable Service*; Dabney, *Systematic Theology*; A. A. Hodge, *Outlines of Theology*; Boyce, *Systematic Theology*; Shedd, *Dogmatic Theology*; Strong, *Systematic Theology*; Charles Hodge, *Systematic Theology*; Berkhof, *Systematic Theology*; Chafer, *Systematic Theology*; Thiessen, *Systematic Theology*; Smith, *Systematic Theology*; Reymond, *Systematic Theology*; Feinberg, *No One Like Him*; Frame, *Doctrine of God*; and Horton, *Christian Faith*.

5. See discussion in Feinberg, *No One Like Him*, 502–3.

βούλομαι in reference to the Spirit; none of which argue for the Son or Spirit's initiation of the decree.

In Matthew 11:27 (cf. Luke 10:22), the Son only chooses to reveal the Father to those that the Father has already given him. Likewise, the many passages in John are in the greater context of the Son only doing "what he sees the Father doing" (John 5:19–20) and doing the "will of [the Father] who sent [him]" (John 5:30). Furthermore, the ones who come to the Son are the ones that the Father has already given him (John 6:37). Similarly, the Spirit individually apportions spiritual gifts "as he wills" (1 Cor 12:11), but it is in the context of God the Father "empowering" gifts in everyone (1 Cor 12:6), who does it by "giving a manifestation of the Spirit."[6] It is why Wayne Grudem concludes,

> Therefore the testimony of Scripture on this matter is consistent. When the Son chooses people for salvation, he is simply following the directives of the Father. He is not acting independently of the Father's authority. Yes, both Father and Son participate in choosing, yet their actions are not identical but distinct. The Father chooses; the Father shows the Son who has been chosen, and the Son chooses those who have been given to him by the Father (John 6:37).[7]

Thus, the consistent testimony of Scripture attributes the divine decree to the person of the Father.

Recently, Robert Culver has argued for the use of the word "plan" rather than decree:

> The word "plan" presents a better face to the reader because the singular number (decree, not decrees) excludes the implication of possible alternate courses for the world in God's mind and it neither suggests nor implies arbitrariness or hesitancy on God's part. God was and is in charge and knows exactly what course the cosmos He made should and will take.[8]

Although in substantial agreement with Culver, I will employ the terms "decree" and "plan" interchangeably, using decree as the more technical term for comprehensive plan of the Father. As such, Scripture characterizes the Father's decree as: (1) wise, (2) eternal and unchangeable, (3) all-inclusive and unconditional, and (4) sovereign.

---

6. Thiselton, *First Corinthians*, 989.
7. Grudem, "Doctrinal Deviations," 23.
8. Culver. *Systematic Theology*, 126.

It Is Wise

From the use of terms like "counsel" and "purpose," the Father's decree is founded in careful thought and deliberation, not arbitrary choices.[9] For example, in Psalm 104:24, commenting on the diversity of God's works, the Psalmist sings, "O Lord, how manifold are your works! In wisdom have you made them all." Likewise, Paul declares that the Father "works all things according to the *counsel* of his will [emphasis mine]" (Eph 1:11),[10] and in Romans, after discussing the sovereign acts of God the Father in his elective purposes (Rom 9–11), Paul concludes with the doxology, "Oh, the depth of the riches and *wisdom* and *knowledge* of God [the Father]! How unsearchable are his judgments and how inscrutable his ways! 'For who has known the *mind* of the Lord, or who has been his *counselor* [emphasis mine]?'" (Rom 11:33–34).[11] Thus, there is a worthy reason to praise the Father as initiator of everything that is a part of his divine plan.

It Is Eternal and Unchangeable

Many passages of Scripture speak of the Father's purposing or planning his works before the foundation of the world: the kingdom prepared for the saints (Matt 25:34), election (Eph 1:4), the names of the saints written in the Lamb's book of life (Rev 13:8; 17:8), and the choice of Christ as redeemer (1 Pet 1:20). These are elsewhere called his "eternal purposes" (Eph 3:11; cf. 2 Tim 1:9). Feinberg insightfully notes that their eternal nature means that they will never change in the future:

> God's plans were made in eternity past, but can they be frustrated at some future time? The psalmist (Psalm 33) instructs us as he praises God for his attributes and his act of creation. He says (vv. 10–11), "The Lord nullifies the counsel of the nations; He frustrates the plans of the peoples. The counsel of the Lord stands forever, the plans of His heart from generation to generation." From this we see not only God's control over world affairs but also that his plans are eternal in that they will continue indefinitely into the future without annulment.[12]

---

9. Shedd, *Dogmatic Theology*, 314.

10. It is clear from the context that the subject of the participle ἐνεργοῦντος is the Father (1:3), who sets forth his "purposes in Christ" (1:9).

11. On the wisdom of the decree, see Chafer, *Systematic Theology*, 1.229.

12. Feinberg, *No One Like Him*, 515.

Thus, there will be no change from within or contingency from without. It is why the Father can affirm, "For I am God, and there is no other; I am God, and there is none like me, declaring the end from the beginning and from ancient times things not yet done, saying, 'My counsel shall stand, and I will accomplish all my purpose'" (Isa 46:9–10).[13]

It Is All-Inclusive and Unconditional

If the Father's plan is eternal, wise and unchangeable, it follows that it must also be all-inclusive and unconditional. For example, from the smallest detail (not even a sparrow falls to the ground apart from the Father—Matt 10:29–30) to the most comprehensive designs (the Father having determined allotted periods and boundaries of every nation of mankind—Acts 17:26), none of his purposes can be thwarted (Job 42:2; Ps 135:6; Isa 14:27). Although the Father's decree is not conditioned upon anything outside of himself, it does not mean that he is the only actor. The Father ordains means as well as ends (Eph 1:4; 2 Thess 2:13; 1 Pet 1:2), and uses various agents to carry out his will, including the Son and the Spirit.[14] Thus, while the Father has even determined the free acts and choices of men, the actors themselves are still responsible (Gen 50:20; Acts 2:23; 3:18; 4:27, 28).[15]

---

13. Though it is not clear from the immediate context that this passage refers to the Father, it is in the context of the four "Servant Songs" (Isa 42:1–9; 49:1–13; 50:4–9; 52:13—53:12), whereby the Father promises to place his Son on center stage as the ideal "servant," and as the one who will bring Jacob back to himself and bring salvation to the ends of the earth (Isa 49:5–6). Terminology apparently coined by Duhm. See Duhm, *Das Buch Jesaja*.

14. See Feinberg's well-reasoned defense in Feinberg, *No One Like Him*, 527–29.

15. Strong, *Systematic Theology*, 1.353–68. On the issue of "determinism," Culver asserts, "There are about three varieties of determinism advocated in the world. This is to say, those who think we have no freedom at all, propose one or all of three causes for this lack of freedom. One is a sort of impersonal, materialistic fate thought to be built into the very fabric of the universe. This is the *moira, aisa* or *fatum* (fate or the fates) of Greek and Roman antiquity. . . . As the ancients became scientific, a second form of determinism—cause-effect in an eternal chain—arose and is still with us as 'scientific or naturalistic determinism', either environmental or hereditary or both. Astrology, which assumes the stars of the sky determine destiny ('your lucky stars') arose very early in human history. It was drawn upon to support the first form of determinism, that is, fate. Both have had revivals in modern times and together reign on most university campuses today. A third form is religious determinism, a major feature of Islam, a non-Trinitarian monotheism. Any strongly held monotheism that has no Savior-God, no wise, loving, holy Father, quickly becomes a hard fatalism, as in the whole Muslim world. The same views develop in forms of Christianity where awareness of God's sovereignty is not matched with awareness of His love, mercy and holiness and does not give sufficient emphasis to that freedom under God that all human beings have as

It Is Sovereign

In Psalm 115:3, in contrast to other gods, the psalmist sings "Our God is in the heavens; he does all that he pleases." As the all-wise God, no one counseled the Lord or taught him anything (Isa 40:12–28; Rom 11:33–35). As the eternal and immutable one, his free and sovereign purposes flow out of his own desires (Eph 1:11) and are accomplished for his name's sake (Isa 48:11; Ezek 20:9).[16] Because the Father determines means as well as ends, he both determines and allows certain aspects within the decree. For example, in Acts 2:23, Peter preaches that Jesus was delivered up according to "the definite plan and foreknowledge of God [the Father];" nevertheless, Jesus was also "crucified and killed by the hands of lawless men." Thus, sinful acts do not frustrate the Father's plans, for he has decreed them. Even still, he is not the author of sin, nor does he tempt anyone to sin (Jas 1:13).[17]

The Decree is Rooted in the Father's Love and Good Pleasure

John Calvin places the Father's particular work from eternity in the doctrines of election and predestination. In his "Articles concerning Predestination," Calvin describes the Father's eternal counsel as "what he willed to be done with the whole human race," and delineates the plan as: 1) the fall of man in Adam, 2) distinction between the elect and the reprobate, 3) adoption of the elect, and 4) a reckoning of the elect as the Father's possession prior to him making the elect members in Christ.[18] Calvin calls this doctrine the "fountain and the first cause;" namely, "God knew before the world was created whom he had elected for salvation."[19] Butin explains Calvin's position: "The gracious will to make the divine nature known to fallen human beings through the gospel stems from the free election of the *hypostatis* of the Father."[20] According to Calvin, the Father's elective work defines the

---

being, by creation, God's image." Culver, *Systematic Theology*, 132.

16. On this point, see Charles Hodge, *Systematic Theology*, 1.535–37 and Erickson, *Christian Theology*, 352.

17. For a thorough argument on God's specific sovereignty over all things, see Frame, *The Doctrine of God*, 47–79.

18. Reid, *Calvin*, 179–80.

19. Commenting on 1 Peter 1:1–2 in Calvin, *Catholic Epistles*, 24.

20. Butin, *Revelation, Redemption, and Response*, 55.

church,²¹ and his purpose will never be changed.²² This is because, for Calvin, the Father gives all of his elect to the Son:

> First, that all who come unto Christ, were before given unto Him by the Father; secondly, that those who were thus given unto Him were delivered, as it were, from the hand of the Father into the hand of the Son, that they may be truly his; thirdly, that Christ is the sure keeper of all those, whom the Father delivered over to his faithful custody and care; for the very end, that He might not suffer one of them to perish.²³

Furthermore, Calvin is careful to root the Father's elective purposes in his eternal love. Meditating on 2 Corinthians 13:14, he says, "For God, viewed in himself, loved us before the creation of the world, and redeemed us for no other reason than this—because he loved us."²⁴ In 2.16.3 of the *Institutes*, he affirms, "Indeed 'because he first loved us', he afterward reconciles us to himself."²⁵

Additionally, Calvin not only ties the Father's elective purposes to his eternal love, but also to his good pleasure: "The intrinsic cause of this is in himself, for he is content with his own secret good pleasure."²⁶ Thus, in

---

21. According to the "Catechism of the Church of Geneva," the church is defined simply as, "the body and society of believers whom God has predestined to eternal life." Reid, *Theological Treatises*, 102.

22. In his *Institutes*, Calvin declares, "God's firm plan that election may never be shaken will be more stable than the very heavens." Calvin, *Institutes*, 3.22.7.

23. Calvin and Cole, *Calvin's Calvinism*, 32.

24. Calvin, *Corinthians*, 404.

25. *Institutes*, 2.16.3. For Calvin, the proof of the Father's love is only understood in Christ. "Christ draws our attention to the eternal counsel of the Father to teach us that the Father cared so much about our salvation that he handed over to us his one and only Son, great as he is. Christ himself, who came into the world to be totally obedient to his Father, confirms that in everything his only aim is to think of us." Calvin, *John*, John 10:18, 249. See also at John 3:35, where all the blessings of the Father's election come through Christ, ibid., 88.

26. *Institutes*, 3.22.7. See also Calvin, *Galatians and Ephesians*, 28, where Calvin defines the Father's "will" as his "good pleasure." He elaborates in his commentary on 2 Thess 1:11–12: "Paul goes to an amazing height in extolling the grace of God, for not contenting himself with the term *good pleasure*, he says that it flows from his goodness, unless perhaps any one should prefer to consider the beneficence as arising from this *good pleasure*, which amounts to the same thing. When, however, we are instructed that the *gracious purpose* of God is the cause of our salvation, and that *that* has its foundation in the *goodness* of the same God, are we not worse than mad, if we venture to ascribe anything, however small, to our own merits? For the words are in no small degree emphatic. He might have said in one word, *that your faith may be fulfilled*, but he terms it *good pleasure*. Farther, he expresses the idea still more distinctly by saying, that God was prompted by nothing else than his own goodness, for he finds nothing in

Calvin's Paterology, the Father purposes and plans salvation for his elect, motivated by love and resulting in his good pleasure. Calvin's categories reveal two of the Father's reasons for conceiving the decree: (1) his love and (2) his good pleasure.

The Father's Plan Is Rooted in His Love

The plan of salvation played out on the stage of creation is an overflow of the *Father's* eternal love for the Son in the Spirit. At the beginning of Galatians, Paul writes that it was the will of the Father for the Son to give himself for sin (Gal 1:4), and that the Father's plan redounds to his glory (Gal 1:5). There is a two-pronged manifestation of the Father's love on display: love for his own glory and love for his elect. Paul reveals that love and election are intertwined. In the letters to the Thessalonians, he writes "We know, brothers *loved* by God, that he has *chosen* you" (1 Thess 1:4), and "we ought always to give thanks to God [the Father] for you, brothers *beloved* by the Lord, because God [the Father] *chose* you as the firstfruits to be saved" (2 Thess 2:13).

According to Paul, the Father's love is not based upon the greatness of the person, since the Father chose "what is *foolish* . . . what is *weak* . . . what is *low* and *despised*" (1 Cor 1:27–28). Nor is it because of any works that the person performs, "in order that God [the Father]'s purpose of election might continue, not because of works but because of him who calls" (Rom 9:11). Rather, the Father's choice flows out of his foreknowledge (Rom 8:29; 11:2).[27] John Murray comments, "[Foreknowledge] means 'whom he set regard upon' or 'whom he knew from eternity with distinguishing affection and delight' and is virtually equivalent to 'whom he foreloved.'"[28] Thus, the Father chose those whom he set his affection upon in eternity past.

Further, his decree manifests itself in eternity past by the sovereign choice of a people from "every tribe and language and people and nation," (Rev 5:9) to be his own children (John 1:12–13), which the Father then gives to his Son (John 6:37; 10:29; 17:2, 6, 9, 24; 18:9). Jesus also reveals a number of realities attached to the decree: (1) All that the Father gives the Son will

---

us but misery. Nor does Paul ascribe to the grace of God merely the beginning of our salvation, but all departments of it." Calvin, *Philippians, Colossians, and Thessalonians*, 320. Calvin writes to Melanchthon that the elect and reprobate are distinguished by this same good pleasure. See Bonnet, *Letters of John Calvin*, 3:62.

27. Προγινώσκω "mean[s] not 'know before'—in the sense of intellectual knowledge, or cognition—but 'enter into relationship with before' or 'choose, or determine, before.'" Moo, *Romans*, 532.

28. Murray, *Romans*, 317.

come (John 6:37), (2) the Son knows them (John 10:27), (3) they will never be snatched out of the Father or Son's hands (John 10:28-29), (4) it is for the purpose of seeing the Father's character (John 17:6),[29] (5) they will be with the Son and see the Father's love and generosity toward the Son (John 17:24),[30] and (6) none will be lost (John 18:9).

What is clear from the preceding passages is that the giving of a people by the Father to the Son not only precedes their salvation, but also directs the motive for the Son's mission, and is why Jesus says in John 6:38-40 that the Father's will determines the success of the decree:

> For I have come down from heaven, not to do my own will but the *will of him who sent me*. And this is the *will of him who sent me*, that I should lose nothing of all that he has given me, but raise it up on the last day. For this is the *will of my Father*, that everyone who looks on the Son and believes in him should have eternal life, and I will raise him up on the last day.

Moreover, in the decree, the Father sets the Son apart for the purpose of redemption (John 10:36), and grants him "authority over all flesh" (John 17:2).[31] Against the idea of this authority being the "authority Jesus enjoys inherent in his being the Son," Carson forcefully argues,

> ... v. 2b refers to the Father's gift, *in eternity past*, of authority over all humanity, on the basis of the Son's *prospective* obedient humiliation, death, resurrection and exaltation. It is nothing less than the redemptive plan of God, for the second part of the verse makes the purpose of this grant clear: it is that the Son might give eternal life to those the Father has given him.[32]

Finally, the Father's sovereign election is rooted in and motivated by his love for sinners. In John 3:16, Jesus tells Nicodemus that the Father in this way "loved the world, that he gave his only son."[33] John, reflecting on this love in 1 John 3:1 calls his readers to consider the greatness of the Father's extravagant love, which is exhibited in their adoption as his children.[34]

---

29. To manifest the Father's name is to reveal his character. Carson, *John*, 558.

30. Köstenberger, *John*, 501.

31. The pronouns are important: "since you [Father] have given him [Son] authority over all flesh, to give eternal life to all whom you [Father] have given him [Son]."

32. Carson, *John*, 555.

33. I take "world" here to be the world system in alienation against God and hostile to him. See Lincoln, *John*, 154.

34. Kruse paraphrases the verse, "Look at the sort of love the Father has given us!" Kruse, *John*, 114.

Further, John defines true love as that which is seen in the Father's eternal act of setting his affection on a people and sending his Son to be the propitiation for their sins (1 John 4:10).[35] Likewise, God's children can only love because of the Father's prior love (1 John 4:19).

Thus, the perfect, eternal love of Father, Son, and Spirit for one another spills over into the Father's designs and purposes to bring a chosen people into this eternal Triune fellowship. Köstenberger and Swain's reflection on the covenant of redemption is helpful:

> In other words, the *pactum salutis* teaches us that the story which unfolds on the stage of history is the story of an intra-trinitarian fellowship of salvation, a fellowship that reaches back "before the world began" (17:5) and that continues even to "the hour" of Jesus' cross, resurrection, and ascension (17:1). In this regard, the claim that the *pactum salutis* is eternal is not so much a claim about "eternity past" as about eternal *persons*, persons whose fellowship remains unbroken throughout the course of redemption and thus guarantees that redemption. . . .[36]

The Father's Plan Brings Him Pleasure

In the same manner, the decree does not issue from the good pleasure of the Triune God's divine nature. Rather, because the Father's plan is motivated by *his* love, it brings *him* good pleasure to design *his* plan for the ages. Paul writes to the Ephesians that the mystery of the Father's will is "according to his purpose, which he set forth in Christ as a plan for the fullness of time, to unite all things in him, things in heaven and things on earth [emphasis mine]" (Eph 1:9–10). In other words, the great pleasure of the Father is to sum up all things in his Son. Later, Paul writes that the Father achieves his plan in Christ (Eph 3:11), and to the Colossians, Paul reiterates that the Father's mystery is Christ (Col 2:2) and the glorious riches of this mystery is Christ in the saints, the hope of glory (Col 1:26–27). Thus, there will be no corner of the world or feature of heaven where Christ's rule will not reach.

Furthermore, in Ephesians 1 (Scripture's most detailed exposition of the Father's design), Paul makes the Father's motive explicit. First, in v. 4, Paul writes that Christians are chosen for the purpose of holiness. When referring to the Father, Paul always uses the verb ἐκλέγομαι as an "indirect

---

35. Marshall, *John*, 214–15. "God's sending provides the fuller demonstration of his loving (cf. Rom. 5:8)." Yarbrough, *1–3 John*, 240.

36. Köstenberger and Swain, *Father, Son, and Spirit*, 170–71.

middle voice," where the Father is acting for himself or in his own interest, indicating it is for his good pleasure.³⁷ The goal is that the Father's elect would be "holy and blameless" before him. Second, in v. 5, Christians are "predestined for adoption as sons." The Father's plan is rooted in his love, which brings him εὐδοκία (1:5). Translated as "purpose" in the ESV, it is used in connection with the Father's will and as Clinton Arnold says, it "refers to the pleasure and delight in one's heart that forms the basis for decision making and action," and is therefore better translated "good pleasure."³⁸ Third, in v. 11, Paul tells the Ephesians that because of the Father's determinations and purposes, they are made to be his own inheritance. The verb here, "κληρόω" is different than in v. 4, where it is "ἐκλέγομαι."

Additionally, it is in the passive voice and should be translated "we are made to be an inheritance (contra ESV which has 'obtained an inheritance')."³⁹ It is why Peter can write in a similar manner in 1 Peter 2:9, "But you are a chosen race, a royal priesthood, a holy nation, a people for his own possession, that you may proclaim the excellencies of him who called you out of darkness into his marvelous light." The Christian community is one which God the Father has singled out and made peculiarly his own.⁴⁰ Thus, the Father, motivated by his love and out of his good pleasure, has planned everything that has or will ever happen, down to the smallest detail, and as Feinberg insightfully observes,

> Since God envisions a whole possible world at once, since his choice of a particular world is based solely on his own purposes and desires, and since it is impossible for an omniscient God to be mistaken about what he really desires or about whether a possible world actually accomplishes his goals, there is no reason for him to change his decree once he makes it.⁴¹

Summary

The decree is a divine act of the Father consistent with the orthodox understanding of inseparable operations. Thus, the Father's decree is shaped by the Father's eternal role within the Godhead as initiator of all divine action.

37. See Wallace, *Greek Grammar*, 419–21.
38. Arnold, *Ephesians*, 83.
39. See Hoehner, *Ephesians*, 227.
40. The implied owner of the noun περιποίησιν is God the Father and the antecedent refers back to 2:4–5 where θεοῦ is in distinction from the Son.
41. Feinberg, *No One Like Him*, 530.

Furthermore, Scripture confirms this by the Father's motives of "love" and "good pleasure." The Father's plan of salvation is an overflow of the Father's eternal love for the Son in the Spirit, and as such, brings him good pleasure in its design and implementation.

Specific Determinations and Allowances in the Father's Decree

In the Scriptures, the Father's decree consists of both determinations and allowances. Calling them the directive and permissive will of God, Paul Enns writes,

> The decree has two aspects. (1) The directive will of God. . . . There are some things in which God is the author; He actively brings about the events. He creates (Isa. 45:18); He controls the universe (Dan. 4:35); He establishes kings and governments (Dan. 2:21); He elects people to be saved (Eph. 1:4).
>
> (2) The permissive will of God. Even though God has determined all things, He may actively bring them about Himself, or He may bring them about through secondary causes. Sinful acts, for example, do not frustrate the plan of God, but neither is God the author of them. They are within the scope of God's decree and are part of His eternal plan and purpose, but man is nonetheless responsible for sinful acts. Hence, "a distinction must be made between the decree and its execution." All acts—including sinful acts—conform to the eternal plan of God, but He is not directly the author of all acts.[42]

Because of this, the Father's plan takes into account man's free choices and the Father will call human beings to account for their sinful choices. A compatibilistic understanding is necessary to explain human freedom and universal divine sovereignty. Bruce Ware explains,

> But not only does the Bible's teaching on the nature of human volition need to be *consistent* with its teaching on divine sovereignty, because the doctrine of sovereignty just surveyed

---

42. Enns, *Moody Handbook of Theology*, 205. Chafer, following Hodge, calls them the "efficacious" and "permissive" decrees. Chafer, *Systematic Theology*, 1.236. Berkhof also uses "permissive" regarding sin: "It should be carefully noted, however, that this permissive decree does not imply a passive permission of something which is not under the control of the divine will. It is a decree which renders the future sinful act absolutely certain, but in which God determines (a) not to hinder the sinful self-determination of the finite will; and (b) to regulate and control the result of this sinful self-determination," Berkhof, *Systematic Theology*, 105.

reveals God's comprehensive and universal control of all that occurs, our human volition must be manifest in a manner that is *compatible* with this strong understanding of divine sovereignty. Human freedom, in a word, must be compatibilistic. That is, comprehensive and universal divine sovereignty must be compatible with the actual and real manner by which human freedom operates [emphasis original].[43]

Most important for our discussion, specific determinations and allowances mentioned in Scripture are always attributed to the Father, whether in connection with creation and providence, the outworking of redemptive history, or the purposed judgment and glory in the consummation of all things.

Creation and Providence

The Father Determined to Create All Things

In Revelation 4:11, those gathered in the throne room of heaven cry out, "Worthy are you, our Lord and God, to receive glory and honor and power, for you created all things, and by your will they existed and were created." That ὁ κύριος and ὁ θεὸς refer to the Father as the one seated on the throne is clear because he is distinguished in the context from the Lamb (Rev 5:5, 7; 6:16; 7:10). Further, it is by the Father's "will (θέλημα)" that all things were created. Stephen Smalley explains,

> The Greek construction of this point is unusual, not to say difficult. First, there is an ambiguity in the preposition διά (*dia*), which means literally *"because of* (your will)." This, in turn, denotes either the operating cause or the intention of creation ("for the sake of your will"; Beasley-Murray 119). Both meanings appear to be present. Creation came about by the operation of God's will; but the universe came into being through him precisely so that his holy purposes for humanity could be accomplished.[44]

Similarly, Isaiah 45:18 declares, "For thus says the LORD, who created the heavens (he is God!), who formed the earth and made it (he established it; he did not create it empty, he formed it to be inhabited!): 'I am the LORD,

43. Ware, "Modified Calvinist Doctrine of God," 98–99. On compatibilism, see also chap. 14 of Feinberg, *No One Like Him*, 677–734, and Feinberg, "God Ordains All Things," 34–35.

44. Smalley, *Revelation*, 125.

and there is no other.'" Although it less clear that the Father is speaking than other passages in Isaiah (Isa 28:16; 44:2; 66:1; cf. Ezek 36:22; Hag 2:6),[45] this pronouncement demonstrates that God has a plan and purpose for the creation.[46] Thus, the Father's decree includes the permanence and stability of the cosmos (cf. Ps 119:90–91; Jer 31:35–37).

The Father Planned Every Detail of His Providential Rule

Following Berkhof,[47] this includes (1) the good actions of men (Eph 2:10–11; Phil 2:13), (2) the wicked actions of men (Prov 16:4; Acts 2:23; 4:27–28; Rev 17:17), (3) events (Prov 16:33; Isa 46:11; Jer 51:12; Dan 2:21; Matt 10:29–30), (4) the means as well as the end (Ps 119:89–91; 2 Thess 2:13; Eph 1:4), (5) the circumstances under which human beings live (Isa 14:26–27; 37:26; Ps 74:17; Acts 17:26; Rom 13:1; Jas 4:13–15; 1 Cor 7:24), and (6) duration of life (Job 14:5; Ps 39:4; 139:16).

From Ephesians 2:10, the Father has decreed the good actions of men and women. Paul writes, "For we are his [the Father's] workmanship, created in Christ Jesus for good works, which God prepared beforehand, that we should walk in them."[48] Also, the Father's plan includes the fall and subsequent evil acts of all people, best illustrated by Acts 2:23: "this Jesus, delivered up according to the definite plan and foreknowledge of God [the Father], you crucified and killed by the hands of lawless men." Nevertheless, James affirms that God the Father is not the author of evil nor does he tempt anyone to sin (Jas 1:13), and therefore people are responsible for their sinful actions.[49] Christ died because of the Father's decision in eternity past, and yet wicked men were held responsible for his death (cf. Acts 4:27–28).

---

45. As argued in chap. 2, it makes good sense here to see *Yahweh* as a reference to the Father, particularly since "thus says the Lord" is clearly the Father in the other mentioned passages. Likewise, the corresponding New Testament phrase τὸν λόγον τοῦ θεοῦ ("word of God") always uses θεός in reference to the Father.

46. On God's purpose in creation, see Young, *Isaiah*, 3:210–12.

47. Berkhof, *Systematic Theology*, 105.

48. The immediate context indicates that that ὁ θεός is in distinction from the Son, and that Christians are the Father's workmanship. On God's sovereignty in the works, see Arnold, *Ephesians*, 141–42.

49. My goal here is not to present a robust theodicy regarding the problem of evil; rather, I am demonstrating that in these passages and the rest of Scripture, it is always the Father who is the one purposing and planning future events, and thus, is always the initiator among the persons of the Godhead. For a thorough examination of the problem of evil, see Frame, *The Doctrine of God*, 160–82.

Furthermore, major events like the rise and fall of nations (Dan 2:21)[50] as well as minor details like the timing of a sparrow's death (Matt 10:29)[51] are under the authority and plan of God the Father. This is because the Father ordains the means as well as the end. For example, in 2 Thessalonians 2:13, Paul says, "God chose you as the firstfruits to be saved, through sanctification by the Spirit and belief in the truth." Here, all three persons of the Godhead are involved in the means of a believer's salvation (sanctification by the Spirit, belief in the truth regarding the Son's work), but it is the Father that chooses who will be saved and the means by which their salvation will be complete.[52]

Finally, the providential circumstances of life are decreed by the Father: he determines the appointed times and boundaries of every nation on the earth (Acts 17:26),[53] he establishes every governmental authority (Rom 13:1),[54] he wills what tomorrow will bring (Jas 4:13–15),[55] and ordains the length of one's life (Ps 139:16). Thus, the Father's purpose will be carried out until all his words are fulfilled (Rev 17:17).[56] In his commentary, Grant Osborne writes,

> In the narrow sense, this goes back to 17:1, where John was promised "the judgment of the great prostitute." In a broader sense, this goes back to the promise of the vindication of the saints in 6:9–11. In 10:7 we are told that "the mystery of God will be completed, just as he announced to his servants the prophets" at the sounding of the seventh trumpet. Thus, in the broadest sense, this points to the fulfillment of all the promises regarding the eschaton and final judgment throughout the Word of God. That would especially be seen in the plural οἱ λόγοι τοῦ θεοῦ, which points to all the prophecies, not just the one of this

---

50. I take *Eloah* here to be the Father because in v. 23, Daniel calls him "God of my fathers." Every use in the New Testament of God of Abraham, God of Isaac, God of Jacob, etc. is a reference to the first person of the Trinity.

51. In this passage, it is explicitly said to be the Father.

52. On the prepositional phrases as means, see Martin, *1, 2 Thessalonians*, 253–54.

53. From the context, θεός is a reference to the Father, since he is the one who raised Christ from the dead and appoints him to be judge (Acts 17:31).

54. The only use of θεός for the Son is in Rom 9:5. Every other use is a reference to the Father.

55. I found no commentaries that argue this is a reference to the Lord Jesus, although it could be argued from James's use in 2:1 and 5:7–8. However, it is less likely since the closer context identifies κύριος with the Father (Jas 3:9), and with God (Jas 4:4, 6–8).

56. In the immediate context θεὸς is in distinction from the Lamb (Rev 17:14). Further, in the book of Revelation, θεὸς is always the first person of the Trinity.

chapter. . . . In other words, the Antichrist and his followers will be participating not only in their own defeat but in what God had planned all along.[57]

My goal here is not to examine the Father's role in the actual work of creation and providence (that is the subject of the next chapter); rather, I have argued from these texts that it is the Father who determined to create all things and who planned every detail of his providential rule.

Redemption

The Father Sovereignly Chose Who Will Be Saved

Paul gives his most concise summary of the Father's plan for redemption in 2 Timothy 1:8–10:

> God [the Father], who saved us and called us to a holy calling [in the believer's experience], not because of our works but because of his own purpose and grace [in eternity past], which he gave us in Christ Jesus before the ages began [in eternity past], and which now has been manifested through the appearing of our Savior Christ Jesus [in redemptive history], who abolished death and brought life and immortality [in the eternal state] to light through the gospel.

The Father's purpose in Christ is to call out his elect, giving them salvation in Christ, which includes a holy calling, spiritual life through the ministry of the Holy Spirit for all eternity. All of this was planned under the authority of the Father "before the ages began." Similarly, when writing to Titus, Paul states that "God's elect" (Titus 1:1) are given the "hope of eternal life" which the Father promised "before the ages began" (Titus 1:2).[58] Peter says the Father's purpose in election is so that his elect would be "his own possession" and that they would "proclaim the excellencies of [the Father] who called [them] out of darkness into his marvelous light" (1 Pet 2:9).[59] Further, Peter connects the Christian's election to the election of Christ, who is "chosen and precious" (1 Pet 2:4, 6) to the Father.[60] This is because the Father does not choose based upon something inherently

---

57. Osborne, *Revelation*, 627–28.

58. Rather than a reference to the Old Testament era, it is proper to take πρὸ χρόνων αἰωνίων as referring to eternity past. See Knight, *Pastoral Epistles*, 284–85.

59. A likely allusion to Isa 43:21. See Schreiner, *1, 2 Peter, Jude*, 115–16.

60. Cf. Luke 9:35, "This is my Son, my *Chosen One*; listen to him!"

good in the person (Rom 9:11; 2 Cor 1:27–28; Jas 2:5).[61] Instead, as we saw earlier in the chapter, the Father's choice is an overflow of his eternal love for the Son in the Spirit, and as such, brings him good pleasure in its design and implementation.

It is why almost every verse of Ephesians 1:3–14 speaks of the Father's design in election: the Father blesses his elect in Christ through the Spirit (v. 3),[62] the Father chose them to be holy and blameless (v. 4),[63] in love the Father predestined his elect to adoption (v. 5),[64] redemption is part of the pleasure of the Father's will (v. 5),[65] election is according to the riches of the Father's grace, freely given in Christ (vv. 6–7),[66] the Father planned to make known his elective purposes in his Son (v. 9),[67] the Father's plan has as its climax the summing up of all things in Christ (v. 10),[68] the elect are predestined to an inheritance "according to the purpose of [the Father] who works all things according to the counsel of his will" (v. 11),[69] and the Father promised to send the Spirit to guarantee redemption for his elect (vv. 13–14).[70]

---

61. For a thorough exegetical defense of unconditional election, see Storms, *Chosen for Life*.

62. πάσῃ εὐλογίᾳ πνευματικῇ means pertaining to the life of the Spirit. See O'Brien, *Ephesians*, 95.

63. The verb is in the middle voice which indicates personal interest in the one chosen. It is not arbitrary. See Hoehner, *Ephesians*, 175.

64. προορίζω is used exclusively of God and in regard to his elect. Taken together with its use in Rom 8:29–30 and 1 Cor 2:7, the Father predetermined the path every Christian would take to be conformed to the image of his Son.

65. κατὰ τὴν εὐδοκίαν is used of the delight the Father takes in his plans. It has warm and personal meaning, and draws attention to God's willingness and joy to do good. τοῦ θελήματος αὐτοῦ is that which is purposed or intended, and stresses the Father's active resolve seen in his redemptive purpose. See Arnold, *Ephesians*, 83–84.

66. O'Brien here is helpful, "This clause stresses that it is in the Beloved, Jesus Christ, that God has poured out all his grace upon us. The verb rendered *freely given* is cognate with the noun *grace*, and emphasizes the abundance of God's gift of salvation as well as implying his generous attitude as the giver." O'Brien, *Ephesians*, 104.

67. That this planning is before the foundation of the world is clear from the context (v. 4).

68. See discussion in Arnold, *Ephesians*, 88–89. Also, cf. Eph 3:9–11 where the Father's "eternal purpose" is realized in Christ.

69. This verse is one of the clearest statements of the Father's initiating role from eternity past. Paul uses three different words that refer to the Father's decree: πρόθεσις, βουλή, and θέλημα. Further, he says the Father's plan encompasses "everything" (τὰ πάντα), including the work of the Son and Spirit. Finally, it is the Father who is doing the work (ἐνεργέω) of putting his plan into effect. Nowhere in the context (or anywhere else in Scripture for that matter) is there any hint that the Son or Spirit plans or purposes redemption.

70. That the promise of the Spirit is a part of the Father's eternal decree, see the

It is important to remember that the Son and Spirit are not resistant to or uninvolved with the Father's decree. Rather, they joyfully fulfill what the Father has planned. Grudem explains,

> Of course, the Son was in full agreement with the Father regarding this plan of salvation. We should never confuse the idea of the Father's *authority* with any thought that the Son disagreed with the Father's plan or reluctantly submitted to the Father's plan. Jesus said, "My food is to do the will of him who sent me and to accomplish his work" (John 4:24). He was the true fulfillment of the words of the Psalmist who said, "I delight to do your will, O my God; your law is within my heart" (Ps 40:8). The Son and Spirit fully agreed with the plans of the Father. But if we are to be faithful to the meaning of this Eph 1:3–5, we still must say that in the eternal councils of the Trinity, there was a role of planning, directing, initiating, and choosing, that belonged specifically to the Father.[71]

Since the goal of election is salvation (1 Thess 5:9; 2 Thess 2:13; Rom 8:33), the Father predestines the path every child of God will take to be conformed into the image of his Son (Rom 8:29). Paul describes the Father's plan as his secret and hidden wisdom (1 Cor 2:7), including everything that the Father has prepared for those who love him (1 Cor 2:9). Paul reveals that a part of the Father's mystery is for believers to know "the riches of his glory for vessels of mercy, which he has prepared beforehand for glory" (Rom 9:23).[72] The Father will make his elect fit for his presence, so that they might glorify him forever. It is why Paul, in chapter 11 of Romans, after investigating the glories of the eternal plan of the Father as revealed in the gospel, cries out "Oh, the depth of the riches and wisdom and knowledge of God [the Father]! How unsearchable are his judgments and how inscrutable his ways . . . for from him and through him and to him are all things. To him be glory forever" (Rom 11:33, 36).[73] Thus, the Father takes the initiative in choosing a people for his glory and pleasure (election), setting his affection upon them in eternity past (foreknowledge), and planning out the path for their holiness and adoption (predestination).

---

section below.

71. Grudem, "Biblical Evidence," 232–33.

72. Moo argues that προετοιμάζω refers to the same thing that προορίζω does in Rom 8:29; namely, "a decision of God in eternity past to bestow his mercy on certain individuals whom he in his sovereign design has chosen." Moo, *Romans*, 608.

73. It is clear from Paul's use of θεός in Romans that it is a reference to the Father. The only use for the Son is found in Rom 9:5.

The Father Planned the Work of His Son

According to Paul in Ephesians 3:11, the Father's *eternal purposes* were "realized in Christ Jesus our Lord."[74] The ascension and exaltation of God the Son after his successful incarnation and work of redemption causes Paul to acknowledge the fulfillment of the Father's divine plan, giving hope to the Ephesian church that the rest of the Father's plan is also certain.[75] Therefore, every element of the Son's work in redemption is part of the Father's decree. The Son came according to the Father's plan (John 4:24; 5:30; 6:38; Heb 10:7, 9) and was crucified as a substitutionary sacrifice for sin (Isa 53:10; Matt 26:39, 42; Mark 14:36; Luke 22:22, 42; Acts 4:23, 28). John Owen (1616–83) helpfully called this the "covenant of redemption,"[76] which is the "covenant made among the members of the Trinity to bring about the redemption of fallen man through the covenant of grace."[77] His thought also made it into the Savoy Declaration in section 8.1, making the covenant explicit: "It pleased God, in his eternal purpose, to chuse [sic] and ordain the Lord Jesus his onely [sic] begotten Son, according to a Covenant made between them both, to be the Mediator between God and Man."[78]

Regarding the Father's part of the covenant, Owen roots it in the truth that the Son is the eternal object of the Father's love. "The Father knows the Son, and the Son knows the Father; the Father loves the Son, and the Son loves the Father; and so, consequently, of the Holy Ghost, the medium of all these actings."[79] Owen subsumes the teaching of Scripture on the love of

---

74. The verses here are the ones that refer to the Father's decree from eternity past in connection with the sending of the Son. I will thoroughly examine the Father's work of providing salvation through the Lord Jesus in chap. 4.

75. See O'Brien, *Ephesians*, 249.

76. Also called the covenant of redemption, *pactum salutis* or *theologoumenon*. The first extended articulation of the doctrine is often ascribed to Johannes Cocceius in his work *Summa Doctrina de Foedere et Testamento Dei*, in his *Opera Theologica*, 8 vols (Amsterdam, 1673). For a history of the doctrine and an attempt at its origins, see Richard A. Muller, "Toward the *Pactum Salutis*."

77. See Fesko, "John Owen," 7–19. Owen has an extensive treatment on the *pactum* in Exercitation 28, "Federal Transactions between the Father and the Son," in his introduction to Hebrews, Owen, *Works*, 19:77–97, as well as in chap. 4 in his *Declaration of the Glorious Mystery of the Person of Christ*, in Owen, *Works*, 1:54–62.

78. The WCF 8.1 reads, "It pleased God, in His eternal purpose, to choose and ordain the Lord Jesus, His only begotten Son, to be Mediator between God and man;" Quoted in Trueman, *John Owen*, 82n60.

79. Owen, *Works*, 8:614. He further elaborates, "And had not the love of God been fixed in the first place in all things upon the person of Christ, there would have been no redundancy to us, nor communication of love unto us. From the first eternal love of God proceeds all love that was in the first creation; and from this second love of God, to

the Father into two categories: (1) The sending of his Son to die for the elect (John 3:16; Rom. 5:8; 1 John 4:9–10), and (2) In choosing sinners for the purpose of participation in the fruits of his love (Eph. 1:3–6).[80]

Furthermore, the covenant flows from the Father's grace and wisdom:

> Its [the covenant's] projection was in the wisdom and love of the Father. Whatsoever is spoken concerning the love, grace, and wisdom of the Father before the world was, was laid out in the projection of this covenant. Take it as it wraps Christ in it,—as it brings forth the forgiveness of sin,—as it is the centre of grace; and it compriseth the whole effect of divine wisdom, as far as the infinitely holy God ever manifested, or ever will manifest to eternity.[81]

Within the terms of the covenant,[82] and always in willing cooperation of the Son and Spirit, the Father appoints the Son to be a surety. "The will of the Father appointing and designing the Son to be the head, husband, deliverer, and redeemer of his elect, his church, his people, whom he did foreknow . . . is that compact (for in that form it is proposed in the Scripture) that we treat of."[83] Owen elsewhere writes, "The Father was the *prescriber*, the promiser, and lawgiver; and the Son was the *undertaker* upon his prescription, law, and promises [emphasis in original]."[84]

The Father then promises to reward the Son for his work of redeeming the elect:

> We may therefore, in the first place, consider the *promises* that in this compact or covenant were made unto the Son upon his undertaking this work. . . . And these promises were of two sorts:—(1.) Such as *concerned his person*; (2.) Such as *concerned the prosperity of the work* which he undertook. Those also which concerned his person immediately were of two sorts:—[1.] Such

---

the person of Christ as incarnate, proceeds all the love in the second creation."

80. Ibid., 2:435–36.

81. Ibid., 8:418.

82. Owen elaborates on Scriptural basis of these terms in *Communion with God*: "The terms of this covenant are at large insisted on, Isa. 53, summed up, Ps. 40:7, 8, Heb. 10:8–10. Hence the Father became to be his God; which is a covenant expression, Ps. 89:26; Heb. 1:5; Ps. 22:1, 40:8, 45:7; Rev. 3:12; Mic. 5:4. So was he by his Father on this account designed to this work, Isa. 42:1, 6, 49:9; Mal. 3:1; Zech. 8:7; John 3:16; 1 Tim. 1:15. Thus the "counsel of peace" became to be "between them both" Zech. 6:13; that is, the Father and Son. And the Son rejoices from eternity in the thought of this undertaking, Prov. 8:22–30." Ibid., 2:177.

83. Ibid., 12:496–97.

84. Ibid., 19:84–85.

as concerned *his assistance* in his work; [2.] Such as concerned *his acceptance* and glory after his work [emphasis in original].[85]

Carl Trueman contends that Owen's contribution to the doctrine is found in his inclusion of the Spirit's work:

> [Owen's contribution] is in his attention to the role of the Holy Spirit with reference to covenant, a point which represents a distinctly Trinitarian advance on the works of Fisher and Bulkeley ... and in so doing, he is being consistent with his basic premise that every external act of God is in its deepest sense an act of the whole Trinity.[86]

Thus, even though the decree, including the covenant of redemption, may be called the Father's work, it is still consistent with the doctrine of inseparable operations.

The Father Purposed Eternal Life through the Spirit's Work

Three times in Scripture the Holy Spirit is called the "promise of the Father" (Luke 24:49; Acts 1:4; 2:33).[87] That the Spirit's work was planned by the Father in eternity past is suggested in James 1:18, "Of his own will he brought us forth by the word of truth, that we should be a kind of firstfruits of his creatures." Richardson's comments are helpful:

> The word of truth is the instrument by which God implants new life in the believer. James's concern was for the unity of knowing the truth and its practical implications of doing the truth (3:12). James later warned against wandering from the truth (5:19). The Word of truth by which God gives birth to new creatures produces a harvest that he had intended since the moment of his first creating. Here is a wonderful uniting of first and second creation. What God brings about in salvation was contained in the original purpose of his creation. Indeed, those saved out of lost humanity will be a firstfruits of God's saving work that reaches every component of creation.[88]

---

85. Ibid., 19:93.
86. Trueman, *John Owen*, 86.
87. The verses here are the ones that refer to the Father's decree from eternity past in connection with the Spirit's work. I will thoroughly examine the Father's work of sending the Spirit in chap. 5.
88. Richardson, *James*, 87.

The Gospel of John makes explicit that God's will is to give eternal life (John 1:13) through the work of the Holy Spirit (John 3:3-8; 6:63). Further, in Acts 13:48, Luke recounts, "And when the Gentiles heard this, they began rejoicing and glorifying the word of the Lord, and as many as were appointed to eternal life believed." Polhill explains, "On their part these Gentiles took an active role in believing, in committing themselves to Christ; but it was in response to God's Spirit moving in them, convicting them, appointing them for life. All salvation is ultimately only by the grace of God."[89] Thus, every aspect of providing redemption through the Son and producing life by the Spirit are a part of God the Father's decree.

Judgment and Glory

The Father Has Appointed a Day of Judgment

Paul, while speaking before the Council of the Areopagus, declares that the Father "has fixed a day on which he will judge the world in righteousness by a man whom he has appointed; and of this he has given assurance to all by raising him from the dead" (Acts 17:31).[90] First, it is important to notice that the Father sets the day and hour of final judgment. In his entry on the use of ἵστημι in Acts 17:31, Walter Grundmann writes,

> He who can put someone in a particular place demonstrates thereby his authority or actual power. It is said of God: τῷ δὲ δυναμένῳ ... ὑμᾶς ... στῆσαι κατενώπιον τῆς δόξης αὐτοῦ ἀμώμους ἐν ἀγαλλιάσει (Jd. 24). This describes the goal of believers to which God has the power to lead them. God sets the day and hour of judgment and its execution, and therewith of the consummation of the world, however it may be conceived: ἔστησεν ἡμέραν ἐν ᾗ μέλλει κρίνειν τὴν οἰκουμένην ἐν δικαιοσύνῃ, Ac. 17:31. To this day of judgment, which is the day of wrath, there applies the question: καὶ τίς δύναται σταθῆναι; (Rev. 6:17 on the basis of Mal. 3:2 etc.). Jesus Christ is appointed Judge acc. to Ac. 17:31.[91]

Second, the Father's authority is also seen in his appointment of the Son as judge. Peter confirms this in Acts 10:42. It is the Lord Jesus himself

---

89. Polhill, *Acts*, 308.

90. The verses here are the ones that refer to the Father's decree from eternity past in connection with the future judgment. I will thoroughly examine the Father's work of perfecting salvation through the consummation of all things in chap. 7.

91. Grundmann, "ἵστημι," in *TDNT*, 7:648.

who commands Peter (and the other apostles) to preach and testify that "he is the one appointed by God [the Father] to be judge of the living and the dead." Further, it is clear from Acts 2:23 and 3:20 that this appointment was a part of the Father's eternal decree, not a decision made later.

Even the path of unbelieving sinners leading up to the judgment day is part of the allowed, permissive decree of the Father. In 1 Peter 2:8, those who "do not believe" (v .7) stumble because they "disobey the word, as they were *destined* to do." The verb τίθημι is often used of what the Father decrees to occur (Acts 1:7; 13:47; 1 Cor 12:18, 28; 1 Thess 5:9; 1 Tim 2:7). Similarly, Romans 9:22 says, "What if God, desiring to show his wrath and to make known his power, has endured with much patience vessels of wrath prepared for destruction." Moo explains,

> In contrast to the active participle "prepared beforehand" in v. 23, Paul here uses a middle/passive participle that does not clearly bring God into the picture. But the parallel with vv. 17–18 suggests strongly that the agent of "prepared" is indeed God: Paul considers the "vessels on whom God's wrath rests" as prepared by God himself for eternal condemnation.[92]

The Father Has Chosen to Bestow Glory and Eternal Life upon His Elect

In Scripture, this end is so certain that Paul can write that those the Father "predestined . . . he glorified" (Rom 8:30)[93] are those whom the Father "prepared beforehand for glory" (Rom 9:23).[94] Therefore the Father has decreed that he will cut short the final days before the return of his Son for the sake of the elect (Matt 24:22; Mark 13:20)[95] and has willed that the Son will lose none of them, but raise them all up on the last day (John 6:39–40).[96] Further, the Father has only purposed to give glory to those whose names are written

---

92. Moo, *Romans*, 607.

93. The subject of the verbs προώρισεν, ἐκάλεσεν, ἐδικαίωσεν, and ἐδόξασεν is θεός (v. 28), who is clearly God the Father in distinction from his Son (v. 29).

94. προετοιμάζω refers to the same thing as προορίζω in Rom 8:29. "A decision of God in eternity past to bestow his mercy on certain individuals whom he in his sovereign design has chosen." Moo, *Romans*, 608.

95. Stein asserts, "This shortening does not involve a sudden change and modification by God of his divine plan for history but reflects a limit that God has set from the beginning on the suffering of his elect." Stein, *Mark*, 606.

96. On unconditional election in the Gospel of John, see Yarbrough, "Divine Election," 47–62.

in the "Lamb's book of life" (Rev 13:8; 17:8; 21:27) before the foundation of the world,[97] and because the Father will keep his promise of giving eternal life, he exercises patience, so that all will reach repentance (2 Pet 3:9).[98]

Paul calls this promise the "hope of eternal life, which God [the Father], who never lies, promised before the ages began" (Titus 1:2; cf. 2 Tim 1:1).[99] Hebrews calls it the "promised eternal inheritance" (Heb 9:15), and John says, "this is the promise he [the Father] made to us—eternal life" (1 John 2:25).[100] The Father's promise includes the "crown of life" (Jas 1:12),[101] inheritance of "the kingdom" (Matt 25:34; Jas 2:5), participation in "the divine nature" (2 Pet 1:4),[102] and a "new heavens and a new earth in which righteousness dwells" (2 Pet 3:13).[103]

Conclusion

In this chapter, I have argued that the consistent testimony of Scripture is that the divine decree is designed and planned by God the Father. It is his wise, eternal, all-inclusive, and sovereign design and will for all that comes to pass, and flows out of his initiating role among the persons of the Godhead, consistent with the orthodox understanding of inseparable operations and the one divine will.

The Father's decree is an overflow of his eternal love for the Son in the Spirit, and as such, brings him good pleasure both in its design and in its implementation. It is no surprise then, that specific determinations and permissions regarding the decree are attributed to the Father, whether

---

97. The genitive τοῦ ἀρνίου is best taken as a genitive of possession: "the book of life belonging to the Lamb." It highlights the initiating role of the Father, for the Father chooses the elect in his Son (Eph 1:4), the Father has the authority to give the elect to his Son (John 6:37–44), and the Father has the authority to grant to the Son the right to give life to whomever he will (John 5:26).

98. For an excellent discussion of how this verse fits into the "two wills" of God, see Piper, "Are There Two Wills in God," 107–31.

99. God the Father is distinguished from Jesus Christ in Titus 1:1 and Titus 1:4.

100. Though αὐτὸς may refer to the Son, it is better to take it here as a reference to the Father, particularly since in 1 John 5:9–11, the Father's testimony concerning his Son is eternal life. Thus "Eternal life is something that comes through Jesus Christ but from God the Father." See Akin, *1, 2, 3 John*, 123.

101. τῆς ζωῆς is an epexegetic genitive: "the crown which is life." See Moo, *James*, 70. Further, the ESV's gloss of "God" for the subject of ἐπηγγείλατο is most likely due to the Jewish reluctance to name God. Davids, *James*, 80.

102. The subject of the verb δεδώρηται is God the Father, whose antecedent is τοῦ θεοῦ (v. 2). See Green, *Jude and 2 Peter*, 181–86.

103. It is God's promise (cf. 3:12). See Kelly, *Peter and of Jude*, 368.

in connection with creation and providence, the outworking of redemptive history, or future judgment and glory in the consummation of all things. Thus, the decree becomes more properly a subject of Paterology rather than theology proper. Finally, in this chapter I have distinguished the decree in eternity from its execution in history, the substance of which we will consider in the next four chapters.

4

The Father's Work of Creating and Preserving the Heavens and the Earth

Introduction

BECAUSE OF HIS PROFOUND and infinite love for the Son and the Spirit, the Father not only plans all that will come to pass (as we examined in the last chapter), but also sets the stage for the display of the Triune Godhead's coequal glory and majesty through the creation of the heavens and the earth. Furthermore, the Father executes his plan through the agency of his Son and Spirit. Therefore, as we shall see below, it is improper to equate the Father with "Creator," as in the popular notion of Father, Son, Spirit as "Creator, Redeemer, Sanctifier." So too, it is erroneous to remove all distinctions appropriate to each person of the Godhead and their respective roles, as in Jürgen Moltmann's "social doctrine of the Trinity." In Moltmann's concern to emphasize the immanence of the Triune God in creation, he has set his theology against the "trinitarian monarchy" of God normally found in studies on theology proper (to Moltmann, particularly exemplified in Karl Barth):

> A social doctrine of the Trinity goes beyond the monarchical doctrine of the Trinity and leads to a pneumatological doctrine of creation. What is normative for all relations in creation is not the structure of command and obedience within the Trinity but the eternal perichoresis of the triunity.[1]

If Moltmann is correct, one would expect Scripture to speak of the Son and Spirit working through the agency of the Father, but instead Scripture shows that it is *always* the Father who initiates the creative work through

---

1. Moltmann, *History and the Triune God*, 127. I am not so much concerned to address Moltmann's "theology of the cross" here as I am to show two different Trinitarian models in creation. For a critique of Moltmann's theology of the cross, see chap. 2 of Ware, *God's Greater Glory*.

the Son and the Spirit, and never vice versa (e.g., John 1:1; 1 Cor 8:6; Heb 1:1-2). Thus, the entire Godhead works to create (and for that matter, to redeem and sanctify) in ways unique and appropriate to each person. For his part, the Father acts through the Son by the Spirit consistent with the eternal *taxis,* and yet the Father, along with the Son and Spirit fully share the divine nature, thereby undoing the dichotomy posed by Moltmann.

Furthermore, the Father not only creates but also providentially governs the heavens and earth through the agency of the Son and Spirit. Here, John Calvin is helpful. In his *Institutes of the Christian Religion*,[2] he arranges the inseparable works of the Trinity under two headings: God as "Creator,"[3] and God as "Governor." At the beginning of his commentary on Genesis, Calvin assigns the work of creation to all three persons of the Godhead,[4] and in 1.13.7 of the *Institutes* he teaches that John 5:17 explains what Moses revealed in Genesis: "Therefore we conclude that God has so spoken that the Word might have his share in the work and that in this way the work might be common to both."[5] His clearest articulation of the Father's united work with the Son in creation is found in his discussion of Hebrews 1:2:

> According to the most usual mode of speaking in Scripture, the Father is called the Creator; and it is added in some places that the world was created by wisdom, by the word, by the Son, as though wisdom itself had been the creator, [or the word, or the Son.] But still we must observe that there is a difference of persons between the Father and the Son, not only with regard to men, but with regard to God himself. But the unity of essence requires that whatever is peculiar to Deity should belong to the Son as well as to the Father, and also that whatever is applied to

---

2. Calvin, *Institutes*.

3. "Calvin appears to studiously avoid using the terms *Father* and *Creator* as synonyms." Butin, *Revelation, Redemption, and Response*, 56. In this regard he is thoroughly exegetical. For example, writing on John 1:3, he says, "The Father made all things by the Son, and all things are made by God through the Son." Calvin, *John*, John 1:3, 16.

4. Calvin, *Genesis*, 18.

5. Calvin, *Institutes*, 1.13.7. This understanding helps give clarity to Calvin's arrangement of the 1559 *Institutes*. Benjamin B. Warfield's interpretation is most popular, "With the edition of 1559 ... a totally new arrangement was introduced, which reduced the whole to a simple and beautiful order—redacted into four books. ... These four books treat in turn of the Father, Son, and Holy Ghost, and the Holy Catholic Church. ... The order was suggested by the consecution of topics in the Apostles' Creed." Warfield and Warfield, *Calvin and Calvinism*, 375. However, Charles Partee has recently made a more compelling argument for bi-partite interpretation, with vols. 1 and 2 expositing "Christ for us," and vols. 3 and 4 expositing "Christ in us." See Partee, *Theology of John Calvin*, 35-40.

God only should belong to both; and yet there is nothing in this to prevent each from his own peculiar properties."[6]

Concluding his discussion of God as Creator in the *Institutes*, Calvin makes the natural transition to God as Governor and asserts that his work as Creator and Governor are inseparably joined: "To make God a momentary Creator, who once for all finished his work, would be cold and barren, and we must differ from profane men especially in that we see the presence of the divine power shining as much in the continuing state of the universe as in its inception."[7] Furthermore, in his commentary on Exodus 3:14, Calvin is careful to attribute the work of governance to the "one God," rather than to the Father alone.[8]

Additionally for Calvin, governance consists in "nourishing and sustaining men"[9] and also "[making] a difference between good and evil, to help the miserable, to punish all wickedness, to check injustice and violence."[10] As such, Calvin subsumes God's role as "Judge" under his work as Governor.[11]

What does this mean for the initiating role of the Father? In this chapter, I will argue that it is demonstrated in both creation and providence through the Trinitarian *taxis*. The Father works through the agency of the Son and Spirit, but the converse is never true. The Son and Spirit never work through the agency of the Father in creation and providence. As discussed in chapter 2, the names Father, Son, and Spirit are fixed in an eternal order. It is altogether expected and appropriate, then, that the Father holds the distinct appropriation of initiating the Triune God's work of creating and preserving the heavens and the earth.

Nevertheless, it is important to remember that the purpose of creation is to display the glory of the Trinity. As such, the initiating work of God the Father does not and cannot devalue the coequal, unrestricted power and

---

6. Calvin, *Hebrews*, 34.
7. Calvin, *Institutes*, 1.16.1.
8. Calvin, *Four Last Books of Moses*, 1:73–74.
9. Calvin, *Psalms*, 2:94–96.
10. Calvin, *Minor Prophets*, 4:217.
11. "[In Dan 7:9,] Daniel now relates how he saw another figure, namely, God sitting on his throne to exercise judgment. We shall see it afterwards concerning Christ, but Daniel now teaches only the appearance of God in his character of a judge. . . . But first it is worth while to consider here, why he says—*the Ancient of days*, meaning the eternal Deity himself, *ascended the throne of judgment*. This scene seems unnecessary, because it is the peculiar office of God to govern the world; and as we know this cannot be done without upright judgment, it follows that God has been a perpetual judge from the creation of the world." Calvin, *Daniel*, 2:31.

undiminished glory of either the Son or Holy Spirit. It is, therefore, just as glorious for the Son and Spirit to be the agents of creation and providence as it is for the Father to oversee creation and providence, commanding and directing the Son and the Spirit. As Calvin says, the heavens and the earth were created as a "theater of God's glory (*theatrum gloriae Dei*)."[12]

Through the Son and Spirit, the Father Created the Heavens and the Earth

"We believe in one God, the Father, almighty, maker of heaven and earth, of all things visible and invisible."[13] On this first sentence of the Nicene-Constantinople Creed, T. F. Torrance writes,

> [Placing this statement at the head of this creed] signifies to us that the doctrine of the Creator belongs to the heart and substance of the Gospel, so that such belief in him is appropriately formulated within the evangelical interrelations of the economic Trinity.[14]

Therefore, according to Torrance, it is improper to equate God the Father alone with Creator. He says,

> Since the Father is never without the Son and the Spirit, all that the Father does is done in, through, and with the Son and the Spirit, and all that the Son and Spirit do is coincident with what the Father does. It is, then, of God the Father in this full sense, in his mutual homoousial and completely perichoretic relations with the Son and in the Spirit that we are to think of him as the Sovereign Creator.[15]

Colin Gunton agrees, adding the doctrine of *ex nihilo* creation to the discussion:

> We shall understand the distinctiveness of the Christian theology of creation only if we realise that these three themes—creation as an article of the creed; creation out of nothing; and creation as the work of the whole Trinity, Father, Son and Holy

---

12. Calvin, *Institutes*, 1.5.8; 1.6.2; 1.14.20; 2.6.1.
13. "Nicene-Constantinople Creed," in Kelly, *Early Christian Creeds*, 297.
14. Torrance, *Christian Doctrine of God*, 203.
15. Ibid., 206.

Spirit—are in some way bound up with each other, both historically and systematically.[16]

It is why the creed goes on to explain that the Son is the one "through whom all things came into existence,"[17] and the Spirit, he is "the Lord and life-giver."[18] Thus, Berkhof concludes,

> The second and third persons are not dependent powers or mere intermediaries, but independent authors together with the Father. The work was not divided among the three persons, but the whole work, though from different aspects, is ascribed to each one of the persons. All things are at once out of the Father, through the Son, and in the Holy Spirit. In general, it may be said that being is out of the Father, thought or the idea out of the Son, and life out of the Holy Spirit. Since the Father takes the initiative in the work of creation, it is often ascribed to Him economically.[19]

Turning to the pages of Scripture, we can see that these assertions hold true.

Trinity and Creation in the Old Testament

In the first three verses of Genesis 1, both the Word of God and the Spirit of God participate in the work of creation:

> In the beginning, God created the heavens and the earth. 2 The earth was without form and void, and darkness was over the face of the deep. And the Spirit of God was hovering over the face of the waters. 3 And God said, "Let there be light," and there was light. (Gen 1:1–3)

On this, Robert Letham comments, "We notice distinctions among God, who created the heavens and earth (v. 1), the Spirit of God, who hovers over the face of the waters (v. 2), and the speech or word of God, issuing the fiat 'Let there be light' (v.3)."[20] Therefore, although it is not demanded by the

---

16. Gunton, *Triune Creator*, 9.
17. Kelly, *Early Christian Creeds*, 297.
18. Ibid., 298. On the Spirit as live-giver, see Oden, *Systematic Theology*, 1:248.
19. Berkhof, *Systematic Theology*, 129.
20. Letham, *Holy Trinity*, 427.

immediate context, Trinitarian echoes exist in this passage that argue for the Father's creation through the Word and by the Spirit.[21]

Similarly, Psalm 33:6 says, "By the *word* of the LORD the heavens were made, and by the *breath* of his mouth all their host (cf. Job 33:4)." Richard Bauckham identifies several passages in the Old Testament where the Word and the Wisdom of God create: "Both the Word and the Wisdom of God take part in the work of creation, sometimes with distinguishable roles (Ps 33:9), sometimes interchangeably (Jer 10:12; 51:15; Ps 104:24; Prov 3:19; 8:30)."[22]

Finally, it is revealed in the New Testament (Heb 1:10-12) that *Yahweh* in Psalm 102:25 is a reference to the Son's role in creation: "Of old you [the Son] laid the foundation of the earth, and the heavens are the work of your hands." Guthrie explains,

> With other NT authors, the author of Hebrews holds the Son as the agent of God the Father in the creation of the universe (1:10; cf. John 1:3; 1 Cor. 8:6; Col. 1:16). Also, the Son is the one to whom all of creation will be subjected in the end (e.g., 1:13; 2:5, 8; cf. 1 Cor. 15:28). . . . Of all things, then, the Son is "Lord," a basic element of early Christian confessions about Christ (e.g., Acts 2:36; Rom. 1:4; 1 Cor. 1:2; Phil. 2:11), and so the author of Hebrews recognizes this divine name from the LXX version of the psalm (101:26) as referring to him.[23]

Nevertheless, the dominant theme of the Old Testament is that the one true and living God, Yahweh-Elohim, made the heavens and the earth (e.g., Gen 2:4; 14:19, 22; 2 Kgs 19:15; Neh 9:6; Job 38-39; Ps 90:2; 121:2; 124:8; 134:3; Isa 37:16; 40:12-31; Amos 4:13). Although, from the perspective of the New Testament, these passages are best understood as references to the first person of the Trinity,[24] the driving force of their Old Testament context is that the heavens and the earth are distinct from yet dependent upon this God for all things, in stark contrast to the false gods made by human hands (Deut 4:28; 1 Chr 16:26; Ps 96:5; 115:4; 135:15; Isa 2:8; 42:8).

Because the Creation is distinct from yet dependent upon the Triune God, this means first that there is a need to distinguish between God's

---

21. For an extended discussion of Trinity and Creation in Gen 1, see Letham, *Holy Trinity*, 425-37.

22. Bauckham, *Jesus and the God of Israel*, 16.

23. Beale and Carson, *New Testament Use of the Old Testament*, 941.

24. Every time the phrase "living God" is used in the New Testament (Matt 16:16; 26:63; Acts 14:15; Rom 9:26; 2 Cor 3:3; 6:16; 1 Tim 3:15; 4:10; Heb 3:12; 9:14; 10:31; 12:22; Rev 7:2), it refers to the Father.

transcendence and his immanence, while also articulating their relationship to one another. As Bruce Ware rightly observes,

> To think of God correctly, then, we must establish our framework for understanding God as containing both of these key elements—both the *transcendent otherness* of God in himself, apart from creation, and also the *immanent nearness* of God with every aspect of the created order [emphasis original].[25]

The transcendence of the one God is not merely that of location; i.e., heaven. Rather, the triune God's transcendence is a reference to his exalted state as sovereign and king (Ps 113:1–4). John Frame explains,

> The transcendence of God is best understood, not primarily as a spatial concept, but as a reference to God's kingship. God's transcendence means that he is sovereign over his creatures.... If, therefore, we are to use the language of transcendence and immanence, it would be best to use *transcendence* for God's royal control and authority, and *immanence* for his covenant presence [emphasis original].[26]

Likewise, the immanence of the one God is not merely that of location; i.e. on the earth. Rather, the triune God's immanence is a reference to his intimate involvement in his creation, especially with his children (Ps 113:5–9).[27] Therefore, transcendence and immanence are relationship terms: the self-sufficient, transcendent, triune God is also the one who has, in his immanence, drawn near to his children, so that they can draw near to him. Michael Horton writes,

> In this trinitarian economy, God is simultaneously transcendent and immanent, utterly distinct from creation yet actively involved in every aspect of its existence and preservation. Gunton elaborates: "[God] is clearly 'without' in the sense of being other, transcendent. He is creator and not creation, but he is also, in realization rather than denial of that transcendence, one who in Christ becomes part of that creation, freely involved within its structures, in order that he may, in obedience to God the Father

---

25. Ware, *God's Greater Glory*, 35.

26. Frame, *Doctrine of God*, 106. In chap. 7, Frame has an excellent discussion of transcendence.

27. Zemek looks at the "grandeur and grace" of transcendence and immanence in his exposition of Ps 113 in Zemek, "Grandeur and Grace," 129–48. His conclusion is that the only proper response is the worship of God in thanksgiving and praise.

and through the power of his Spirit, redirect the creation to its eschatological destiny."[28]

Furthermore, transcendence must precede immanence. Ryan Lister argues,

> It is because of his being "high above the nations" that the Lord is able to raise the poor from the dust (Ps 113:4–9). It is because the Lord dwells in the high and holy places that he is able to bring respite to the contrite and lowly spirit (Isa 57:15). Through the knowledge of the transcendent realities of God's nature, we are able to appreciate fully what it means for God to be in relationship with the world, and, in particular, his people.[29]

Finally, Ware rightfully acknowledges God's relationship to his creation:

> First, in light of God's transcendent self-existence and infinite self-sufficiency, we must resist the temptation to imagine God's relationship with the world as somehow contributing to meeting some deficiency in God himself. To put this differently, the dependence relationship between God and the world is asymmetrical: we (the world) depend on God for absolutely everything; God depends on the world not one bit.[30]

It follows from this that creation was accomplished *ex nihilo*.[31] As Horton asserts,

> Creation does not take place within God's being, as neo-Hegelian theologies assume. Yet it also does not generate itself. Nor is the world a self-sustaining mechanism in the way that deism supposed. It is not only brought into being but sustained in being and becoming and finally brought to its consummated goal by the Father, in the Son, through the Spirit. Creation is rightly described by Christians as one of God's external works (*opera ad extra*)—that is, one of the contingent and freely chosen relations to which is not God—rather than being one of his internal works (*opera ad intra*), that is, necessary intratrinitarian relations and attributes.[32]

28. Horton, *Christian Faith*, 331. He is quoting Gunton, *Triune Creator*, 24.
29. Lister, *Presence of God*, 46.
30. Ware, *God's Greater Glory*, 43.
31. For a nuanced defense of creation *ex nihilo*, see Feinberg, *No One Like Him*, 552–57. See also Bavinck, *In the Beginning*, 34–39.
32. Horton, *Christian Faith*, 327–28.

Thus, creation is one of the divine acts of the Triune God initiated by the Father.

Trinity and Creation in the New Testament

Turning to the New Testament, the Father's initiating role becomes explicit. To begin with, many passages speak of God the Father as the Creator. For example, he is called the "sovereign Lord" (Acts 4:24)[33] and "living God" (Acts 14:15), the "Lord of heaven and earth" who "gives to all mankind life and breath and everything" (Acts 17:24-25; cf. Eph 3:9; 1 Tim 4:3-4; 6:13), the "Creator" (Rom 1:25), the "molder" and "potter" (Rom 9:20-21), and "builder" (Heb 3:4). Therefore, at the beginning of creation, it is the Father who maintains the right and authority to declare all things "good" (Gen 1:4, 10, 12, 18, 21, 25, 31).

Additionally, Jesus testifies that the Father created humanity from the beginning "male and female" (Matt 19:4; Mark 10:6), and is the one who made their "outside" and "inside" (Luke 11:40), both material and immaterial.[34] Therefore Paul can say that the Father gives names to every grouping of angels in heaven and humanity on earth (Eph 3:15).[35]

Finally, the book of Revelation bears strong witness to the Father's role in creation. In Revelation 4:11, the Father is worthy of worship because creation was initiated by him and only continues to exist only because of him.[36] As Creator, God the Father has made all three spheres of life on earth: "heaven and what is in it, the earth and what is in it, and the sea and what is in it" (Rev 10:6; cf. 14:7; Acts 4:24). As such, the reality of God the Father as Creator means he is the "Alpha and the Omega," the one "who is and who was and who is to come, the Almighty" (Rev 1:8),[37] the "beginning and the end" (Rev 21:6).[38]

---

33. In their prayer, Peter and John are addressing the Father as the sovereign Lord. Further, he is distinguished from both the Holy Spirit (v. 25) and Jesus (v. 27).

34. See Bock, *Luke 9:51—24:53*, 1113-14.

35. Lincoln rightly argues that the term ὀνομάζεται "evokes some of the OT connotations of 'naming' in terms of exercising dominion over or even bringing into existence." Lincoln, *Ephesians*, 203.

36. For a discussion on why preservation precedes creation in the phrase "they existed and were created" (ἦσαν καὶ ἐκτίσθησαν), see Beale, *Revelation*, 335.

37. The identity of the Lord God (κύριος ὁ θεός) as Father is not immediately apparent from the context. Lenski identifies this as Jesus in Lenski, *Revelation*, 51. However, κύριος ὁ θεός is only ever used of the Father in Revelation (Rev 1:8; 4:8; 11:17; 15:3; 16:7; 18:8; 21:22; 22:5). The clearest use is Rev 21:22, "And I saw no temple in the city, for its temple is the Lord God the Almighty (κύριος ὁ θεός) and the Lamb."

38. This context identifies the Alpha and Omega as the Father more clearly. He is the one who will finally dwell among men (Rev 21:3). He is the one seated on the throne

The Father Creates through the Son

As mentioned earlier, it is improper to see only the Father as Creator, for Scripture also testifies to the Son's role in creation. 1 Corinthians 8:6 says, "yet for us there is one God, the Father, from whom are all things and for whom we exist, and one Lord, Jesus Christ, through whom are all things and through whom we exist."

The Lord Jesus Christ is the agent "διά (through)" whom all things were made. Paul Rainbow, in his dissertation "Monotheism and Christology in 1 Corinthians 8:4–6" speaks of the preposition's importance:

> The preposition διά in contrast to ἐξ and εἰς, gives to the Lord a penultimate role in both the divine operations of creation and redemption; the ultimate source and goal is the Father. These features of v 6 must be read in the larger context of Paul's language about Christ in I Corinthians, where we find the statements, "Christ is God's" (3.23); "the head of Christ is God" (11.3); "when all things are subjected to him, then the Son himself will also be subjected to him who put all things under him, that God may be everything to every one" (15.28).[39]

But lest it mean falling into the error of Arianism, Rainbow also emphasizes the importance of the Father and Son's relationship to "all things":

> Both stand together on the side of the creator rather than the creation. Even as God is the unique object of Christian hope, so also is the Lord the unique object of Christian hope. The variation of prepositions from ἐξ and εἰς to διά distinguishes God and the Lord from each other, but not with respect to the external relations which they unitedly bear to created reality.[40]

It is why Peter can tell the crowd at Solomon's portico, "you killed the Author of life [Jesus], whom God [the Father] raised from the dead" (Acts 3:15).[41] Further, in John 1:3 and 10, the Father is indirectly described as the Creator, while the Son is described as the one through whom the Father makes "all things."[42] Thus, the Son is the agent of creation, while the Father

---

(Rev 21:5), and the one who will be a God with "sons" (Rev 21:7).

39. Rainbow, "Monotheism and Christology," 169–70.

40. Ibid., 172.

41. The word has a double nuance, meaning "leader" and "originator." Here, he is not only the agent creating biological life, but also the origin of new life in him. See Scott, "Archēgos," 47–54.

42. In 1:3, 10, the construction (διά + genitive) indicates agency, demonstrating that the Son's role is a means to the larger purposes. See Wallace, *Greek Grammar*, 433–34.

is the initiator and director of the project. Morris brings out the importance of this distinction:

> [John] does not say that all was made "by" him, but "through" him. This way of putting it safeguards the truth that the Father is the source of all that is. The relation of the first two Persons of the Trinity in the work of creation is of interest. There is a careful differentiation of the parts played by the Father and the Son (1 Cor 8:6). Creation was not the solitary act of either. Both were at work (and for that matter, still are; cf. 5:17, 19). The Father created, but he did it "through" the Word.[43]

In Colossians 1:16, Paul uses a different preposition, "ἐν αὐτῷ," to emphasize that all things were created "within the sphere" of Christ,[44] complementing his argument later in the sentence that "all things were created through him (δι' αὐτοῦ) and for him (εἰς αὐτόν)."[45] The author of Hebrews also argues that creation has Christ as its goal and origin: "but in these last days he has spoken to us by his Son, whom he appointed the heir of all things, through whom also he created the world" (Heb 1:2).

Nevertheless, the Son is not inferior to the Father, for although he is the agent of creation, he is also the "beginning of the new creation" (Rev 3:14),[46] and therefore shares the divine title, the "Alpha and the Omega, the first and the last, the beginning and the end" (Rev 22:13).[47] Boxall writes,

> This [use of the title for the Son] should not surprise us, given that the Lamb has already shared God's throne, and that the two can be spoken of together using a singular pronoun (see on 22:3). Each successive occurrence of this divine title has expanded upon it to explicate its meaning; this third and final occurrence adds the first and the last (1:17; 2:8; cf. Isa. 41:4; 44:6;

---

43. Morris, *John*, 71.

44. Harris writes, "'All things in heaven and on earth' were created *in* God's beloved Son (v. 13), not in the sense that he was the preexistent or ideal archetype of creation but in the sense that creation occurred 'within the sphere of' Christ. In his person resided the creative energy that produced all of creation." Harris, *Colossians & Philemon*, 44–45.

45. Although εἰς αὐτόν may simply be equivalent to αὐτῷ, meaning for his benefit and glory, it is better to take it as meaning that Christ is the ultimate goal of creation, paralleling Eph 1:10. See Hoehner's discussion in Hoehner, *Ephesians*, 219–25.

46. Beale, *Revelation*, 297–301. Beale has a compelling excursus in his commentary entitled, "The Old Testament Background of Christ's Titles in 3:14."

47. In the context, Jesus is the one speaking (v. 16), the one who is coming soon (v. 12), and is thus, along with the Father (1:8; 21:6), the "Alpha and the Omega, the first and the last, the beginning and the end."

48:12; the second instance at 21:6 had already added the phrase the beginning and the end). Christ is present as both the pre-existent agent of creation (see 3:14) and the one who is coming in judgement and salvation at its climax.[48]

The Father Creates by the Spirit

As mentioned above, most of the references to the Spirit's role in creation are found in the Old Testament (Gen 1:2; 2:7; Job 33:4; Pss 33:6; 104:30). Sinclair Ferguson's measured words are instructive:

> This is not to claim that the Old Testament provides a detailed analysis of the role of the Spirit of God in creation, or that the enigmatic statement in Genesis 1:2 alone is adequate to ground the idea that the Spirit of God is a distinct divine hypostasis. Much remains opaque. What is of interest is that the activity of the divine *ruach* is precisely that of extending God's presence into creation in such a way as *to order and complete what has been planned in the mind of God*. This is exactly the role the Spirit characteristically fulfills everywhere in Scripture. In the New Testament the Spirit undertakes this role in the accomplishment of redemption: the Father sends, the Son comes, the Spirit vindicates (1 Tim. 3:16); the Father plans, the Son sacrifices and rises, the Spirit applies (*e.g.* 1 Pet. 1:1–2) [emphasis original].[49]

It is not surprising, then, that in turning to the New Testament, the emphasis is on the Spirit as the one who creates new life as well. For example, in Jesus's conversation with Nicodemus (John 3:5–8), he says that unless the Spirit gives new life, a person cannot enter the kingdom of God. Later, in a conversation with his disciples (John 6:63), he tells them unless the Spirit teaches them, they cannot comprehend his words because, "It is the Spirit who gives life."[50]

Paul makes a similar argument in 2 Corinthians 3:6, when he says, "the letter kills, but the Spirit gives life." Murray Harris explains,

---

48. Boxall, *Revelation*, 316.
49. Ferguson, *Holy Spirit*, 21.
50. Contra the view that this is the human spirit, Morris says, "The antithesis between flesh and spirit would lead us to think that the spirit of man is meant. But the human spirit is not life-giving. There is unquestionably a reference to the Holy Spirit, the Life-Giver. This is the case in John's previous contrast between flesh and spirit in 3:6." Morris, *John*, 385.

When Paul observes here that the Spirit "imparts life" or when he describes the Spirit as "life-giving" (τῆς ζωῆς, Rom. 8:2; cf. Gal. 5:25), he is affirming that one characteristic—perhaps the principal characteristic—of the Spirit is that he perpetually grants the physical and spiritual life of which he is the source.[51]

Colin Gunton is even more emphatic:

> The Spirit is the Lord and giver of life, and this means both the everyday life of the mortal and the transformed life of the one whose mortality has put on immortality. The bearing of this transformation is first of all on the destiny of the human being. For Paul, the giving of the Spirit to the community that is the Church is a guarantee of precisely this. . . .
>
> Thus the new creation is both continuous with and a transformation of the old: "sown . . . perishable, . . . raised imperishable; . . . sown in dishonour, . . . raised in glory; . . . sown in weakness, raised in power, . . . sown a natural body, . . . raised a spiritual body [that is, one filled with the Spirit]" (1 Cor. 15:42–4).[52]

Summary

Creation is initiated by the Father, and accomplished through the Son by (or in) the Spirit. Basil of Caesarea argued that this held true for the unseen as well as the seen:

> In their [angels] creation, consider for me the initial cause of their existence (the Father), the Maker (the Son), the Perfecter (the Spirit). So the ministering spirits exist by the will of the Father, they are brought into being by the energy of the Son, and they are perfected by the presence of the Spirit.[53]

Once again, it is important to reiterate that the Son and Spirit are not therefore inferior. As Bavinck explains,

> In this context the Son and the Spirit are not viewed as secondary forces but as independent agents or "principles" (*principia*),

---

51. Harris, *Second Corinthians*, 273–74.
52. Gunton, *Father, Son, and Spirit*, 118.
53. Basil, *On the Holy Spirit*, 71. Basil, *De Spiritu Sancto*, XVI.38.

as authors (*auctores*) who with the Father carry out the work of creation, as with him, they also constitute the one true God.⁵⁴

Thus, God the Father does not require angels or any other inferior powers to assist him, for there are only two realities: the Triune Godhead who creates and their creation. As a consequence, it is precisely this reality that upholds creation *ex nihilo*.

Through the Son and Spirit, the Father Providentially Governs the Universe

Just as the Father creates through the Son and Spirit, so too through them he providentially governs the heavens and earth. Colin Gunton, in his book, *The Triune Creator* makes the case that creation and providence ought to be considered together:

> The chief difference between the concepts of creation and providence is, then, first that providence presupposes creation, presupposes that there is something to provide for; while, second, creation presupposes providence, for although it is a finished act, it is not the finished act of the deist machine maker, but of one who has in view the care for and governing of the creation. . . . Providence is what God makes of the created world which has been given its own being distinct from him. There is a different form of relationship: interaction as distinct from origination.⁵⁵

Because of this, Gunton not only forms a Trinitarian doctrine of creation (as the title suggests), but also fashions a Trinitarian doctrine of providence:

> Because the doctrines of the Son and the Spirit enable us to articulate an understanding of the way in which God works in and towards the world, our understanding of the divine work of creation is not limited to the beginning and the end. In various ways God can be understood to continue to be involved in the world, guiding its movement and enabling anticipations of its final perfection to take place. From christology and pneumatology together flow those further aspects of the doctrine which

---

54. Bavinck, *In the Beginning*, 40.
55. Gunton, *Triune Creator*, 179.

are indicated by words like "conservation," "preservation," "providence," and "redemption."[56]

T. F. Torrance agrees,

> Like his creative activity God's providential activity has positive Trinitarian content, for through their perichoretic interrelations the Father, the Son, and the Holy Spirit are creatively and redemptively at work in fulfilling God's eternal purpose of love for his creation and for men, women and children within it.[57]

Therefore, God the Father, through the agency of the Son and Spirit continually oversees and directs the creation both by preserving its existence and by governing it in such a way as to fulfill all his plans within his decree. The biblical examination that follows will begin with the general areas of providence found in the Old Testament (preservation and government), and then turn to the New Testament in order to articulate a consistent Trinitarian *taxis* of providence: initiated by the Father and accomplished through the Son by (or in) the Spirit.

Trinity and Providence in the Old Testament

The Old Testament demonstrates that the universe is not a random jumble of accidental occurrences but rather an intricately designed system controlled by the loving authority of God the Father, which means that the Father's providential rule is not mechanical or merely causal. As Bruce Ware says,

> God continually oversees and directs all things pertaining to the created order in such a way that 1) he preserves in existence and provides for the creation he has brought into being, and 2) he governs and reigns supremely over the entirety of the whole of creation in order to fulfill all of his intended purposes in it and through it.[58]

My goal in what follows is not to flesh out a robust doctrine of providence.[59] Rather, I want to inspect those passages and events in the Old Testament that bear witness to God the Father's providential care, particularly seen from the lens of New Testament understanding.

---

56. Ibid., 10.
57. Torrance, *Christian Doctrine of God*, 221.
58. Ware, *God's Greater Glory*, 17.
59. For example, see Helm, *Providence of God*, and Berkouwer, *Providence of God*.

The Father Preserves His Creation

In a classic verse on divine providence, Nehemiah writes,

> You are the LORD, you alone. You have made heaven, the heaven of heavens, with all their host, the earth and all that is on it, the seas and all that is in them; and you preserve all of them; and the host of heaven worships you. (Neh 9:6)

From this verse alone, it is not immediately apparent that *Yahweh* is a reference to the Father. However, in the next verse, *Yahweh* is described as the one who "chose Abram" (Neh 9:7), and in the New Testament, the consistent testimony is that the first person of the Trinity is the one who spoke to Abraham (Luke 1:55; 73; Acts 3:13, 25; 7:2, 8, 17, 32; Gal 3:8, 18; Heb 6:13), and the one Abraham believed (Rom 4:3; Gal 3:6; Jas 2:23). Even Jesus calls the Father, the "God of Abraham" (Matt 22:32; Mark 12:26; Luke 20:37). Therefore, it is right to think of the Father as the one who not only made the heavens, the earth, and the seas but also the one who "preserve[s] all of them."

Furthermore, in the Old Testament, the Holy Spirit is implicitly tied to the work of preservation. In one of the premier psalms on providence (Ps 104), the psalmist praises *Yahweh* for his provision of water (vv. 10–13), food (vv. 14–15, 27–28), and shelter (vv. 16–18). He then ties the preservation of life to the work of the Spirit:

> When you hide your face, they are dismayed; when you take away their breath, they die and return to their dust. When you send forth your *Spirit*, they are created, and you renew the face of the ground. (Ps 104:29–30)

Also, in his conversation with Job, Elihu says that the Father preserves the very life of man by the Spirit:

> If he [God, the Almighty] should set his heart to it and gather to himself his *spirit* and his *breath*, all flesh would perish together, and man would return to dust (Job 34:14–15).[60]

Therefore, all creatures are dependent upon the Father to send forth his Holy Spirit, so that they can exist and live. Christopher Wright concludes,

> So the Creator Spirit is also the provider Spirit. Or, to put it more formally, in this psalm we have moved from the doctrine of creation to the doctrine of providence. God not only brings

---

60. On this passage as a reference to the Holy Spirit, and for the variety of uses of רוּחַ in the book of Job, see Clarke, "Job 27:3," 111–21.

all things into existence, he also sustains all things by his power. Day by day, season by season, year by year, from age to age, the Spirit of God is there, sustaining and renewing the earth. God the Creator, God the provider—both are truths that the Bible links with the Holy Spirit.[61]

Above all, in his providence, the Father demonstrates his care for those created in his image. As Michael Bird notes,

> God is particularly concerned with the well-being of humanity as they are the summit of his creating activity (Gen 1:26–27; Ps 8:4–6). God sends rain for the sustenance of all peoples (Job 5:10; 37:13; Ps 135:7; Zech 10:1; Matt 5:45). Human beings have the spheres of their existence fixed by the Lord (Acts 17:26). God determines the constancy of the universal laws of nature that govern the earth and seas: "I have . . . made my covenant with day and night and established the laws of heaven and earth" (Jer 33:25).[62]

Finally, the Father sometimes preserves his people through miracles, which are described as his "mighty deeds," "signs," and "wonders."[63] From the perspective of the New Testament, the Father was the one who (1) preserved Noah and his family in the flood, and (2) acted to deliver his people out of Egypt in the Exodus. In Hebrews 11:7, the Father warns Noah about the flood.[64] Then, the Father waited patiently while the ark was prepared (1 Pet 3:20),[65] and preserved Noah and his family "when he brought a flood upon the world of the ungodly" (2 Pet 2:5; cf. 3:5–6).[66] Thus, *Yahweh*, the one in whose eyes "Noah found favor" (Gen 6:8) is, in these biblical passages, God the Father.

In the same way, the New Testament attributes the deliverance of Israel from Egypt as a work of the Father. He spoke to Moses at the burning

---

61. Wright, *Knowing the Holy Spirit*, 21.

62. Bird, *Evangelical Theology*, 143.

63. The New Testament repeatedly attributes miracles to the work of the Father (John 3:2; 10:37–38; Acts 2:19, 22; 4:30; 15:12; 19:11; 1 Cor 12:28; Gal 3:5; Heb 2:4). On the definition of miracles, see Frame, *Doctrine of God*, 241–60.

64. In chapter 11 of Hebrews, every use of θεός is refers to the Father. He is distinguished from Jesus in Heb 12:2.

65. In the immediate context, θεός is in distinction from Jesus Christ (1 Pet 3:18, 21; 4:1), and therefore a reference to the Father.

66. In 2 Peter, θεός is used one time for the Son (2 Pet 1:1) in the context of the phrase "God and Savior, Jesus Christ." However, when θεός stands by itself, it is a reference to the Father (2 Pet 1:2, 21; 2:4; 3:5, 12; esp. 1:17).

bush (Acts 7:31–36),⁶⁷ and "with uplifted arm he led them" out of Egypt (Acts 13:17; cf. Heb 8:9),⁶⁸ miraculously providing bread from heaven to feed them in the wilderness (John 6:32).⁶⁹ To be sure, he did it through the agency of his Son, for the rock that gave them drink was Christ (1 Cor 10:4),⁷⁰ and even Jude asserts that the Lord Jesus "saved a people out of the land of Egypt" (Jude 5).⁷¹ It is why Moses responds in prayer: "O Lord GOD, you have only begun to show your servant your greatness and your mighty hand. For what god is there in heaven or on earth who can do such works and mighty acts as yours" (Deut 3:24).

Michael Horton's analysis of miracles is helpful:

> The question is not whether God is involved in every aspect of our lives but how God is involved. Therefore, with respect to providence, the question is never whether causes are exclusively natural or supernatural, but whether God's involvement in every moment is providential or miraculous [emphasis original].⁷²

The Father Governs His Creation through the Son and Spirit

Embedded in the proper name "Lord" (*Yahweh*, κύριος) is the concept of sovereign governance.⁷³ G. K. Beale writes,

---

67. Throughout his speech to the high priest, Stephen is speaking of the Father, which is made clear by the Trinitarian shape of his heavenly vision (7:55), and his confession, "Behold, I see the heavens opened, and the Son of Man standing at the right hand of God" (Acts 7:56).

68. Paul, in his witness to the Jews in Antioch Pisidia speaks of the Father's work in the history of Israel, distinguishing him from the Savior Jesus (Acts 13:23).

69. The implication in Jesus's thinking is that just as the Father gave his Son, the "true bread from heaven," so too he gave the manna in the wilderness.

70. As mentioned in chap. 2, Paul uses the Song of Moses in Deut 32:4 (cf. 1 Cor 10:4) to conclude "the Rock was Christ."

71. It is difficult to determine if the proper reading is Ἰησοῦς or κύριος. For our purposes, regardless of the noun used, the second person of the Godhead is the referent (cf. "Master and Lord, Jesus Christ," in Jude 4), and thus the agent not only of Israel's salvation but the agent of destruction for "those who did not believe."

72. Horton, *Christian Faith*, 369. It is important to also keep Frame's balanced thinking in mind: "I do not believe, however, that Scripture warrants a sharp distinction between providence and miracle. Indeed, in Scripture the language of miracle is used for providential events, and providential events have much the same use as miracles." Frame distinguishes providence from miracles as "extraordinary" vs. "ordinary" manifestations of God's lordship. Frame, *Doctrine of God*, 261.

73. Contrary to this position is open theism. Sanders, *God Who Risks*. Refutations

> The Old Testament is the story of God, who progressively reestablishes his new-creational kingdom out of chaos over a sinful people by his word and Spirit through promise, covenant, and redemption, resulting in worldwide commission to the faithful to advance this kingdom and judgment (defeat or exile) for the unfaithful, unto his glory.[74]

Therefore, in the Old Testament, the Father's lordship is explained by his role as king and his role as lawgiver. Additionally, Thomas Schreiner brings out the importance of humanity in God's lordship:

> Focusing on God as King in the abstract apart from human beings does not do justice to the breadth found in the Scriptures. For the central message of Scripture also includes human beings—the crown of creation—who are created in God's image. Since God is King and Lord, it is his purpose and design that he be glorified in all things and by all people. . . . The sovereignty of God and his kingship take place in history, in the story recounted in the Scriptures, revealed supremely in the ministry and person of Jesus Christ.[75]

It is why the Old Testament Psalmist can declare, "The LORD sits enthroned over the flood; the LORD sits enthroned as king forever" (Ps 29:10), "For the LORD, the Most High, is to be feared, a great king over all the earth" (Ps 47:2; cf. 47:1–9), "The LORD reigns; he is robed in majesty; the LORD is robed; he has put on strength as his belt. Yes, the world is established; it shall never be moved" (Ps 93:1), and "The LORD has established his throne in the heavens, and his kingdom rules over all" (Ps 103:19).

That these uses of *Yahweh* ought to be understood as a reference to the Father are best seen in the extended treatment of Psalm 95 by Hebrews 3:7—4:7. The author of Hebrews quotes Psalm 95:11, also alluding to Genesis 2:2 on the basis of verbal analogy, to help define God's "rest" (Heb 4:3–5). Further, in the context of Hebrews, θεός is identified as the Father in distinction from Jesus his Son (Heb 4:14), who is Christ (Heb 3:6, 14), the high priest who gives the ultimate rest. Finally, as I argued in chapter 2, when the New Testament quotes the Old Testament, the Father is customarily the referent when the proper names of God are used. Thus, *Yahweh* in Psalm 95 is properly identified as the Father, who is worthy of praise:

---

of open theism include Ware, *God's Lesser Glory*; Frame, *No Other God*; and Piper, Taylor, and Helseth, *Beyond the Bounds*.

74. Beale, *New Testament Biblical Theology*, 16.

75. Schreiner, *King in His Beauty*, xiii–xiv.

> For the LORD is a great God, and a great King above all gods. In his hand are the depths of the earth; the heights of the mountains are his also. The sea is his, for he made it, and his hands formed the dry land. (Ps 95:3–5)

Other passages confirm the Father's authority in his governing providence. When the disciples ask Jesus if he will restore the kingdom to Israel (Acts 1:6), Jesus responds by saying, "It is not for you to know times or seasons that the Father has fixed by his own authority" (Acts 1:7). The Father is the one who has providentially determined the times and dates according to *his own authority* (ἐξουσίᾳ). It is only then, under his authority, that his kingdom will come (Matt 6:10). Even Nebuchadnezzar acknowledges this in his prayer of repentance:

> All the inhabitants of the earth are accounted as nothing, and he does according to his will among the host of heaven and among the inhabitants of the earth; and none can stay his hand or say to him, "What have you done?" (Dan 4:35)

Daniel continually speaks of the Father's kingship and kingdom throughout his book: "the God of heaven will set up a kingdom that shall never be destroyed" (Dan 2:44), "His [the Most High God] kingdom is an everlasting kingdom" (Dan 4:3), "his [the Most High] kingdom endures from generation to generation" (Dan 4:34), "his [one like a son of man] kingdom [given by the Ancient of Days (v. 13)] one that shall not be destroyed" (Dan 7:14), "the saints of the Most High shall receive the kingdom and possess the kingdom forever, forever and ever" (Dan 7:18), "their [the Most High and his saints] kingdom shall be an everlasting kingdom, and all dominions shall serve and obey him" (Dan 7:27). There is a clear flow of thought throughout Daniel that God Most High, the Ancient of Days, the Father gives a kingdom to his Son (one who is like a son of man) and therefore the saints not only receive this kingdom but also reign in this kingdom.[76]

In Deuteronomy, the Father himself says, "See now that I, even I, am he, and there is no god beside me; I kill and I make alive; I wound and I heal; and there is none that can deliver out of my hand" (Deut 32:39). The use of the near context (32:35) quoted in the New Testament (Rom 12:19; Heb 10:30), demonstrate that *Yahweh* is a reference to the Father. Finally, all of the Father's governance is done on behalf of his goal to display his glory by saving a people and summing up all things in his Son (Eph 1:9–10). Stephen Wellum and Peter Gentry bring out this detail:

---

76. On the relationship between these passages, see Hamilton, *With the Clouds of Heaven*, 71–77.

God's kingly work in creation is never presented as an end in itself; rather it is the beginning of God's eternal plan (Eph 1:11; Rev. 4:11) in time, which he now directs and governs toward a specific *telos*. In this way, creation leads to providence, and both creation and providence establish the eschatological direction of God's plan, particularly worked out in terms of specific covenantal relationships God enters into with his creation, which, in the end, all leads to a specific goal centred in Christ (cf. Col 1:15–20). In light of such teaching, even though the specific *wording*, "kingdom of God," is not found until much later in Scripture, the *idea* is taught in the opening pages of the Bible [emphasis original].[77]

Thus, the Father governs the creation through his Son and Spirit and will establish a kingdom that will never end.

Trinity and Providence in the New Testament

In the New Testament, the Father's providence is never apart from his Son or Spirit. In fact, a clear Trinitarian *taxis* emerges. The Father providentially preserves and governs through the Son and by (or in) the Holy Spirit. To begin with, many biblical passages speak of the Father's work in providence.

For example, in the Sermon on the Mount, Jesus says the Father "makes his sun rise on the vile and on the good, and sends rain on the just and on the unjust" (Matt 5:45). A little later, he says, "Look at the birds of the air: they neither sow nor reap nor gather into barns, and yet your heavenly Father feeds them. Are you not of more value than they" (Matt 6:26), and "But if God [the Father] so clothes the grass of the field, which today is alive and tomorrow is thrown into the oven, will he not much more clothe you, O you of little faith . . . your heavenly Father knows that you need them all" (Matt 6:30–32; cf. Luke 12:24, 28). In another sermon, Jesus tells his audience, "Are not two sparrows sold for a penny? And not one of them will fall to the ground apart from your Father" (Matt 10:29; cf. Luke 12:6).

So too Barnabas and Paul, in response to the crowd's idolatrous worship of them in Lystra, argue for the Father's work in providence: "Yet he [the Father] did not leave himself without witness, for he did good by giving you rains from heaven and fruitful seasons, satisfying your hearts with food and gladness" (Acts 14:17).[78] Paul also argued for the Father's providence in

---

77. Gentry and Wellum, *Kingdom through Covenant*, 592.

78. The antecedent of the pronoun is found in v. 15, "living God." Every time the phrase "living God" is used in the New Testament (Matt 16:16; 26:63; Acts 14:15; Rom

his address on Mars Hill. It is clear from the context that Paul has the Father in mind because in v. 31 he says it is God who "has fixed a day on which he will judge the world in righteousness by a man [Jesus his Son] whom he has appointed; and of this he has given assurance to all by raising him from the dead." So, Paul writes,

> And he [the Father] made from one man every nation of mankind to live on all the face of the earth, having determined allotted periods and the boundaries of their dwelling place, that they should seek God, and perhaps feel their way toward him and find him. Yet he is actually not far from each one of us, for "In him we live and move and have our being;" as even some of your own poets have said, "For we are indeed his offspring." (Acts 17:26–28)

It is also why Paul can argue that the Father predestines the inheritance of his elect, and it is "according to the purpose of him [the Father] who works all things according to the counsel of his will" (Eph 1:11; cf. Rom 8:28). Thus, for Paul, providence is clearly a work initiated by the first person of the Trinity.

The author of Hebrews agrees, "For land that has drunk the rain that often falls on it, and produces a crop useful to those for whose sake it is cultivated, receives a blessing from God [the Father]" (Heb 6:7). In the context, God is distinct from the Son of God (v. 6), and the Holy Spirit (v. 4). Likewise, James tells his audience, "Every good gift and every perfect gift is from above, coming down from the Father of lights with whom there is no variation or shadow due to change" (Jas 1:17).[79] On this passage Ware writes,

> Imagine the breadth and significance of this claim. Where does every single good gift originate? From the Father. Even the gift of the Son who provides our salvation? Yes, he is a gift from the Father (John 3:16; 1 John 4:10). And the gift of the Spirit who works in our hearts to transform us, to gift us, to minister in the body of Christ? Yes, he too is from the Father (Acts 1:4; 2:33). Every good gift, in all of life, comes ultimately from the Father.[80]

9:26; 2 Cor 3:3; 6:16; 1 Tim 3:15; 4:10; Heb 3:12; 9:14; 10:31; 12:22; Rev 7:2), it refers to the Father.

79. θεός is always a reference to God the Father in the book of James, who uses κύριος for Jesus: "Lord Jesus Christ" (1:1), and "our Lord Jesus Christ, the Lord of glory" (2:1).

80. Ware, *Father, Son, and Spirit*, 54.

The Father Providentially Governs through the Son

Even though the Father is clearly the initiator, Scripture is clear that the he does not work apart from his Son. Two passages make this eminently clear: Colossians 1:17 and Hebrews 1:3. In Colossians 1:17, Paul writes, "And he [Jesus] is before all things, and in him all things hold together." Peter Lewis explains what it means for Jesus to hold all things together:

> First of all, Christ is said to be not only the explanation of the origins of all existence outside of God, but also the full and ultimate explanation of its continuance. He is "the innermost, animating, cohesive principle of power, of the entire cosmos." ... However, we must not think merely in terms of the origin and support of creation. There is something even higher! What we have here is the doctrine of *providence* in its most personal and purposeful form. He who keeps all things in being is leading all things toward their goal in him.[81]

Further, Paul's broader discussion of Jesus as κύριος (Col 1:3) argues for the Son's mediatorial governance in providence under the Father's authority. The Son, as the Father's agent in creation, is also the Father's agent in providence. Arthur Wainwright reflects,

> One of the avenues through which early Christians approached their belief that Christ was an agent in creation was the doctrine of Christ's Lordship over all things in heaven and on earth. ... Paul believed that God had put all things in subjection under Christ's feet (Eph. 1:22; I Cor. 15:27). In virtue of this power Christ sustained the created world. There is "one Lord Jesus Christ, through whom are all things and we through him" (I Cor. 8:6). "In him all things consist" (Col. 1:17). The Lordship of Christ is not merely a title by which he receives tributes of service and adoration. He gives life to the world which is held together by him.[82]

In Hebrews 1:3, the author writes, "He [the Son] is the radiance of the glory of God and the exact imprint of his nature, and he upholds the universe by the word of his power." Thus, God the Father is both creator (v. 2) and upholder of the universe (v. 3), and he exercises both functions through the agency of his Son.[83] Furthermore, Peter O'Brien argues that

---

81. Lewis, *Glory of Christ*, 245. Lewis is quoting J. Weiss, in turn quoted in Paul Beasley-Murray, "Colossians 1:15–20," 174.

82. Wainwright, *Trinity in the New Testament*, 149–50.

83. See comments in Ellingworth, *Hebrews*, 100–101.

φέρω means the Son not only upholds all things, but does so with a goal and purpose in mind:

> Not only is Jesus Christ the agent of creation (v. 2c); he also sustains the universe he has made. This Lord is not like the god of the deists, who, having created the world, then proceeded to let it run on its own. He is personally and continually involved in sustaining it. The verb used here, *phero*, has the primary sense of "sustain or uphold." The immediate context, however, suggests the additional nuance of the Son's 'carrying' all things to their appointed end or goal. The notion of direction or purpose seems to be included. The author, then, is not referring to the passive support of a burden like the Greek god Atlas bearing the dead weight of the world on his shoulders. Rather, the language implies a "bearing" that includes movement and progress towards an objective. Montefiore comments: "What is here being ascribed to the Son is the providential government of the universe, which is the function of God himself."[84] Moreover, if this nuance of direction is present, then the Son's bearing all things (i.e., time and space) to their appointed end looks forward to his work of redemption, which is described in the next line (v. 3c). The Son's sustaining all things is not simply the backdrop to or the precursor of his redemptive work. His cleansing of sins is an important objective of Christ's providential work.[85]

The Father Providentially Governs by the Spirit

Although the Holy Spirit's role in providence is less explicit, the implication from the New Testament is that the Spirit is the one by (or in) whom the Father preserves and governs. As we saw in chapter 2, just as the Father and Son have life in themselves, so too the Spirit is the "living water" (John 4:14; 7:38–39), "who gives life" (John 6:63). The Spirit is typified by water, which in the New Testament is a symbol for cleansing and refreshing, without which life does not long endure. Thus, the Father is the source of all life, but mediates the preservation of that life by his Spirit.[86]

---

84. O' Brien is referencing Montefiore, *Hebrews*, 35, cited by Ebert, "Wisdom in New Testament Christology," 89.

85. O'Brien, *Hebrews*, 56–57. See also Allen, *Hebrews*, 121.

86. A corollary would be the Spirit-empowered skill of artisans in the Old Testament to shape, mold and make beautiful the elements of the created world (Exod 31:3; 35:31).

Fire is another image of the Father's preservation by the Spirit. As Thomas Oden says,

> The fire of the Spirit can symbolize protection, as in the pillar of fire that guided Israel in the desert (Exod. 13:21; Zech. 2:5), or purifying discipline, as in a refiner's fire (Mal. 3:3; Titus 2:14). Those who attest the Spirit's life are destined to "suffer grief in all kinds of trials. These have come so that your faith—of greater worth than gold, which perishes even though refined by fire—may be proved genuine" (1 Pet. 1:6, 7; Wm. Penn, *No Cross, No Crown*). Zealous service of the Spirit is likened to fire, where love is flaming into human warmth and fervent prayer (Ambrose, *Duties III.18*, NPNF 2 X, p. 84). With the memory of such metaphors in the background, the gifts at Pentecost were described as "tongues of fire that separated and came to rest on each of them" (Acts 2:3).[87]

Even in the Old Testament, the Spirit's role in providence is to sustain everything made (Ps 104:30). Finally, the Spirit's mediatorial governance is witnessed in the men he empowered to rule. Joseph, Daniel, and Moses were endued with the Holy Spirit and enabled to govern with unusually great measure (Gen 41:38; Dan 4:8-9; Num 11:25-29).[88] Also, after David's sin with Bathsheba, he cried to the Lord, "Cast me not away from your presence, and take not your Holy Spirit from me" (Ps 51:11). David understood his kingship was only effective if the Spirit empowered him to govern and rule in the approving presence of *Yahweh*.

It is why Michael Horton argues that not only the Son, but also the Holy Spirit are involved in the doctrine of providence:

> It is the Spirit who is at work within the field spoken into existence by the Father in the Son (Ro 8:26-28; Isa 32:15; 2Co 3:17). It is the Spirit who so orchestrates the unfolding plot of redemption around the Son to the glory of the Father that the past becomes a living promise and the future becomes a revivifying reality. Because the Father works not only *upon* but *within* history by his Spirit, and does all things in his Son, God's providence cannot be conceived merely in terms of immediate cause and effect.[89]

Thus, the Holy Spirit is the one by whom the Father works to providentially sum up all things in his Son (Eph 1:9-10).

---

87. Oden, *Systematic Theology*, 3:44.
88. See Ferguson, *Holy Spirit*, 21-22, and Erickson, *Christian Theology*, 883-84.
89. Horton, *Christian Faith*, 350.

Conclusion

In this chapter, I have argued that there is a consistent display of the Father's initiating role within the works of creation and providence: the Father creates, preserves, and governs *through* the Son and *by* (or *in*) the Holy Spirit. However, although a *taxis* exists within the works of creation and providence, there is no diminishing of glory due all three persons of the Godhead. It is why the Creed includes in its sentence on the Holy Spirit the assertion, "who with the Father and the Son together is worshipped and glorified."[90] In fact, the goal and purpose of creation and providence is for the Triune God's glory to be exhibited in a Christocentric Trinitarian manner.

The Father, the one "from [whom] and through [whom] and to [whom] are all things. To [whom] be [the] glory forever" (Rom 11:36) is the one who purposed and planned to "unite all things" in his Son (Eph 1:10), therefore he poured out his Spirit to create life (Gen 2:7; Job 33:4; Ps 33:6), sustain life (Gen 1:2; 104:30), and give new life (John 6:63; 2 Cor 3:6). At the end of the age, "at the name of Jesus every knee [will] bow, in heaven and on earth and under the earth, and every tongue confess that Jesus Christ is Lord, to the glory of God the Father" (Phil 2:10–11).

Basil of Caesarea in "On the Holy Spirit" describes his Trinitarian devotion with two phrases: "Glory to the Father through [*dia*] the Son in [*en*] the Holy Spirit," [worship of God as revealed in Creation] and "Glory to the Father with [*meta*] the Son together with [*syn*] the Holy Spirit" [worship of God in Godself *en se*].[91] He argues that both are necessary to balance the equality of the divine persons while still worshiping each in their proper order.[92]

In the next chapter, we will see that the gospel message of redemption comes *from* the Father *through* the Son *by* the power of the Holy Spirit, and in chapter 8, we will see that our response must correspond to that *taxis*: to the praise of the Father's glory (Eph 1:3–14), through union with the Son and in praise of his atoning work at the cross (Phil 2:9–11), by the empowering, indwelling ministry of the Holy Spirit (Phil 3:3). "For *through* him [Jesus] we both have access *in* one Spirit *to* the Father" (Eph 2:18).

---

90. "Nicene-Constantinople Creed," in Kelly, *Early Christian Creeds*, 297.

91. Basil, *On the Holy Spirit*, 29–30. Basil, *De Spiritu Sancto*, I.3.

92. See Wainwright's discussion in Wainwright, "Trinitarian Worship," 209–21. In it, Wainwright writes, "Christian worship, like the salvation it celebrates and advances, is summed up in the movement "from the Father, through Christ, in the Holy Spirit, to the Father [*a Patre, per Christum, in Spiritu Sancto, ad Patrem*]" (211). See also, Parry, *Worshipping Trinity*, 83.

5

The Father's Work of Providing Salvation in Redemptive History through the Sending of the Son

Introduction

GOD THE FATHER, WHO through the Son and Spirit created all things, gives life to all things and calls them good, who "dwells in unapproachable light" (1 Tim 6:16), who has authority to give names to every grouping of angels in heaven and humanity on earth (Eph 3:15), and who is "over all and through all and in all" (Eph 4:6), promised in redemptive history to bring salvation through his Messiah. Therefore, the Father begins the work of providing salvation with a promise of the gospel. After the fall, the Father did not abandon his creation, but rather makes this promise first to Abraham (Gen 12:1–3), and then, through the prophets to the people of God (Heb 1:1).

Next, the Father sends his Son at the high point of the ages (Heb 9:26), bringing fulfillment to the promises and securing salvation through the substitutionary sacrifice for sin at the cross (2 Cor 5:21; Phil 2:6–8). In doing so, the Father makes his Son the focal point for the display of his glory (Phil 2:10–11), raising him up and exalting him to his right hand (Heb 10:12; 12:2; 1 Pet 3:22), thus setting him over all things (Eph 1:22).

In this chapter, I will argue that the Father's role in redemptive history is to initiate all the divine works tied to the promise and coming of the Messiah, including the promise to Adam and Eve, the promise to Abraham, the giving of the old covenant through Moses, the promise to David, the promise of a new covenant, and finally the sending of his Son to be the Messiah.

Through the Prophets the Father Promised a Messiah

In Hebrews 1:1-2, the author writes, "Long ago, at many times and in many ways, God [the Father] spoke to our fathers by the prophets, but in these last days he has spoken to us by his Son." All the Father's promises and prophecies were heading to the culminating revelation of his Son as the Messiah.[1] However, this does not mean that the Father somehow spoke apart from the Son in the Old Testament. As David Allen remarks,

> Amazingly, the author viewed the revelation of the Son as God's "speech" to us, and thus it is an appropriate metaphor for all that God does through Christ in the world and not just in reference to the words of Christ. Additionally, when Scripture speaks of the "word of the LORD" addressed to and through Old Testament prophets, the Son, as the second Person of the Trinity, is always involved as well. As the author made clear in Heb 11:3, it was God's speech that created the universe. Thus, the word that God now speaks through his Son is in no way discontinuous with God's word spoken through the prophets or even in creation. This indicates that the author of Hebrews considered speech to be an appropriate metaphor for divine revelation beyond that which is merely verbal.[2]

The Father's climactic revelation has come through his Son, not only in his words, but also through all of his Messianic works of incarnation, crucifixion, resurrection and exaltation.[3] The apostle Paul refers to these promises in the Old Testament as the Gospel that belongs to the Father (1 Thess 2:2, 8, 9; 2 Cor 11:7; Rom 1:1; 15:16; 1 Tim 1:11),[4] that is his secret and hidden wisdom (1 Cor 2:7), a mystery hidden for ages in him (Eph 3:9) that was promised beforehand through his prophets (Rom 1:2), and is concerning his Son (Rom 1:3). The Father reveals his gospel in the prophetic writings (Rom 16:26), which are variously referred to as the word from him (1 Thess 2:13; 1 Cor 14:36; 2 Cor 2:17; 4:2; Rom 9:6; Col 1:25; Titus 1:3; 2:5;

---

1. For a discussion of the comparison and contrast between the two ways of the Father's speaking in the prophets and his Son, see Ellingworth, *Hebrews*, 91 and Johnson, *Hebrews*, 65.

2. Allen, *Hebrews*, 104. See also, Johnson, *Hebrews*, 66, 70.

3. O'Brien, *Hebrews*, 51.

4. I take the genitive phrase εὐαγγέλιον τοῦ θεοῦ and its variants to be a possessive genitive (gospel belonging to God) or less likely a genitive of source (gospel from God), although they are closely related. This is in contrast to εὐαγγέλιον τοῦ Χριστοῦ, which is better understood as an objective genitive, the gospel about/concerning Christ.

4:5; 2 Tim 2:9),[5] the oracles from him (Rom 3:2), the teaching about him as Savior (Titus 2:10),[6] and the Scripture breathed out by him (2 Tim 3:16). Therefore, it is God the Son who has the role of communicating the person and work of the Father as revealed in the gospel. Furthermore, Peter speaks of the Spirit's agency in inspiration: "For no prophecy was ever produced by the will of man, but men spoke from God [the Father] as they were carried along by the Holy Spirit" (2 Pet 1:21), and is why Scripture sometimes attributes the same prophecy to both the Father and the Holy Spirit (e.g., Acts 4:25; Heb 3:7; 10:15).[7] Thus, we may say that "the Lord GOD does nothing without revealing his secret to his servants the prophets" (Amos 3:7), and this he does through the Son and by the Holy Spirit.

The public discourses in Luke-Acts, likewise, give consistent evidence that the gospel promises originate from the Father. Mary's magnificat (Luke 1:46–55) speaks of the Father's "remembrance of his mercy." Zechariah's prophecy at the birth of his son (Luke 1:68–78) praises the Father for keeping his "promise," remembering his "holy covenant" with Abraham. Peter, in his sermon at Pentecost (Acts 2:14–39), speaks of the oath God the Father made to Abraham concerning the Christ (Acts 2:30–31). Peter also, in his sermon at Solomon's portico (Acts 3:12–26) argues that the Father "foretold by the mouth of all the prophets that his Christ would suffer" (Acts 3:18). Paul at Antioch says, "And we bring you the good news that what God promised to the fathers" (Acts 13:32), and again at his defense before Agrippa, "And now I stand here on trial because of my hope in the promise made by God to our fathers" (Acts 26:6).

Finally, Stephen's testimony at his martyrdom (Acts 7:2–53) is perhaps the most thorough in its summary: (1) the Father makes his promises to Abraham (Acts 7:2–8), (2) the Father preserves his people through Joseph (7:9–16), (3) the Father delivers his people through Moses (7:17–43), (4) the Father makes his presence manifest among his people in the temple (7:44–50), (5) the Father finally fulfills his promises in his Son, the Messiah (7:51–53). After his testimony, Stephen receives a Trinitarian vision remarkably consistent with the divine *taxis*. "Full of the Holy Spirit," Stephen sees the glory of God the Father and Jesus standing at the Father's right hand (Acts 7:55).[8] I want to now briefly examine each major milestone in greater detail.

---

5. I take this to be a genitive of source (or origin). It may be even more nuanced and what Wallace calls a genitive of production "the word produced by God." For genitive of production, see Wallace, *Greek Grammar*, 104–6.

6. See Lenski, *Colossians, Thessalonians, Timothy, Titus and Philemon*, 917.

7. For the Spirit's role in the inspiration of Scripture, see vol. 4 of Henry, *God, Revelation, and Authority*.

8. The Spirit's new-covenant ministry is to glorify the Son (John 15:26), who is at

The Father's Promises from Adam to Abraham

Genesis 3:15 is the *protoevangelium*, the first promise made in reference to mankind's restoration after the fall.[9] In it, the Father promises to give the woman a descendant (later revealed to be his own Son) who will crush the serpent's head, and in doing so will receive a bruise upon his heel, and is why the apostle Paul can write, "For as in Adam all die, so also in Christ shall all be made alive" (1 Cor 15:22).[10] Paul more frequently, however, narrows the focus on the promise given to Abraham. The Father is the one who preached the gospel beforehand to Abraham (Gal 3:8).[11] The Father made both a promise and a covenant with Abraham (Gal 3:17–18, 21), and gave it to him personally (Gal 3:20).[12] Though Abraham did not deserve this blessing (Rom 4:2), Abraham believed the Father's promises (Rom 4:3, 17) regarding the Messiah without wavering (Rom 4:20), fully convinced the Father was able to do what he promised (Rom 4:21). Since the Father is faithful to his promises (2 Cor 1:18; Rom 3:3), Abraham was justified by faith (Rom 4:3) as an example of all who would believe. In the same way, the author of Hebrews points out that the Father "swore by himself" (Heb 6:13), and "guaranteed it with an oath" (Heb 6:17) when he made his promise to Abraham, so James writes that because Abraham believed the Father, he was called "a friend of God" (Jas 2:23).[13]

---

the Father's right hand, which in turn, terminates in praise to the Father (Phil 2:11; 1 Pet 4:11).

9. It is most likely a reference to the Father since he makes a promise about his Son, who will be the descendent of the woman. Further, as argued in chap. 4, the Father is the one who spoke in Gen 1–2.

10. The verb ζωοποιέω is never used in other passages to describe those outside of Christ. However, Paul is probably not dealing with the eternal destinies of those who do not believe. Rather, he is simply saying there is no resurrection of the dead (just or unjust; cf. John 5:28–29; Acts 24:15) apart from Christ.

11. The context of θεός in every use in Galatians demonstrates that ὁ θεὸς is a reference to the Father in distinction from the Son (e.g., see use in Gal 1:1–4).

12. The relationship between the two clauses in this verse is greatly debated. I take the two phrases together to mean that the Father, when he gave the law, used a mediator; however, when he gave the promise to Abraham, he spoke it directly and no human mediation was involved. See Dunn, *Galatians*, 191.

13. As argued in chap. 2, the consistent testimony of the New Testament is that the one speaking in Gen 12 and Gen 15 was the first person of the Trinity.

The Father's Giving of the Old Covenant through Moses

Since the Father promised through his prophets that he would send his Messiah to restore what was lost in the fall, the Pharisees rightly believed that God the Father spoke to Moses (John 9:29). Accordingly, in the Gospel of John, the Father told Moses two important things: (1) the Law (John 1:17; cf. Heb 9:20), and (2) the promise of a deliverer (John 5:46).[14] The Father first speaks to Moses and calls him to prophetic ministry at the burning bush (Exod 3:1–4:17). At the bush, he reveals the divine name, *Yahweh* (Exod 3:15; cf. Acts 7:31–35),[15] emphasizing his covenant keeping presence with his people.[16] The Father gives Moses the pattern for the tabernacle (Acts 7:44; Heb 8:5), and appoints the priesthood (Heb 5:1, 4). It is no surprise then that Zechariah and Elizabeth, descendants of Aaron, are described as "righteous before God [the Father], walking blamelessly in all the commandments and statutes of the Lord [the Father]" (Luke 1:6).[17] Further, Zechariah served as a priest before the Father, and was providentially on duty in the temple when an angel promised that Zechariah's son, John would be the forerunner of the Messiah (Luke 1:8–17). In similar manner (as will be examined fully in chap. 8), the new-covenant church as both temple and priesthood serves God the Father through Jesus Christ in the power of the Holy Spirit. Concerning the new-covenant temple, Paul writes, "In him [Christ] you also are being built together into a dwelling place for God [the Father] by the Spirit" (Eph 2:22). Concerning the priesthood, Peter writes, "you yourselves like living stones are being built up as a spiritual house [the indwelling work of the Spirit], to be a holy priesthood, to offer spiritual sacrifices acceptable to God [the Father] through Jesus Christ" (1 Pet 2:5). The Father accomplishes this by raising up another prophet like

---

14. This deliverance was typified by two events in the wilderness: the bronze serpent (John 3:14) and the manna (John 6:31).

15. There is a connection in both the Exodus and the Acts account with the "angel of the Lord." Although it is possible that the angel here is a created being, since Stephen also says the Law was "delivered by angels" (Acts 7:53; cf. Gal 3:19; Heb 2:2), more likely the traditional view is correct that in this case it is a theophany of the pre-incarnate Son of God. In many passages the "angel of the Lord" is identified with God and speaks as God (e.g., Gen 16:7–13; 21:17–20; 22:12; 31:11–13; Judg 6:11–27). If this is the case, it is another instance of the Father's initiating role in sending the Son as his messenger.

16. The glory of God's presence at the burning bush that Moses experiences culminates in the glory of *Yahweh* filling the tabernacle (Exod 40:34-38).

17. In this context, both θεός and κύριος are references to the first person of the Trinity. In the infancy chapters of Luke (1–2), θεός is always a reference to the Father. κύριος is used of him 25 times and twice for Jesus (1:43 and 2:11). See Nolland, *Luke 1—9:20*, 27.

Moses (Deut 18:15-22; cf. 34:10-12) through the incarnation and ministry of his Son (Acts 3:22; 7:37).

The Father's Promise to David

In Paul's sermon to the synagogue of Antioch in Pisidia, he reminds his listeners of their redemptive history, bringing to their attention that God the Father raised up David to be their king (Acts 13:22). Paul explains, "Of this man's offspring God has brought to Israel a Savior, Jesus, as he promised" (Acts 13:23). After explaining the crucifixion, Paul connects the resurrection to the Father's promise to David: "And as for the fact that he [the Father] raised him from the dead, no more to return to corruption, he [the Father] has spoken in this way, 'I will give you the holy and sure blessings of David'" (Acts 13:34).[18] Peter, in his sermon at Pentecost adds, "Being therefore a prophet, and knowing that God had sworn with an oath to him that he would set one of his descendants on his throne" (Acts 2:30). David's role as prophet is important, because it demonstrates that the Father spoke through David's mouth "by the Holy Spirit" (Acts 4:25) concerning his Son (Acts 4:26-27). The Father's initiatory work through the Spirit is thus evident in the giving of prophecy.

The Father's Promise of the New Covenant

The Father also spoke through other prophets; therefore, Philip said to Nathaniel, "We have found him of whom Moses in the Law and also the prophets wrote, Jesus of Nazareth, the son of Joseph" (John 1:45). In the same manner, the apostle John appeals to Isaiah and concludes, "Isaiah said these things because he saw his [the Son's] glory and spoke of him" (John 12:41).[19] It is why the Father speaks through Isaiah to say, "Behold,

---

18. The citation comes from Isa 55:3 LXX. "This seems to indicate that God, having made promises to David, pledged himself to keep them, if not in David's lifetime, in the ongoing future of his people." Beale and Carson, *New Testament Use of the Old Testament*, 586.

19. The passage in mind is Isaiah 6. John quotes from Isa 6:10 in John 12:40, and then speaks of the Son's preincarnate glory. The throne room scene in Isaiah 6 is staggering. The Lord on the throne who is thrice holy, whose glory fills the earth (Isa 6:3), will be rejected by the people (Isa 6:10). In the context of the Johannine pericope points the finger to the Pharisees' rejection of Jesus as Messiah when he heals the man who was born blind (John 9:39-41), as well as their response to Jesus other "signs" in the Gospel of John. See Beale and Carson, *New Testament Use of the Old Testament*, 479-83.

the virgin shall conceive and bear a son, and they shall call his name Immanuel" (Isa 7:14; Matt 1:22–23).

The final prophet before Christ is John the Baptist, described in John 1:6, "There was a man sent from God [the Father], whose name was John."[20] John the Baptist himself was not the Messiah (John 1:21; 3:28), but he pointed to the promised Messiah as the "Lamb of God" (John 1:29; cf. Matt 11:10; Mark 1:2; Luke 1:15–17; 7:27), the one "who ranks before me" (John 1:30). Consequently, John says, "I myself did not know him [as the Messiah], but he [the Father] who sent me to baptize with water said to me, 'He on whom you see the Spirit descend and remain, this is he [the Messiah] who baptizes with the Holy Spirit.' And I have seen and have borne witness that this is the Son of God" (John 1:33–34).[21] Thus, the Father sent the prophets and spoke through them for the purpose of promising a Messiah, and pointing to his incarnate Son as the fulfillment of that promise.

Furthermore, Hebrews makes clear that the new covenant promised to Jeremiah was made by the Father.[22] Quoting Jeremiah 31:31–34 (cf. Heb 8:8–12), the author of Hebrews argues that Jesus is mediator of this new covenant (Heb 8:6), which is given by *Yahweh* (Heb 8:8), who in this context is the first person of the Trinity. In Hebrews 10:15–17, the author adds the agency of the Holy Spirit in the giving of Jeremiah's new-covenant promise: "And the Holy Spirit also bears witness to us; for after saying, 'This is the covenant that I will make with them after those days, declares the Lord' . . . then he [the Holy Spirit] adds, 'I will remember their sins and their lawless deeds no more.'" Finally, the author urges his audience to "hold fast the confession of our hope without wavering" (Heb 10:23), for he who promised is faithful; namely, the Father. It is why Paul Ellingworth writes,

> The basis for believers' endurance is the reliability of God's promise. Πιστός is used of Jesus in → 2:17; 3:2; cf. 3:5), but promising is for Hebrews a prerogative of God, either directly (6:13) or by implication through scripture (12:26). The closest parallel is → 11:11, of God's promise to Abraham (or Sarah); cf. 6:13. In the present verse, the content of the promise is not mentioned; the appeal is rather to God's nature as worthy of trust. As in → 6:8, no verb is expressed; the statement that God is faithful

---

20. The divine passive ἀπεσταλμένος is made explicit in the prepositional phrase "from God." Köstenberger and Swain conclude, "Hence, God is shown to take the initiative not only in creation but also in redemptive history." Köstenberger and Swain, *Father, Son, and Spirit*, 50.

21. When John the Baptist said, "I did not know him," (John 1:31, 33) he meant in Jesus's capacity as Messiah. See Morris, *John*, 132–34.

22. The new covenant will be examined in greater detail in chap. 6.

is axiomatic (e.g., Dt. 7:9; 32:4; Ps. 145:13 [LXX 144:13a]; 1 Cor. 1:9; 2 Cor. 1:18), and forms the basis and motive for the readers' faithfulness.[23]

Thus, the words of Scripture, though mediated through the Son and Spirit, are initiated by the Father.

The Father Sends His Son to be the Messiah

Because the gospel message is the testimony about God concerning his Son (1 Cor 2:1),[24] the good news is not only about promise but also about fulfillment. Paul writes to the Corinthians that the promises of the Father find their "Yes" in the Son (2 Cor 1:20). To the Romans, Paul explains that Christ became a servant to demonstrate the Father's truthfulness and "confirm the promises to the patriarchs" (Rom 15:8). Furthermore, it reveals the righteousness of the Father (Rom 1:17), because it explains how he could pass over the sins of the patriarchs and still be "just and the justifier of the one who has faith in Jesus" (Rom 3:26).

At exactly the right time in human history and according to his goodness and loving-kindness (Titus 3:4), the Father sends the Son (Gal 4:4), who is his image (2 Cor 4:4; Col 1:15),[25] who is in the form of the Father (Phil 2:6),[26] who is equal to the Father (Phil 2:6), and in whom all the fullness of the Father was pleased to dwell (Col 1:19).[27] The Father sends the Son to become a man (Rom 8:3) and to become the mediator between God and man (1 Tim 2:5). In John's Gospel, sixteen of the twenty-one chapters describe the Father's sending of the Son, and by implication, initiating, directing and guiding all the Son's activities and experiences.[28] Concerning the Synoptic Gospels, Simon Gathercole writes,

23. Ellingworth, *Hebrews*, 526.

24. There is both a textual issue (τὸ μυστήριον/μαρτύριον τοῦ θεοῦ) as well as decision to be made on the use of the genitive. I take the ESV reading "testimony" to be correct rather than "mystery." The genitive is an objective genitive "the testimony about God." See Fee, *First Corinthians*, 91.

25. The use of εἰκὼν means Christ is an exact, as well as visible, representation of God the Father. See Kittel, "εἰκὼν" in *TDNT*, 2.388–90, 395–96.

26. The use of μορφή means Christ possesses the very nature of God. See discussion in Hawthorne, *Philippians*, 81–84.

27. "The totality of divine essence and power is resident in Christ . . . and all of the attributes of God . . . are disclosed in him." Bruce, *Colossians, Philemon, and Ephesians*, 73–74.

28. Cf. John 3:34; 4:34; 5:23–24, 30, 36–38; 6:29, 38–39, 44, 57; 7:16, 28–29, 33; 8:16, 18, 26, 29, 42; 9:4; 10:36; 11:42; 12:44–45, 49; 13:20; 14:24; 15:21; 16:5; 17:3, 8, 18,

> Very common in the Synoptics is the implication of the Father's authority over the Son and the corresponding obedience of the Son to the Father. All things are given to the Son by his Father (Matt. 11.27 par. Luke 10:10; Matt. 28.18), and he continues to depend on the Father in prayer (e.g., Mark 1.35). Perhaps most clearly of all, the Son is frequently described as *sent* by the Father: once or twice in Mark, twice in Matthew, four times in Luke. Sending clearly presupposes an authority of the sender over the envoy.... As a result, it can be concluded that the order Father-Son-Spirit in Matt. 28.19 is not incidental; rather, it is born out of the early Christian thinking that the Father has authority over the Son, who in turn has authority over the Spirit.[29]

Millard Erickson disagrees, arguing from inseparable operations that the sending of the Son was "done by the Father but on behalf of the Trinity. In a very real sense, all of them sent the Son, and all had jointly decided that he would go."[30] Summarizing Augustine's *On the Trinity* saying,

1. The Son is from the Father, an apparent reference to the idea of eternal generation of the Son by the Father.
2. All works attributed to any one member of the Trinity are to be interpreted as actually being the work of all of them.
3. Statements about the Son's obedience or submission to the Father are to be understood as referring to the Son's incarnate state and are not to be read back into the eternity preceding his coming.
4. Consequently, while it is said that the Father sent the Son because they are referred to respectively as the Father and the Son, it can as well be said that the Son also sent himself.
5. There is therefore no evidence of an eternal functional subordination of the Son to the Father, whereby the Son must always do the Father's will.[31]

A major problem with this argument is that there is not one Scripture passage that teaches the Son sent himself or even that the Spirit sent the Son. The consistent testimony is that the Father sent the Son. Furthermore, Erickson's summary removes the nuance of distinct appropriations found

---

21, 23, 25; 20:21.

29. Gathercole, *Preexistent Son*, 72–73.
30. Erickson, *Who's Tampering with the Trinity*, 135.
31. Ibid., 158–59.

in the doctrine of inseparable operations.³² Conclusively, Stephen Wellum, in his review of Erickson's book, says, "I find no evidence of this [that the Son sent himself] in Augustine, let alone in Scripture."³³ Jesus, in John 8:42, argues the opposite, "I came not of my own accord [ἀπ' ἐμαυτοῦ], but he [the Father] sent me."

Finally, Michael Ovey notes the asymmetry about sending:

> The use of the individual personal names of "Father" and "Son" suggest that the sending cannot just be taken as "the triune God generically" sending the Son. Rather the sending is in the context of the personal relationship between the individual persons of Father and Son. Since that relationship of Father and Son is eternal, this sending is not reducible simply to the human nature. And sending has something irreducibly asymmetrical about it: someone sends, and someone else is sent.³⁴

In the remainder of this section, I will argue that the Father not only initiated the coming of Christ, but also sanctioned and validated his Son's ministry and message by the Spirit. Four periods in Jesus's life substantiate this assertion: (1) his incarnation, (2) his ministry, (3) his death, and (4) his resurrection and exaltation.

In the Incarnation

In the incarnation, the Father reveals himself through his unique son. Just as seen with all of the Father's other works, the Father's motive in sending the son is abounding love (John 3:16-17), and in the incarnation, the Father's love has gone public (1 John 4:9).³⁵ The Father desires to manifest his presence and glory through the Son, therefore John not only states a truth about the Father, "No one has ever seen God [the Father]" (John 1:18; cf. 1 John 4:12),³⁶ he also affirms a truth about the Son's incarnation, "The only God, who is at the Father's side, he has made [the Father] known."

---

32. See McCall "Relational Trinity," 121. Here McCall demonstrates that inseparable operations does not entail indistinguishable operations.

33. Wellum, "Irenic and Unpersuasive," 46.

34. Ovey, *Your Will Be Done*, 88.

35. Brown, *John*, 551.

36. John 1:18 (cf. 1 John 4:12), lends weight to the evidence that some of the Old Testament theophanies were "christophanies," particularly when the "angel of the Lord" is mentioned (Gen 16:7-14; 21:17-19; 22:11-18; 31:11-13; 32:24-30; 48:15-16; Exod 3:2-6; 14:19-22; Josh 5:13-16; Judg 2:1-5; 6:11-14; 13:2-23; Ezek 40:1-47:12; Zech 1:1—6:8).

Furthermore, by using the word "dwelt" (σκηνόω) for the incarnation, John is pointing back to the Old Testament tabernacle,[37] and is proclaiming that the manifest glory of *Yahweh* in the Old Testament tabernacle[38] is the same glory revealed in the incarnate Son. Additionally, John chooses to highlight two attributes of the Father's glory: "grace and truth" (John 1:14, 17). John's choice is not arbitrary. Rather, in them John specifically refers to the revelation given to Moses in Exodus 33–34. There, the Father's glory (Exod 33:18) is equivalent to his name (Exod 33:19), and the Father reveals his name to Moses as,

> The LORD, the LORD, a God merciful and gracious, slow to anger, and abounding in *steadfast love* and *faithfulness*, keeping steadfast love for thousands, forgiving iniquity and transgression and sin, but who will by no means clear the guilty, visiting the iniquity of the fathers on the children and the children's children, to the third and the fourth generation [emphasis mine]. (Exod 34:6–7)

When the Father tells Moses he abounds in steadfast love (*hesed*) and faithfulness (*emeth*), John translates it "grace and truth" (χάριτος καὶ ἀληθείας).[39] Therefore, Jesus can proclaim, "I have come in my Father's *name*," (John 5:43) and the crowd on Palm Sunday can rightly declare, "Blessed is he who comes in the *name* of the Lord" (John 12:13). Jesus is the one on whom the Father has set his seal (John 6:27),[40] and as such, is the "Holy One" (Mark 1:24; Luke 4:34; John 6:69; cf. Luke 2:22–23) that God the Father has set apart to be the "Christ, the Son of God, who is coming into the world" (John 11:27).

According to Philippians 2:6, the Son did not consider equality with God the Father a thing to be grasped,[41] therefore, he became incarnate. The author of Hebrews quotes Psalm 40:6–8 to make the same point:

---

37. Morris, *John*, 91.

38. In John 2:16–17, Jesus makes reference to the temple as the Father's house, the dwelling place for his manifest glory.

39. Brown, *Epistles of John*, 416–19.

40. Of this passage, Carson says, "The idea is that God has certified the Son as his own agent, authorizing him as the one who alone can bestow this food. God has attested the Son, in much the same way that someone who accepts the Son's testimony thereby attests or certifies (the same verb) that God himself is truthful. *When* God 'placed his seal of approval' on the Son is not specified. If we are to think of a specific time (though the aorist tense of the verb does not require that we so limit ourselves), perhaps the reference is to Jesus' baptism (cf. 1:31–34)." Carson, *John*, 284.

41. Regarding ἁρπαγμός, the meaning can be in an active sense to denote "the act of snatching or seizing," or in a passive sense to signify "that which is seized." Both

Consequently, when Christ came into the world, he said, "Sacrifices and offerings you have not desired, but a body have you prepared for me; in burnt offerings and sin offerings you have taken no pleasure. Then I said, 'Behold, I have come to do your will, O God, as it is written of me in the scroll of the book.'" (Heb 10:5–7; cf. 10:8–9)

Thus, the Son freely became incarnate as an act of obedience to the Father.

The Spirit was also involved as the Father's agent in the incarnation. The angel explains to Mary, "The Holy Spirit will come upon you, and the power of the Most High [the Father] will overshadow you; therefore the child to be born will be called holy—the Son of God" (Luke 1:35). That the Father, not the Holy Spirit, is the initiator of the incarnation is clear by the angel's concluding statement, "For nothing will be impossible with God [the Father]" (Luke 1:37).

The Father, thus, sends the eternal Son to become the incarnate Son in order to reveal a true knowledge of himself and thereby give eternal life to his adopted sons.[42] Jesus says in John 7:28 (cf. John 8:26–27), that he knows the Father because he comes from him and was sent by him. Jesus, as the true bread of God the Father "comes down from heaven and gives life to the world" (John 6:32–33), he is the one who has the words of eternal life (John 6:69), and he is the one who declares, "this is eternal life, that they know you the only true God, and Jesus Christ whom you have sent" (John 17:3; cf. 1 John 5:20). It is also why John writes, concerning Jesus, the following words at the beginning of his first epistle,

> That which was from the beginning, which we have heard, which we have seen with our eyes, which we looked upon and have touched with our hands, concerning the word of life—the life was made manifest, and we have seen it, and testify to it and

---

translations, active and passive, are plausible from the word itself. However, in the broader context of v. 6, the concessive use of ὑπάρχω strongly argues for a passive translation of ἁρπαγμός. Furthermore, in the context of v. 7, the tension needs to be maintained between the contrasting ἀλλά. Finally, the context leans toward the fact that it was not his deity, but rather his obedience that compelled his incarnation and passion. Therefore, the best translation of ἁρπαγμός is passively, "a thing to be grasped." For a strong argument that "equality with God" is distinct from Christ's existing in the "form of God," see Burk, "Christ's Functional Subordination" 82–107.

42. During the life of Christ, this claim did not go unopposed. The Pharisees said, "This man is not from God" (John 9:16) and "we do not know where he comes from" (John 9:29). In doing so, they revealed they did not know the Father (John 17:25).

proclaim to you the eternal life, which was with the Father and was made manifest [by the Father] to us (1 John 1:1–2).[43]

In the Life and Ministry of Jesus

In the life and ministry of Jesus, the Father pours out his Spirit on the Son, so that the Son can perform the Father's works and speak the Father's words. Nevertheless, the Father's authority over the Son in no way demands that the Son be inferior. In John 5:18, even Jesus's opponents understood that in calling God his Father, Jesus was "making himself equal with God [the Father]." Further, John's reflective statements of John 3:31–35 are instructive: "He [Jesus] who comes from above is above all. . . . He [Jesus] who comes from heaven is above all" (v. 31). Clearly, the Son is above all in that he descended from heaven (John 3:13), and thus has authority to speak about the things he has seen and heard in the heavenly sphere.[44] Nevertheless, the Father has authority in that he sent the Son and in his love, "has given all things into his hand" (John 3:35; cf. John 13:3).[45] Included in the gift of "all things" is the empowering of the Spirit in the life and ministry of Jesus (Matt 3:16–17; 12:18; Luke 3:22; 4:18–19; Acts 10:38). John teaches that the Father gave to the Son the "Spirit without measure" (John 3:34),[46] and so too, the Father is always with him (John 8:29; 16:32). Therefore, the Son is always portrayed as equal to the Father but also dependent upon him and obedient to him.[47]

Curiously, Marianne Meye Thompson argues that since there is an absence of the word "obey" in the Gospel of John, the emphasis is not on submission. Instead she argues from John 10:18 that the Son's obedience is "an *enactment* or *expression* of the Father's will, rather than as submission

---

43. φανερόω is in the passive voice, indicating it is the Father who made the Son manifest, not the Son who made himself appear. In cf. 1 John 4:9–10, 14; 5:11 the Father's implicit role in 1 John 1:2 is made explicit.

44. Carson, *John*, 213.

45. Fisher brings out an implication in this passage "This exaltation of the Son in the area of his authority has been delegated to him by the Father. Thus, it is assumed that 'above all' (2x) refers to everything and everyone except the Father." Fisher, "God the Father," 150.

46. Grammatically, the one who gives the Spirit could be understood as the Son; however, v. 35 makes it clear that the Father, who gives all things to the Son, is the one who gives the Spirit. See Carson, *John*, 212.

47. For an excellent study on the authority of the Father seen in his sending of the Son, see Cowan, "Father and Son," 47–64.

or acquiescence to it [emphasis original]."⁴⁸ Therefore, in Thompson's thinking, the Son is not under the authority of the Father, for "the notion of hierarchy or 'superiority' is subsumed into the Father's life-giving, not 'command-giving,' persona."⁴⁹ Christopher Cowan's response to Thompson is worth quoting at length:

> Several responses are necessary. First, granting the absence of the actual words "obey," "obedience," and "obedient" (ὑπακούω, ὑπακοή, and ὑπήκοος) in John's Gospel, it is hard to see the relevance of this in light of the clear evidence for the presence of the *concept*. Both Meyer and Thompson acknowledge that John speaks of Jesus's "doing the will" (ποιεῖν τὸ θέλημα) of the one who sent him (4:34; 6:38). Yet the same phrase is used with respect to others "doing God's will" (7:17; 9:31; cf. 1 John 2:17) and is clearly intended to refer to their *obedience* to God. ... Thus, arguments that point to the lack of these words in the Gospel to describe Jesus's actions hardly seem persuasive when one realizes that they are not even a part of John's vocabulary. To "do God's will" and "keep God's word/commandments" are simply the Johannine formulas for expressing obedience to God [emphasis original].⁵⁰

The Son's unity with and dependence upon the Father and his empowering Spirit causes the Son to assert, "the Son can do nothing of his own accord, but only what he sees the Father doing. For whatever the Father does, that the Son does likewise" (John 5:19).⁵¹ In the next verse, the Father's love for the Son explains why the Son can do everything the Father does. Additionally, the Father's love is presented in a continual display to the Son of all his works (John 5:20). The Son's life and ministry was therefore, a demonstration of the Father's works (John 10:32–33), and characterized as something he "must" do (John 9:4).⁵² The Father gave the Son authority to

48. Thompson, *Promise of the Father*, 150.
49. Ibid.
50. Cowan, "Father and Son," 56–57.
51. Commenting on this verse, Köstenberger and Swain write, "The Father enjoys *personal* priority in the *taxis* (order) of the triune life, not ontological superiority, for the Father and the Son hold all things in common: one divine name (17:11), one divine power (5:19, 21–22), one divine identity (10:30)." Köstenberger and Swain, *Father, Son, and Spirit*, 123.
52. In John's Gospel, the works of the Father through the Son circle around seven specific signs. They are: (1) water changed to wine (John 2:1–11), (2) healing of the nobleman's son (John 4:46–54), (3) the healing of the man at the pool (John 5:1–18), (4) the feeding of the five thousand (John 6:1–14), (5) walking on the water (John 6:16–21), (6) healing of the blind man (John 9:1–41), and (7) raising of Lazarus (John 11:1–44).

perform miracles (Matt 9:8; Mark 5:19 where credit is given to the Lord; Luke 5:17; Acts 2:22) and forgive sin (Mark 2:7, 10; Luke 5:21, 24). Thus, the Son laid aside his own will to do the will of the Father (John 6:38), to accomplish his work (John 4:34; cf. Heb 3:1–6), and to "always do the things that are pleasing to him" (John 8:29). In short, Jesus said, "but I do as the Father has commanded me, so that the world may know that I love the Father" (John 14:31; cf. John 15:10).

Just as the Son came to perform the Father's works, he also came to speak the Father's words. Prior to the start of his public ministry, Jesus battled the temptations of Satan with the Spirit-inspired words of God the Father (Matt 4:3–10; Luke 4:3–12). At his baptism and transfiguration, the Father told the witnesses, "You are/This is my beloved Son, with you/whom I am well-pleased" (Mark 1:11; 9:7; cf. Matt 3:17; 17:5; Luke 9:35; 2 Pet 1:17–18), so to hear the Father we must "listen to him" (Matt 17:5; Mark 9:7; Luke 9:35; cf. Deut 18:15). Jesus preaches the Father's Gospel (Mark 1:14–15; Luke 4:43) and sent his own disciples to do so as well (Luke 9:2, 60; John 20:21). If someone rejects the words of Jesus, they are ultimately rejecting the words of the Father who sent him, "The one who hears you hears me, and the one who rejects you rejects me, and the one who rejects me rejects him who sent me" (Luke 10:16). The same teaching appears in several forms throughout the Gospels (Matt 10:40; 18:5; Mark 9:37; Luke 9:48; John 5:23; 12:44–45; 13:20). Thus, even Jesus's teaching was initiated by the Father (John 7:16), for he speaks what he has seen in the Father's presence (John 8:38), he speaks what the Father has commanded (John 12:49), and those who are "friends" of Jesus are informed of all the Father says (John 15:15; 17:14).[53] Further, the Father's words of are absolute truth (John 8:40; cf. Matt 22:16; Mark 12:14) and they are "eternal life" (John 12:50). The

---

Regarding these signs, Nicodemus tells Jesus, "Rabbi, we know that you are a teacher come from God, for no one can do these signs that you do unless God is with him" (John 3:2). Morris affirms that the signs not only point to the Father, but originate with him as well. "Perhaps it would be true to say that where John sees miracles from one point of view as σημεῖα, activities pointing people to God, from another he sees them as ἔργα, activities that take their origin in God. Morris, *John*, 612. These signs were worked out in the sovereign, providential timing of the Father (John 9:3), and in response to Jesus' prayer (John 11:21–22, 41–42). Therefore, the works testify that the Father has sent the Son (John 5:36–38; 10:25) and that the Father and Son are one (John 10:37–38).

53. "The Paraclete whom Jesus sends will in the wake of the cross and resurrection complete the revelation bound up with the person and work of Christ (14:26; 16:12–15), thereby making Jesus' disciples more informed, more privileged, more comprehending than any believers who ever came before (cf. 1 Pet. 1:10–12)" Carson, *John*, 523. It is staggering to think that just as the Father loved the Son, the Son has loved his people (John 15:9).

Father authenticates the words of Jesus through the empowering ministry of the Holy Spirit (John 3:34), and so, to hear the Son is to hear the Father.

Two interconnected aspects of Jesus's teaching touch on the Father's initiating authority: (1) the kingdom of God, and (2) the use of parables. To begin with, Jesus prayed that the Father's kingdom would come (Matt 6:9–10),[54] which has "drawn near," is "at hand," and has "come upon" the world in the life and ministry of Jesus (Matt 3:2; 4:17; 10:7; 12:28; Luke 10:9, 11, 20).[55] To the followers of Jesus, the Father gives the "secret of the kingdom," but for those outside of Christ, "everything is in parables" (Matt 13:11; Mark 4:11; Luke 8:10).[56] It is why Jesus thanks the Father, "I thank you, Father, Lord of heaven and earth, that you have hidden these things from the wise and understanding and revealed them to little children; yes, Father, for such was your gracious will" (Matt 11:25–26; Luke 10:21). In that context, Jesus understands that his authority to "choose to reveal" the knowledge of the Father is only because "all things have been handed over" to him by the Father (Matt 11:27; Luke 10:22).

In all that the Son accomplished and taught he sought to glorify God the Father (John 17:4). Throughout the Gospels, as people see the ministry of Jesus, they respond in praise to the Father (Matt 9:8; 15:31; Mark 2:11–12; Luke 5:24–26; 7:15–16; 9:42–43; 13:12–13; 17:14–16; 18:42–43; 19:37; 23:47). Significantly, in Luke's Gospel the pattern is: people see the works of Christ, and glorify the Father; that is, until the Son's exaltation (Luke 24:51). Then, Christ's disciples "worship him" (Luke 24:52). Nevertheless, Luke is sure to mention in the next verse, "and [his disciples] were continually in the temple blessing God [the Father]" (Luke 24:53). Jesus rebukes his enemies for not understanding the purpose of the incarnation: The Son doing the works of the Father, giving life and exercising judgment so that "all may honor the Son, just as they honor the Father. Whoever does not honor the Son does not honor the Father who sent him" (John 5:23). Therefore, in Jesus's glorification of the Father, the Father glorified the Son (John 8:49–50, 54–55). A good example of this is seen in the resurrection of Lazarus. When Jesus first heard of Lazarus' death, he said, "This illness does not lead to death. It is for the glory of God, so that the Son of God may be glorified through it" (John 11:4). After Lazarus was raised, Jesus said to Martha, "Did I not tell you that if you believed you would see the glory of

---

54. The genitive phrase βασιλεία τοῦ θεοῦ is a possessive genitive. The kingdom which belongs to God the Father.

55. For the already/not yet aspect of the "kingdom of God," see Ladd, *Gospel of the Kingdom*.

56. In these passages δέδοται is a divine passage, with God the Father as the implied actor.

God?" Furthermore, the mutual glorification of Father and Son culminates in the work of the cross: "Father, the hour has come; glorify your Son that the Son may glorify you" (John 17:1).

In the Crucifixion

In the crucifixion of Jesus, the Father gives the Son to be the Savior of the world by making him to be a substitutionary, propitiatory sacrifice for his elect. John gives a summary statement of his own eyewitness testimony: "we have seen and testify that the Father has sent his Son to be the Savior of the world" (1 John 4:14). The Father sent him into the world, and brought him to the hour of his betrayal and death (John 12:27–28), in order to glorify him. Jesus said, "Now is the Son of Man glorified, and God is glorified in him. If God is glorified in him, God will also glorify him in himself, and glorify him at once" (John 13:31–32). The author of Hebrews testifies to this as well, "But we see him who for a little while was made lower than the angels, namely Jesus, crowned with glory and honor because of the suffering of death, so that by the grace of God he might taste death for everyone" (Heb 2:9). The Father is the one who crowned him with glory and honor.[57]

Therefore, in sending the Son, the Father fulfills his "plan and foreknowledge" (Acts 2:23; cf. Acts 4:28) delivering him up to death to be a sin offering (2 Cor 5:21; Rom 8:3, 32). Furthermore, the Son offered himself up (John 10:17–18) through the anointing ministry of the Holy Spirit (Heb 9:14),[58] which he received from the Father. As a result of the cross, the Father condemned sin (Rom 8:3), and as the "Lamb of God,"[59] (John 1:29, 36) he is the gift provided by the Father in order to "take away the sin of the world" (John 1:29).[60] This the Father does by putting his Son forward as a

---

57. The author of Hebrews has changed the two aorist verbs in the psalm quotation (in Heb. 2:7), ἠλάττωσας and ἐστεφάνωσας to perfect passive participles in v. 9: ἠλαττωμένον and ἐστεφανωμένον. The passive voice indicates that God the Father is the initiator of these actions (as the Old Testament citation of Psalm 8:5 explicitly says. See O'Brien, *Hebrews*, 98–99.

58. See Ellingworth, *Hebrews*, 456–58.

59. Substitutionary atonement is often criticized in Johannine studies; nevertheless, it is the teaching of Scripture. For a defense of substitutionary atonement in the Gospel of John, see Gieschen, "The Death of Jesus," 243–61, and Carey, "Lamb of God and Atonement Theories," 97–122. For a more general defense, see Jeffery, Ovey, and Sach, *Pierced for Our Transgressions*.

60. Burge, *John*, 74.

means of propitiation (Rom 3:25; 1 John 4:10; cf. 1 John 2:2).[61] Thus, as the Son is "lifted up" (John 8:28), he fully satisfied the Father's righteous requirement through drinking the "cup that the Father has given [him]" (John 18:11),[62] and entrusting himself to the Father's loving care as he breathes his last words, "Father, into your hands I commit my spirit" (Luke 23:46).

The cross is a demonstration of the Father's love, not only for his Son, but also for sinners (Rom 5:8). In Christ, the Father made a way for reconciliation (2 Cor 5:19; Rom 5:10; Eph 2:16; Col 1:20, 22),[63] so that he might bring sinners to himself (1 Pet 3:18; Rom 5:2; Eph 2:18; 3:12). In Christ, the Father is able to declare a sinner righteous (Rom 3:24; 5:9).[64] In Christ, the Father makes peace (Col 1:20), and in Christ, the Father forgives (Col 2:13-14). Jesus appeared to "destroy the works of the devil" (1 John 3:8), putting an end to the works that are hostile to God the Father, and is therefore able to give "eternal life to all whom [the Father] has given him" (John 17:2).[65] Thus, by his blood, Jesus "ransomed people for God [the Father] from every tribe and language and people and nation" (Rev 5:9), giving them a new status as the Father's possession.[66] It is worth repeating that the

---

61. ἱλαστήριον means the satisfaction of the righteous wrath of the Father toward sin. The Father himself here takes the initiative to send the Son to be the means of satisfaction. See Schreiner, *Romans*, 191-92. For a thorough lexical treatment of ἱλασμός, see Morris, *Apostolic Preaching of the Cross*, 155-74.

62. The Old Testament allusions associate the cup with suffering and with the wrath of God the Father (Ps 75:8; Isa 51:17; Jer 25:15; Ezek 23:31-33). The book of Revelation has similar connections (Rev 14:10; 16:19), which fit well with the doctrine of propitiation. Moreover, it is important to see that it is the Father's loving plan that sends the Son to be the propitiation for sin, and therefore, the Father's wrath must be carefully nuanced with his love.

63. In Romans 5, reconciliation is "the supreme manifestation of the love of God toward men." See Murray, *Redemption, Accomplished and Applied*, 38.

64. δικαιόω means to pronounce, accept and treat as righteous. It is a forensic declaration, not a creative act, and it is a full and free justification based on Christ's blood and imputed righteousness alone. See Owen, *Doctrine of Justification* in vol. 5 of Owen, *Works*.

65. In this passage, life is only given to the Father's elect. Köstenberger notes, "This indicates again the subordination of the Son to the Father (see 14:28), a voluntary submission that pertains not just during Jesus' earthly ministry, but eternally (so 1 Cor 15:28; cf. 11:3).... John juxtaposes, without embarrassment, God's sovereign election of certain ones to eternal life, his universal love for the world and his condemnation of those who reject his mercy (Carson 1991: 555)." Köstenberger, *John*, 487. Closely connected to the Father's universal love and particular election is the Son's universal love and particular redemption. Jesus says in John 10:14-15, "I am the good shepherd. I know my own and my own know me, just as the Father knows me and I know the Father; and I lay down my life for the sheep."

66. Osborne, *Revelation*, 260.

Father's authority over the Son in the incarnation and crucifixion in no way diminishes the majesty or glory of Christ. Richard Bauckham's comments on Philippians 2:6–11 are helpful:

> But, since the exalted Christ is first the humiliated Christ, since indeed it is because of his self-abnegation that he is exalted, his humiliation belongs to the identity of God as truly as his exaltation does. The identity of God—who God is—is revealed as much in self-abasement and service as it is in exaltation and rule. The God who is high can also be low, because God is God not in seeking his own advantage but in self-giving.[67]

It is why all "blessing and honor and glory and might" are forever due the one "who sits on the throne" and "the Lamb" (Rev 5:13).

In the Resurrection and Exaltation

In the resurrection and exaltation, the Father raised up the Son from the dead, exalting the Son to his throne and granting the Son the authority to rule over all nations, appointing him as the eternal high priest at his right hand. The Father accepts his Son's sacrifice, demonstrating his approval by raising Christ from the dead (Acts 2:24, 32; 3:15; 4:10; 5:30; 10:40; 13:30, 33–35; 17:31; Gal 1:1; 1 Thess 1:10; 1 Cor 15:15; 2 Cor 4:14; 13:4; Rom 6:4; 10:9; Col 2:12; Heb 5:7; 13:20; 1 Pet 1:21). Peter writes that the Father not only raised him from the dead but also "gave him glory" (1 Pet 1:21). Therefore, as a part of the resurrection, the Father publicly revealed Christ to be his Son (Rom 1:4),[68] and Jesus, as the Christ, lives by the power of the Father (2 Cor 13:4), and lives to honor and glorify him (Rom 6:10).[69]

In the Johannine literature, although both the Father and the Son accomplish the resurrection of Christ,[70] emphasis is on the Son's authority to raise himself from the dead. For example, speaking of his body, Jesus says in John 2:19, "Destroy this temple, and in three days *I* will raise it up." In the same passage, the Father is identified as the one who accomplishes the resurrection through the use of the divine passive ἠγέρθη (v. 22).[71] Likewise, the strongest statement from Jesus is found in John 10:17–18, "For this reason

---

67. Bauckham, *Jesus and the God of Israel*, 45.

68. ὁρίζω can mean "appointed," but better to mean "marked out" or "designated." I have translated it above as publicly revealed. See Morris, *Romans*, 44.

69. See Moo, *Romans*, 379.

70. For the Spirit's work in the resurrection of Jesus, see Rom 1:4 and 8:11.

71. Lenski, *John*, 220–21.

the Father loves me, because I lay down my life that I may take it up again. No one takes it from me, but I lay it down of my own accord. I have authority to lay it down, and I have authority to take it up again." Yet, the Son's authority is not absolute in the resurrection, it is granted. Jesus concludes in v. 18, "This charge I have *received* from my Father [emphasis mine]." Thus, the Father has granted to the Son the authority to be "the resurrection and the life" for himself and for all who will believe in him (John 11:25).

After the resurrection, Jesus returned to the Father in heaven (John 7:33; 13:3; 16:5, 17, 28; 17:11, 13; 20:17), and was exalted as king and lord at the right hand of the Father (Matt 22:44; Mark 12:36; Luke 20:42-43; 22:69; Acts 2:33-36; 5:31; 7:55-56; Rom 8:34; Col 3:1; Heb 1:3, 13; 8:1-2; 10:12; 12:2; 1 Pet 3:22). In doing so the Father placed everything under the Son's feet (Eph 1:22), disarming demonic forces by triumphing over them in Christ (Eph 3:10; Col 2:15),[72] and giving his Son the name above all names (Phil 2:9). The Father's works in Christ are in keeping with his purpose to sum up all things in his Son (Eph 1:10) because his eternal purposes are accomplished in the Lord Jesus (Eph 3:11).[73] All of this discloses the Father's mighty work in redemption. The message of the cross (1 Cor 1:18) revealed in the gospel is the power of God for salvation (Rom 1:16); for Christ is the "power of God and the wisdom of God" (1 Cor 1:24, 30), and the Father gives the growth of the gospel (1 Cor 3:6-7). Thus, as the "King of Israel" (John 1:49) and the Anointed One on whom the angels of God ascend and descend (John 1:51),[74] the Father is the one who has given the Son authority to forever rule over the "kingdom of God" (Matt 28:18; John 3:3, 5), which is why Jesus can call it "my kingdom" (John 18:36).[75]

Nowhere in John's literature is this more clearly seen than the throne room visions of Revelation. The one "who is to rule all the nations with a rod of iron," and who is "caught up to God [the Father] and his throne" (Rev 12:5), this one is "Jesus Christ the faithful witness, the firstborn of the dead, and the ruler of kings on earth" (Rev 1:5).[76] Jesus, thus, can claim the

---

72. Though the terms can be used for earthly rulers, Paul's usage of the words as well as the contextual emphasis on Christ's authority over them as a result of his exaltation argues for them to be evil demonic powers. See Arnold, *Ephesians*, 112-13.

73. With the emphasis in this context on fulfillment the use of ποιέω argues for the Father "bringing his plan to realization in Christ." See O'Brien, *Ephesians*, 248.

74. For the connection of Jacob's ladder with this statement of Christ, see Carson, *John*, 163-64. Carson concludes, "What the disciples are promised, then, is heaven-sent confirmation that the one they have acknowledged as the Messiah has been appointed by God."

75. John, though aware of the kingdom terminology used by the Synoptic authors, seems to favor eternal life terminology. See Borchert, *John 1-11*, 172.

76. Since Jesus here is displayed as the promised Davidic King, he has the authority

titles, "King of kings, and Lord of lords" (Rev 19:16), and "the Alpha and the Omega, the first and the last, the beginning and the end" (Rev 22:13).

In Revelation 1, John describes the exalted Christ,

> In the midst of the lampstands [I saw] one like a son of man, clothed with a long robe and with a golden sash around his chest. The hairs of his head were white, like white wool, like snow. His eyes were like a flame of fire, his feet were like burnished bronze, refined in a furnace, and his voice was like the roar of many waters. In his right hand he held seven stars, from his mouth came a sharp two-edged sword, and his face was like the sun shining in full strength. When I saw him, I fell at his feet as though dead. But he laid his right hand on me, saying, "Fear not, I am the first and the last, and the living one. I died, and behold I am alive forevermore, and I have the keys of Death and Hades." (Rev 1:13–18)

John sees the fulfillment of Jesus prayer in John 17:5, "Father, glorify me in your own presence with the glory that I had with you before the world existed." It is no wonder then that John fell at his feet like a dead man. His glory as the exalted God-man is like the Father's glory, which John sees in chapter 4:

> At once I was in the Spirit, and behold, a throne stood in heaven, with one seated on the throne. And he who sat there had the appearance of jasper and carnelian, and around the throne was a rainbow that had the appearance of an emerald. Around the throne were twenty-four thrones, and seated on the thrones were twenty-four elders, clothed in white garments, with golden crowns on their heads. From the throne came flashes of lightning, and rumblings and peals of thunder, and before the throne were burning seven torches of fire, which are the seven spirits of God. (Rev 4:2–5)

Even though John is surprised that there is no one worthy to open the scroll in the Father's "right hand" (Rev 5:1),[77] it should be no surprise to the reader that the one worthy is the "Lion of the tribe of Judah, the Root of

---

to grant kingship to the Father's children (Rev 1:6).

77. Beale gives weight to John's fears: "In John's moment of despair, this meant for him that history would not be governed to the benefit of God's people, there would be no protection for God's children in the hours of bitter trial; no judgments upon a persecuting world; no ultimate triumph for believers; no new heaven and earth; no future inheritance!" Beale, *Revelation*, 348–49.

David" (Rev 5:5), the one who has conquered death and now has rights over the earth and all of redemptive history.[78]

The further description of the Son as "a Lamb standing, as though it had been slain, with seven horns and with seven eyes, which are the seven spirits of God sent out into all the earth" (Rev 4:6), ties the Father and Son to the ministry of the Spirit. Just as the Father has authority over the "seven spirits," so too the risen and exalted Christ, as a man, has authority to send the "seven spirits of God [the Father]" out into all the earth.[79] It is why Jesus, after appearing to his disciples, tells them he will send "the promise of my Father upon you" (Luke 24:49; Acts 1:4; cf. Acts 2:33). As we will see in the next chapter, the Father, through the Son, pours out his promised Spirit to usher in the new covenant. Thus, the Father desires to placard his Son before the world as a demonstration of his lavish love and faithfulness to his promises. It is no surprise that in the throne room of heaven the continuous response of the heavenly court is unceasing worship of the Father and the Son:

> And I heard every creature in heaven and on earth and under the earth and in the sea, and all that is in them, saying, "To him who sits on the throne and to the Lamb be blessing and honor and glory and might forever and ever!" And the four living creatures said, "Amen!" and the elders fell down and worshiped. (Rev 5:13–14)

Finally, the book of Hebrews speaks at length about the Son's high priestly ministry, which flows from his exaltation to the right hand of the Father. In chapter 1, as part of Christ's exaltation, the Son is promised an eternal throne (Heb 1:8) and an anointing with immeasurable gladness (Heb 1:9). As he appears before the Father's throne in chapter 2, he sings out in praise to the Father (Heb 2:12) and presents the "children God has given [him]" back to the Father (Heb 2:13). According to the author, it was only possible to become a "merciful and faithful high priest" because he became incarnate, "like his brothers in every respect" (Heb 2:17). After his resurrection, the author reminds his audience that "Jesus, the Son of God"

---

78. I take the scroll to be the title deed of the earth and the Father's redemptive plan of events that are to reveal his remaining mystery, so that everything promised to Adam in the garden and lost in the fall is restored through the last Adam, the Lord Jesus Christ, in the new heavens and new earth. See Osborne, *Revelation*, 247–50.

79. In Revelation this is also clear from the letters to the seven churches. The Son's message is sent to the churches by the Spirit: "let him hear what the Spirit says to the churches" (Rev 2:7, 11, 17, 29; 3:6, 13, 22). Jesus is the one who "has [possesses] the seven spirit of God and the seven stars" (Rev 3:1), and thus has authority over the Spirit to send him.

is the "great high priest who has passed through the heavens" (Heb 4:14). Most important for our discussion, the author writes, "Christ did not exalt himself to be made a high priest, but was appointed by [the Father]" (Heb 5:5), and he was "designated by God [the Father] a high priest after the order of Melchizedek" (Heb 5:10). In chapter 7, the author of Hebrews concludes: "Consequently, he is able to save to the uttermost those who draw near to God through him, since he always lives to make intercession for them." (Heb 7:25).

Thus, the Father's initiating role extends past the incarnation and humiliation on earth, into the exaltation and session of the Son, and as we shall see in chapter 7, into eternity future.

Conclusion

In this chapter, I have argued that all the Father's works in redemptive history display his initiatory role within the Trinity, which is also consistent with the eternal *taxis* discussed in chapters 2. The text never teaches that the Son and Spirit give Scripture through the agency of the Father, nor do they send the Father. Rather, the Father is the one who is consistently said to send the Son, and the Son asks the Father to send the Spirit (which we will examine in greater detail in the next chapter). Thus, the Father's work as the planner and purposor remains consistent from eternity past into redemptive history through the sending of the Son and the pouring out of the Spirit, a subject to which we now turn.

6

The Father's Work of Producing Salvation in His Elect and Conviction in the World through the Pouring Out of the Holy Spirit

Introduction

THE FATHER CONTINUES HIS work of salvation by seeking worshipers and drawing his elect into his own kingdom through the proclamation of the gospel and the pouring out of the Holy Spirit (John 6:44; 2 Thess 2:14; Acts 10:44). Through the Spirit (2 Cor 1:22), the Father unites believers to his Son (1 Cor 1:30; 2 Cor 1:21; Col 1:27), giving them a new identity (John 1:12; Rom 5:1), a new nature (John 1:13; 1 Pet 1:3), a new community (Eph 2:19), and a new relationship with him (Gal 4:9; 1 John 4:7; 5:20). In doing so, the Father will sanctify his children completely through his word and his Spirit (John 17:17; 2 Cor 3:18), filling them with all his fullness (Eph 3:19) and conforming them into the image of his Son (Rom 8:29). Furthermore, the Father will keep and seal them (Eph 1:13; Jude 24), and no one will ever snatch them out of his hand (John 10:29). On the other hand, those who refuse to believe the Spirit of truth's (John 14:17) witness to the gospel of Christ (John 15:26) demonstrate they do not love the Father (John 15:23–24). Consequently, they are under his wrath (John 3:36; Rom 1:18) and will never know him (Titus 1:16; 1 John 4:8) or possess eternal life (Matt 25:46; John 17:3).

In this chapter, I will argue that all of the works of the Father through the agency of his Spirit display a fixed *taxis* within the Trinity. The Father remains the initiator, for the Son asks the Father to pour out the gift and promise of the Holy Spirit. As John writes,

- And I will ask the Father, and he will give you another Helper, to be with you forever. (John 14:16)

- But the Helper, the Holy Spirit, whom the Father will send in my name, he will teach you all things and bring to your remembrance all that I have said to you. (John 14:26)
- But when the Helper comes, whom I will send to you from the Father, the Spirit of truth, who proceeds from the Father, he will bear witness about me. (John 15:26)

Commenting on these three verses, Christopher Cowan remarks,

> Jesus tells his disciples that he will ask the Father to send the Holy Spirit to be with them (John 14:16, 26). But, the giving of the Holy Spirit occurs after Jesus's resurrection. This promise to ask the Father seems to imply a continued dependence on him after his resurrection (and, most likely, after his ascension; cf. Acts 2:1–4). While Father and Son are equally senders of the Spirit (John 14:26; 15:26), according to John, the Spirit's coming involves Jesus's making a request of his Father.[1]

The Father Seeks Worshippers and, through the Spirit, Draws Them to Himself

As we saw in chapter 3, the Father's calling is rooted in his eternal plan. To the Romans, Paul writes, "those whom [the Father] predestined he also *called*, and those whom he called he also justified, and those whom he justified he also glorified" (Rom 8:30). Furthermore, the Father's calling is based on his sovereign grace (Acts 2:39; Gal 1:6, 15; 2:21; Eph 2:8)[2] and the exercise of his will (Matt 11:25–26; Luke 10:21).[3] Using Moses's conversation with the Father as an example (cf. Exod 33:19), Paul speaks the Father's words, "I will have mercy on whom I have mercy, and I will have compassion on whom I have compassion" (Rom 9:15).[4] Thus, the Father has the authority to show mercy to whomever he wills and to harden whomever he wills (Rom 9:18).[5]

---

1. Cowan, "Father and Son," 63.

2. The verb καλέω is part of Paul's vocabulary for emphasizing the Father's divine initiative in salvation. See Bruce, *Galatians*, 80.

3. By using εὐδοκία here, Jesus is combining the ideas of both decision and approval of his will. It is what brings the Father good pleasure and satisfaction. See Nolland, *Matthew*, 471.

4. Except for Rom 9:5 (where θεὸς is used for the Son), every other use in the chapter is a reference to the Father.

5. Nevertheless, humans are still morally responsible for their actions. As Douglas Moo brings out: "It is imperative that we maintain side-by-side the complementary

The Father, then, calls believers (Gal 5:8) into his own kingdom and glory (1 Thess 2:12) and into the fellowship of his Son (1 Cor 1:9) through the gospel (2 Thess 2:14). The Father loves his children (Jude 1) and calls them for his own purposes (Rom 8:28), including holiness (1 Thess 4:7; Rom 1:7; 1 Pet 1:15) and peace (1 Cor 7:15). Therefore, Paul's desire for the Thessalonian church was that, "God [the Father] may make [them] worthy of his *calling* and may fulfill every resolve for good and every work of faith by his power [emphasis mine]" (2 Thess 1:11). In this way, the Father is keeping those whom he calls safe and unharmed until the day of redemption for his Son, Jesus Christ (Jude 1).[6] What is impossible for man is possible for God the Father (Matt 19:26; Mark 10:27; Luke 18:27).

Furthermore, the Father accomplishes all of this through the agency of his Holy Spirit. For example, while speaking to the woman at the well, Jesus mentions the Father's design for the incarnation and subsequent sending of the Spirit: "But the hour is coming, and is now here, when the true worshipers will worship the Father in spirit and truth, for the Father is seeking such people to worship him" (John 4:23). In the same passage, Jesus tells her that if she knew the gift of God (the Holy Spirit) and who was speaking to her (the Messiah), she would have asked him to give her the living water of the Holy Spirit (John 4:10).[7]

Later, in the upper room discourse with his disciples, Jesus reveals a number of truths regarding the Father's sending of the Spirit: (1) the Father gives the Helper (the Spirit) in response to the Son's request (John 14:16), (2) the Spirit's indwelling ministry gives knowledge of Jesus's identity and the Christian's unity with him (John 14:20; 15:26; cf. 1 John 3:24; 4:2–3; 4:13),[8] (3)

---

truths that (1) God hardens whomever he chooses; (2) human beings, because of sin, are responsible for their ultimate condemnation. Thus, God's bestowing of mercy and his hardening are not equivalent acts. God's mercy is given to those who do not deserve it; his hardening affects those who have already by their sin deserved condemnation." Moo, *Romans*, 599–600.

6. The participle τετηρημένοις is understood to either mean "kept for Jesus Christ" with the Father as the agent (dative of advantage) or "kept by Jesus Christ" with the Son as the agent (instrumental). Although either decision is possible, Bauckham's discussion of Old Testament parallels with Israel lends weight to the notion that just as the Father loved and guarded Israel, so too he has loved and is keeping his people in the new covenant. Bauckham, *2 Peter and Jude*, 26. See also the discussion in Davids, *2 Peter and Jude*, 38–39.

7. In John 7:38–39, the apostle John gives us the key to understanding "living water" as the "Holy Spirit."

8. John teaches that all the persons of the Trinity indwell the believer through the ministry of the Spirit, and ties it to the replacement of the temple in Jerusalem with Jesus first, and then believers in union with him. For a comprehensive study on the relationship between the temple and indwelling, see Hamilton, *God's Indwelling*

the Spirit brings to the Apostles' remembrance everything Jesus taught (John 14:26),[9] (4) Jesus is also involved in the sending of the Spirit (John 15:26),[10] (5) the Spirit will convict the world concerning sin, righteousness and judgment (John 16:8–11),[11] and (6) the Father gives all things to the Spirit, who then reveals them to the disciples (John 16:15; cf. 1 John 4:1).

Thus, the Father takes the initiative in salvation by seeking his elect, sending his Spirit to do his convicting and revelatory work of glorifying the Son's person and work as the Messiah (John 16:8; 1 Thess 1:5). Furthermore, the Father takes the initiative in drawing a sinner to himself. A person cannot receive the testimony about Christ unless "it is given [by the Father to] him from heaven" (John 3:27). However, Jesus teaches, "all that the Father gives [him] will come to [him]" (John 6:37). Moreover, they cannot come unless the Father (ostensibly by the Spirit) sovereignly draws them (John 6:44),[12] and grants it (John 6:65). The Father does this by "teaching" (again, presumably by the Spirit), so that "everyone who has heard and learned

---

Presence, particularly chap. 6. In it, Hamilton also deals with the relationship between regeneration and indwelling.

9. In the context, the Spirit's ministry of revelation is for the Apostles and their subsequent writing of the New Testament Scriptures. In John's experience, he speaks of the Spirit's revelatory ministry at the beginning and end of his Apocalypse. In Rev 1:9–10, "I, John . . . was on the island called Patmos on account of the word of God and the testimony of Jesus. I was in the Spirit on the Lord's day . . ." and in Rev 22:6, "These words are trustworthy and true. And the Lord, the God of the spirits of the prophets, has sent his angel to show his servants what must soon take place." In these passages, all three persons of the Godhead are at work in the giving of Scripture. The revelation belongs to the Son (Rev 1:1) and are his words (Rev 2:18; 3:1, 14). The Father gave this to the Son (Rev 1:1), and they reveal the Father's mystery (Rev 10:7), which is what must soon take place (Rev 22:6). The Spirit then brings to the Apostles's remembrance what Jesus taught (John 14:26), and guides him into all the truth that is to be revealed (John 16:13).

10. "If the Spirit is not to be described begotten lest he appear to be another Son, what word is to be used? Gregory found in John 15:26 the statement that the Spirit "proceeds (ἐκπορεύεται) from the father" (Gregory of Nazianzus, Oration 31:8). This is for the most part a sheer terminological fiat: Gregory knew that the Scriptures bear witness to a distinction between the Son and the Spirit, and he elevated a rather undistinguished word from the Gospel of John to the status of a technical term in the doctrine of the Trinity, thereby defining the Spirit as "the one who proceeds from the Father." Sanders, *Image of the Immanent Trinity*, 179.

11. For the interpretive possibilities and challenges to this passage, see Aloisi, "Paraclete's Ministry of Conviction," 55–69.

12. ἕλκω is a strong word, emphasizing the effectual calling of the Father's elect. Carson, *John*, 293. Carson also insists "with no less vigour that John emphasizes the responsibility of people to come to Jesus, and can excoriate them for refusing to do so (*e.g.*, 5:40)."

from the Father comes" to the Son (John 6:45),[13] and in receiving the Son, they receive the Father who sent him (Matt 10:40).

Through the Spirit, the Father Unites Believers to his Son

Not only does the Father draw his elect through the agency of the Holy Spirit, he also, by the Spirit, unites believers to Christ. The Father accomplishes this union in order to bring Christians into an experience of the unity (John 17:21), glory (John 17:22), and love (John 17:23, 26) that exists within the Triune relationship of Father, Son, and Spirit. Furthermore, John ties it to the Father's mission of seeking worshipers, which is accomplished through the union of believers with Christ. Robert Peterson's analysis of union with Christ in the gospel of John is helpful:

> Because of the Father's love for the Son and their love for the world and because of the Son's incarnation, death, and resurrection, believers are in the Father and the Son. They are mutually indwelt by the Trinitarian persons as an act of grace insofar as creatures can partake of the divine life (cf. 2 Pet. 1:4). John includes the Holy Spirit in the mission of God. Jesus will ask the Father to send the Spirit to indwell and be with believers, and they will know him (John 14:17). Although John does not correlate the Spirit's work and union with Christ as does Paul, John provides the raw materials for systematic theology to do so.[14]

Historically, in the Reformed tradition, union with Christ has been divided into two aspects: new identity (or status) and new nature. Those who believe the gospel then are *accepted* by the Father because of their new position in Christ (legal union), and they are *alive* to the Father because of their new nature in Christ (vital union).[15] Scripture also speaks of two more implications that come through union with Christ: (1) the Father places believers into the church, giving them a new community in Christ, and (2) the Father calls believers his children, bringing them into a new relationship

---

13. This "hearing" is also tied to the Son's drawing. Jesus says in John 10:27, "My sheep hear my voice," and in John 12:32, "And I, when I am lifted up from the earth, will draw all people to myself." The Son's emphasis of the Son's drawing is on all people without distinction; that is, both Jew and Gentile, but still has an element of individual "drawing" of those the Father has given him.

14. Peterson, "Union with Christ," 28.

15. For recent works on union with Christ, see Macaskill, *Union with Christ*; Campbell, *Paul and Union with Christ*.

in Christ. In what follows, I will explore these two aspects and implications of union with Christ, covering a well-worn path of soteriological studies. What is perhaps new, is the pateriological focus; namely, it is the first person of the Trinity who through the Son and by the Spirit secures the believer's union with Christ.

The Father Accepts Believers because They Have a New Identity in Christ

It is clear from the passages that follow that the Father is the one who justifies, reconciles, redeems, and forgives. Furthermore, these declarations flow from the Father's initiating role within the Trinity. Nevertheless, the Father never works apart from the Son or the Holy Spirit. Rather, it is through union with Christ accomplished by the pouring out of the Spirit, that the Father gives the Christian a new identity.

First, because of the Son's substitutionary work at Calvary, the Father is able to justify the ungodly and count them righteous (Rom 4:5).[16] In Romans, Paul teaches that the "righteousness of God" is the righteous activity of God worked out for a sinner's justification by the obedience and blood of Christ on the cross (cf. Rom 5:9),[17] which is why Paul can also write that justification is "in Christ" (Rom 3:24; cf. Gal 2:17).[18] Furthermore, in 1 Corinthians 6:11, Paul includes the Holy Spirit in the work of justification: "you were justified in the name of the Lord Jesus Christ and by the Spirit of our God."[19] On this passage, Roy Ciampa and Brian Rosner write,

> It is foundational to Paul's understanding of salvation that it involves the cooperative work of all three persons of the Godhead, to use the language of Chalcedon. 1 Corinthians 1:4–7, 2:4–5, 2:12, and 6:19–20 are other places in the letter (cf. 2 Cor. 1:21–22) where salvation is predicated either explicitly or implicitly on the threefold work of the triune God.[20]

---

16. Colin Kruse writes, "God's acquittal of the wicked and repentant is based upon the fact that he has provided an atoning sacrifice so that he can be both just and the justifier of those who have faith in Jesus (3:26). Kruse, *Romans*, 206–7.

17. See Moo, *Romans*, 73–75.

18. Constantine Campbell argues that Christ is the agent of justification in that it is the "redemption associated with Christ" that justifies. See Campbell, *Paul and Union with Christ*, 114–15.

19. See also Romans 8:4 and 14:17 where justification and righteousness is connected to the Holy Spirit.

20. Ciampa and Rosner, *First Corinthians*, 244.

Not only that, the prepositional phrases used regarding justification reveal the Father as initiator in the divine work. God the Father produces salvation, including justification "in the name of the Lord Jesus" and "by the Spirit."[21] Because the Father justifies by grace through faith (Gal 3:6, 8, 11; Rom 3:24, 26; 8:33; Titus 3:7), the Christian has peace with the Father (Rom 5:1), is saved from his wrath (Rom 5:9) and becomes an "[heir] according to the hope of eternal life" (Titus 3:7). The antecedent to ἐκείνου is God our Savior (Titus 3:4), who regenerates *by* the Holy Spirit (Titus 3:5) poured out *through* Jesus Christ (Titus 3:6).

Second, the Father reconciles believers to himself through the death of his Son.[22] Again in Romans, Paul connects reconciliation to the death of Christ (Rom 5:10), arguing that believers are only reconciled to the Father "*through* the Lord Jesus Christ (Rom 5:11; cf. 2 Cor 5:18–20; Eph 2:16; Col 1:20–22). Colin Kruse insightfully notes,

> The juxtaposition of justification (5:9) and reconciliation (5:10) is noteworthy, and raises the question of distinctions between the two concepts. As used by Paul, the terms are very close but nevertheless distinct. Justification is essentially a legal term relating to decisions in a court of law, whereas reconciliation is a personal term relating to the restoration of relationships. But Paul's understanding of God as the justifier of sinners cannot be separated from his understanding of God as reconciler. For Paul God is not the detached judge dispensing judgment, but the lover of sinners desiring reconciliation with them.[23]

The Holy Spirit is not explicitly tied to the work of reconciliation, but due to its close connection with justification and part of the broader work of salvation, 1 Corinthians 6:11 applies the agency of the Spirit to this aspect of the atonement as well.

Finally, out of the abundant riches of his grace, the Father lavishes redemption and forgiveness upon his children (Eph 1:7–8) by cancelling the certificate of debt that was against them, nailing it to the cross (Col 2:13–14).[24] The Father, therefore, qualifies his children to share in the inheritance of the saints (Col 1:12), delivering them from "the domain of darkness" and

---

21. See Fee, *First Corinthians*, 246.
22. On reconciliation, see Morris, *Apostolic Preaching of the Cross*.
23. Kruse, *Romans*, 238.
24. A χειρόγραφον was a document containing a signed certificate of debt in which the signature legalized the debt. It is the obligation of every person to keep the law of God, whether the Jewish obligation to keep the Mosaic Law or the Gentile obligation to keep the moral law. See O'Brien, *Colossians, Philemon*, 124–25.

transferring them into "the kingdom of his beloved Son" (Col 1:14; cf. 1 Cor 1:30). Further, Paul in Ephesians teaches two phases to this redemption. In chapter 1, he refers to the first phase as a sealing in Christ "with the promised Holy Spirit" when a person "believes" (Eph 1:14; cf. 2 Cor 1:22; 5:5). The second phase is yet future when Christ returns and is called the "day of redemption" (Eph 4:30; cf. Rom 8:23). Peter O'Brien explains,

> Believers have already experienced a present redemption which includes the forgiveness of sins (1:7); but one element of that redemption is yet to be realized. On the final day, God will 're-deem' his own possession, and the guarantee he has given of this is his sealing of them with the Spirit. The mention of a future redemption is consistent with other references to the future in Ephesians (cf. 1:10, 14; 2:7; 5:5, 27; 6:8, 13), and shows that Paul did not envisage salvation as being fully or completely realized. There is a fulfilment yet to come, and believers eagerly await it. For the moment, however, the apostle's gaze is on the presence of the Spirit in their midst. They are to live out the future in the here and now until that 'day' of redemption arrives, and this reminder that the Holy Spirit is God's own seal should be an incentive to holy living and speaking.[25]

Thus, the Father's acceptance of the believer is often described by the new reality of "grace and peace," and is why Paul begins almost every one of his letters with the blessing, "Grace and peace from God our Father" (2 Thess 1:2; 1 Cor 1:3; 2 Cor 1:2; Rom 1:7; Eph 1:2; Col 1:2; Phlm 1:3; Phil 1:2; 1 Tim 1:2; Titus 1:4; 2 Tim 1:2; cf. 1 Pet 1:2; 2 Pet 1:2; 2 John 1:3). The Father's grace (1 Cor 3:10; 15:10; Col 1:6) is his kind intention and disposition to act for the benefit of his elect, which is why Paul teaches the Corinthians, "God [the Father] is able to make all grace abound to you, so that having all sufficiency in all things at all times, you may abound in every good work" (2 Cor 9:8). The Father's peace (1 Thess 5:23; 2 Thess 3:16; 2 Cor 13:11; Rom 15:33; 16:20; Phil 4:9) flows from his character and he grants it abundantly to his children,[26] which is why Paul writes to the Philippians, "And the peace of God [the Father], which surpasses all understanding, will guard your hearts and your minds in Christ Jesus" (Phil 4:7).

Even grace and peace takes on a Trinitarian shape in the book of Revelation. John writes to the churches of Asia Minor, "Grace to you and peace

---

25. O'Brien, *Ephesians*, 349.

26. "The peace which God gives excels and surpasses all our own intellectual calculations and considerations, all our contemplations and premeditated ideas of how to get rid of our cares.... What God gives, surpasses all that we ask or think (cf. Eph 3:20)." Müller, *Philippians and Philemon*, 142.

from him who is and who was and who is to come [the Father], and from the seven spirits [the Holy Spirit] who are before his throne, and from Jesus Christ the faithful witness, the firstborn of the dead, and the ruler of kings on earth" (Rev 1:4–5). The Gospel, then includes the good news that the Father, through the pouring out of the Holy Spirit, seals believers in his Son, giving them a new identity and standing before him.

The Father Enlivens Believers, Giving Them a New Nature in Christ

When the Father supplies the Spirit (Gal 3:5; 1 Thess 4:8; 1 Cor 2:12; Rom 5:5), he not only grants a new identity, he also imparts new life, giving believers a new nature in Christ. Further, according to Titus 3:6, the Father pours out his Holy Spirit "through Jesus Christ our Savior." The use of διά with genitive object demonstrates that the Father pours out the Spirit through the agency of the Son, and therefore the *taxis* is preserved (cf. John 15:26). Consequently, both the Father and Son send the Spirit.[27] As such, the Father (and Son) send the Spirit to "anoint" believers (2 Cor 1:21) and indwell them (John 3:5–6, 8; 1 Cor 3:16; 6:19; Rom 8:9; Jas 4:5),[28] bringing new life into existence (John 6:40; Rom 4:17; Eph 1:17; 2:4–5, 9; Col 2:12–13; Titus 3:4–5; 1 Pet 1:3).[29]

Thus, by the Father's will, sinners are given the new nature: "who were born, not of blood nor of the will of the flesh nor of the will of man, but of God [the Father]" (John 1:13; cf. Jas 1:18).[30] From the near context, inseparable operations are preserved, for the Son in v. 12 also "gave the right to become children of God."

Also, in keeping with the divine *taxis*, those who are Christ's "sheep," to whom Christ gives eternal life (John 10:27–28), are those that the Father gives him (John 10:29). John explains why in his first epistle: "And this is the testimony, that God [the Father] gave us eternal life, and this life is in his Son. Whoever has the Son has life; whoever does not have the Son of God does not have life" (1 John 5:11–12). Consequently, eternal life is from the

---

27. It is helpful to see that the Spirit is not only called the "Spirit of God" (Matt 3:16; 12:28; 8:9, 14; 15:19; 1 Cor 2:11, 14; 7:40; 12:3; Eph 4:30; Phil 3:3; 1 John 4:2; Rev 3:1; 4:5; 5:6) but also the "Spirit of Christ" (Rom 8:9; cf. Acts 16:7; Phil. 1:19; 1 Pet. 1:11).

28. οἰκέω is a settled residence. Every believer has the Holy Spirit resident within them. See Moo, *Romans*, 490.

29. On "eternal life," see Kruse, *John*, 184–87.

30. That this is the Father is clear from the previous verse (Jas 1:17), where he is called the "Father of lights."

Father, revealed in the Son, and inextricably tied to Spirit-given belief (John 20:31; 1 John 5:13) and knowledge (John 17:3; 2 Cor 4:6) through "the living and abiding word of God" (1 Pet 1:23; cf. Jas 1:18).[31] Thus, all the Trinity at the direction of the Father, is at work to give new life to those the Father places in Christ by the Spirit.

The Father Places Believers into the Church, Giving them a New Community in Christ

The church belongs to the Father (Gal 1:13; 1 Thess 2:14; 2 Thess 1:4; 1 Cor 1:2; 1 Cor 11:16, 22; 15:9; 2 Cor 1:1; 1 Tim 3:5, 15).[32] Furthermore, Scripture calls the church the Father's field (1 Cor 3:9), the Father's building (1 Cor 3:9), the Father's household (Eph 2:19; 1 Tim 3:15; cf. Matt 12:4; Heb 3:6), and the Father's temple (1 Cor 3:16–17; 2 Cor 6:16; cf. 1 Pet 2:5–6). Even in this relationship, the Trinitarian *taxis* is preserved, for the church belonging to God the Father is also called generally the church of Christ (Rom 16:16; 1 Thess 1:1; 2 Thess 1:1) and more specifically the church that is "in Christ" (Gal 1:22; 1 Thess 2:14).[33] Also, the Father who arranges members in his church and gives gifts to them as he chooses (1 Cor 12:18, 24, 28), empowers them through union with the Lord Jesus Christ by the agency of the Holy Spirit. Paul writes to the Corinthians, "Now there are varieties of gifts, but the same *Spirit*; and there are varieties of service, but the same *Lord*; and there are varieties of activities, but it is the same *God* who empowers them all in everyone [emphasis mine]" (1 Cor 12:4–6). Concerning the relationship of this *taxis* to inseparable operations, Anthony Thiselton writes,

> The unity and grace of God as one, who nevertheless dispenses his gifts in variety through Christ as Lord by the Holy Spirit calls attention to God as "author, authorizer, destiny and judge . . . (Rom. 12:1–2; 13:1–4; 1 Thess. 4:3; 1 Cor. 6:13–14; 8:6; 12:4–6). 1 Cor. 7 in particular shows the Pauline tendency "to trace everything back to God."[34]

Thiselton then quotes from 1:30 in Athanasius's *Epistle to Serapion*:

---

31. Including both his spoken word and his written one. See Blum, *1, 2 Peter*, 227.

32. ἐκκλησία τοῦ θεοῦ is best understood as a possessive genitive, "the church belonging to God." See Hiebert, *Thessalonian Epistles*, 112.

33. Green, *Thessalonians*, 142.

34. Thiselton, *First Corinthians*, 934, quoting Richardson, *Paul's Language about God*, 237.

The gifts which the Spirit divides to each are bestowed from the Father (παρὰ τοῦ πατρός) through the Word (διὰ τοῦ λόγου). For all things that are of the Father are of the Son also; therefore those things which are given from the Son in the Spirit are gifts of the Father. And when the Spirit is in us, the Word also, who gives the Spirit, is in us, and in the Word is the Father.[35]

Thiselton concludes:

> In the exegesis of Athanasius, Paul views the Father as the source of spiritual gifts (*from* God); the Son, Christ, as their mediator (*through* Christ as Lord); to be "activated" by the agency of the Holy Spirit (*by* the Spirit). . . . Thus *in the experience of the believer* the persons of the Trinity are inseparable, even if apart from such experience distinctions of personhood can be made [emphasis original].[36]

Important to this discussion is the meaning of κεφαλή (headship).[37] Paul writes that Christ is "head over all things (Eph 1:22; cf. 4:15)," including "all rule and authority" (Col 2:10) and the church, which is his body (Eph 5:23; Col 1:18; 2:19). Nevertheless, Paul also writes that "the head of Christ is God [the Father]" (1 Cor 11:3). In fact, 1 Corinthians 11 is one of the main passages used to demonstrate an authority-submission structure in relationships where there is equality of being, both between men and women as well as within the Godhead.[38] For example, Bruce Ware writes,

> It seems that 1 Corinthians 11:3 suggests this [*taxis* within the Godhead] and then applies this same *taxis* to God-designed human relationships. For all eternity, the order establishes that

---

35. Ibid., 935.
36. Ibid.
37. For the meaning of κεφαλή as authority, see Schreiner, "Head Coverings," 124. See also Thiselton, *First Corinthians*, 812–26 and Keener, *1–2 Corinthians*, 92–93. Most egalitarians would argue that κεφαλή means "source" rather than "authority." In doing so, they would argue that there is no intended structure of authority and submission in these passages. Consequently, women have a right to lead in the church just as men.
38. Recently, Kyle Claunch has written a substantial essay answering the question, "Does 1 Corinthians 11:3 ground gender complementarity in the immanent Trinity?" His answer is yes, albeit indirectly. He concludes: "1 Corinthians 11:2–16 is best understood according to a gender complementarian reading; the submission of woman to man ("man is the head of woman") is grounded, in part, in the submission of the Son to the will of the Father ("God is the head of Christ"); the statement "God is the head of Christ" pertains directly to Christ in his incarnate state, in which his human will is submitted to the divine will of the Father; nevertheless, the submission of Christ to the Father, per his human will, is the analogical expression of the immanent Trinitarian taxis of the one eternal divine will." Claunch, "God is the Head of Christ," 93.

God is the head of Christ; within the created sphere, there is an ordering such that Christ is the head of man; and within human relationships, the order establishes that man is the head of woman. Intrinsic to God's own nature is a fundamental *taxis*, and he has so designed creation to reflect his own being, his own internal and eternal relationships, in part, through created and designed relationships of *taxis*.[39]

Furthermore, Michael Bird and Robert Shillaker point out that the authority-submission structure is by way of analogy, not equivalence:

> Peter Bolt's article on 1 Cor 11:3 has also shown that God being the head of Christ was largely interpreted by patristic authors with the language of hierarchy and also with the concept of origination, which is tantamount to equality in being and subordination in role. What is more, as Bolt points out, what we have in 1 Cor 11:3 and in its patristic interpretation is analogy but not equivalence. Nobody ever says that the husband is the head of the wife because God is the head of Christ. There is an analogy or parallel between male-female relationships and the Father-Son relationship, but no causality.[40]

In this way, the marriage relationship becomes an analogy, not only of the relationship between Christ and the church (Eph 5:23), but also the relations between the Father and Son (also by implication, the Holy Spirit). Thus, the Father chooses to give a people to his Son, also appointing him head over the church of God, which is this new community in Christ. The Father accomplishes this by the empowering agency of his Holy Spirit (1 Cor 12:13), so that those in Christ are given a "manifestation of the Spirit for the common good (1 Cor 12:7), so that they may hold fast to the "Head" and grow with a "growth which is from God [the Father]" (Col 2:19).

The Father Calls Believers his Children, Bringing them into a New Relationship in Christ

Through the work of the Holy Spirit, the Father adopts Christians, calling them his sons (Gal 3:26; 4:5; 2 Cor 6:16, 18; Rom 9:8; Eph 1:5; Phil 2:15). As sons, believers are heirs through the work and grace of God the Father (Gal

---

39. Ware, *Father, Son, and Spirit*, 72. Contrary to this position would be those who argue that the Trinity is not a model for social relationships. For example, see Johnson, "Trinitarian Agency," 108–32.

40. Bird and Shillaker, "Subordination in the Trinity," 302–3. The article they are referring to is Bolt, "Three Heads in the Divine Order," 147–61.

4:7).⁴¹ John explains this implication of union with Christ in his prologue to his Gospel: "But to all who did receive him [Christ], who believed in his name, he gave the right to become children of God" (John 1:12). When John says, "the right" to become children, John's first thought is of status, and when he uses the verb "become," he is teaching that through faith in Christ, there is a change in that status.⁴² The status is for everyone, including both Jews and Gentiles (John 11:52), and the change is immediate, though not yet fully completed by the Father (1 John 3:2).⁴³

The Father knows his children (Gal 4:9; 2 Cor 5:11)⁴⁴ and loves them (1 Thess 1:4; 2 Thess 2:16, 3:5); therefore, nothing can separate them from his love in Christ Jesus (Rom 8:39) and through the Spirit's power will overcome every obstacle to their salvation (Rom 8:13, 37). Even when they sin and disobey, as a perfect Father, he disciplines them (Heb 12:5-7, 9). According to the author of Hebrews, the Father "disciplines us for our good, that we may share his holiness" (Heb 12:10). Therefore, as his children walk through life in a fallen world, the Father imparts comfort for the present and hope for the future (2 Thess 2:16–17; 2 Cor 1:2–3; 7:6).

To the Corinthians, Paul described the Father as the "God of all *comfort*" (2 Cor 1:2), and to the Romans he described him as the "God of *hope*" (Rom 15:13). The Father's hope will never put his children to shame (Rom 5:5). Since the Father is for his children (Rom 8:31), he will give them all things in Christ (Rom 8:32), supplying every one of their needs according to his glorious riches (Phil 4:19; Jas 1:17), causing all things to work out for their good (Rom 8:28), granting victory to them over every enemy and peril (1 Cor 15:57; 2 Cor 1:10; 2:14), and inviting them to draw near (Heb 4:16; 7:19, 25; 10:21–22) so that he might answer their prayer (1 Pet 3:12).

In response to their prayers, the Father can do "far more abundantly than all that [his children] ask or think" (Eph 3:20), because it is not their strength, but his power at work on their behalf (Eph 3:20; 1 Cor 2:5; 2 Cor 4:7; Rom 16:25). That is why Paul prays for the Ephesians that they would know "what is the immeasurable *greatness* of his *power* toward [those] who believe, according to the *working* of his great *might* that he *worked* in Christ when he raised him from the dead and seated him at his right hand in the

---

41. By using the phrase διὰ θεοῦ, Paul sees adoption as a sovereign gracious work of the Father, which is not based in any way on our work or merit. See Longenecker, *Galatians*, 175.

42. Morris, *John*, 87.

43. For the divine passive here, see Yarbrough, *1–3 John*, 177–78.

44. "The Father's children have become objects of his favorable attention and he has revealed himself to them." Burton, *Galatians*, 229.

heavenly places" (Eph 1:19–20).[45] Furthermore, the Spirit bears witness to the Christian's spirit that they are children (Rom 8:16) and heirs of the Father (Rom 8:17). As such, the Father has prepared amazing things for his children (1 Cor 2:9), also revealing them through his Spirit (1 Cor 2:10–11). Thus, the Father gives the Christian a new status as his child, ushering them by the Spirit into a new relationship in Christ.

Through the Spirit, the Father Will Sanctify Believers Completely

In union with Christ, along with a new status and new nature, the Father continues the work of progressive sanctification in his saints through the ministry of his Holy Spirit. Writing to the Thessalonians, Paul teaches that the Father has destined his children for salvation (1 Thess 5:9; 2 Tim 1:9), he sanctifies them completely (1 Thess 5:23; Rom 6:22), and will be faithful to do it (1 Thess 5:24). That is because, according to Paul, believers have already put on the new self, "which is created after the likeness of the Father in true righteousness and holiness" (Eph 4:24)[46] and is "being renewed in knowledge after the image of its Creator" (Col 3:10). Once again, it is important to see that the Father does this through the agency of the Son and Spirit. The author of Hebrews prays that the Father would "equip [the saints] with everything good that [they] may do his will, working in [them] that which is pleasing in his sight, *through Jesus Christ* [emphasis mine]" (Heb 13:21; cf. Heb 9:14). After all, Christ is the archetype of the *Imago Dei*, the one who is the "image of God," (Col 1:15; Heb 1:3) and the one into whose image all Christians will be conformed (1 John 3:2; 1 Cor 13:12).[47] Furthermore, it is the Spirit's leading that is evidence a believer has been born of God (Rom 8:14) and it is the Spirit who is the agent of spiritual transformation (2 Cor 3:18).[48]

Also, in John 17:17, Jesus prays to the Father, "Sanctify them in the truth; your word is truth." Here, Jesus ties the sanctifying work of the Father to both the word and the Spirit with a clear emphasis on mission (John

---

45. Paul emphasizes the importance of the Father's power by: (1) Placing it last in the list of his prayer requests for the Ephesians, (2) Using the expression "ὑπερβάλλον μέγεθος", and (3) Piling up words for God's strength and work including four nouns: δύναμις, ἐνέργεια, κράτος, ἰσχύς, and one verb: ἐνεργέω.

46. ἐνδύσασθαι is an aorist middle infinitive signifying its completion when the believer was converted. See Hoehner, *Ephesians*, 609–10.

47. Kruse, *Letters of John*, 116.

48. Harris, *Second Corinthians*, 317–19.

17:18, 23; cf. Acts 20:32). Regarding this passage, David Peterson summarizes, "We might say that the Spirit works through the apostolic word to sanctify or consecrate a people to God 'in the truth.'"[49] The sanctifying work of the Father is additionally seen in his role as the "vinedresser" (John 15:1). Every branch "that does bear fruit (has life in it) he prunes, so that it may bear more fruit" (John 15:2). The Father is glorified by the manifestation of life, and for that reason, will continue to prune so that his children will continue to bear more and more fruit (John 15:8). In 1 John, the implications are manifold: First, "No one born of God makes a practice of sinning" (1 John 3:9; 5:18), but instead "practice righteousness" (1 John 3:10). Second, "whoever loves has been born of God" (1 John 4:7–8). Third, "everyone who believes that Jesus is the Christ has been born of God" (1 John 5:1). Finally, "everyone who has been born of God overcomes the world" (1 John 5:4). Thus, the Father, through union with Christ and by the agency of the Holy Spirit will sanctify believers completely.

Through the Spirit, the Father Will Keep His Children

As Jesus prepares to leave his disciples, he asks the Father to "keep them in [his] name" (John 17:11) and to "keep them from the evil one" (John 17:15). John describes this keeping as the Father's divine protection through the ministry of the Son, and as a result of the Spirit's work in the new birth: "We know that everyone who has been born of God [by the Spirit] does not keep on sinning, but he who was born of God [the Son] protects him, and the evil one does not touch him" (1 John 5:18).[50] In the book of Revelation, this keeping is pictured as "the seal of the living God" (Rev 7:2–3; cf. 8:4), and later described as the Lamb's name and "his Father's name written on their foreheads" (Rev 14:1; cf. 22:4). It is a clear mark of both ownership and security,[51] and is why Jesus can claim that his sheep "will never perish" and never be snatched out of the Father and Son's hands (John 10:28–29).

Furthermore, the Father's keeping is not governed by subjective experience, for John says, "whenever our heart condemns us, God [the

---

49. Peterson, *Possessed by God*, 32. He connects the Spirit to "truth" from his identifier as the "Spirit of truth" (John 14:17; 15:26; 16:13), as the one who reminds the Apostles of everything Jesus said (14:26), from his testimony on behalf of the Son (15:26–27), and from his guiding them into all the truth (16:13–15). Ibid., 31–32.

50. For the "one born of God" as Jesus, see Yarbrough, *1–3 John*, 316–17.

51. Beale, *Revelation*, 734.

Father] is greater than our heart" (1 John 3:20).[52] In fact, John later speaks of those who are born of God as "overcomers" (1 John 5:4), and as a result, are called to a life of perseverance in the faith: "Here is a call for the endurance of the saints, those who keep the commandments of God and their faith in Jesus" (Rev 14:12).

Anthony Hoekema captures the balance of divine sovereignty and human responsibility well:

> The doctrine of the perseverance of true believers is one of the most comforting teachings of Scripture. We learn from it that God by his power keeps his people from falling away from him, that Christ will never permit anyone to snatch them out of his hand, and that the Holy Spirit seals them for the day of redemption. Our heavenly Father holds us securely in his grasp; that is our ultimate comfort in life and death. We rest finally not on our hold of God but on God's hold of us.
>
> Yet this doctrine also urges us to persevere in the faith—and this is our challenge. We can only persevere through God's strength and by his grace. But to teach this doctrine in such a way as to present only its comfort and not its challenge, only the security and not the exhortation, is to teach it one-sidedly. And the Bible constantly warns us against such one-sidedness.[53]

Because it is the Father's will that "one of the little ones" should never perish (Matt 18:14), the Father guards his children by his power. Nevertheless, as Peter writes, they are guarded "through faith" (1 Pet 1:5). Therefore, the Father guards his people both through his power and by means of their faith.[54] Ultimately, however, it is accomplished by the Father. In 2 Peter 1:3–4 Peter encourages his audience: "His [the Father's] divine power has granted to us all things that pertain to life and godliness, through the knowledge of him who called us [the Father] to his own glory and excellence, by which he has granted to us his precious and very great promises, so that through them you may become partakers of the divine nature,

---

52. For the exegetical difficulties of this passage, see Marshall, *Epistles of John*, 197–98. He concludes, "So here too John is telling his readers that they can safely entrust themselves to the judgment of God who knows all about them, and consequently, they can set their hearts at rest, even though they feel self-condemned."

53. Hoekema, *Saved by Grace*, 255.

54. For all the exegetical possibilities of διὰ πίστεως in 1 Peter 1:5, see Horrell, "Whose Faith(fulness)," 110–15. Horrell acknowledges the possibility that the reference here is to God's faithfulness, but tentatively concludes that a reference to the faith of believers probably is more likely, particularly because of the larger context of 1 Pet 1:7–9, where the believer's faith is in view.

having escaped from the corruption that is in the world because of sinful desire." Although Ἰησοῦ τοῦ κυρίου ἡμῶν is the nearest antecedent (2 Pet 1:2), it is better to understand the Father as the one who is using his divine power and the Father as the one who calls (cf. 1 Pet 1:15; 2:9; 5:10, where the Father is the one who calls). As we saw earlier in the chapter, the Father calls believers into union and fellowship with his Son by the agency of the Holy Spirit. Here, the Father does so in order that his children will become "partakers of the divine nature."[55] Peter did not mean that believers will share in the Triune God's essence in every respect, such that they become divine. Rather, that they will be morally perfected, sharing in righteousness and holiness, experiencing the full restoration of the *Imago Dei*, thereby partaking of the moral excellence and immortality of Christ.[56] Thus, the Father is able through union with the Son and by the agency of the Holy Spirit to "keep [believers] from stumbling and to present [them] blameless before the presence of his glory with great joy" (Jude 24), and therefore reveals that he is to be praised through Jesus Christ for all "glory, majesty, dominion, and authority" (Jude 25).[57]

Unbelievers are under the Father's Wrath

The Father's relationship to the world stands in stark contrast to his relationship with his children. Paul's opening chapter of Romans reveals the indictment: "For the wrath of God is revealed from heaven against all ungodliness and unrighteousness of men, who by their unrighteousness suppress the truth" (Rom 1:18).[58] Furthermore, they do not honor the Father (Rom 1:21), thank him (Rom 1:21; 2:4) or acknowledge him (Rom 1:28), and therefore reveal that they hate him (Rom 1:30; Rom 8:7). Because of this, they "exchanged the truth of God [the Father] for a lie and worship and serve the creature rather than the Creator" (Rom 1:25; cf. Luke 16:15; John 5:44).[59]

John makes it an issue of love. Because they love the world (John 3:19; 1 John 2:15–16), they do not have the love of God the Father in them

---

55. On the doctrine of *theosis* from this passage, see Robert V. Rakestraw, "Becoming Like God," 257–69.

56. See Starr, *Sharers in Divine Nature*.

57. For these appellations of "glory, majesty, dominion and authority" being *through* Jesus Christ our Lord, see also Rom 7:25; 16:27; 2 Cor 1:20; Col 3:17; 1 Pet 4:11.

58. It is clear from Rom 1:1, 4, 7–9 that θεός is a reference to the Father distinguished from the Son.

59. In this context, τὸν κτίσαντα is a reference to the Father. For all three persons involved in creation, see chap. 4.

(John 5:42; 1 John 2:15; 4:8).[60] Jesus makes love the litmus test of hearing and obeying the Father's words (John 8:47; 14:23–24; cf. Matt 15:6; Mark 7:8, 13; Rom 8:8; 2 John 1:9). Therefore, the fruit of this life apart from the knowledge and love of the Father is a life of evil (3 John 1:11; cf. Rom 3:23)[61] and a life without love for others (1 John 3:10; 4:20).

Consequently, Scripture even speaks to those who profess to know the Father but deny him by their works (Titus 1:16). They honor the Father with their lips but their hearts are far from him (Isa 29:13; Matt 15:8; Mark 7:6). It is why James says, "You believe that God is one; you do well. Even the demons believe—and shudder" (Jas 2:19). The demons illustrate perfectly the deficiency of verbal profession without obedience. James then concludes, "faith apart from works is dead" (Jas 2:26).[62] According to Jesus, because some professing believers do not know the Father (or the Son), they believe it to be an act of worship to kill Christians (John 16:2–3).[63]

It is important at this point to reaffirm the Trinitarian shape of their unbelief. They do not honor the Father because they do not honor the Son (John 5:23) or love him (John 8:42), revealing that they hate both the Father and the Son (John 15:23–24). Furthermore, they deny that Jesus is the Christ, and in doing so deny the Father (1 John 2:22; cf. Jude 4) and therefore do not have a relationship with him (1 John 2:23).[64] In the same manner, they have no relationship with the Spirit. They do not "walk by the Spirit" (Gal 5:16), they are not "led by the Spirit" (Gal 5:18), they do not "live by the Spirit" or "keep in step with the Spirit (Gal 5:25), and therefore bear no "fruit of the Spirit" (Gal 5:22).[65] Judas is a prime example of this in the Gospel, for the Father as the vinedresser takes away the one who does

---

60. The context of 1 John 4:8 makes clear that θεός is not in the generic or as Trinity because this same God "sent his Son into the world" (v. 9) "to be the propitiation for our sins" (v. 10). Furthermore, he has given us "his Spirit" (v. 13). Trinitarian understanding helps us here to see that this love has been manifested in the immanent Trinity from all eternity, and thus is an attribute of the Triune God's nature as well as an action between Father, Spirit, and Son.

61. See Marshall, *Epistles of John*, 92.

62. See Davids, *James*, 125–26.

63. Λατρεία and its verbal cognate λατρεύω is the predominant word in the New Testament for religious or cultic service and translates the Hebrew verb עָבַד (abad), which was used of the Levitical priestly service in the temple. As such, the killing of Christians here is believed by unbelievers to be a sacrificial offering to God the Father. For a discussion of the word-group see Peterson, *Engaging with God*, 64–68.

64. Marshall, *Epistles of John*, 73n16.

65. See discussion in Moo, *Galatians*, 371–72.

not bear fruit (John 15:2).⁶⁶ This Trinitarian shape of unbelief is seen most explicitly in Rom 8:8–9:

> Those who are in the flesh cannot please God [the Father]. You, however, are not in the flesh but in the Spirit, if in fact the Spirit of God dwells in you. Anyone who does not have the Spirit of Christ does not belong to him [the Son].

The *taxis* in this passage is again upheld. Unbelievers (those in the flesh) cannot please the Father because they do not possess the indwelling ministry of God's Spirit. Because the Spirit is also Christ's Spirit, unbelievers do not belong to the Son either, and thus, the Father's wrath is revealed against them (Rom 1:18) and remains on them (John 3:36).

Consequently, the Father opposes the proud in their unbelief (Jas 5:4; cf. 1 Pet 3:12), blinding their hearts so that they have no desire for him or his salvation (John 12:40). giving them up to impurity (Rom 1:24), dishonorable passions (Rom 1:26) and a debased mind (Rom 1:28). Further, the Father is patiently enduring "vessels of wrath" and they prepare themselves for destruction by their sinful, rebellious lifestyle (Rom 9:22; cf. 2:5),⁶⁷ promising that while they live in unbelief, they will never enter his rest (Heb 3:18; 4:3–5).

Conclusion

In this chapter, I have argued that all the Father's works in the experience of the believer are consistent with the Trinitarian *taxis*. Both the Father and Son send the Spirit in the new-covenant age, but the reverse is never the case. Rather, the Son asks the Father (as initiator) to pour out the gift and promise of the Holy Spirit (John 14:16, 26; 15:26).

The Father, therefore, draws through the Spirit, grants union with Christ through the Spirit (bestowing a new status and new nature on believers), and the Father continues the work of progressive sanctification in his saints through the ministry of his Holy Spirit. Thus, the Father is able through union with the Son and by the Holy Spirit to "keep [believers] from stumbling and to present [them] blameless before the presence of his glory with great joy" (Jude 24). In these works, the Father initiates, inseparable operations are affirmed, and the divine *taxis* is upheld. Finally, as we shall see in the next chapter, the Father will be initiating all divine work into eternity future.

---

66. For the meaning of αἴρω as "cut off" rather than "lift up," see Carson, *John*, 518. For Judas as the referent, see Köstenberger, *John*, 452.

67. I take καταρτίζω to be in the middle voice meaning that people have prepared themselves for destruction by their own sinful choices. See Morris, *Romans*, 368.

7

The Father's Work, through the Son and Spirit, of Perfecting Creation and Salvation through Judgment and the Restoration of All Things

Introduction

THE FATHER WILL COMPLETE the work of salvation by sending his Son a second time to gather his elect (Matt 24:31; Mark 13:27) and raise the dead (Acts 24:15; Rev 20:4–5), bringing them before the Father's judgment seat (Rom 14:10). There, through the agency of the Son, the Father will righteously judge, giving eternal rewards to his children and punishment to the lost (Matt 25:46; Acts 10:42; 17:31; 2 Cor 5:10; Rev 11:18; 20:11). The Father will make all things new (Rev 21:5) and will dwell on earth to reign, giving his children the consummation of their adoption (Rev 21:3; 22:4). Then, the Son himself will hand over all things to the Father (1 Cor 15:28), and for all eternity, the Father will be continually revealing the incomparable riches of all that he graciously accomplished for his children in and through Christ by the power of the Holy Spirit (Eph 2:7). Thus, they will always be with him and they will worship him (Eph 3:21; Jude 25; Rev 22:5).

In chapters 4–6, I have argued that all the Father's works of creation, providence, and redemption are accomplished through the agency of the Son and by the agency of the Holy Spirit. Furthermore, the finer details of the Father's working (e.g., giving Scripture, promising a Messiah, uniting believers to his Son, pouring out his Spirit, keeping and sanctifying his children, etc.) display a consistent *taxis* within the persons of the Trinity.

In this chapter, I will argue that the Father will initiate all divine work necessary to consummate the economy of redemption and fulfill his decree. Thus, the Father's role as initiator remains consistent from eternity past, through redemptive history, into eternity future and is never reversed. It is worth repeating that Scripture proves and affirms the equal glory and coeternal majesty of the Father, Son, and Holy Spirit, and that they share full unity in regard to the divine name, the divine nature, and divine action; particularly because 1 Corinthians 15:28 has been used in history to argue for the inferiority of the Son.[1]

It is why Wesley Hill argues for "asymmetrical mutuality"; that is, "*mutual* in that the identities of God and Jesus are inseparably bound up with one another's. And yet it is asymmetrical insofar as God is determined in his relation to Jesus specifically as 'father' (or 'sender,' 'the one who raised . . . ,' etc.) while Jesus is determined in his relation to God specifically as the one who was 'sent,' 'raised,' and so on."[2] Concerning 1 Corinthians 15:28 he writes,

> The one who is "God and Father" (15:24) is not the one who comes to be designated "Son" (v. 28). Nor is there any doubt that the Son is the one who subordinates himself to God, and not vice versa. And yet the Son remains *the Son* in his subordination to the Father. To conclude, in other words, from the Son's irreducible distinction from the Father that his inextricable identity *with* the Father is somehow mitigated or diminished is to confuse affirmations that belong on parallel rather than intersecting planes. The Son is still the Son when God is all in all, which means that the Father is still the Father when he at last enjoys full eschatological sovereignty, God and Christ remain basic to one another's identities, and so a "redoubled" form of speech is necessary to receive the theological pressure of 1 Cor 15:24–28. Explicating this text requires the reference both to what unites God and Christ on the sovereign side of the Sovereign-ruled (or Creator-creature) divide as well as to what distinguishes God and Christ in terms of their personal uniqueness.[3]

Thus, though the Father and Son (and by implication, Spirit) are co-equal, there will remain for eternity future, "eschatology distinct roles for God and Christ."[4] However, before I discuss the "end" (1 Cor 15:24) in detail, I will address the Father's role in sending the Son a second time, to raise the just and the unjust (through the Son and Holy Spirit), to judge the living and the dead (through the agency of the Son and Spirit), and to usher in his kingdom, making all things new (again through the Son and Spirit).

1. For example, see Origen's refutation of heretics on this passage in Origen, *On First Principles*, 3.5.6–7.
2. Hill, *Paul and the Trinity*, 133.
3. Ibid., 132–33.
4. Ibid., 131.

The Father Sends His Son a Second Time to Bring Salvation through Judgment

James Hamilton has recently argued that the center of biblical theology is "God's glory in salvation through judgment."[5] Therefore, the second coming of Jesus Christ serves two purposes: bringing salvation to his elect and pouring out his wrath upon the guilty. "And will not God [the Father] give justice to his elect, who cry to him day and night?"[6] According to Jesus in the Gospels, this day of Christ's return is yet future (Matt 23:39; Mark 8:38; 13:19–20; Luke 9:26; 13:35) and known only to the Father (Matt 24:36; Mark 13:32). Clearly, this limitation is within the realm of the Son's humanity,[7] but it demonstrates that even after his exaltation, the Father will still initiate the Son's return. Further, the Father will give justice to his elect, and this day will come "speedily" (Luke 18:7–8).[8] Peter explains that any delay is because the Lord [the Father] is patient, "not wishing that any should perish, but that all should reach repentance" (2 Pet 3:9).[9]

When that day finally comes, it is a day of salvation for God's elect. Through the second coming of his Son, the Father will resurrect the dead and transform the living (Matt 22:31–32; Mark 12:26–27; Luke 20:37–38; 1 Thess 4:14; 2 Thess 1:6–7; 2 Cor 4:14; 13:4). The Father, who started the work in his children, will bring it to a complete and perfect end at the day of Christ's glorious appearing (Phil 1:6). Furthermore, this resurrection is accomplished through the agency of his Son (John 5:21, 25). Jesus affirms this resurrection occurs on the "last day" (John 6:39), and John says seeing Jesus at his return will cause the believer's transformation: "Beloved, we are God's children now, and what we will be has not yet appeared; but we know

---

5. Hamilton, *God's Glory in Salvation through Judgment*.

6. ποιέω τὴν ἐκδίκησιν means "to vindicate," in the sense of punishing offenders and/or of rescuing those who are in trouble (cf. Acts 7:24). Here in the context, the emphasis is on the latter, but the former is implied in the fact that his elect are crying out to him to hurry.

7. Since the second century AD, Arians use these verses to demonstrate the Son's subordination to the Father. However, commentators are fairly unanimous on ascribing the limitation of omniscience to the humanity of Jesus, not his divinity. See discussion in Edwards, *Mark*, 406–8.

8. ἐν τάχει can mean "soon" or "suddenly." Here, I take it to mean soon. I. Howard Marshall's explanation from Delling is helpful: "To the elect it may seem to be a long time until he answers, but afterwards they will realise that it was in fact short (Delling, 219f.)." Marshall, *Luke*, 676.

9. κυρίῳ here is a reference to God the Father. In chaps. 2–3, when Peter wants to distinguish his use of κύριος for the Son, he uses the phrase "Lord and Savior Jesus Christ" (2:21; 3:18) and "Lord and Savior" (3:2). All other uses of κύριος refer to the Father.

that when he appears we shall be like him, because we shall see him as he is" (1 John 3:2).[10] Revelation calls it the "first resurrection," which will result in the saints becoming "priests of God and of Christ, and they will reign with him for a thousand years" (Rev 20:6).[11]

Also, as explained in chapter 4, just as the Holy Spirit is the Lord and giver of life in the first creation, it is by the Spirit that the Father, through the Son, consummates eternal life (John 6:63; 2 Cor 3:6). Paul writes in Rom 8:11, "If the Spirit of him [the Father] who raised Jesus from the dead dwells in you, he [the Father] who raised Christ Jesus from the dead will also give life to your mortal bodies through his Spirit who dwells in you." Paul is completely convinced of the Father's faithful working, therefore he tells the Philippians that he presses on "toward the goal for the prize of the upward call of God [the Father] in Christ Jesus" (Phil 3:14),[12] and to the Galatians writes, "the one who sows to the Spirit will from the Spirit reap eternal life" (Gal 6:8).[13] Thus, the Father's children will receive his gift of glorification when he sends Jesus back to the earth a second time, and the Father gives this gift through the agency of his Son and Spirit.

When that day comes, it is also a day of judgment for the ungodly. In the book of Revelation, the return of Christ is described as the "great day of [the Father and Son's] wrath" (Rev 6:16–17) and "the great day of God Almighty" (Rev 16:14).[14] Throughout the Revelation, the Father's wrath is pictured with several images, including plagues (Rev 15:1), bowls full of wrath (Rev 15:7–8; 16:1), and most notably, as a winepress.[15]

In Revelation 14:19, the "grape harvest of the earth" is thrown into the "winepress of the wrath of God."[16] In the next verse, the image changes suddenly from the treading of grapes to a military slaughter. Ladd comments, "the thought is clear: a radical judgment that crushes every vestige of evil

---

10. The ὅτι clause refers to ἐσόμεθα, not οἴδαμεν. See Marshall, *Epistles of John*, 173.

11. I take the resurrection in this passage to be physical, and thus the millennium to be a future reign of Christ on the earth after his return. See Osborne, *Revelation*, 706–7.

12. In this context, the perfect tense of the participle πείθω has a stative aspect expressing Paul's certainty and conviction. See O'Brien, *Philippians*, 63.

13. That the future aspect of eternal life is implied here, Bruce, *Galatians*, 265.

14. Throughout Scripture, it is also called the "day of the Lord" (Isa 13:6, 9; Jer 46:10; Ezek 30:3; Joel 1:15; 2:1, 11, 31; 3:14; Amos 5:18, 20; Obad 15; Zeph 1:7–8, 14; Mal 4:5; Acts 2:20; 1 Cor 5:5; 1 Thess 5:2; 2 Thess 2:2; 2 Pet 3:10); the "day of God" (2 Pet 3:12; Rev 16:14); the "day of Jesus Christ" (Phil 1:6); the "day of our Lord Jesus Christ" (1 Cor 1:8); the "day of Christ" (Phil 1:10; 2:16); "that day" (1 Thess 5:4; 2 Thess 1:10; 2:3; 2 Tim 1:12, 18; 4:8); and the "day of wrath" (Rom 2:5).

15. See Bauckham, *Theology of the Book of Revelation*, 94–98.

16. The harvest of grapes in the Old Testament is a symbol of judgment (Isa 63:2–3; Joel 3:13; cf 19:13, 15).

and hostility to the reign of God."[17] In Revelation 16 is a corresponding image where the Father forces "Babylon the great" to drink the "wine of the fury of his wrath" (Rev 16:19). Both images are combined in Revelation 19's return of the Son: "He will tread the winepress of the fury of the wrath of God the Almighty" (Rev 19:15), and in a quite graphic manner, make the unbelievers to be the "great supper of God [the Father]" for the carrion birds (Rev 19:17).[18]

In this judgment, the Father demonstrates his justice and righteousness (Rev 18:5, 8; 18:20), for these are not innocent people. They have made themselves drunk on the immorality of the "great prostitute" (Rev 17:2; 18:3), they have persecuted and killed the saints (Rev 16:6), and they refused to repent (Rev 16:9, 11, 21) or worship God the Father (Rev 9:20; 13:4, 8, 12, 15; 14:11; 16:2; 19:20). Thus, angelic testimony says, "Just are you, O Holy One, who is and who was, for you brought these judgments. . . . Yes, Lord God the Almighty, true and just are your judgments" (Rev 16:5, 7). So too the great multitude of heaven affirms, "Hallelujah! Salvation and glory and power belong to our God, for his judgments are true and just" (Rev 19:1–2). It is why the author of Hebrews speaks to their Trinitarian shaped offense:

> How much worse punishment, do you think, will be deserved by the one who has trampled underfoot the *Son of God*, and has profaned the blood of the covenant by which he was sanctified, and has outraged the *Spirit of grace*? For we know him [the Father] who said, "Vengeance is mine; I will repay." And again, "The Lord will judge his people." It is a fearful thing to fall into the hands of the *living God* [emphasis mine]. (Heb 10:29–31)

Thus, the Father will both save and judge by sending his Son a second time to save his elect and pour out his wrath upon his enemies.

In the Final Judgment, the Father Judges Righteously through the Son

On Mars Hill, Paul told the crowd, "The times of ignorance God [the Father] overlooked, but now he commands all people everywhere to repent, because he has fixed a day on which he will judge the world in righteousness by a man [Jesus] whom he has appointed; and of this he has given assurance to all by raising him from the dead" (Acts 17:31; cf. Acts 10:42). In Romans, Paul further explains that the Father judges through the agency of the Son:

17. Ladd, *Revelation*, 202.
18. Beale, *Revelation*, 965.

"on that day when, according to my gospel, God judges the secrets of men by Christ Jesus" (Rom 2:16). In this work, the Father fulfills the Messianic promise laid out in Psalm 2:6–9, where the Father has authority to grant the nations to the Son and then through whom the Father executes his judgment. He says to the Son, "Ask of me, and I will make the nations your heritage, and the ends of the earth your possession" (Ps 2:8).

Therefore, in the context of this final judgment, the Father is the final one to whom the whole world is held accountable (Rom 3:19), for he is the one who will judge the world (Rom 3:6). It is why James declares, "There is only one lawgiver and judge, he who is able to save and to destroy" (Jas 4:12; cf. Matt 10:28; Luke 12:5).[19] Consequently, with Christ as the Father's representative, all will stand before the judgment seat of the Father (Rom 14:10), give an account for their actions (Rom 14:12), and receive what they deserve (Rom 2:6–11). It is why Paul can also call it the "judgment seat of Christ" (2 Cor 5:10). Tom Schreiner explains,

> All believers will stand before God's judgment seat. The verb παραστησόμεθα (parasitēsometha, we shall stand) is a technical term for standing before a judge (Acts 27:24; Pol. Phil. 6.2; cf. BAGD 628; MM 494–95). This text also has a remarkable oscillation between Christ and God. Paul specifically mentions θεός in verse 3, while in verse 4 the κύριος is likely Christ (contra Fitzmyer 1993c: 690). Similarly, in verses 6–9 the κύριος is Christ, but those who live to the Lord give thanks to "God" (v. 6). It is surprising, given the emphasis on the lordship of Christ, that the judgment seat is God's in verse 10. It is also likely that the κύριος in the OT citation is God rather than Christ since believers stand before God's judgment seat (v. 10) and give account to God (v. 12). The alternation between God and Christ does not signal confusion on Paul's part. Instead, it demonstrates the very close relationship between them. Christ functions as God's representative in the judgment, hence judgment in Paul can be ascribed either to Christ (2 Cor. 5:10) or to God (Rom. 14:10).[20]

Because the Father's justice will be vindicated at the judgment seat (2 Thess 1:5),[21] there will be both rewards for his children and punishment for the ungodly. Jesus taught that after he returns, we will sit on his glorious throne, bring the nations before him, separating the sheep from the goats

---

19. The use of νομοθέτης with κριτής makes it a reference to the Father, who is the giver of Scripture and therefore has the authority to judge based upon its demands.

20. Schreiner, *Romans*, 722.

21. See Bruce, *1 & 2 Thessalonians*, 148.

(Matt 25:31-46; cf. 2 Tim 4:1). Concerning this time, the angelic court of Revelation 11 worships God the Father, singing to him,

> We give thanks to you, Lord God Almighty, who is and who was, for you have taken your great power and begun to reign. The nations raged, but your wrath came, and the time for the dead to be judged, and for rewarding your servants, the prophets and saints, and those who fear your name, both small and great, and for destroying the destroyers of the earth (Rev 11:17-18).[22]

This *taxis* is maintained in the handing out of the rewards. The Father initiates the rewards based upon their good works (Matt 5:12; 6:1, 4, 6, 18; Luke 6:23, 25; 1 Cor 3:14; Heb 11:6; 2 John 8), and this he does through the Son (Matt 25:34; Col 3:24). Although the Father's rewards are based upon good works, his children will have no fear of facing the Father's wrath, for the Father has already justified them by the blood of his Son (Rom 5:9). Therefore, Paul writes to the Thessalonians that they are worthy of the kingdom according to the "righteous judgment of God" (2 Thess 1:5) because they manifest perseverance and faith during suffering (2 Thess 1:4).[23]

Likewise, the *taxis* is maintained in the dispensing of punishment. The retributive justice of the Father through the Son (Matt 16:27; John 5:22, 27; 8:16) at his second coming culminates in what Revelation calls, "the great white throne" of the Father (Rev 20:11).[24] Because the wicked have no inheritance in God's kingdom (1 Cor 6:9-10; Eph 5:6; Col 3:5-6), they receive eternal punishment (Matt 25:46) described as "eternal fire" (Matt 25:41; cf. Luke 16:22-28), "unquenchable fire" (Mark 9:43, 48), and "outer darkness" (Matt 8:12; 22:13; 25:30) where they will "drink the cup of God [the Father's] wrath (Rev 14:10) and be "tormented day and night forever and ever" (Rev 20:10). It is why eternal punishment is therefore called "the second death" (Rev 20:14; 21:8). Christopher Cowan rightly concludes,

> So, the Father has given the Son authority to render judgment— a judgment that lies outside of the sphere of his earthly ministry. Therefore, even at the consummation, the Son's role as

---

22. That this is a reference to the Father is clear from the use of κύριε ὁ θεὸς ὁ παντοκράτωρ. κύριος ὁ θεός is only ever used of the Father in Revelation (Rev 1:8; 4:8; 11:17; 15:3; 16:7; 18:8; 21:22; 22:5). The clearest use is found in Revelation 21:22, where the Lord God is in distinction from the Lamb (the Son), "And I saw no temple in the city, for its temple is the Lord God the Almighty and the Lamb."

23. See Wanamaker, *Thessalonians*, 220-23.

24. Throughout the book of Revelation, the throne belongs to the Father.

judge will be one that has been delegated to him by his Father (cf. 1 Cor. 15:22–28).[25]

But what about the Holy Spirit? Although there are no specific texts that say the Holy Spirit will participate in the future judgment, a few passages hint at his potential role. For example, Isaiah 42:1 (cf. Isa 11:4–5) speaks of the Spirit-empowered Messiah who "will bring forth justice to the nations." Furthermore, those who "blaspheme the Spirit will not be forgiven . . . in this age or the age to come" (Matt 12:31–32; Mark 3:29; Luke 12:10). In the context, blasphemy against the Spirit was attributing Jesus's work to the devil rather than to God the Holy Spirit. R. T. France writes, "the juxtaposition of τὸ πνεῦμα τὸ ἅγιον with πνεῦμα ἀκάθαρτον (v. 30 [of Mark 3]) suggests that this allegation involves a total perversion of the truth and a repudiation of the rule of God."[26] Therefore, it seems that the Son judges from the throne in the power of the Holy Spirit to render justice, providing the reward of eternal life to those who are the Father's elect (cf. John 6:63), and bearing witness against those who reject the Son.

Finally, it seems that John the Baptist speaks of the Spirit's role in the final judgment when he says, "I baptize you with water for repentance, but he who is coming after me is mightier than I, whose sandals I am not worthy to carry. He will baptize you with the Holy Spirit and fire" (Matt 3:11; cf. Luke 3:16). Grant Osborne comments,

> The mention of "and fire" has caused some controversy. Some think them antithetical, with the Spirit coming on the faithful and the fire of judgment on the unfaithful. This would certainly fit the context of judgment. More and more, the two are being seen as a hendiadys ("spirit-fire"—note that one preposition introduces both, indicating that they are a unity). Still, there is a question whether the "Spirit-fire" refers to judgment or the refining fire of the Spirit. But this disjunction is unnecessary. It is best to see both nuances: those who accept the message of the kingdom are purified by the Spirit while those who reject it face judgment. Both nuances fit the OT background as well as the Judaism of Jesus' day (e.g., Qumran; cf. 1QS 4:20–21).[27]

Thus, the Spirit's role in the judgment is to be the executor of the Father's judgment through the Son, and once again, the *taxis* is affirmed.

---

25. Cowan, "Father and Son," 62–63.
26. France, *Mark*, 177.
27. Osborne, *Matthew*, 116.

As an Inheritance, the Father Gives His Kingdom to His Children

Adam was created to serve as a king, ruling over the earth, displaying the "image of God" in it, and fruitfully filling the earth with many other king-priests (Gen 1:26-28). T. Desmond Alexander concludes, "Behind these commands lies the expectation that an ever-growing human population of royal-priests will create a magnificent temple-city, which will eventually fill the earth."[28] For Adam, then, all his life was to be given over in worship of the Father as a kingdom of priests.

Because the people's service was often given over in idolatry to the worship of other gods (Deut 7:16; 2 Kgs 10:18-19, 21-23; Jer 2:20), the Father promised to send his Son to be the true worshipping king-priest who would bring in an eternal kingdom (Dan 2:44; 4:3, 34; 6:26-27; 7:14). For example, in the four "Servant Songs" of Isaiah (Isa 42:1-9; 49:1-13; 50:4-9; 52:13—53:12), the Messiah is portrayed as the ideal king–priest that Israel failed to be. Furthermore, the songs have a logical flow to them: (1) describing the Father's provision of a servant, sovereignly chosen (42:1-4)[29] and therefore effective (42:5-9),[30] (2) describing the quality of the Father's servant, without blemish (49:1-4)[31] and of infinite worth (49:5-13),[32] (3) describing the willingness of the Father's servant, without rebellion (50:4-6) and not ashamed (50:7-9), and (4) describing the Father's satisfaction with his servant, exalted for his work (52:13-15),[33] given as a penal substitutionary

---

28. Alexander, *From Paradise to Promised Land*, 126. In his footnote, he recommends Dumbrell's article, which develops the idea that Adam is a king-priest with the role of expanding Eden into a worldwide sanctuary. See Dumbrell, "Genesis 2:1-17," 53-65.

29. Young, *Isaiah*, 3:109.

30. The Father makes him an effective servant by pouring out the Spirit upon him (Isa 42:1). See Oswalt, *Isaiah*, 2:110-12.

31. Young says, "In this verse divine jealousy and exclusiveness are revealed. Idolatry may be tolerant of other religions, but the religion of the Lord is not tolerant. Worship and praise must be given to the Lord alone; it cannot be shared with idols. True religion possesses a divine exclusiveness. Yet, because glory and praise belong to God, He is able to carry through His work with the servant; were He to forfeit that which is His due alone, He would be as impotent as the graven images." Young, *Isaiah*, 3:123.

32. Seen in the fact that he is the only place of salvation not only for Israel, but for the nations as well.

33. "High . . . lifted up . . . exalted" is a trio which many link with the threefold exaltation of Jesus Christ in resurrection, ascension, and heavenly enthronement of Phil 2:9-11 and Acts 2:33.

sacrifice (53:1-6), willing to be a substitute (53:7-9),[34] and prosperous in his sacrifice (53:10-12).

Coming to the New Testament, it is no surprise then, that Jesus is the Son of Man, who "did not come to be served, but to *serve*, and to give his life a ransom for many" (Matt 20:28; cf. Mark 10:45). As the second Adam (Rom 5:12-21; 1 Cor 15:22, 45), Jesus is the perfect king-priest, who is the image of God the Father (John 1:14, 18; Col 1:15; Heb 1:3). As the true and perfect king of the universe, he will reign forever with a scepter of righteousness over the new heavens and the new earth (Matt 2:2; 27:11; Rev 19:11, 14). As a perfect high priest, he offered perfect worship through a supreme sacrifice and brought his sheep near to God the Father (Eph 5:2; 1 Tim 2:5; Heb 6:20; 9:11, 26-27; 10:12).[35] And thus, forevermore the Lamb stands alongside the Father as the one to whom all worship is due (Rev 5:13; 7:10; 21:22; 22:3).

Furthermore, just as the Holy Spirit empowers the Son to be a king-priest, he also empowers the saints to live forever as king-priests who worship the Triune God by serving the Father. As those united to Christ, the Spirit empowers new-covenant saints to be king-priests (1 Pet 2:9; Heb 10:19, 22; Rev 1:6), and as such, they share in the kingly reign of Jesus (Heb 2:5-8; Jas 2:5), since they have been raised with him in the heavenly places (Eph 2:6; cf. Rev 22:5). They also share to some degree in his authority over evil spiritual forces (Eph 6:10-11; Jas 4:7; 1 Pet 5:9; 1 John 4:4). As priests, then, the children of God will eternally worship and offer prayer to the

---

34. Oswalt says, "He is not a victim caught in the great gears of a remorseless destiny, but a person of worth and dignity even in the midst of degrading circumstances." Oswalt, *Isaiah*, 391.

35. His office of prophet is often paired with king and priest. As the perfect prophet, he is the one who most fully reveals the Father and declares his word to us (Deut 18:15; Acts 3:22-23; John 1:18; 8:28; 12:49). Interestingly, Adam could be considered the first prophet, in that he had true knowledge of God and always spoke truthfully about God and his creation until the fall. It could also be argued that one of the new-covenant blessings is that in Christ, not only are all the Father's children kings and priests, but they are also all prophets. In Num 11:29, Moses states, "I wish that all the Lord's people were prophets," (and by implication were filled with the Spirit) and in Joel 2:28-29, this blessing was predicted for the messianic age. In Acts 2:16-21, Peter declares that in the church this prophecy is now fulfilled. In Christ, every believer is led by the Holy Spirit to discern the truth (1 John 2:20, 27), and is directed to admonish with the word of Christ (Col 3:16), as well as to instruct (Rom 15:14) and encourage other believers (Heb 3:13). Because of the Spirit's indwelling ministry, every believer must read, ponder, and love the Word of God, be able to interpret it properly, and be skillful in applying it to their own questions and needs and to those around them. In the future kingdom, could it be possible that our prophetic ministry will not end? Our knowledge will then be perfect and we shall know as we are known (1 Cor 13:12). We will speak only truth about God and his world, and in us the original prophetic purpose, which God had for Adam, will be fulfilled.

Father as they behold his face and dwell in his presence (Rev 22:3–4). This means that priestly service goes beyond the scope of this age and is part of the future inheritance, so that for all eternity they will be with the Father and serve him:

> Therefore they are before the throne of God [the Father], and *serve* him day and night in his temple; and he who sits on the throne will shelter them with his presence. They shall hunger no more, neither thirst anymore; the sun shall not strike them, nor any scorching heat. For the Lamb in the midst of the throne will be their shepherd, and he will guide them to springs of living water, and God will wipe away every tear from their eyes [emphasis mine]. (Rev 7:15–17)

At the final judgment, the saints receive their reward from the Father, illustrated in the "conqueror" passages of Revelation. Through the mediation of the Son, the Father's gives his children (1) the right to eat from the tree of life (Rev 2:7; cf. Rev 22:14), (2) the crown of life so as not to be hurt by the second death (Rev 2:10–11; cf. 20:6; Jas 1:12), (3) a new status pictured by the hidden manna, a white stone, and a new name (Rev 2:17; cf. 22:4), (4) authority to rule over the nations (Rev 2:26; cf. 19:6; 22:5), (5) the white garments of righteousness (Rev 3:5; cf. 19:6–8), (6) a secure standing in the new creation (Rev 3:12; cf. 21:2, 22; 22:4), and (7) the right to sit with Christ on his throne (Rev 3:21; cf. 19:6; 22:5). These rewards point to the realities Adam enjoyed in the Garden, and thus, the inheritance of eschatological promises to restore and transform what was lost in the fall.[36]

The creation is then transformed into the new heavens and earth (2 Pet 3:13; 21:1) and the garden is transformed into the New Jerusalem (Rev 21:2, 10–11; 22:1–5).[37] There will no longer be the need for a temple, because the new creation becomes the temple (Rev 21:22).[38] The identity of the one who does this is in Rev 21:5: "And he who was seated on the throne said, 'Behold, I am making all things new.'" God the Father, once again

---

36. The removal of curse is seen in the promises of Rev 7:16, "They shall hunger no more, neither thirst anymore; the sun shall not strike them, nor any scorching heat" and Rev 21:4, "He will wipe away every tear from their eyes, and death shall be no more, neither shall there be mourning, nor crying, nor pain anymore."

37. For the Old Testament allusions to the first creation and the garden, see Due, *Created for Worship*, Ross, *Recalling the Hope of Glory*, 489–98, and Bauckham, *Theology of the Book of Revelation*, 126–43.

38. Beale notes, "In the former world everything unclean was kept away from the temple where God's presence dwelled. But there will be no uncleanness in the new world (cf. 21:27), so that the perimeters of the new temple will be able to encompass the entirety of the cosmos." Beale, *Revelation*, 1091.

through the agency of his Son (John 14:2), and by the power of his Spirit (Rom 8:20–23)[39] is the creator of the new heavens and new earth, and he makes it a place fit for his presence (Rev 21:3; cf. 7:14–17), and there his children will see the Father's face (Rev 22:4).

It is important to recognize that in Revelation 22:1, not just the Father, but all three persons of the Godhead will forever dwell among their people: "Then the angel showed me the river of the water of life [a reference to the Holy Spirit],[40] bright as crystal, flowing from the throne of God [the Father] and the Lamb." All three persons of the Godhead will manifest their love and life to the saints: "For the Lamb in the midst of the throne will be their shepherd, and he will guide them to springs of living water [the Holy Spirit], and God [the Father] will wipe away every tear from their eyes" (Rev 7:17). Thus, the saints will serve (Rev 7:15) and worship (Rev 22:3) the Father day and night forever.[41]

And yet, the final "conqueror" passage in Revelation 21:7 concludes that the reward the saints receive is God the Father himself: "The one who conquers will have this heritage, and I will be his God and he will be my son." Concerning this passage, Samuel Rico writes,

> The imagery of "living water" (ὕδωρ ζωῆς) in the Apocalype (Rev 21:7; 22:17) echoes the OT thirst motif (where God is the object of the thirst), and it echoes Jesus' thirst motif. Revelation's teaching that God is the believer's portion and inheritance and the one who satisfies the thirsty, is an echo that reverberates throughout Scripture. This echo sounds in the Torah, continues through the Prophets and Psalms, appears again in the early church, and finds its consummation in the Apocalypse.[42]

Thus, as the initiator, it is ultimately the Father who grants his kingdom to his children (Matt 13:43; 25:34; Luke 13:29; 14:15; Gal 5:21; 2 Thess 1:5; 1 Cor 6:9; 15:50; Eph 5:5), and who will make known his glorious riches to them for all eternity (Rom 9:23).

---

39. Paul connects the Spirit's ministry in Romans 8 with the new birth and the new creation, tying it back to the first creation and physical birth. Just as the Spirit is the author and giver of life in the first creation, he too is the author and giver of eternal life in the new heavens and new earth.

40. Discussed in the section below.

41. We can see the same Triune presence in the worship found at the end of Rev 5:13 since the Lamb has the Spirit *in* him (Rev 5:6).

42. Rico, "Thirsting for God," 429. In this article, Rico argues that the Levitical inheritance motif frames the background for understanding the saints' reward in the Apocalypse; namely, God himself.

God the Father as "All in All"

From the preceding discussion, an important question arises; namely, how does the eternal reign of Christ (as well as the eternal reign of the Spirit) and the eternal reign of believers relate to the eternal reign of God the Father? Craig Keener poses the problem in his article "Subordination within the Trinity" when he writes,

> In some sense the messianic king and Son of man must reign forever (Isa 9:7; Dan 7:14; Lk 1:32–33), but Jewish people also usually affirmed that God himself would reign more directly in the final time (Exod 15:18; Ps 146:10; Mic 4:7).[43]

A few passages shed some light on this relationship. In the context of his discussion on true greatness in the kingdom, Jesus tells his disciples, "You are those who have stayed with me in my trials, and I assign to you, as my Father assigned to me, a kingdom, that you may eat and drink at my table in my kingdom and sit on thrones judging the twelve tribes of Israel" (Luke 22:28–30). In v. 29, the Son confers on his disciples the right to rule, just as the Father confers on the Son the right to rule.[44] In this, the Father clearly has the initiating authority; for, on another occasion, Jesus tells his disciples "You will drink my cup [of suffering], but to sit at my right hand and at my left is not mine to grant, but it is for those for whom it has been prepared by my Father" (Matt 20:23; cf. Mark 10:40). The Son has been granted all authority (Matt 28:18) by the Father, but it does not include authority over the Father or apart from the Father's authority. In Revelation 3:21, Jesus rephrases this concept, "The one who conquers, I will grant him to sit with me on my throne, as I also conquered and sat down with my Father on his throne."

Because the Son shares the throne with his Father, Gilbert Bilezikian argues against ordering of divine authority in eternity future. Bilezikian writes,

> We discover in Scripture not only that Christ is sitting at the right hand of God but also that he is sitting at the center of God's throne. This is not an incidental reference but a heavy emphasis made especially in the book of Revelation. In Rev 3:21 Christ says, "I overcame and sat down with my Father on his throne." Only Christ may join the Father on his throne. Victorious believers are invited to become guest participants in the reign of

---

43. Keener "Subordination within the Trinity," 51. Keener references Moffat's commentary on 1 Corinthians: Moffatt, *First Corinthians*, 250.

44. "διατίθημι," in BDAG, 238.

Christ on a different throne. In 7:17 the Lamb is at the center of the throne of God. In 12:5 the Son who will rule all the nations with an iron scepter is "taken up to God and to his throne." In 22:3 we are told that there will be one throne in the heavenly Jerusalem, the eternal city of God. It is "the throne of God and of the Lamb." Contrary to Grudem's suggestion [the Son is at the right hand of the Father], God is not on the throne with the Son apart from him or below the throne in a position of subordination. According to Scripture, both God the Father and God the Son occupy the same throne for eternity. They are "equal in power and glory."[45]

I appreciate Bilezikian's concern that both the Father and Son are equal in power and glory, and in his mind, the Son forever sitting at the Father's right hand rather than fully sharing his throne undermines the Son's equal status as God. Nevertheless, the full testimony of Scripture is both that the Son reigns forever (and by implication, the Spirit) in one divine rule and monarchy, and that it is an ordered rule. Michael Ovey's recent work on the divine monarchy paves a path forward for a resolution to this tension. Ovey appeals to Augustine's various debates with the Arians and then concludes:

> Overall, we note in Augustine a real concern to preserve the biblical data, notably the asymmetry of relations between the Persons. Augustine is insistent that the Trinity is not a community of three friends, but a trinity of Father, Son and Spirit. Within this framework of relational asymmetry, he wants to preserve the Father as "beginning" (*principium*), and it is hard to miss the parallels with the Cappadocian insistence on the Father as Cause (*Aitia*).[46]

Ovey then turns to the Gospel of John and contends that this asymmetrical and co-relative relationship of Father and Son contains a deep but asymmetrical love:

---

45. Bilezikian, "Hermeneutical Bungee-Jumping," 63. In his book *Who's Tampering with the Trinity*, Millard Erickson agrees that these passages seem to contradict a uniform picture of the Son sitting at the Father's right hand. See Erickson, *Who's Tampering with the Trinity*, 114. Giles proceeds even further, arguing for an exchange of authority, "If this is the case, what Paul is teaching is that at the resurrection God the Father freely makes God the Son ruler over all, and at the end, God the Son freely gives back this rule to God the Father. Rather than speaking of fixed roles, or of an eschatological subordination of the Son, or of the demise of the Trinity, this text indicates a changing of roles in different epochs by two omnipotent divine persons." Giles, *Jesus and the Father*, 115.

46. Ovey, *Your Will Be Done*, 74.

> The Father's love is paternal in that he loves his Son and accordingly, as a father, is lavishly generous both in eternity and within time: in eternity, he gives the Son the same kind of life that he has himself, life-in-himself (uncreated life); and within the framework of created space and time he gives his Son all things in creation as his to rule over. The Son's love is filial in that he loves the Father and reveals this by his obedience to his Father and his will.[47]

For Ovey, this Trinitarian account demonstrates how other-personed love and authority between ontological equals is both possible and holy, and shows how obedience and humility are divine virtues worthy of emulation.[48] Ovey concludes,

> If there is such a divine monarchy [with *taxis*], we have to see how it is that the monarchical prerogatives of the Son are consistent rather than competitive with, or independent of, those of the Father. For it is the unity of the divine monarchy that contributes so decisively both to the certainty of salvation and also to the certainty of justice being rendered to earthly power-holders.[49]

To be clear, the Father, Son, and Holy Spirit are fully God, and therefore, all three persons possess all authority over the creation. They made the worlds (chap. 3), they providentially govern the worlds (chap. 3), they have accomplished redemption (chaps. 4–6) and they will make all things new (chap. 7). Yet within the Godhead, the Son and Spirit maintain an authority that is consistent with, rather than competitive to the initiating authority of the Father. It is with this in mind that we turn to 1 Corinthians 15:24–28.

1 Corinthians 15:20–28

In this passage, Paul provides an explanation of the Father's role in eternity future. In brief, I will argue that the Father, who put everything under the authority of his Son (1 Cor 15:27), will receive back the kingdom from Christ at the end of the age (1 Cor 15:24).[50] Even the Son will be subject to the Father (1 Cor 15:28), so that the Father will be "all in all" (1 Cor 15:28).

---

47. Ibid., 77.
48. Ibid., 115–16.
49. Ibid., 122.
50. Grosheide, *First Corinthians*, 365.

First, however, we must be clear on the meaning of "all in all" (1 Cor 15:28). For example, Barrett remarks:

> The end is that God may be all in all. "All in all," then, is to be understood in terms of Rom. 11:36; 1 Cor. 15:54-7; "soteriologically, not metaphysically" (Bachmann; cf. Knox, *Gentiles*, p. 128). It is not the absorption of Christ and mankind, with consequent loss of distinct being, into God; but rather the unchallenged reign of God alone, in his pure goodness.[51]

Therefore, many commentators conclude that ἐν πᾶσιν is most likely neuter plural ("all in all") rather than masculine plural ("everything to everyone").[52] Thus, "all in all," points to the final supremacy of θεός.

This leads us naturally to the use of θεός in this passage, particularly in v. 28. Since at least the time of Augustine, theologians have understood θεός here to be a reference to the Trinity.[53] For example, Lenski writes, "From that moment onward ὁ Θεός, the Triune God in all three persons conjointly, one God, shall stand supreme amid glorified humanity in the new heaven and the new earth."[54] If θεός is a reference to the Trinity, then these verses must be describing Jesus in his humanity handing over the kingdom to the Godhead. Dahms gives a historical summary:

> Marcellus of Ancyra (died c. 374) interpreted the passage to mean that "the Son represents a temporal, revelational interim" [G. C. Berkouwer, *The Return of Christ* (Grand Rapids: Eerdmans, 1972) 430]. For him, only the Logos is eternal. "The Son of God" refers only to the incarnate Logos. Augustine held that "in so far as he is God" he is not put under the Father, but in so far as he is a man, a servant and a priest, "he with us will be put under him" [Augustine, *On the Trinity*, 1.10–11]. John Calvin asserted that the subjection of the Son will be "in respect of his human nature." "Christ's humanity will then no longer be interposed to keep us back from a closer view of God." He will not "resign the kingdom, but will transfer it in a manner from his humanity to his glorious divinity" [John Calvin, *Commentary on the Epistles of Paul the Apostle to the Corinthians* (Grand Rapids: Eerdmans,

---

51. Barrett, *First Corinthians*, 361.

52. See Ciampa and Rosner, *First Corinthians*, 779; Ellingworth, *First Corinthians*, 350; Thiselton, *First Corinthians*, 1239.

53. Augustine's, *On the Trinity* ends with the acclamation of "the one God, the Trinity," as he who remains "all in all." See Augustine, *On the Trinity*, 15.28.51.

54. Lenski, *First and Second Corinthians*, 686. More recently, see Erickson, *Who's Tampering with the Trinity*, 249; cf. also page 136–38 and 164–65; and Belleville, "'Son' Christology," 69–70.

1948) 2.26, 32–33] C. Hodge advances the interpretation that "the subjection here spoken of is not predicated of the eternal Logos, the second person of the Trinity. . . . The word *Son* here designate(s), not the Logos as such, but the Logos as incarnate. . . . It is not the subjection of the Son as Son, but of the Son as Theanthropos [emphasis original]" [Charles Hodge, *An Exposition of the First Epistle to the Corinthians* (Grand Rapids Eerdmans, 1959), 333–34].[55]

In chapter 2, I argued against θεός as a reference to the Trinity, but the argument bears repeating. First, if θεός here were a reference to the full Trinitarian God, it would be the only usage in the entire Pauline corpus.[56] As a divine proper name, θεός customarily refers to the Father and exceptionally refers to the Son or Holy Spirit. Furthermore, the implied personal and relative pronouns (in the masculine singular) in 1 Corinthians 15:24–28 argue that θεός is a reference to the Father: (1) the implied subject of the verb θῇ (v. 25) is identified as the implied subject of ὑπέταξεν (v. 27), both of which are taken from Psalm 110 where the Father puts the Messiah's enemies under his feet, (2) the subject of the verbless clause ἐκτὸς (v. 27) and the participle τοῦ ὑποτάξαντος is God the Father, for it is clear that the Father is not subject to Christ, (3) the implied subject of the participle τῷ ὑποτάξαντι (v. 28) is the Father, consistently arguing in these verses that the Father puts all things in subjection under the Son. Therefore, the referent to these pronouns is identified as θεός of v. 28, who is the Father.

If the person of the Son (ὁ υἱὸς, v. 28) gives up the kingdom to the person of the Father, then is it only in his human nature as the Davidic Messiah, or does it also include his divine nature as the second person of the Godhead? In the context, Paul is quoting from Psalm 110 (v. 25) and Psalm 8 (v. 27), where the Davidic king rules God's kingdom as regent.[57] Also, Paul uses the terminology Χριστός, arguing that he is the second Adam (vv. 22–23). So, at the very least, Paul is speaking of the man Jesus. Nevertheless, as James Hamilton argues in his recent article,

> Paul does not appear to be discussing the difference between the human Jesus and the divine Jesus, nor is he making a statement

55. Dahms, "Subordination of the Son," 352.

56. See chap. 1 of Harris, *Jesus as God*. After studying all the uses of θεός in the Septuagint, extra-biblical literature, and the New Testament, he concludes, "When (ὁ) θεός is used, we are to assume that the NT writers have ὁ πατήρ in mind unless the context makes this sense of (ὁ) θεός impossible (47). On the footnote to this sentence he writes, "In the NT θεός regularly refers to the Father alone and apparently never to the Trinity (47n112).

57. Beale and Carson, *New Testament Use of the Old Testament*, 745–46.

about how all three members of the Trinity are involved in everything one member does. He is discussing the order of the events at the end and the way that Christ "must reign until he has put all his enemies under his feet" (1 Cor. 15:25).[58]

Furthermore, Hamilton argues, the statement that the Son will be "subjected" to the Father (v. 28) must be understood in light of the statement in 15:27 that the Father will not be subject to the Son.[59] He summarizes,

> There is a way of talking about these realities that both upholds orthodoxy and accounts for everything the text says, but it is a way that Giles is not willing to grant: in what they are, Christ and the Father are ontologically equal; in what they do, Christ is functionally subordinate to the Father. The Arians would not have affirmed ontological equality.[60]

Thus, Hamilton is summarizing the asymmetrical nature of the eternal *taxis* consistent with inseparable operations. The Father will, for all eternity, be the initiator of the one work of divine rule.

Finally, the use of αὐτὸς ὁ υἱὸς ("the Son himself," v. 28) is theologically significant. The absolute use of the title without any genitival modifiers is used only here in the writings of Paul.[61] Ciampa and Rosner, in their commentary, explain the significance:

> Since the language of "Father" and "Son" is covenantal language, it reminds us that the Son's role in the biblical and covenantal meta-narrative was always that of restoring and reflecting the glorious reign of the Father over all of his dominion. Paul simply takes us to the ultimate conclusion of the biblical narrative of redemption and restoration, which is that the creation which went astray and which the Son was commissioned to redeem and restore has come full circle to its complete submission to God—and beyond. But it was always about bringing creation to perfect submission to God. . . . This verse does not demean or marginalize Christ, but emphasizes that his mission will be fully and perfectly accomplished.[62]

Thus, the person of the Son, as the God-man, hands over his kingdom to the Father at the end, not in an absolute sense, such that his sovereignty

---

58. Hamilton, "That God May Be All in All," 100.
59. Ibid., 101.
60. Ibid., 106.
61. Garland, *1 Corinthians*, 713.
62. Ciampa and Rosner, *First Corinthians*, 778.

is temporary, rather with the idea that for all eternity the Father (with the Son and Spirit alongside him) will reign over the new creation. John Frame concludes,

> As the servant of God, who remains eternally man as well as God, Jesus demonstrates his obedience by subjecting himself and his kingdom to the headship of God the Father.[63]

Revelation provides further evidence.

Revelation 11:15–19

At the end of the age, "The kingdom of the world has become the kingdom of our Lord and of his Christ, and he shall reign forever and ever" (Rev 11:15). Beale notes the implications of the passage:

> It is not clear whether it is "our Lord" or "his Christ" who "will reign forever and ever." It may well be that "the singular comprehends God and his Christ as an inseparable unity" (for the same phenomenon see on 22:3). But vv 16–17 show that it is the Lord whose eternal reign is focused on here (5:12–13, like Luke 1:33, shows that the Lamb shares in this endless rule, and therefore would be included here). The consummated fulfillment of the long-awaited messianic kingdom prophesied in the OT finally has come to pass (12:10 makes the same point). It is difficult to say how Christ's delivering up the kingdom to the Father and subjecting himself to the Father at the consummation in 1 Cor. 15:24–28 relates to the present text. Perhaps Christ gives up the redemptive-historical phase of his rule and then assumes an eternal rule alongside but in subjection to his Father.[64]

Rather than seeing the singular subject as a comprehensive term for both the Father and the Son, it is better to understand the singular subject to be κύριος. That the Messiah will reign with the Father is implicit, for the throne where the Lamb sits is ultimately the Father's throne.[65] As Ladd says, "Even if the immediate agent is the Messiah, the kingdom is still God's rule; and the subject of 'he shall reign for ever and ever' is God."[66] It is also made clear in vv. 16 and 17 where the heavenly court falls down and worships God the Father saying, "We give thanks to you, Lord God Almighty, who is

---

63. Frame, *Doctrine of God*, 683.
64. Beale, *Revelation*, 611.
65. See Bratcher and Hatton, *Handbook on Revelation*, 176.
66. Ladd, *Revelation*, 161–62.

and who was, for you have taken your great power and begun to reign." The phrase "Lord God Almighty" or "Lord God" is only ever used of the Father in the book of Revelation (Rev 1:8; 4:8; 11:17; 15:3; 16:7; 18:8; 21:22; 22:5) with its clearest use in Revelation 21:22 where the Father is distinguished from the "Lamb." It says, "And I saw no temple in the city, for its temple is the Lord God the Almighty and the Lamb."

Furthermore, the kingdom of God the Father is the driving goal of the book (Rev 1:6, 9; 5:10; 11:17; 12:10; 19:6; 20:4). Finally, in Revelation 22:5, the kingdom is given to the saints to rule over with authority: "And night will be no more. They will need no light of lamp or sun, for the Lord God will be their light, and they will reign forever and ever." Thus, the eternal reign of believers is ultimately under the eternal reign of the Triune God, with the Father initiating the eternal work of divine rule.

Revelation 22:1–5

Revelation 22:1 paints a beautiful picture of this eternal *taxis*: "Then the angel showed me the river of the water of life [the Spirit], bright as crystal, flowing from the throne of God [the Father] and the Lamb [the Son]." The throne in Revelation is the place of authority, and here we see all three persons of the Godhead revealing themselves from that throne. The first is the Holy Spirit, pictured as living water flowing from the Father and Son. An ancient picture from the days of the new covenant promised in Ezekiel (Ezek 36:25–27), John 7:37–39 makes clear that "living waters are a reference to the Holy Spirit (cf. John 3:5; 4:10–24; 1 John 5:7–8 where water is symbolically tied to the Spirit). This would mean that John used the same imagery for the Trinity earlier in the book of Revelation: "For the Lamb in the midst of the throne will be their shepherd, and he will guide them to springs of living water [the Holy Spirit], and God [the Father] will wipe away every tear from their eyes" (Rev 7:17).

In both passages, the Spirit is the giver of life. Revelation 22:2 continues this theme for the river provides nourishment, watering the "tree of life," whose leaves are for "the healing of the nations," and gives sense to the Spirit's appeal of 22:17, "The Spirit and the Bride say, 'Come.' And let the one who hears say, 'Come.' And let the one who is thirsty come; let the one who desires take the water of life without price." For all eternity, the Spirit appeals to the saints to come and drink fully of him, partake of him, and be filled by him, so that they might serve, worship, and reign as king-priests in the kingdom (22:5).

As to the Lamb sharing the throne with the Father (22:1), Hamilton's insight is instructive:

> Here the reference to God is clearly a reference to the Father, and the reference to the Lamb is likewise a reference to Jesus. This would indicate that the *role* of Christ as the Redeemer remains relevant in eternity future. . . . Both are God, as 22:3 speaks in the singular of *his* servants worshipping *him*, referring back to both God and the Lamb. And yet the hierarchy and roles seen from Revelation 4–5, where the Lamb approached the one on the throne, remain in that depiction of the new heaven and new earth. So it would seem natural to conclude that by continuing to depict Jesus as the Lamb in Revelation 22:3, John is saying in a different way what Paul said in 1 Corinthians 15:24 and 28—that Christ has rendered the kingdom to the Father and been subjected to him. Thus, Christ's kingdom is everlasting, but he reigns in the kingdom he has delivered to the Father, in which he is subject to the Father.[67]

Thus, the divine work of eternal rule will be exercised by Father, Son and Spirit for all eternity, and it will reflect the eternal *taxis*: rule initiated by the Father, accomplished through the Son, and perfected by the Spirit.

Conclusion

This chapter has argued that the Father initiates all work necessary to consummate the ages, from the sending of his Son a second time to bring salvation through judgment, in judging both the saints and the ungodly through the agency of his Son and Spirit, in providing the saints their inheritance of a kingdom, and in the eternal rule of the divine monarchy. In no way does the Father's initiating role attack the equal glory and coeternal majesty of the Son and Spirit, for they share full unity in regard to the divine name, nature and actions.

The Father's role of initiator is also understood through the use of κράτος in the doxologies of the New Testament. In 1 Timothy 6:15–16, Paul reminds Timothy that the Father will display the appearing of the Lord Jesus at the proper time because the Father is "the blessed and only Sovereign, the King of kings and Lord of lords, who alone has immortality, who dwells in unapproachable light, whom no one has ever seen or can see. To him be honor and eternal dominion [κράτος]. Amen." Peter affirms the same in 1 Peter 5:10–11. After a little suffering, the Father, "who has called you to

---

67. Hamilton, "That God May Be All in All," 107.

his eternal glory in Christ, will himself restore, confirm, strengthen, and establish you. To him [the Father] be the dominion [κράτος] forever and ever. Amen." Finally, Jude 24–25, "Now to him [the Father] who is able to keep you from stumbling and to present you blameless before the presence of his glory with great joy, to the only God, our Savior, through Jesus Christ our Lord, be glory, majesty, dominion [κράτος], and authority [ἐξουσία], before all time and now and forever. Amen."

As the next chapter will show, these doxologies do not mean that the Father will receive *more* glory than the Son or Spirit. Rather, the glory due the Triune God is consistent with the eternal *taxis*. Just as all divine works come from the Father through the Son by the Spirit, the response of worship corresponds to that *taxis*: by the Spirit through the Son to the Father. Therefore, just as all divine work begins with the Father (in order, not in time), all worship terminates with him (not to the exclusion or detriment of the Son and Spirit), which is why, for all eternity future, the Father will, through the work of the Spirit in his children, showcase his Son as glorious. Paul elegantly captures this in Ephesians 2:7, "in the coming ages he [the Father] might show the immeasurable riches of his grace in kindness toward us in Christ Jesus." As the successive ages of eternity future roll on like waves on a seashore, the Father will, by the indwelling Spirit, continually be showing his children the extraordinary riches of his grace, which have been purposed from eternity past in his kind intentions, and which find their revelation in his Son.

8

Worship as a Response to the Father's Work through the Son and Spirit

Introduction

THE FATHER, SON, AND Spirit are glorious, and they love their glory with infinite passion (Exod 15:11; Isa 48:9–11).[1] More specifically, their glory consists in the awesome and abundant beauty that emanates from the sum total of all their attributes working together in perfect accord.[2] In other words, all divine work is for the sake of their divine name (Ezek 36:20–23; Ps 115:1): both creation (Ps 19:1; Isa 43:7, 21) and redemption glorifies the Triune God (Eph 1:5–6, 12, 14), for the indwelling Spirit through union with Christ empowers the Father's children to live for the "glory of God," both individually (1 Cor 10:31; 1 Pet 4:11) and corporately (Eph 3:10); and the ultimate goal in the new heavens and earth is for the redeemed to see and enjoy the glory of the Triune God forever (Hab 2:14; Rev 22:3–5).[3]

---

1. In response to the question, why did God create the world, and how is mankind to join him in fulfilling that end, Jonathan Edwards wrote his important and unrivaled work, *A Dissertation Concerning the End for Which God Created the World*. In it, he argues that first, the internal (intrinsic) glory of God might be magnified in all of creation, and second, that all the Father's elect would rejoice in God above everything (ascribed glory). Jonathan Edwards, *Works*, 8:404–63.

2. For a brief, but thorough, biblical theology of "glory," see Gaffin, "Glory," in *New Dictionary of Biblical Theology*, 507–11.

3. It is important to see the contrast between the intrinsic glory that the Triune God has possessed from all eternity and the ascribed glory that is due him for creation and redemption. This is clear in John 17:4–5 where in v. 4, all the works of Jesus bring ascribed glory to the Father, whereas in v. 5, Jesus desires to be glorified with the intrinsic glory he had with the Father before the world existed. For a good discussion of this contrast, see Carson, *John*, 556–57. The Spirit's intrinsic glory is not explicitly mentioned; however, in the book of Revelation, as the "seven spirits" (Rev 1:4), he is intimately tied to "the one who sits on the throne," and as the "seven horns and seven eyes" (Rev 5:6), he is intimately connected to "the Lamb." For a thorough discussion of the Spirit in the book of Revelation, see Bauckham, *Theology of the Book of Revelation*, 109–25.

Nevertheless, a God who is not known cannot be worshipped, and thus any discussion surrounding worship requires a number of explanatory assertions. First, it is necessary for God to reveal himself to his people. Paul, writing to the Corinthians, assumes that the world cannot know God through their own wisdom (1 Cor 1:21). God the Father, then, takes the initiative both to seek worshippers (John 4:23) and to draw them to himself (1 Pet 2:9–10). The Father accomplishes this through the ministries of his Son (John 1:18; 6:44, 65; 2 Cor 4:3–4) and his Spirit (1 Cor 2:14).

Second, as discussed in chapter 4, in God's self-revelation there is a need to distinguish between his transcendence and his immanence, while also articulating their relationship to one another. The transcendence and immanence of the Triune God is not only that of location (in heaven and on earth respectively). God's transcendence is a reference to his eminent position as sovereign and king (Ps 113:1–4),[4] and his immanence is tied to his intimate involvement in his creation, especially with his children (Ps 113:5–9).[5] Thus, transcendence and immanence are relationship terms: the self-sufficient transcendent God is also the one who has, in his immanence, drawn near to his children, so that they can draw near to him.

Third, and most important for our discussion, the Father cannot be known apart from his Trinitarian role among and relationships to his Son and Spirit. I have argued that God exists eternally as three distinct, yet inseparable persons known to us as the Father, the Son, and the Holy Spirit, who are one regarding the divine name, the divine nature and divine action. Nevertheless, a consistent Trinitarian *taxis* exists among the persons of the Godhead, such that the Father occupies the first place within the operational ordering of the personal names (e.g., Father-Son-Spirit). The Father also holds the first position of relational order among the divine persons (e.g., unbegotten, eternal generation, eternal procession). This means that the distinct personal appropriations of the Father within the inseparable operations of divine action are always as the initiator. The Father is the master designer and architect of the ages (chap. 3), and through the Son and Spirit makes creation (chap. 4) the stage upon which he placards the gospel story of salvation. The Father purposed this in eternity past (chap. 3), revealed it in the sending of the Son and Spirit (chaps. 5–6), and will complete it in the eternal state through the Son and Spirit (chap. 7). These realities establish a robust Paterology that have argued for my claim that the Father is the initiator of all divine activity.

---

4. See chap. 7 of Frame, *Doctrine of God*.
5. See Zemek, "Grandeur and Grace," 129–48.

Furthermore, it is this Trinitarian *taxis* that informs our worship. For example, defending against the charge of Arianism, Basil the Great, in *On the Holy Spirit*, describes his Trinitarian devotion with two phrases: "Glory to the Father through [διά] the Son in [ἐν] the Holy Spirit," (worship of God as revealed in Creation) and "Glory to the Father with [μετά] the Son together with [σύν] the Holy Spirit" (worship of God in Godself—*en se*). Both are necessary in order to balance the equality of the divine persons while still worshiping each in their proper order. Therefore, the gospel message of redemption comes *from* the Father *through* the Son *in* the power of the Holy Spirit, and our response must correspond to that *taxis*: to the praise of the Father's glory (Eph 1:3–14), through union with the Son and in praise of his atoning work at the cross (Phil 2:9–11), by the empowering, indwelling ministry of the Holy Spirit (Phil 3:3).[6] Note Paul's careful use of prepositions in Eph 2:18: "For *through* him [Jesus] we both have access *in* one Spirit *to* the Father [emphasis mine]."

Letham argues, however, "Trinity has in practice been relegated to such an extent that most Christians are little more than practical modalists."[7] Giving examples from current hymnody, Letham concludes that general theistic worship is deficient worship.[8] As a remedy, Tom Smail, in his book *The Forgotten Father*, speaks to the necessity of the *taxis* for worship. He writes,

> It [the gospel] is not first a Jesuology (a doctrine about Jesus) or a pneumatology (a doctrine about the Spirit) but it is a theology or even a patrology—a doctrine about God the Father. It starts not with the cross of Jesus or with the gift of the Spirit, but with the Father who so loved the world that he gave his Son in his Spirit. And it achieves its purpose, not when the body of Christ is gloriously renewed in every part without spot or wrinkle (Ephesians 5.27), not even when the enthroned Christ has subdued all his enemies and brought every knee to bow before him (Philippians 2.11), but rather when that same Christ "hands over the kingdom to God the Father, after he has destroyed all dominion, authority, and power" (I Corinthians 15.24). "When he has done this, then the Son will himself be made subject to

---

6. Ware argues for this Trinitarian *taxis* in worship. See Ware, "Christian Worship and Taxis," 28–42. For a book-length study of worship with Trinitarian taxis in mind, see Parry, *Worshipping Trinity*.

7. Letham, *Holy Trinity*, 407. See also Torrance, *Worship*, 19–41.

8. Letham, *Holy Trinity*, 421–22.

him who put everything under him, so that God may be all in all" (I Corinthians 15.28).[9]

Smail's diagnosis is further exacerbated by worship definitions that are either too narrow or too nonspecific.[10] Definitions of worship, such as Hustad's, then are delightfully refreshing: "Christian worship is the affirming, transforming response of human beings to God's self-revealing and self-giving, through Jesus Christ, in the power of the Holy Spirit."[11] His definition includes worship as a response and worship within a Trinitarian structure. However, because worship also shapes our spirituality,[12] it is necessary to integrate the mind (understanding), heart (inward affections), and body (outward behavior) into the definition. Accordingly, Torrance writes,

> Christian worship is, therefore, our participation through the Spirit in the Son's communion with the Father, in his vicarious life of worship and intercession. It is our response to our Father for all that he has done for us in Christ. It is our self-offering in body, mind and spirit, in response to the one true offering made for us in Christ, our response of gratitude (*eucharistia*) to God's

---

9. Smail, *Forgotten Father*, 20. Christ-centeredness has become a *shibboleth* among certain evangelical circles and has, sadly, become Christomonism apart from the Father or Spirit. It is often measured by how often Jesus Christ is mentioned rather than in the context of the Father's desire to make the Son the direct object of the church's worship and to sum up all things in him as his Messiah, and therefore the Father sent the Spirit to bear witness to this reality.

10. For some, worship is synonymous with music in the corporate gathering or is the formalized liturgy. For others, worship is defined merely as a feeling of veneration or adoration or simply a response to who God is, what he says, and what he does. For a discussion on the difficulty of defining worship and why some definitions are inferior, see Oliver, "Development and Evaluation of Worship Theology," 19–36. I was in the first worship class he taught at The Cornerstone Seminary in Vallejo, while he was developing the research for his dissertation, and am indebted to him for a number of emphases in this chapter, particularly the importance of "remembrance" discussed below.

11. Hustad, *True Worship*, 272. Hustad's definition is an expansion of Evelyn Underhill's: "The total adoring response of man to the one Eternal God self-revealed in time," in Underhill, *Worship*, 61.

12. By this I mean living a Spirit-directed life in both understanding and experience within the context of Scripture, e.g. Gal 2:20. McClendon's definition is helpful: "Biblical spirituality seeks to ground one's understanding and experience in the normative standard of God's Word. Biblical spirituality is anchored in the belief that the biblical text is foundational to the Christian life. Scripture is not to be subjected to or brought on par with one's personal subjective knowledge of or experience with God. Thus, the Bible should be used to shape and correct one's cultural understanding and expression of the Christian faith." McClendon, "Galatians 2:20," 3.

grace (*charis*), our sharing by grace in the heavenly intercession of Christ.[13]

Finally, due to the biblical language of both the Old and New Testament, it is necessary to add the concepts of remembrance, submission, and service into the definition,[14] noting that there is a proper order of remembrance › submission › service. Thus, this chapter will examine worship of the Father as a proper response to his works by considering the following definition:

> Worship is the Spirit-illumined calling of the saints to *remember* the greatness and goodness of God the Father in the face of Jesus Christ so that they will cultivate Spirit-wrought *submission* in their hearts that draws them near to the Father through lordship of the Son so that, in turn, they may be commissioned to use their lives in Spirit-empowered *service* for the glory of Christ, to the praise of the Father.

In doing so, I will argue that the eternal *taxis* in the Godhead complements and reflects the *taxis* of worship that is due our Triune God.

The Spirit-Illumined Calling of the Saints to *Remember* the Greatness and Goodness of God the Father in the Face of Jesus Christ

Remembrance is a key theme in worship and, biblically speaking, is not for its own sake as a mental exercise, but rather to effect an appropriate external action.[15] Furthermore, the concept of remembrance is reflected in the biblical words "meditate," "know," "lay something upon the heart," and "do not forget." Merrill, in his important article on the subject, argues, "Every word of praise, every petition, every act of ritual and ceremony, every obedient work—all these are worship and all are triggered by remembrance and depend on remembrance, if they are to be carried on into the future as part of the living tradition and mission of the Church."[16]

---

13. Torrance, *Worship*, 15.

14. See Oliver, "Development and Evaluation of Worship Theology," 36–51.

15. For Old Testament usage, see Eising, "זָכַר" in *TDOT*, 4:64–82, and Yamauchi, "זָכַר" in *TWOT*, 1:241-43. In the New Testament, see Michel, "μιμνῄσκομαι," in *TDNT*, 675.

16. Merrill, "Remembering," 36.

All Worship Terminates with the Father

The Father initiated worship when he made man, and even after the fall, the Father is committed to seeking worshippers (John 4:23). The Old Testament narrative ties this to the Father's own "remembering."[17] He remembers (זָכַר) his covenants "with every living creature" (Gen 9:15–16) and with his chosen people (Exod 2:24; 6:5; Lev 26:42, 45; Deut 4:31; Pss 98:3; 105:8; 106:45; 111:5; 115:12; Ezek 16:60).[18] In return, the Father expects his name to be remembered as a part of his covenant people's regular worship. Ralston says,

> The prerequisite of covenant relationship with God introduces a third concept: "remember" *(zakar* and *mimneskomai).* A central theme of Old Testament covenant, it views a covenant relationship in three directions simultaneously. Looking to the past, one recalls the covenant's inauguration, keeping in mind the nature of the relationship, its promises, and stipulations. In the present, it asks if the covenant responsibilities are being fulfilled and demands integrity of both parties. In the future, it anticipates God's unfulfilled covenant promises and confidently expects their blessings. Remembrance permeates all Old Testament worship institutions, both seasonal (Exodus 13:3, 9) and Sabbath (Exodus 20:8). When tied to an action, it denotes an obligatory act of consecration to be repeated as a center of the gathering of God's people. Conversely, when one "forgets," the relationship has been forfeited by a failure by one party to fulfill their part of the covenant.[19]

Thus, in the Pentateuch, the Father ties his blessing to their remembrance of him (Exod 20:24), and the Passover feast was to be a remembrance of God's deliverance out of Egypt (Exod 12:14), and as the manifestation of his greatness (who he is) and goodness (what he has done), it was to

---

17. In chap. 2, I noted every NT use of the OT where the names *Elohim, Yahweh,* and *Adonai* (when it is a divine name) refer to God the Father. I am assuming that the pattern found in the NT use of the OT is consistent with the passages I use that are not quoted in the New Testament. Therefore, it is most appropriate when we read about God in the Old Testament and the second or third person is not explicitly identified through New Testament revelation, that we should have God the Father in mind. In this context, in particular, it is the covenant keeping one who is the God of Abraham and Isaac and Jacob, who Jesus identifies in the NT as the 1st person of the Trinity (Matt 22:32; Mark 12:26; Luke 20:37; cf. Acts 3:13; 7:32; Jas 2:23).

18. Likewise, the prayers of the Old Testament saints were often for God not to forget his covenant with his people (Judg 9:2; 16:28; 1 Sam 1:11; 2 Kings 20:3; 2 Chr 6:42; Neh 5:19; 13:14, 31; Pss 25:6; 89:50; 106:4; 119:49; 132:1; Isa 38:3; Jer 14:21; Lam 5:1). For an in-depth study of God remembering, see Merrill, "Remembering," 30–32.

19. Ralston, "'Remember' and Worship," 80.

be the high point on the calendar for personal and corporate worship.[20] In the historical narratives, remembrance as worship is seen on three general occasions: (1) the setting up of stones as altars (Josh 8:30-35; 22:34) or "stones of remembrance" (Josh 4:1-9; 1 Sam 4:1; 1 Sam 7:12), (2) the giving of farewell speeches (Deut 33; Josh 23:1-16; 1 Sam 12:6-18), and (3) the offering of dedications (1 Kgs 8:1-65).[21] In the Psalms (the songbook of Israel's corporate worship) remembrance permeates the people's praise for God's covenant love (חֶסֶד), and is with those who remember his precepts (Ps 103:17-18).[22] Furthermore, remembrance demands submission and undivided loyalty (Ps 22:27-28), and obedience naturally flows from remembrance (Ps 119:55). Finally, in the prophets, remembrance is tied to the greatness of who God is (Isa 46:8-9; Jonah 2:7) and the goodness of what he has done (Isa 63:7; Zech 10:9).

Several Old Testament words related to worship circle around the orbit of remembrance. Regarding נָגַד (*nagad*), the people were to "make known" God's excellencies before their brethren (Ps 145:4). In turn, they were then to "declare" his glory to the nations (Isa 66:19).[23] Regarding הָלַל (*halal*), the people were to be deeply thankful and satisfied in the greatness and goodness of who God is and what he has done for his people (e.g., Ps 105). In 1 Chronicles 16:4 it says David "appointed some of the Levites as ministers before the ark of the Lord, to invoke [*zakar*], to thank [יָדָה *yada*], and to praise [*halal*] the Lord, the God of Israel."[24]

Turning to the New Testament use of the Old Testament, the evidence becomes even more apparent: all worship terminates with God the Father. Paul, reflecting on Abraham's faith, says that as Abraham remembered the promises of God the Father, rather than wavering, his faith grew stronger (Rom 4:20), causing him to respond by giving glory to God the Father.[25] Paul later reflects on the Father's purpose for Pharaoh's oppression of Israel: "For this very purpose I have raised you up, that I might show my power in

---

20. See Vickers, "The Lord's Supper," 319-21.

21. See Pierce, *Enthroned on Our Praise*, 112-18.

22. See Hyde, "Remembrance of the Exodus in the Psalms," 404-14.

23. *"nagad,"* in these contexts is in the hiphil stem and gives the sense of presenting God prominently or meaningfully before someone. See *HALOT*, 666.

24. From these two passages, a number of synonyms emerge as a worshipful remembrance of God: רָנַן *ranan* "to cry out, shout for joy," שִׁיר *shir* "to sing," בָּרַךְ *barak* "to kneel, bless, praise," גָּדַל *gadal* "to praise, magnify," רוּם *rum* "to exalt," זָמַר *zamar* "to sing, sing praise, make music," and יָדָה *yada* "to praise, give thanks."

25. The dative τῇ πίστει is most like a dative of reference, rather than a dative of cause or means. It is not that he grew strong because of faith, but rather it was his faith that grew strong. See discussion in Moo, *Romans*, 285-86.

you, and that my name might be proclaimed [in a way to be remembered] in all the earth" (Rom 9:17). Paul, in thinking of his own people, says they have a praiseworthy devotion ("zeal") for God, but not according to real, practical knowledge (Rom 10:2).

Jesus' indictment is just as severe: "You hypocrites! Well did Isaiah prophesy of you, when he said: 'This people honors me [the Father] with their lips, but their heart is far from me; in vain do they worship me, teaching as doctrines the commandments of men" (Matt 15:7–9; cf. Mark 7:6–7; Isa 29:13). That Jesus has the Father in mind is clear from the earlier context of Matthew 15, when he accuses the Pharisees and scribes of breaking the commandment of "God" (Matt 15:3). The Thessalonians were commended for their faith in the Father (1 Thess 1:8; 2:13). The Corinthians were urged to be reconciled to the Father (2 Cor 5:20) and not receive the Father's grace in vain (2 Cor 6:1). Paul, himself, was continually taught to hope in the Father and not rely on himself. He writes, "Indeed, we felt that we had received the sentence of death. But that was to make us rely not on ourselves but on God [the Father] who raises the dead. He delivered us from such a deadly peril, and he will deliver us. On him we have set our hope that he will deliver us again" (2 Cor 1:9–10). Thus, to truly know and honor God the Father by remembering his greatness and goodness is to obey his commands, and many of those are summed up in believing the Father's promises regarding his Messiah (cf. Heb 10:23; 37–38; 11:4–7, 10–11, 19, 25, 27; 1 Pet 1:21).

The Father Reveals Himself through the Son and Thus Makes His Son the Direct Object of the Church's Worship

Although the Father is the focus for all of worship, to worship him to the exclusion of the Son is to fall into the same error as Paul's Jewish countrymen. Don Carson makes a strong case that *Christian* worship is no less Christ-centered than God-centered:

> The set purpose of the Father is that all should honor the Son even as they honor the Father (John 5:23). Since the eternal Word became flesh (John 1:14), since the fullness of Deity lives in Christ in bodily form (Col 2:9), since in the light of Jesus' astonishing obedience (even unto death!) God has exalted him and given him "the name that is above every name, that at the name of Jesus every knee should bow, in heaven and on earth and under the earth" (Phil 2:9–10), and since the resurrected Jesus quietly accepted Thomas's reverent and worshiping words, "My Lord and my God!" (John 20:28), contemporary Christians

follow the example of the first generation of believers and worship Jesus without hesitation.[26]

Andrew Fuller agrees when he writes, "A jealousy for the honour of the Father, at the expense of that of the Son, was the error and overthrow of the Jewish nation."[27] The Father desired to manifest his presence and glory through the Son, not apart from him. In John 1:18, John first states a truth about the Father, "No one has ever seen God [the Father]," and then affirms a truth about the Son's incarnation, "The only God, who is at the Father's side, he has made [the Father] known." Previously, in v. 14, John had identified what it was that the Son made known; namely, the Father's glory.[28] Thus, the Father, sends the eternal Son to become the incarnate Son in order to reveal a true knowledge of himself and thereby give eternal life to his adopted sons, so that they in turn will remember him.

This means that the concept of remembrance in the New Testament must have greater precision. Remembrance in the New Testament is remembering the greatness and goodness of God the Father, particularly in the person and work of his Son, Jesus Christ. It is also why it is proper to say that Christ is the direct object of the church's worship, and why corporate worship ought to include a rehearsal of the gospel for the purpose of remembrance.[29] Paul understands that good doctrine produces good doxology, and so concludes Romans with the words,

> Now to him who is able to strengthen you according to my gospel and the preaching of Jesus Christ, according to the revelation of the mystery that was kept secret for long ages but has now been disclosed and through the prophetic writings has been made known to all nations, according to the command of the eternal God, to bring about the obedience of faith—to the only wise God be glory forevermore through Jesus Christ! Amen. (Rom 16:25–27)

Even at the beginning of the Son's incarnation, those who saw him were led to praise the Father, and Luke records several these encounters for us. First is Mary, who "magnifies the Lord" and "rejoices in God [her] Savior"

---

26. Carson, *Worship by the Book*, 41.

27. Fuller, *Works*, 3:698. See also Fuller, *Works*, 2:161, 2:181, and 2:346.

28. As seen in chap. 2, by using the word "dwelt" (σκηνόω), John is pointing back to the Old Testament tabernacle, and is proclaiming that the manifest glory of *Yahweh* in the Old Testament tabernacle is the same glory revealed in the incarnate Son.

29. Chappell makes the case that the liturgy of our corporate services should take its shape from the gospel in Chapell, *Christ-Centered Worship*. More recently, see Cosper, *Rhythms of Grace*.

(Luke 1:46–47), for the Father "helped his servant Israel, in remembrance of his mercy" (Luke 1:54). Next is Zechariah, who sees the infant, John the Baptist, and is filled with the Spirit to bless the "Lord God of Israel" who "raised up a horn of salvation" in "the house of his servant David" (Luke 1:68–69). Even the angelic host, at the birth of Christ, sings "Glory to God [the Father] in the highest" (Luke 2:14). Likewise, Simeon (Luke 2:27–32) and Anna (Luke 2:36–38) see Jesus and glorify the Father.

Throughout the Gospels, as people see the ministry of Jesus, they respond in praise to the Father (Matt 5:16; 9:8; 15:31; Mark 2:11–12; Luke 5:24–26; 7:15–16; 9:42–43; 13:12–13; 17:14–16; 18:42–43; 19:37; 23:47). Significantly, in Luke's Gospel the pattern is: people see the works of Christ, and glorify the Father; that is, until the Son's exaltation (Luke 24:51). Then, Christ's disciples "worship him" (Luke 24:52). Nevertheless, Luke is sure to mention in the next verse: "and [his disciples] were continually in the temple blessing God [the Father]" (Luke 24:53). Jesus rebukes his enemies for not understanding the purpose of the incarnation. The Son does the works of the Father, giving life and exercising judgment so that "all may honor the Son, just as they honor the Father. Whoever does not honor the Son does not honor the Father who sent him" (John 5:23).

The man Christ Jesus, empowered by the Spirit, lived a perfect life of remembrance before the Father, and as such was and remains the ideal worshipper.[30] As one born under the Law, he obeyed the Law completely, and is seen worshipping in the synagogue (Matt 4:23; 9:35; 12:9; 13:54; Mark 1:21, 39; 3:1; 6:2; Luke 4:15–16, 44; 6:6; 13:10; John 6:59), at Passover (Matt 26:17–19; Mark 14:12–16; Luke 2:41; 22:7–15; John 2:13, 23; 6:4; 11:55; 13:1) and other festivals (John 7:1–10; 10:22), and in the temple (Matt 21–25; Luke 2:42–50; 19:47; 20:1; 21:37; John 18:20). Jesus rebuked Satan for tempting him to false worship: "You shall worship the Lord your God and him only shall you serve" (Matt 4:10; cf. Luke 4:8), and he drove out the money-changers for making the house of the Father a den of thieves (Matt 21:12; Mark 11:15; John 2:14–17), thus restoring the court of the Gentiles for a brief time to the place of worship the Father intended it to be.

Jesus lived in remembrance of and perfect obedience to all the Father's commands he learned from the Scriptures (Matt 20:28; Mark 10:45; John 4:34; 5:30; 6:38; 14:31; Heb 10:7, 9), and prayerful dependence upon the Father to empower him by the Holy Spirit (Matt 14:23; 26:36; Mark 1:35; 9:29; Luke 3:21; 5:16; 6:12; 9:18; John 17).[31] His honor of the Father does

---

30. See Peterson, *Engaging with God*, 138–42.
31. For Jesus living his life as a Spirit-empowered man, see Ware, *The Man Christ Jesus*.

not cease after his resurrection and exaltation. Due says, "The book of Acts and the various New Testament letters portray a raised and glorified Jesus who continues to serve God as the man in heaven, and to lead creation in its praise."[32] This is chiefly manifest in his high-priestly ministry (Heb 4:14–16; 7:25; 8:1). He is the "minister in the holy places, in the true tent that the Lord set up, not man" (Heb 8:2), and sings out to the Father, "I will tell of your name to my brothers; in the midst of the congregation I will sing your praise" (Heb 2:12), and sings out over us, "Behold, I and the children God has given me" (Heb 2:13).[33]

What does this mean for those who have placed faith in Christ? First, and foremost, the Lord's Supper was instituted as one of the enduring ordinances of the church, given for the purpose of *remembering* the goodness and greatness of God the Father, as revealed in the person and work of the Lord Jesus Christ (Luke 22:19; 1 Cor 11:24ff). Furthermore, for the new-covenant believer, studying the Old Testament sacrificial system and Law should be a reminder that Christ's sacrifice for sin is perfect and sufficient (Heb 10:3, 10, 14, 18).

The Father has commanded his children to listen to his Son (Matt 17:5; Mark 9:7; Luke 9:35; John 10:16; 18:37), and so remembering the words of Jesus is necessary for faith and life (John 2:22). It is why Peter writes; "In both of them I am stirring up your sincere mind by way of reminder, that you should remember the predictions of the holy prophets and the commandment of the Lord and Savior through your apostles" (2 Pet 3:1–2; cf. 1:12–13).[34]

Consequently, the New Testament response of remembrance is fleshed out by several words related to worship. For example, the people "praised" and "glorified" (δοξάζω) God the Father for who he is and what he has done in Christ (Matt 23:47; Luke 2:20; Acts 11:18; Rom 15:6, 9; Rev 15:3–4).[35] They sang "hymns" (ὑμνέω) of praise and celebration (Acts 16:26; Eph 5:19;

---

32. Due, *Created for Worship*, 141.

33. For extended discussions of the high-priestly ministry of Christ and its connection to his eternal worship of the Father, see Torrance, *Worship*, 43–67, Peterson, *Engaging with God*, 228–34, and Due, *Created for Worship*, 153–65.

34. Leivestad says, "Remembering persons from redemptive history can have a similar function (e.g., Lot's wife in Luke 17:32; cf. the examples in Heb 11). Likewise remembering the courage and blamelessness of the Apostles (Acts 20:31; 1 Thess 2:9) or the works of faith, hope, and love in the congregation (1 Thess 1:3) becomes a continual source of strength." See Leivestad, "μνημονεύω," in *EDNT*, 2:435.

35. Synonyms that also emerge from the New Testament in remembrance of the Father are: αἰνέω "laud, praise," ἐπαινέω "praise, extol," and εὐλογέω "praise, commend, extol, bless."

Col 3:16).³⁶ They reacted with "rejoicing" and "gladness" (χαίρω) when a sinner came to understand the person and work of Christ (Acts 13:48; 1 Pet 4:13; Rev 19:7). The Father commands remembrance, the self-giving of Christ compels it, and the Holy Spirit enables it.

The Father Makes Genuine Worship Possible by the Spirit's Work of Regeneration

The Psalmist sings praises and gives thanks to the Father because "He has caused his wondrous works to be remembered" (Ps 111:4). It should be no surprise, for the Father had promised Moses this very thing (Exod 20:24). By the end of the Pentateuch, Moses gives the people a final warning about forgetting God. He says ironically that though they saw the works of *Yahweh* (Deut 29:2), he had not given them "a heart to understand or eyes to see or ears to hear" (Deut 29:4) in order to "know that I am the Lord your God" (Deut 29:6). Their idolatry was seen in not remembering the Father (Deut 29:24–28), and so he will "circumcise" their hearts (Deut 30:6), causing them to remember who he is and what he has done (Deut 30:10–14).³⁷

Though still very much a secret in Deuteronomy (Deut 29:29), the Father continues to reveal more about his "new covenant." In Isaiah, the Father remembers when he brought his people out of Egypt and put his Spirit in their midst (Isa 63:11), and therefore promises a future outpouring of the Spirit (Isa 44:1–8), which will bring the Father's forgiveness (Isa 44:22; cf. Jer 31:31–34), and their response of worship (Isa 44:23). In Ezekiel, the Father promises to give them a new heart by placing his Spirit in his people (Ezek 36:26–27), which will cause his name to be vindicated and worshiped before the world (Ezek 36:22–23). Though, the resulting remembrance of *Yahweh* is implied, the Father explicitly tells them: "Then you will remember your evil ways, and your deeds that were not good, and you will loathe yourselves for your iniquities and your abominations" (Ezek 36:31), thus tying their confession and repentance of idolatry inextricably with their remembrance and worship.³⁸

---

36. Of particular note is that the content of Spirit-filled hymns of Eph 5:19, with which we are to encourage one another, are hymns full of the gospel, the word regarding Christ in Col 3:16. We are to stir one another up to remember these things when we gather together.

37. See Sailhamer, *Pentateuch as Narrative*, 471–78.

38. For an insightful study on remembrance in Ezekiel, see De Vries, "Remembrance in Ezekiel," 58–64. De Vries concludes: "Thus it appears that what Israel remembers and forgets, and what Yahweh remembers and forgets, is vitally connected with her past history, her present peril, and her future hopes. Because this nation has forgotten

As discussed in chapter 6, the promised "new covenant" is brought in by Christ through the pouring out of the Spirit; consequently, new-covenant worship begins at the point where the Holy Spirit produces regeneration, bringing to the human mind and heart the true knowledge of the Father as he has revealed himself in the person and work of his Son. In Philippians 3:3, Paul writes, "For we are the circumcision, who worship by the Spirit of God and glory in Christ Jesus and put no confidence in the flesh."[39] Furthermore, Paul teaches that this circumcision is synonymous with regeneration: "And you, who were dead in your trespasses and the uncircumcision of your flesh, God made alive together with him, having forgiven us all our trespasses" (Col 2:13).

Looked at from another angle, genuine worship of and communion with the Father can only happen through the Spirit's work of uniting the believer to Christ,[40] and therefore why Paul declares, "For through him [Christ] we both have access in one Spirit to the Father" (Eph 2:18). Owen calls this kind of worship "gospel worship,"[41] which is a high privilege and results in communion with the Father:

> Wherefore, as a Father is he the ultimate object of all evangelical worship, of all our prayers. So is it expressed in that holy and

---

what she should have remembered, and remembered what she should have forgotten, she is under divine judgment at this awful hour. Yahweh will judge her, scouring her as a caldron on the fire, yes, even melting her to ashes [24:1–14], yet he cannot and will not forget her. Though she be dead as dry bones, he will raise her again [37:1–14]. He will not consign her with the heathen to the place of no-remembrance. Rather, he will restore her after a while, remembering her in his covenant mercy and making her to remember him." Ibid., 64.

39. The circumcision Paul speaks of is the promise of Deut 30:6. Paul, in Rom 2:29, teaches that this circumcision is "a matter of the heart, by the Spirit, not by the letter," and is what enables every regenerate person to be "ministers of a new covenant, not of the letter, but of the Spirit. For the letter kills, but the Spirit gives life" (2 Cor 3:6). One of the unique aspects of apostolic ministry was the writing of new-covenant revelation. In John 14:26, Jesus promised his disciples, "But the Helper, the Holy Spirit, whom the Father will send in my name, he will teach you all things and bring to your remembrance all that I have said to you." In the context of John 14:26, I take this to be a promise to the Apostles that they would be reminded of everything that Jesus taught them, so that they could write the New Testament. As a result, we now have the inspired New Testament preserved for us so we can bring to remembrance what the Father says in the Scriptures through his Son, and as the Spirit gives us illumination of the Word, we can worship our Triune God rightly: the glory of the Father manifested by the praise of the Son in the power of the Spirit.

40. For the relationship of union with Christ to the mutual indwelling of the Trinity, and their implications for the corporate gathering of worship, see Best, *Unceasing Worship*, 48–57.

41. Owen, *Works*, 18:45.

divine description of it given by the apostle, Eph. 2:18. "Through Christ we have access by one Spirit unto the Father." No tongue can express, no mind can reach, the heavenly placidness and soul-satisfying delight which are intimated in these words. To come to God as a Father, through Christ, by the help and assistance of the Holy Spirit, revealing him as a Father unto us, and enabling us to go to him as a Father, how full of sweetness and satisfaction is it![42]

If the Spirit's ministry is to placard and exalt Christ, to the praise of the Father's glory, how ought we to worship the Spirit? Wainwright says,

With the dubious exceptions of 1 Corinthians 6:19-20 and Philippians 3:3, there is no case in the New Testament where the Holy Spirit is an object of worship as distinct from an enabling medium. Yet we have seen the systematic logic of a move from agency to being. And there are notable examples in liturgical history for praise and prayer addressed specifically to the Holy Spirit.[43]

Parry perceptively argues that the Spirit's ministry of drawing attention to Christ means that any worship of the Spirit must always be connected to the Father and the Son, and be biblically informed.[44] Therefore, although there is no passage in Scripture that teaches the direct worship of the Spirit, he ought to be honored, prayed to, and thanked for his role within the divine economy and for his relation to the other two persons of the Trinity. Thus, as Basil has so helpfully articulated, worship is on the one hand to the Father through the Son in the Holy Spirit, and at the same time to the Father with the Son together with the Holy Spirit.[45]

---

42. Ibid., 4:292-93. Owen believed union with Christ was the foundation of communion with the entire Godhead and is the premise of his work, *Communion with God*. The longer title is instructive: *Of Communion with God the Father, Son, and Holy Ghost, Each Person Distinctly, in Love, Grace, and Consolation; or, The Saints' Fellowship with the Father, Son, and Holy Ghost Unfolded*.

43. Wainwright, "Trinitarian Worship," 213.

44. Parry, *Worshipping Trinity*, 94-95.

45. The New Testament evidence for personal prayer to Jesus is also evident, when κύριος is a reference to the Son: Acts 7:59-60; 13:2; 2 Cor 12:8; 1 Thess 3:11-13; 2 Thess 2:16-17; 3:5, 16; 1 Tim 1:12; 2 Tim 1:16-18; 4:22; cf. the benediction of "grace" in Rom 16:20; 1 Cor 16:23; Gal 6:18; Phil 4:23; 1 Thess 5:28; 2 Thess 3:18; Phlm 25.

Spirit-Wrought *Submission* in Their Hearts That Draws Them Near to the Father through the Lordship of the Son

Submission (חוה, προσκυνέω) is one of the main word groups from both the Old and New Testaments that are translated as "worship."[46] From these words come a heart attitude of adoration and homage to God the Father as king. More than the physical posture of bowing down, this heart attitude is one that approaches the king and says, "I am yours, and do with me what you want." This expression of awe and grateful submission is a recognition of God's gracious character and rule.[47]

The Father Draws Near to Us So That We May Draw Near to Him

In his work, *Recalling the Hope of Glory*, Ross demonstrates that the Garden of Eden was the first sanctuary, where mankind had access to God and was able to draw near and have communion with him.[48] After the fall, it is through Moses that the Father initiates the revelation of the tabernacle, the priesthood, and the sacrificial system as the means by which his people can draw near and approach him as the Holy One who dwells in their midst and desires relationship with them. The tabernacle is described as a royal house (Exod 25:1—26:30) with the abundant use of gold and precious stones. The items in this house, an ark (or chest), a table, and a lampstand, were common items found in every house at that time, and presence of bread on the table and light in the lampstand were reminders that Yahweh was there always, both day and night.[49]

Furthermore, the tabernacle was a holy house (Exod 26:31—31:18). The veil between the holy place and the most holy place separated the manifest presence of God from the people. The sacrificial system and the rules for clean and unclean living further demonstrated the holiness of God and sinfulness of the people. However, the complicated arrangement and

---

46. Recent dispute has arisen over the etymology of the Old Testament word. In most lexicons, it is considered a Hithpael of שָׁחָה *shachah*, but is considered by some on the basis of Ugaritic evidence to be an Eshtaphal stem of חוה *chawa*. See discussion on Yamauchi, "חוה" in *TWOT*, 267–69.

47. See discussion in Peterson, *Engaging with God*, 55–74.

48. Ross, *Recalling the Hope of Glory*, 90–108. See also Sailhamer, *Pentateuch as Narrative*, 98–100.

49. See Alexander, *From Paradise to the Promised Land*, 224–36. For an extensive study on the symbolism of the earthly temple and its pattern after the heavenly temple, see Beale, *Temple and the Church's Mission*, 29–49.

rules of the tabernacle were not to exclude the people from God, but rather give them a proper way to approach the Holy One through the blood of an atoning sacrifice. Thus, the tabernacle was also a meeting house (Exod 29:42–46). In Deuteronomy 12:5, God says he would permanentize his dwelling for the people in the land of promise: he will choose it, he will put his name there, and he will make his habitation there.[50]

The heart attitude of submission and fearing the Lord, then, were closely related ideas. David sings out in Psalm 5:7, "But I, through the abundance of your steadfast love, will enter your house. I will bow down [*chawa*] toward your holy temple in the fear of you." Likewise, the Psalmist commands, "Oh come, let us worship [*chawa*] and bow down; let us kneel before the Lord, our Maker! For he is our God, and we are the people of his pasture, and the sheep of his hand" (Ps 95:6–7). Peterson's thoughts on his word study are helpful:

> Part of the ritual of worship came to stand for the whole, so that bending over to the LORD came to represent devotion and submission to him as a pattern of life. Particularly by means of sacrifice and praise in the temple cult at Jerusalem. God's dominion over the whole creation, his gracious rule over his chosen people, and his kingly presence in their midst was acknowledged. Such homage to God is essentially what is meant when the English word "worship" translates *hištaḥăwâ* and *proskynein* in the Old Testament.[51]

It Is through Submission to Christ as Lord That We May Confidently Draw Near to the Father

The translation of "submission (προσκυνέω)" as worship in the New Testament causes a new pattern to emerge. The exalted Christ now stands next to God the Father as the one worshipped (Luke 24:52; Rev 5:13). As *Immanuel*, his royal presence and authority is far greater than that of the Old Testament temple (Matt 1:23), and so he replaces the temple as the place where the Father dwells (John 1:14, 18; Col 1:15; 2:9; Heb 1:3). Jesus

---

50. Later established in Jerusalem, it is no surprise then that in Revelation, the creation is transformed into the new heavens and earth (Rev 21:1) and the garden is transformed into the New Jerusalem (Rev 21:2, 10–11; 22:1–5). There will no longer be the need for a temple, because the new creation becomes the temple (Rev 21:22). See Due, *Created for Worship*, 226–28, Ross, *Recalling the Hope of Glory*, 489–98, and Bauckham, *Theology of the Book of Revelation*, 126–43.

51. Peterson, *Engaging with God*, 63.

himself told the Pharisees "I tell you, something greater than the temple is here" (Matt 12:6),[52] and so he received the worship of those who bowed down in submission to him (Matt 14:33; 28:9, 17; Luke 24:52), expressing their trust as those who saw God the Father reflected in Jesus. He is the one to whom every knee should bow and every tongue confess is Lord, to the glory of God the Father (Phil 2:10–11). Praise is often connected with the Father's work through Christ in salvation: "The God and Father of the Lord Jesus, he who is blessed forever" (2 Cor 11:31), "To the only wise God [the Father] be glory forevermore through Jesus Christ" (Rom 16:27), "Blessed be the God and Father of our Lord Jesus Christ" (Eph 1:3), "Every tongue confess that Jesus Christ is Lord, to the glory of God the Father" (Phil 2:11). For all eternity, the Christian's service will be a life of worship, walking in a manner worthy of the Father. Thus, Paul can write to the Ephesians, "To [the Father] be the glory in the church and in Christ Jesus throughout all generations, forever and ever" (Eph 3:21).

Therefore, Jesus can tell the Samaritan woman in John 4:20–24 that the place of worship, either Jerusalem or Gerazim or any other "holy site," is no longer important. Rather, through belief in Jesus as the Messiah (and by implication, a submission to him as Lord), "true worshipers will worship the Father in spirit and truth" (John 4:23). Encapsulated in this verse, Jesus teaches Trinitarian worship. Those who worship the Father will do so by a regenerated human "spirit" that has experienced the "living water" (John 4:10–14) of the Holy Spirit,[53] and will worship the Father through the truth that is only found in Christ Jesus. There is only one proper response to the Father's glorious and eternal lordship. To the Romans, Paul writes, "Oh, the depth of the riches and wisdom and knowledge of God! How unsearchable are his judgments and how inscrutable his ways" (Rom 11:33), and then three verses later, "For from him and through him and to him are all things. To him be glory forever" (Rom 11:36). In fact, Paul's regular response is praise, "To the Father belongs glory forever and ever" (Gal 1:5, 24), "The Father is blessed forever" (Rom 1:25), "To our God and Father be glory forever and ever" (Phil 4:20), "to the praise of his [the Father's] glory" (Eph 1:12,14).

---

52. Beale notes, "On him, not on the Temple, rests the 'Shekinah' glory in an even greater way than previously in the temple (echoing perhaps the prophecy of Hag 2:9, 'the latter glory of this house will be greater than the former'). Therefore, not only is Jesus identified with the temple because he is assuming the role of the sacrificial system, but he is also now, instead of the temple, the unique place on earth where God's revelatory presence is located. God is manifesting his glorious presence in Jesus in a greater way than it was ever manifested in a physical temple structure." Beale, *Temple and Church's Mission*, 178.

53. In John 7:38–39, the apostle John gives us the key to understanding "living water" as the Holy Spirit.

Regarding the use of submission in book of Revelation, Nützel perceptively writes,

> The use of προσκυνέω in Revelation has two centers of gravity: the worship of God and the Lamb in the heavenly liturgy (4:10; 5:14; 7:11; 11:16; 19:4) and the worship of the dragon, the "beast from the sea," and his image on earth (13:4, 8, 12, 15; 19:20; cf. 20:4), worship described as a distortion of the heavenly liturgy (cf. 13:1–8; 5:6–14). This anti-divine cult leads to ruin (14:9, 11; 16:2; 19:19–21), rejection of it to life (20:4). Only worship of God allows one to come through judgment by God (14:7). When at the end all nations worship the victorious God (15:4), the heavenly worship will fill the New Creation. Only God and the Lamb are worthy of worship, so the angels ward off any homage to themselves (19:10b; 22:8f.). Only blasphemers throw themselves down before demons and idols (9:20).[54]

Thus, submission to the lordship of Christ in the power of the Spirit is the only means possible for true worship of the Triune God.

It Is by the Spirit That We Draw Near with Family Affections for God as Father

The Spirit's indwelling ministry gives knowledge of Jesus' identity and the Christian's unity with him (John 14:20; 15:26; cf. 1 John 3:24; 4:2–3; 4:13), and gives genuine hope because the Spirit brings God's fatherly love to us (Rom 5:5). It is why Paul writes to the Ephesians: "In him [Christ] you also are being built together into a dwelling place for God [the Father] by the Spirit" (Eph 2:22).[55] It is why Peter writes, "you yourselves like living stones are being built up as a spiritual house, to be a holy priesthood, to offer spiritual sacrifices acceptable to God through Jesus Christ" (1 Pet 2:5). By the Spirit and through the Son, this "holy house" is a family house, which will bring glory to the Triune God as the Father's adopted children draw near to him.[56]

---

54. Nutzel, "προσκυνέω," in *EDNT*, 3:174.

55. In this new privileged position as the temple, believers are dear to the Father (Eph 2:19) as fellow citizens and family, they are secure in Christ (Eph 2:20), who is the cornerstone of the new temple, and they are growing into a temple in the Spirit (Eph 2:21), which will one day fill the earth.

56. Interestingly, Due believes that this wider theology of the temple leads Jesus to mean the new-covenant people as temple rather than the building in Jerusalem when he quotes Ps 69:9, saying, "Zeal for your house will consume me" (John 2:17). "While Jesus was full of zeal for the Jerusalem temple as the dwelling place of his Father's name,

The Father expects his children to respond to this new relationship by knowing him for who he really is. Therefore, as those known by him (Gal 4:9), the Father wants his children to *know* him as a loving, gracious Father and to *know* who they are in Christ. In his letter to the Ephesians, Paul prays two different prayers for them, but they require the same response. Paul wanted the Ephesians to know what is true of them in relation to the Father. In the first prayer, Paul wanted the Ephesians to know the hope to which the Father had called them (Eph 1:18), to know that they are the Father's glorious inheritance (Eph 1:19), and to know what is the immeasurable greatness of the Father's power toward them (Eph 1:19). In the second prayer, Paul wanted them to know Christ's love for them so that they would be filled with the Father's fullness (Eph 3:19). To the Colossians, Paul had a similar prayer, that they would know the Father and know his will (Col 1:9-10; 2:2), and by that knowledge, that they would be strengthened with the Father's power (Col 1:11, 29).

In Romans 8:14-17, Paul describes this new relationship of adoption. First, he says that those who are obedient to the Father and who bow the knee to Christ can do so only because they "are led by the Spirit of God" (Rom 8:14). They are killing sin (Rom 8:13) and will be heirs of God the Father and fellow heirs with Christ (Rom 8:17).[57] As his children, the Father also wants them to know that they are led by his Spirit (Rom 8:14), therefore he stirs up family affections through his Spirit so that his children would not live in the fear of a slave but in the affection of a son and that they would instinctually cry out "Abba Father" (Rom 8:15-16). Paul argues, then, that being led by the Spirit leads to the mortification of sin by trusting in the surpassing worth of the Father's love. Thus, integral to our communion with the Father is a lifestyle of praying to him (Matt 6:6, 9; 9:38; 18:19; Mark 9:47; 11:25; Luke 11:2, 9, 13; 1 Thess 5:16-18; 2 Cor 9:14; Rom 15:30; Eph 2:18; 3:12; Col 4:3; Phil 4:6; Jas 1:5, 7; 1 Pet 5:6-7), hoping in him (Luke 12:32; 2 Cor 1:9-10; 1 Tim 4:10; 6:17; 2 Tim 1:12; Heb 10:36) and giving thanks to him (1 Thess 1:2; 2:13; 3:9; 2 Thess 1:3; 2:13; 8:16; 9:15; Rom 6:17; 7:25; Eph 5:20; Col 1:12; 3:16-17; Heb 12:28-29).[58]

---

that which ultimately consumes him is the passion for the new, spiritual temple which would become 'the dwelling of God in the Spirit' (Eph. 5:22). The zeal for this temple would take him to the cross as the atoning Lamb of God, there to make a once-for-all sacrifice for sin to seal the new covenant in his blood." Due, *Created for Worship*, 132.

57. Moo says "We are sons of God by virtue of our belonging to *the* Son of God, and we are heirs of God only by virtue of our union with the one who is the heir of all of God's promises, Jesus Christ, God the Son [emphasis original]." Moo, *Romans*, 505.

58. As mentioned in n. 49 of this chapter, personal prayer to Jesus is also evident in the New Testament (Acts 7:59-60; 13:2; 2 Cor 12:8; 1 Thess 3:11-13; 2 Thess 2:16-17; 3:5, 16; 1 Tim 1:12; 2 Tim 1:16-18; 4:22), and by application he ought to be honored,

Finally, the Spirit enables the believer to draw near to the Father through a new and "living way" found in the Son (Heb 10:19).[59] The author of Hebrews teaches that our approach ought to be one of "confidence" and "boldness," which stand in stark contrast to the restrictions placed on the people of God in the earthly temple under the old covenant. We now have great confidence because our high priest has gone before us and left the way open (Heb 10:20–21) and the Spirit has washed our hearts clean (Heb 10:22), exhorting the children of God to "with confidence draw near to the throne of grace, that we may receive mercy and find grace to help in time of need" (Heb 4:16). We have a Father who has drawn near to us through his Son. He has made us to be his temple, the place where his glory dwells, and therefore invites us to draw near to him as our perfect Father. This response brings all honor and glory to our Triune God.

Living in Spirit-Empowered *Service* for the Glory of Christ, to the Praise of the Father

All of the church's service flows from the fountain of Spirit-empowered worship, adoration, and passion for the glory of the Triune God to be known by others in the face of Christ (Rom 12:1; Heb 13:15; Eph 5:18–20). The Old Testament word for service, עָבַד (*abad*) and its New Testament counterpart λατρεύω, along with their cognates, are often translated "worship" when about God.[60] More importantly, they are tied to the concept of priesthood, and therefore, tie the purpose of mankind to service in the Father's presence and enjoyment of every provision he has given for life.

Mankind Was Created to Worship as a Kingdom of Priests

In Genesis 2:15, it says, "The Lord God took the man and put him in the garden of Eden to work it and keep it." The two responsibilities, "to work" and "to keep," taken together point to man's work as priestly in nature

---

prayed to and thanked for his role within the divine economy and his relationship to the Father and Spirit.

59. Dahl identifies two implications of the Christian who draws near. First, it is as members of a priestly community and so there is a corporate element of the church gathered. Second, it also means the church scattered to "go to him [Jesus] outside the camp and bear the reproach he endured" (Heb 13:13). Dahl, "A New and Living Way," 401–12.

60. See Kaiser, "עָבַד" in *TWOT*, 639, and "λατρεύω," in BDAG, 586.

rather than simply agricultural. The first word "work" (*abad*) is often used for spiritual service in the Old Testament, specifically for the priestly duty of the Levites (Num 3:7–8; 4:23–24, 26).[61] The second word, "keep" (שָׁמַר, *shamar*) was also used for the Levites responsibility to guard the tabernacle (Num 1:53), and are paired together to speak of priestly ministry: "They shall keep guard [*shamar*] over him and over the whole congregation before the tent of meeting, as they minister [*abad*] at the tabernacle. They shall guard [*shamar*] all the furnishings of the tent of meeting, and keep guard [*shamar*] over the people of Israel as they minister [*abad*] at the tabernacle" (Num 3:7–8). Thus, Adam was the archetypical priest.[62]

The Father's design was reiterated to Israel at Sinai: "Now therefore, if you will indeed obey my voice and keep my covenant, you shall be my treasured possession among all peoples, for all the earth is mine; and you shall be to me a kingdom of priests and a holy nation" (Exod 19:5–6). This service was not to merely be a duty, but rather a joy-filled, liberating experience (Exod 3:12; 4:23; 7:16; 10:26; Ps 22:30). Their lives were to be completely given over to God the Father in total allegiance (Deut 10:12-13; Josh 22:5). However, their service was often given over in idolatry to the worship of other gods (Deut 7:16; 2 Kgs 10:18-19, 21-23; Jer 2:20).

The Father Sends His Son to Be the True Worshipping King-Priest Who Is Also Worthy to be Worshipped

In the Old Testament, the most significant use of the term "servant" is as a messianic description. The Father expected Israel to be his "servant" to show the light of his glory and even fitted them with his truth (Isa 41:8–9), and yet Israel as a servant of the Lord proved to be deaf to the voice of God and blind to their commission (Isa 42:18–24), and thus were wicked servants who discarded the kindness and gentleness of the Holy One to chase after worthless idols, to follow "empty wind" (Isa 41:29).

In response, the Father places his Son on center stage as an ideal "servant," and as one who will bring Jacob back to himself and bring salvation to the ends of the earth (Isa 49:5–6). As noted in the previous chapter, as the Messiah is the ideal servant, he is also the ideal king-priest, the Son of Man, the second Adam, who will reign forever, serve forever, and worship forever,

---

61. It was also used for those who were called "the servant of *Yahweh*" in unique roles such as Abraham, Isaac, Jacob, Moses, Joshua, Caleb, David, Hezekiah, Eliakim, and Zerubbabel. God often called the prophets, "my servants" or "his servants."

62. See Ross, *Recalling the Hope of Glory*, 105–8, Alexander, *From Paradise to Promised Land*, 123–25, and Due, *Created for Worship*, 41–42.

and therefore, stands alongside the Father as the one to whom all worship is due. Smith reflects,

> The ascended Christ is the operative agent of Christian worship: Christ our high priest calls us into worship and then leads us into the presence of the Creator God. Our worship is a participation in the communion that has existed for all of eternity within the triune God. The sacramental actions of the church make this reality visible and enable this reality to be embodied – and thus to be lived.[63]

The Holy Spirit Empowers Us to Live Forever as King-Priests Who Serve the Father and Son

Also, in the previous chapter, we saw that those united to Christ are empowered by the Spirit in the new covenant to be king-priests who share in the present and future reign of Christ, since they have been raised to the heavenly places in Christ. With that future inheritance in mind, their present duty is to continually offer themselves, and all that they do or have, as sacrifices to the Father through the Son.

The Christian's worship is a life of service (Matt 5:33; 6:24; 22:21; Mark 12:17; Luke 16:13; Luke 20:25; 1 Thess 1:9; 2 Cor 6:4; 2 Tim 1:3), a calling (1 Cor 7:17, 24; 2 Cor 10:13; Phil 3:14), and a commissioning (2 Cor 2:17) by the Father to steward his mysteries (1 Cor 4:1; cf. Jude 3), be ministers of a new covenant (2 Cor 3:6; 4:1), and be ambassadors for Christ (2 Cor 5:20). As such, believers make the Father's appeal to a lost world, "Be reconciled to the Father" (2 Cor 5:20). Furthermore, any fruit they bear is terminates in the Father's glory (Rom 7:4). Therefore, Paul commands Christians to do all for the Father's glory (1 Cor 6:20; 10:31; 2 Cor 1:20; 9:13; Rom 15:6-7; Phil 1:11) and to rejoice in the Father (Rom 5:2,11). In Paul's thinking, the Christian life is one of good works, which the Father prepared beforehand (Eph 2:10), which are done through his power (Phil 2:12-13), and which is why a life walked in a manner worthy of the Father brings him great pleasure (Phil 2:13; 4:18; 1 Tim 5:4). Therefore, the Father wants his children to live their lives in a manner worthy of him (1 Thess 2:12; 4:1). But note that it is not to the exclusion of the Son or Spirit, for Paul also wrote that Christians are to "walk in a manner worthy of the Lord [Jesus]" (Eph 4:1), and to "keep in step with the Spirit" (Gal 5:25). Thus, it is a Trinitarian shaped life of service "worthy of the gospel" (Phil 1:27).

63. Smith, "Sacraments and the Embodiment of Our Trinitarian Faith," 189.

In Romans 6, Paul describes one of the aspects of servanthood as worship. In v. 11, he teaches Christians to consider themselves as dead to sin and alive to the Father. In v. 13, because of their new sphere of existence, Christians are to place themselves at the Father's disposal,[64] and yield their members as weapons of righteousness for the Father to be used for his purposes. In v. 16, Paul says the result of this slavery (Rom 6:22) to the Father is, as Murray says, a "righteousness in all its aspects and culminating, indeed, in the consummated righteousness of the new heavens and new earth."[65] Later in the letter, Paul returns to this theme and tells the Romans to "present [their] bodies as a living sacrifice, holy and acceptable to God the Father, which is [their] spiritual worship" (Rom 12:1).

This is not simply a "spiritualization" of the traditional terminology of cultic worship. Instead, this "spiritual act of worship" or "reasonable service" means the offering is no longer a slain animal but the believer's whole life as a sacrifice to God. Much like Jesus' teaching in John 4:20–24, Paul shifts the meaning of worship away from the location of the temple in Jerusalem to the believer's life of "spirit and truth." Schreiner notes, "The terms ἁγίαν and εὐάρεστον have cultic associations as well. The former term denotes the idea that the sacrifice is dedicated to God, while the latter evokes OT notions of sacrifices that are pleasing and fragrant to God."[66] Furthermore, the use of λογικός here is probably best translated reasonable rather than spiritual since it is the appropriate response to the mercies of God the Father.[67] Thus, the Christian ought to see their priestly ministry as service for the Father, enabled by the Spirit's indwelling and acceptable through the finished work of Christ.

Picking up the same priestly imagery, Peter also speaks of servanthood as worship. In 1 Peter 2:4–5, believers are "living stones" that come to Jesus Christ the "living stone." Once again, implicit is the Spirit's work of regenerating those "chosen" by God the Father (1 Pet 2:4, 9) and uniting them to the Son. Furthermore, the Father has chosen them for a purpose; namely, "to offer spiritual sacrifices acceptable to God [the Father] through Jesus Christ." As already seen in Romans 6 and 12:1, the new-covenant sacrifices consist in offering up our entire life for the Father's use (cf. 1 Cor 10:31). The

---

64. Though the verb παραστήσατε is an aorist infinitive, it is connected to a present tense prohibition in the first clause, and therefore the command to "yield themselves" remains in force throughout the life of the believer. See Moo, *Romans*, 385.

65. Murray, *Romans*, 231.

66. Schreiner, *Romans*, 644.

67. Cranfield thinks "understanding" is the best translation: "the intelligent understanding worship, that is, the worship which is consonant with the truth of the gospel." Cranfield, *Romans*, 2:602–5.

author of Hebrews adds 1) praise and thanks: "Through him [Christ] then let us continually offer up a sacrifice of praise to God [the Father], that is, the fruit of lips that acknowledge his name" (Heb 13:15), and 2) acts of love: "Do not neglect to do good and to share what you have, for such sacrifices are pleasing to God" (Heb 13:16; cf. Phil 4:18; Jas 1:27). Thus, as the Father's priests, the Christian's new-covenant sacrifices are offered within a *taxis* of Trinitarian worship.

Closely tied to the priestly duty of spiritual sacrifices is the duty to offer up spiritual gifts (Heb 5:1). Just as the Levitical priests were to offer both gifts and sacrifices, so too the new-covenant priests are to offer spiritual gifts to their brethren. Just like the sacrifices, the gifts are acceptable to God the Father through Jesus Christ. In 1 Corinthians 12:4–6, Paul teaches that the Father is the source of spiritual gifts, and in 1 Corinthians 12:7 he gives them for the common good. Though there is a great diversity of gifts (1 Cor 12:8–11), every gift is necessary (1 Cor 12:12–19) and every gift is interdependent upon one another (1 Cor 12:20–30).

Finally, since every sacrifice and gift the church offers as priests of the Father are only acceptable through Jesus Christ, believers are dependent upon the Spirit to produce spiritual fruit. In 1 Corinthians 12:31, Paul concludes his talk on gifts, and then says, "*And I will show you a still more excellent way.*" He continues in 1 Corinthians 13:1–3, to explain that spiritual gifts (and by implication, spiritual sacrifices) without spiritual fruit (here "love"; cf. Gal 5:22–23) are worthless. Thus, the litmus test of priestly service is love; for God and for others (Matt 22:37–39; cf; Mark 12:30–33; Luke 10:27; Deut 6:5; Lev 19:18), which is only possible through union with Christ and the indwelling ministry of the Holy Spirit.

Conclusion

If worship can be defined Trinitarianly as,

> the Spirit-illumined calling of the saints to *remember* the greatness and goodness of God the Father in the face of Jesus Christ so that they will cultivate Spirit-wrought *submission* in their hearts that draws them near to the Father through lordship of the Son, so that, in turn, they may be commissioned to use their lives in Spirit-empowered *service* for the glory of Christ, to the praise of the Father.

And if there is a proper order of the biblical terminology of remembrance › submission › service, then there are necessary implications for specific acts of worship, both for the individual and for the corporate gathering. Individually, the believer by the Spirit is united to the Lord Jesus Christ and is therefore a temple, a priest, and a sacrifice to the praise of the Father's glory. Thus, every believer should live his or her life in "unceasing worship."

Corporately, everything the church places into their liturgy should be informed by the gospel as an explanation of the new covenant, and shaped by the *taxis* of Christocentric Trinitarianism: *from* the Father, *through* the Son, *by* the Spirit back *to* the Father, *through* the Son, *by* the Spirit. For the Lord's Supper, this means the saints should resist the urge to merely recollect Jesus, but as Letham says, "In the Eucharist the faithful feeding on Christ in faith by the Holy Spirit, and thus in union with Christ the Son we share in his access to the Father."[68] For preaching, this means the pastor must constantly place before the people the goodness and greatness of the Father in the face of Christ Jesus. As he does so, he can be assured the Spirit will do his ministry of glorifying the Son.[69]

For singing of corporate praise, this means that focus on one person of the Trinity to the exclusion of the others, or relying upon songs that are vague or confused regarding God are inadequate. Rather, as Kauflin says, "A faithful worship leader magnifies the greatness of God in Jesus Christ through the power of the Holy Spirit by skillfully combining God's Word with music, thereby motivating the gathered church to proclaim the gospel, to cherish God's presence, and to live for God's glory."[70] For prayer, this means through Christ and with Christ, in the power of the Spirit, the children of God confidently address him as Father (Matt 6:9–13). Therefore, as the saints gather and are equipped for the "work of ministry" (Eph 4:12), they scatter for mission as an act of worship as ambassadors of the Father. Köstenberger and Swain write,

> The church's mission not only flows from and through the love of the triune God; it also flows *to* the love of the triune God. The Father, after all, seeks *worshippers* (4:23). The Father sent the Son to make his great and holy name known to his people (1:18; 17:6). The church's mission therefore ultimately consists in reaping a worldwide harvest of worshippers (4:35–38) gathered by the Son, through the Spirit, to serve and adore the "Holy Father" (17:11; cf. Isa. 6:3; 66:19–21; Rev. 22:3–4).

68. Letham, *Holy Trinity*, 423. See also Letham, *Lord's Supper*.

69. Azurdia argues that the Holy Spirit is the Christocentric Spirit and therefore to be Spirit-empowered in preaching, the preacher must get in line with the Spirit's ministry of glorifying the Son. Azurdia, *Spirit Empowered Preaching*.

70. Kauflin, *Worship Matters*, 55. As the core of his book, Kauflin explores this definition over ten chapters.

One day the church's mission will be consummated in trinitarian worship (Rev. 22:1–5). This means that, even now, as the church engages in the worship of the Holy Trinity, she engages not simply in the *means* of her mission, but in the very *end* of her mission: the *Gloria Dei*.[71]

Thus, this consistent Trinitarian *taxis* that exists among the persons of the Godhead informs our worship, and is therefore immensely practical. For all eternity, as the exalted saints will live Spirit-empowered lives united to the glorified and risen Christ. They will serve as king-priests of the Father day and night in his new creation before his throne, and the Father will shelter them with his presence. "For from him and through him and to him are all things. To him be glory forever. Amen" (Rom 11:36). All of this redounds to the praise of our Triune God.

---

71. Köstenberger and Swain, *Father, Son, and Spirit*, 164.

9

Conclusion

BECAUSE STUDIES DEVOTED EXCLUSIVELY to the person and work of God the Father are almost nonexistent (historically subsumed under Theology Proper, and as such, neglected in favor of studies on the Trinity), the development of Paterology as a discipline is greatly needed within the academic community. This book reflects my contribution to the field, and my desire to answer Gerald Bray's lament, "Who has written anything on the work of the Father, considered as one of the Trinity and not just as a personification of the divine?"[1] As such, I have focused on the Father's roles and relationships with the Son and Spirit, not only within the economy of redemption, but also from eternity past, arguing that the Father is the initiator of all divine action.

In our Paterology, we must never lose sight of the fact that the doctrine of the person and work of the Father is not so much an intellectual exercise as an exposition of the character of a person. Our theology ought to be put into practice, and be done for the benefit of the church. This means for those of us who are Christ-centered in our preaching and practice, we must be careful not to become Christomonistic, to the exclusion of the Father and Spirit. The Father's desire is to make the Son the direct object of the church's worship and to sum up all things in him as his Messiah, and therefore the Father sent the Spirit to bear witness to this reality through the church. In Emmanuel Durand's essay on the Father, he reflects on the reality that Jesus did not keep his disciples for himself, but rather sends them on to the Father. He says,

> The ultimacy of the Father in divine revelation prohibits the disciples from remaining fixed exclusively on Christ. Christ's departure to be with the Father is an integral part of his mission in respect to us. In theological terms one could say that the irreducibly Christocentric character of revelation is simultaneously ordered toward a paternal teleology.[2]

1. Bray, *God Has Spoken*, 206.
2. Durand, "Theology of God the Father," 372.

Thus, the eternal *taxis* in the Godhead complements and reflects the corresponding *taxis* of worship that is due our Triune God.

In our Paterology, we must also take care to correct the view of God that Father as distant and wrathful, and so implacable toward his elect that none would dare to draw near to him. It is misunderstanding of the Father that makes any run from him, for when a sinner understands the gospel rightly, they see that the Father so loved this fallen world, he sent his Son. For the believer, then, communion with God the Father is one of the greatest privileges and realities that should cause them to approach the Father's throne of grace with confidence. The Father has planned it, he has sent his Son to procure it, and he has poured out his Spirit as the pledge and seal that he will make all things new.

Jesus explained the Father's character with a parable:

> And he said, "There was a man who had two sons. And the younger of them said to his father, 'Father, give me the share of property that is coming to me.' And he divided his property between them. Not many days later, the younger son gathered all he had and took a journey into a far country, and there he squandered his property in reckless living. And when he had spent everything, a severe famine arose in that country, and he began to be in need. So he went and hired himself out to one of the citizens of that country, who sent him into his fields to feed pigs. And he was longing to be fed with the pods that the pigs ate, and no one gave him anything.
>
> But when he came to himself, he said, 'How many of my father's hired servants have more than enough bread, but I perish here with hunger! I will arise and go to my father, and I will say to him, "Father, I have sinned against heaven and before you. I am no longer worthy to be called your son. Treat me as one of your hired servants."' And he arose and came to his father. But while he was still a long way off, his father saw him and felt compassion, and ran and embraced him and kissed him. And the son said to him, 'Father, I have sinned against heaven and before you. I am no longer worthy to be called your son.' But the father said to his servants, 'Bring quickly the best robe, and put it on him, and put a ring on his hand, and shoes on his feet. And bring the fattened calf and kill it, and let us eat and celebrate. For this my son was dead, and is alive again; he was lost, and is found.' And they began to celebrate." (Luke 15:11–24)

The younger brother comes back expecting to be a slave, but is received as a son. The father doesn't approach him in a halfhearted, uncommitted manner. He is far different from the "elder brother," who is full of pride, proclaiming his own self-righteousness (Luke 15:25–30). Instead, he was moved with compassion, ran and grabbed his son in his arms and kissed him. He called for a robe and ring of honor, restored his son in the household, and threw a party of celebration. This is our heavenly Father. He clothes us in the robes of Christ's righteousness, uniting us to his Son, and he pours out his Spirit into our hearts to seal our adoption and to stir up family affections so that we cry out "Abba, Father!"

> Now to [the Father] who is able to keep you from stumbling and to present you blameless before the presence of his glory with great joy, to the only God, our Savior, through Jesus Christ our Lord, be glory, majesty, dominion, and authority, before all time and now and forever. Amen. (Jude 24–25)

Bibliography

Achtemeier, Paul J. *Peter 1: A Commentary on First Peter*. Hermeneia. Minneapolis: Fortress, 1996.
Akin, Daniel L. *1, 2, 3 John*. New American Commentary. Nashville: Broadman & Holman, 2001.
Alden, Robert L. *Job*. The New American Commentary. Nashville: Broadman & Holman, 1993.
Alexander, T. Desmond. *From Paradise to the Promised Land: An Introduction to the Pentateuch*. Grand Rapids: Baker Academic, 2012.
Alexander, T. Desmond, and Brian S. Rosner. *New Dictionary of Biblical Theology*. Leicester, UK: IVP, 2000.
Alford, Henry. *Alford's Greek Testament: An Exegetical and Critical Commentary*. Grand Rapids: Guardian, 1976.
Allen, David L. *Hebrews*. Nashville: B & H, 2010.
Allen, Leslie C. *Jeremiah*. Old Testament Library. Richmond, VA: Westminster John Knox, 2008.
———. *Joel, Obadiah, Jonah and Micah*. The New International Commentary on the Old Testament. Grand Rapids: Eerdmans, 1994.
Aloisi, John. "The Paraclete's Ministry of Conviction: Another Look at John 16:8-11." *Journal of the Evangelical Theological Society* 47, no. 1 (2004) 55–69.
Aquinas, Thomas. *Summa Theologica*. Translated by Fathers of the English Dominican Province. London: Burns Oates & Washbourne, n.d.
Arnold, Clinton E. *Ephesians*. Zondervan Exegetical Commentary Series on the New Testament. Grand Rapids: Zondervan, 2010.
Ashley, Timothy R. *The Book of Numbers*. The New International Commentary on the Old Testament. Grand Rapids: Eerdmans, 1993.
Astley, Jeff, David Brown, and Ann Loades. *Creation: A Reader*. Problems in Theology. London: T. & T. Clark, 2003.
Athanasius. *De decretis*. In *NPNF2*.
———. *De synodis*. In *NPNF2*.
———. *Four Discourses Against the Arians*. In *NPNF2*.
———. *Letters to Serapion on the Holy Spirit*. In *Letters of St. Athanasius Concerning the Holy Spirit*. Translated by C. R. B. Shapland. New York: Philosophical Library, 1951.
———. *Statement of Faith*. In *NPNF2*.
Attridge, Harold W. *Hebrews*. Hermeneia. Minneapolis: Fortress, 1989.
Augustine of Hippo. *On the Trinity*. In *NPNF1*.
Ayres, Lewis. *Augustine and the Trinity*. Cambridge: Cambridge University Press, 2010.

———. *Nicaea and Its Legacy: An Approach to Fourth-Century Trinitarian Theology.* Oxford: Oxford University Press, 2004.

Azurdia, Arturo G. *Spirit Empowered Preaching: The Vitality of the Holy Spirit in Preaching.* Fearn, UK: Mentor, 1998.

Baars, Arie. "'Opera Trinitatis Ad Extra Sunt Indivisa' in the Theology of John Calvin." In *Calvinus Sacrarum Literarum Interpres*, edited by H. J. Selderhuis, 131–41. Göttingen: Vandenhoeck & Ruprecht, 2008.

Badcock, Gary D. "Whatever Happened to God the Father?" *Crux* 36, no. 3 (2000) 2–12.

Baddeley, Mark. "The Trinity and Subordinationism: A Response to Kevin Giles." *Reformed Theological Review* 63, no. 1 (2004) 29–42.

Balserak, Jon. *Divinity Compromised: A Study of Divine Accommodation in the Thought of John Calvin.* Studies in Early Modern Religious Reforms. Dordrecht: Springer, 2006.

Bancroft, Emery H. *Elemental Theology, Doctrinal and Conservative.* Grand Rapids: Zondervan, 1945.

Barackman, Floyd H. *Practical Christian Theology: Examining the Great Doctrines of the Faith.* Grand Rapids: Kregel, 2001.

Barker, Kenneth L. *Micah, Nahum, Habakkuk, Zephaniah.* The New American Commentary. Nashville: Broadman & Holman, 1999.

Barnes, Michel Rene. "Augustine in Contemporary Trinitarian Theology." *Theological Studies* 56, no. 2 (1995) 237–50.

Barnett, Paul. *The Second Epistle to the Corinthians.* The New International Commentary on the New Testament. Grand Rapids: Eerdmans, 1997.

Baron, Lori. "Interpreting the Shema: Liturgy and Identity in the Fourth Gospel." *Annali di storia dell'esegesi* 27, no. 2 (2010) 53–60.

———. "The Shema in John's Gospel against Its Backgrounds in Second Temple Judaism." PhD diss., Duke University, 2015.

Barr, James. "Abba Isn't 'Daddy.'" *Journal of Theological Studies* 39 (1988) 28–47.

Barrett, Charles K. *Acts.* Vol. 1. International Critical Commentary. Edinburgh: T. & T. Clark, 1994.

———. *Acts.* Vol. 2. International Critical Commentary. Edinburgh: T. & T. Clark, 1994.

———. *The Epistle to the Romans.* Rev. ed. Black's New Testament Commentary. London: Continuum, 1991.

———. *The First Epistle to the Corinthians.* Black's New Testament Commentary. London: Continuum, 1968.

Barrick, William D. "Inspiration and the Trinity." *The Master's Seminary Journal* 24, no. 2 (2013) 179–97.

Barth, Karl. *The Theology of John Calvin.* Translated by Geoffrey William Bromiley. Grand Rapids: Eerdmans, 1995.

Basil of Caesarea. *The Book of Saint Basil on the Spirit.* In *NPNF2*.

———. *On the Holy Spirit.* Translated by Stephen M. Hildebrand. Yonkers, NY: St. Vladimir's Seminary Press, 2011.

Bates, Matthew W. *The Birth of the Trinity: Jesus, God, and Spirit in New Testament and Early Christian Interpretations of the Old Testament.* Oxford: Oxford University Press, 2015.

Bauckham, Richard J. *2 Peter and Jude*. Word Biblical Commentary. Nashville: Thomas Nelson, 1983.

———. *Jesus and the God of Israel: God Crucified and Other Studies on the New Testament's Christology of Divine Identity*. Milton Keynes, UK: Paternoster, 2009.

———. *The Theology of the Book of Revelation*. Cambridge: Cambridge University Press, 1993.

Bavinck, Herman. *In the Beginning: Foundations of Creation Theology*. Translated by John Bolt and John Vriend. Grand Rapids: Baker, 1999.

———. *Reformed Dogmatics*. Vol. 2. *God and Creation*. Translated by John Bolt and John Vriend. Grand Rapids: Baker Academic, 2004.

———. *The Doctrine of God*. Translated by William Hendriksen. Carlisle, PA: Banner of Truth Trust, 1977.

Beale, G. K. *The Book of Revelation: A Commentary on the Greek Text*. New International Greek Testament Commentary. Grand Rapids: Eerdmans, 1999.

———. *The Temple and the Church's Mission: A Biblical Theology of the Dwelling Place of God*. Downers Grove, IL: IVP Academic, 2004.

Beale, G. K., and D. A. Carson. *Commentary on the New Testament Use of the Old Testament*. Grand Rapids: Baker Academic, 2007.

Beeke, Joel R., and Mark Jones. *A Puritan Theology: Doctrine for Life*. Grand Rapids: Reformation Heritage, 2012.

Beeley, Christopher A. "Divine Causality and the Monarchy of God the Father in Gregory of Nazianzus." *Harvard Theological Review* 100, no. 2 (2007) 199–214.

Belleville, Linda L. "'Son' Christology in the New Testament." In *The New Evangelical Subordinationism*, edited by Denis Jowers and Paul House, 59–81. Eugene, OR: Pickwick, 2012.

Belt, H. van den, ed. *Restoration through Redemption: John Calvin Revisited*. Studies in Reformed Theology vol. 23. Leiden: Brill, 2013.

Bennett, William. "The Sons of the Father: The Fatherhood of God in the Synoptic Gospels." *Interpretation* 4, no. 1 (1950) 12–23.

Bergen, Robert D. *1, 2 Samuel*. The New American Commentary. Nashville: Broadman & Holman, 1996.

Berkhof, L. *Systematic Theology*. Grand Rapids: Eerdmans, 1939.

Berkouwer, G. C. *The Providence of God*. Grand Rapids: Eerdmans, 1952.

Best, Harold M. *Unceasing Worship: Biblical Perspectives on Worship and the Arts*. Downers Grove, IL: IVP, 2003.

Bigg, Charles. *A Critical and Exegetical Commentary on the Epistles of St. Peter and St. Jude*. International Critical Commentary. Edinburgh: T. & T. Clark, 1910.

Bilezikian, Gilbert. "Hermeneutical Bungee-Jumping: Subordination in the Godhead." *Journal of the Evangelical Theological Society* 40, no. 1 (1997) 57–68.

Billings, J. Todd. *Calvin, Participation, and the Gift the Activity of Believers in Union with Christ*. Changing Paradigms in Historical and Systematic Theology. Oxford: Oxford University Press, 2007.

———. "John Calvin: United to God through Christ." In *Partakers of the Divine Nature*, edited by Michael J. Christensen and Jeffery A. Wittung, 200–218. Grand Rapids: Baker Academic, 2007.

Bird, Michael F. *Evangelical Theology: A Biblical and Systematic Introduction*. Grand Rapids: Zondervan, 2013.

Bird, Michael F., and Robert Shillaker. "The Son Really, Really Is the Son: A Response to Kevin Giles." *Trinity Journal* 30, no. 2 (2009) 257–68.
———. "Subordination in the Trinity and Gender Roles: A Response to Recent Discussion." *Trinity Journal* 29, no. 2 (2008) 267–83.
Block, Daniel Isaac. *The Book of Ezekiel*. Grand Rapids: Eerdmans, 1997.
———. "How Many Is God? An Investigation into the Meaning of Deuteronomy 6:4-5." *Journal of the Evangelical Theological Society* 47, no. 2 (2004) 193–212.
———. *Judges, Ruth*. The New American Commentary. Nashville: Broadman & Holman, 1999.
Bloesch, Donald G. *God, the Almighty: Power, Wisdom, Holiness, Love*. Downers Grove, IL: IVP, 1995.
Blum, Edwin A. *1, 2 Peter*, The Expositor's Bible Commentary. Grand Rapids: Zondervan, 1981.
Boa, Kenneth, and William Kruidenier. *Romans*. Holman New Testament Commentary. Nashville: Broadman & Holman, 2000.
Bock, Darrell L. *Luke 1:1—9:50*. Baker Exegetical Commentary on the New Testament. Grand Rapids: Baker Academic, 1994.
———. *Luke 9:51—24:53*. Baker Exegetical Commentary on the New Testament. Grand Rapids: Baker Academic, 1994.
Boice, James Montgomery. *Foundations of the Christian Faith: A Comprehensive & Readable Theology*. Downers Grove, IL: IVP, 1986.
Borchert, Gerald L. *John 1–11*, New American Commentary. Nashville: Broadman & Holman, 1996.
Boulton, Matthew. *Life in God: John Calvin, Practical Formation, and the Future of Protestant Theology*. Grand Rapids: Eerdmans, 2011.
Boxall, Ian. *The Revelation of Saint John*. Black's New Testament Commentary. London: Continuum, 2006.
Boyce, James Petigru. *Abstract of Systematic Theology*. Philadelphia: American Baptist Publication Society, 1887.
Boyer, Steven D. "Articulating Order: Trinitarian Discourse in an Egalitarian Age." *Pro Ecclesia* 18, no. 3 (2009) 255–72.
à Brakel, Wilhelmus. *The Christian's Reasonable Service*. Morgan, PA: Soli Deo Gloria, 1993.
Bratcher, Robert G., and Howard Hatton. *A Handbook on the Revelation to John*. UBS Handbook Series. New York: United Bible Societies, 1993.
Bray, Gerald Lewis. *The Doctrine of God*. Downers Grove, IL: IVP Academic, 1993.
———. *God Has Spoken: A History of Christian Theology*. Wheaton, IL: Crossway, 2014.
———. "The Trinity and Subordinationism: The Doctrine of God and the Contemporary Gender Debate." *Churchman* 117, no. 3 (2003) 267–72.
Breneman, Mervin. *Ezra, Nehemiah, Esther*. The New American Commentary. Nashville: Broadman & Holman, 1993.
Brown, Colin, ed. *The New International Dictionary of New Testament Theology*. 4 vols. Exeter, UK: Paternoster, 1975.
Brown, Raymond Edward. *The Epistles of John*. Garden City, NY: Doubleday, 1982.
Bruce, F. F. *1 & 2 Thessalonians*. Word Biblical Commentary. Waco, TX: Word, 1982.
———. *The Acts of the Apostles: The Greek Text with Introduction and Commentary*. Grand Rapids: Eerdmans, 1990.

———. *The Epistle of Paul to the Galatians: A Commentary on the Greek Text*. The New International Greek Testament Commentary. Exeter, UK: Paternoster, 1982.

———. *The Epistle to the Hebrews*. The New International Commentary on the New Testament. Grand Rapids: Eerdmans, 1964.

———. *The Epistles to the Colossians, to Philemon, and to the Ephesians*. The New International Commentary on the New Testament. Grand Rapids: Eerdmans, 1984.

Brunner, Emil. *Dogmatics*. Philadelphia: Westminster, 1950.

Bruno, Christopher R. *"God Is One": The Function of* Eis Ho Theos *as a Ground for Gentile Inclusion in Paul's Letters*. London: T. & T. Clark, 2013.

Burge, Gary M. *John*. The NIV Application Commentary. Grand Rapids: Zondervan, 2000.

Burk, Denny. "Christ's Functional Subordination in Philippians 2:6." In *The New Evangelical Subordinationism*, edited by Dennis Jowers and Paul House, 82–107. Eugene, OR: Pickwick, 2012.

Burton, Ernest De Witt. *A Critical and Exegetical Commentary on the Epistle to the Galatians*. International Critical Commentary. Edinburgh: T. & T. Clark, 1921.

Buswell, J. Oliver. *A Systematic Theology of the Christian Religion*. Grand Rapids: Zondervan, 1962.

Butin, Philip Walker. *Revelation, Redemption, and Response: Calvin's Trinitarian Understanding of the Divine-Human Relationship*. New York: Oxford University Press, 1995.

Butner, D. Glenn, Jr. "Eternal Functional Subordination and the Problem of the Divine Will." *Journal of the Evangelical Theological Society* 58, no. 1 (2015) 131–49.

Calvin, John. *Acts*. Crossway Classic Commentaries. Wheaton, IL: Crossway, 1995.

———. *Commentaries on the Catholic Epistles*. Translated by John Owen. Grand Rapids: Baker, 1996.

———. *Commentaries on the Epistles of Paul the Apostle to the Corinthians*. Vol. 2. Translated by John Pringle. Grand Rapids: Baker, 1996.

———. *Commentaries on the Epistles of Paul the Apostle to the Philippians, Colossians, and Thessalonians*. Translated by John Pringle. Grand Rapids: Baker, 1996.

———. *Commentaries on the Epistles of Paul to the Galatians and Ephesians*. Translated by William Pringle. Grand Rapids: Baker, 1996.

———. *Commentaries on the Epistles to Timothy, Titus, and Philemon*. Translated by William Pringle. Grand Rapids: Baker, 1996.

———. *Commentaries on the Four Last Books of Moses Arranged in the Form of a Harmony*. Vols. 1, 3, 4. Translated by Charles William Bingham. Grand Rapids: Baker, 1996.

———. *Commentaries on the Twelve Minor Prophets*. Vols. 1, 4, 5. Translated by John Owen. Grand Rapids: Baker, 1996.

———. *Commentary on the Book of Psalms*. Vols. 1, 2. Translated by James Anderson. Grand Rapids: Baker, 1996.

———. *Commentary on the Book of the Prophet Daniel*. Vol. 2. Translated by Thomas Meyers. Grand Rapids: Baker, 1996.

———. *Commentary on the Epistle of Paul the Apostle to the Hebrews*. Translated by John Owen. Grand Rapids: Baker, 1996.

———. *Commentary on the Epistle of Paul the Apostle to the Romans*. Translated by John Owen. Grand Rapids: Baker, 1996.

———. *Commentary on a Harmony of the Evangelists Matthew, Mark, and Luke*. Vols. 1, 3. Translated by William Pringle. Grand Rapids: Baker, 1996.
———. *Genesis*. Crossway Classic Commentaries. Crossway, 2001.
———. *The Gospel according to John*. Grand Rapids: Eerdmans, 1991.
———. *Institutes of the Christian Religion*. Translated by John Thomas McNeill. London: SCM, 1961.
———. *Letters of John Calvin*. Translated by Jules Bonnet. Bellingham, WA: Logos Bible Software, 2009.
Calvin, John, and Hendry H. Cole. *Calvin's Calvinism: A Treatise on the Eternal Predestination of God*. Bellingham, WA: Logos, 2009.
Calvin, John, and Joel R. Beeke. *The Soul of Life: The Piety of John Calvin*. Profiles in Reformed Spirituality. Grand Rapids: Reformation Heritage, 2009.
Campbell, Constantine R. *Paul and Union with Christ: An Exegetical and Theological Study*. Grand Rapids: Zondervan, 2012.
Capes, David B. "The Lord's Table: Divine or Human Remembrance?" *Perspectives in Religious Studies* 30, no. 2 (2003) 199–209.
Carey, George Leonard. "The Lamb of God and Atonement Theories." *Tyndale Bulletin* 32 (1981) 97–122.
Carson, D. A. *The Gospel according to John*. The Pillar New Testament Commentary. Grand Rapids: Eerdmans, 1991.
———. *Worship by the Book*. Grand Rapids: Zondervan, 2002.
Chafer, Lewis Sperry. *Systematic Theology*. Dallas: Dallas Seminary Press, 1947.
Chambers, Talbot W. "'The Everlasting Father.'" *Journal of the Society of Biblical Literature and Exegesis* 1 (1881) 169–71.
Chappell, Bryan. *Christ-Centered Worship: Letting the Gospel Shape Our Practice*. Grand Rapids: Baker Academic, 2009.
Chen, Diane G. "Ancient Near Eastern Literature and the Hebrew Scriptures about the Fatherhood of God." *Shofar: An Interdisciplinary Journal of Jewish Studies* 24, no. 4 (2006) 192–94.
———. *God as Father in Luke-Acts*. Studies in Biblical Literature 92. New York: Lang, 2006.
Childs, Brevard S. *The Book of Exodus: A Critical, Theological Commentary*. Philadelphia: Westminster, 1974.
Chung, Sung Wook. *John Calvin and Evangelical Theology: Legacy and Prospect, in Celebration of the Quincentenary of John Calvin*. Louisville: Westminster John Knox, 2009.
Ciampa, Roy E., and Brian S. Rosner. *The First Letter to the Corinthians*. The Pillar New Testament Commentary. Grand Rapids: Eerdmans, 2010.
Clancy, Robert A. D. "The Old Testament Roots of Remembrance in the Lord's Supper." *Concordia Journal* 19, no. 1 (1993) 35–50.
Clarke, Rosalind. "Job 27:3: The Spirit of God in my Nostrils." In *Presence, Power, and Promise: The Role of the Spirit of God in the Old Testament*, edited by David G. Firth and Paul D. Wegner, 111–21. Downers Grove, IL: IVP Academic, 2011.
Claunch, Kyle. "God is the Head of Christ: Does 1 Corinthians 11:3 Ground Gender Complementarity in the Immanent Trinity?" In *One God in Three Persons*, edited by Bruce Ware and John Starke, 65–94. Wheaton, IL: Crossway, 2015.

———. "What God Hath Done Together: Defending the Historic Doctrine of the Inseparable Operations of the Trinity." *Journal of the Evangelical Theological Society* 56, no. 4 (2013) 781–800.
Clines, David J. A. "The Image of God in Man." *Tyndale Bulletin* 19 (1968) 53–103.
Cole, R. Dennis. *Numbers*. The New American Commentary. Nashville: Broadman & Holman, 2000.
Cooper, Lamar Eugene. *Ezekiel*. The New American Commentary. Nashville: Broadman & Holman, 1994.
Cocceius, Johannes. *Summa Doctrina de Foedere et Testamento Dei*. In Cocceius, *Opera Theologica*, 8 vols. Amsterdam, 1673.
Cosper, Mike. *Rhythms of Grace: How the Church's Worship Tells the Story of the Gospel*. Wheaton, IL: Crossway, 2013.
Cowan, Christopher. "The Father and Son in the Gospel of John." In *One God in Three Persons*, edited by Bruce Ware and John Starke, 47–64. Wheaton, IL: Crossway, 2015.
———. "'I Always Do What Pleases Him': The Father and Son in the Gospel of John." In *One God in Three Persons*, edited by Bruce Ware and John Starke, 47–64. Wheaton, IL: Crossway, 2015.
Craigie, Peter C. *The Book of Deuteronomy*. The New International Commentary on the Old Testament. Grand Rapids: Eerdmans, 1976.
Cranfield, C. E. B. *A Critical and Exegetical Commentary on the Epistle to the Romans*. New International Critical Commentary. 2 vols. Edinburgh: T. & T. Clark, 1975–79.
Culver, Robert Duncan. *Systematic Theology: Biblical and Historical*. Fearn, UK: Mentor, 2005.
Currid, John D. *A Study Commentary on Genesis*. EP Study Commentary. Darlington, UK: Evangelical, 2003.
Dabney, Robert Lewis. *Lectures in Systematic Theology*. Grand Rapids: Zondervan, 1972.
Dahl, Nils. "The Neglected Factor in New Testament Theology." *Reflection* 73, no. 1 (1975) 5–8.
———. "A New and Living Way: The Approach to God according to Heb 10:19–25." *Interpretation* 5, no. 4 (1951) 401–12.
Dahms, J. V. "The Subordination of the Son." *Journal of the Evangelical Theological Society* 37, no. 3 (1994) 351–64.
D'Angelo, Mary Rose. "Intimating Deity in the Gospel of John: Theological Language and 'Father' in 'Prayers of Jesus.'" *Semeia* no. 85 (1999) 59–82.
Davids, Peter H. *The Epistle of James: A Commentary on the Greek Text*. The New International Greek Testament Commentary. Grand Rapids: Eerdmans, 1982.
———. *The First Epistle of Peter*. The New International Commentary on the New Testament. Grand Rapids: Eerdmans, 1990.
———. *The Letters of 2 Peter and Jude*. The Pillar New Testament Commentary. Grand Rapids: Eerdmans, 2006.
Davis, Barry C. "Is Psalm 110 a Messianic Psalm?" *Bibliotheca sacra* 157, no. 626 (2000) 160–73.
Davis, John Jefferson. "Who's Tampering with the Trinity?" *Priscilla Papers* 25, no. 4 (2011) 28–30.

Dean, Benjamin. "Person and Being: Conversation with T. F. Torrance about the Monarchy of God." *International Journal of Systematic Theology* 15, no. 1 (2013) 58–77.

Deane-Drummond, Celia. *Creation through Wisdom: Theology and the New Biology.* London: T. & T. Clark, 2000.

DeClaissé-Walford, Nancy L., Rolf A. Jacobson, and Beth LaNeel Tanner. *The Book of Psalms.* The New International Commentary on the Old Testament. Grand Rapids: Eerdmans, 2014.

De Petris, Paolo. *Calvin's Theodicy and the Hiddenness of God: Calvin's Sermons on the Book of Job.* European university studies. Series XXIII, Theology vol. 926. New York: Lang, 2012.

De Vries, Simon J. "Remembrance in Ezekiel." *Interpretation* 16, no. 1 (1962) 58–64.

Dodd, C. H. *The Johannine Epistles.* London: Hodder and Stoughton, 1966.

Dowey, Edward A. *The Knowledge of God in Calvin's Theology.* New York: Columbia University Press, 1952.

———. *The Knowledge of God in Calvin's Theology.* Exp. ed. Grand Rapids: Eerdmans, 1994.

Doyle, Robert C. "Basic Expectations, Strategies and Consequences: Towards Understanding the Triune God in the Company of John Calvin." *Reformed Theological Review* 68, no. 3 (2009) 151–74.

Due, Noel. *Created for Worship: From Genesis to Revelation to You.* Fearn, UK: Christian Focus, 2005.

Duhm, Bernard. *Das Buch Jesaja, Handkommentar zum Alten Testament.* Göttingen: Vandenhoeck & Ruprecht, 1892.

Dumbrell, W. J. "Genesis 2:1–17: A Foreshadowing of the New Creation." In *Biblical Theology: Retrospect and Prospect*, edited by S. J. Hafemann, 53–65. Downers Grove, IL: IVP Academic, 2002.

Duncan, J. Ligon, Dan Kimball, Michael Lawrence, Mark Dever, Timothy C. J. Quill, Dan Wilt, and J. Matthew Pinson. *Perspectives on Christian Worship: 5 Views.* Nashville: B & H Academic, 2009.

Dunn, James D. G. *The Epistle to the Galatians.* Black's New Testament Commentary. London: Continuum, 1993.

Durand, Emmanuel. "A Theology of God the Father." In *Oxford Handbook of the Trinity*, edited by Gilles Emery and Matthew Levering, 371–86. Oxford: Oxford University Press, 2011.

Ebert, D. J. "Wisdom in New Testament Christology, with Special Reference to Hebrews 1:1–4" PhD diss., Trinity Evangelical Divinity School, 1998.

Eckman, David. *Knowing the Heart of the Father.* Singapore: Imprint Edition, 2008.

Edgar, Brian. *The Message of the Trinity: Life in God.* Downers Grove, IL: IVP, 2004.

Edwards, Mark. "Exegesis and the Early Doctrine of the Trinity." In *Oxford Handbook of the Trinity*, edited by Gilles Emery and Matthew Levering, 80–91. Oxford: Oxford University Press, 2011.

Edwards, James R. *The Gospel according to Mark.* Pillar New Testament Commentary. Grand Rapids: Eerdmans, 2001.

Edwards, Jonathan. *Works of Jonathan Edwards.* 26 vols. New Haven, CT: Yale University Press, 1957.

Eising, H. "זָכַר" In *TDOT*, 4:64–82.

Ellingworth, Paul. *The Epistle to the Hebrews*. New International Greek Testament Commentary. Grand Rapids: Eerdmans, 1993.
Ellis, Brannon. *Calvin, Classical Trinitarianism, and the Aseity of the Son*. 1st ed. Oxford: Oxford University Press, 2012.
Elshout, Bartel. "The Unique Relationship between the Father and the Son in the Gospel of John." *Puritan Reformed Journal* 3, no. 1 (2011) 41–55.
Elwell, Walter A., and Barry J. Beitzel. *Baker Encyclopedia of the Bible*. Grand Rapids: Baker, 1988.
Emery, Gilles, and Matthew Levering, eds. *The Oxford Handbook of the Trinity*. Oxford: Oxford University Press, 2011.
Enns, Paul P. *The Moody Handbook of Theology*. Chicago: Moody, 1989.
Erickson, Millard J. *Christian Theology*. Grand Rapids: Baker Academic, 2013.
———. *God in Three Persons: A Contemporary Interpretation of the Trinity*. Grand Rapids: Baker, 1995.
———. *Who's Tampering with the Trinity? An Assessment of the Subordination Debate*. Grand Rapids: Kregel, 2009.
Eugenio, Dick Osita. "Communion with God: The Trinitarian Soteriology of Thomas F. Torrance." PhD diss., University of Manchester, 2011.
Fay, Ron C. "Father, Son and Spirit in Romans 8: Paul's Understanding of God with Special Reference to the Roman Recipients." PhD diss., Trinity Evangelical Divinity School, 2006.
Fee, Gordon D. *The First Epistle to the Corinthians*. The New International Commentary on the New Testament. Grand Rapids: Eerdmans, 1987.
Feinberg, John S. "God Ordains All Things." In *Predestination and Free Will: Four Views of Divine Sovereignty and Human Freedom*, edited by David Basinger and Randall Basinger, 17–44. Downers Grove, IL: IVP, 1986.
———. *No One Like Him: The Doctrine of God*. The Foundations of Evangelical Theology. Wheaton, IL: Crossway, 2001.
Fensham, F. Charles. *The Books of Ezra and Nehemiah*. The New International Commentary on the Old Testament. Grand Rapids: Eerdmans, 1982.
Ferguson, Sinclair B. *The Holy Spirit*. Downers Grove, IL: IVP Academic, 1996.
———. *John Owen on the Christian Life*. Edinburgh: Banner of Truth, 1987.
Fesko, J. V. "John Owen on Union with Christ and Justification," *Themelios*, 37, no. 1 (2012) 7–19.
Fisher, Matthew C. "God the Father in the Fourth Gospel: A Biblical Patrology." PhD diss., Southeastern Baptist Theological Seminary, 2003.
Foerster, Werner, "κύριος." In *TDNT*, 3:1039–95.
Forsyth, Peter T. *God the Holy Father*. Blackwood, Australia: New Creation, 1987.
Foster, Edgar G. "Metaphor and Divine Paternity: The Concept of God's Fatherhood in the Divinae Institutiones of Lactantius (250-325 Ce)." PhD diss., University of Glasgow, 2008.
Foster, Paul. "Why Did Matthew Get the Shema Wrong? A Study of Matthew 22:37." *Journal of Biblical Literature* 122, no. 2 (2003) 309–33.
Fox, Michael V. *Proverbs 1–9*. Anchor Yale Bible Commentary. New Haven, CT: Yale University Press, 2000.
———. *Proverbs 10–31*. Anchor Yale Bible Commentary. New Haven, CT: Yale University Press, 2009.

Frame, John M. *The Doctrine of God. A Theology of Lordship*. Phillipsburg, NJ: P & R, 2002.

France, R. T. *The Gospel of Mark*. New International Greek Testament Commentary. Grand Rapids: Eerdmans, 2002.

Fuller, Andrew. *The Works of Andrew Fuller*. Edinburgh: Banner of Truth Trust, 2007.

Gabriel, Andrew K. *Barth's Doctrine of Creation: Creation, Nature, Jesus, and the Trinity*. Eugene, OR: Cascade, 2014.

Gaffin, R. B., Jr., "Glory." In *New Dictionary of Biblical Theology*, edited by T. Desmond Alexander, Brian S. Rosner, D. A. Carson, and Graeme Goldsworthy, 507–11. Downers Grove, IL: IVP Academic, 2000.

Galot, Jean. *Abba, Father, We Long to See Your Face: Theological Insights into the First Person of the Trinity*. New York: Alba House, 1992.

Garland, David E. *1 Corinthians*. Baker Exegetical Commentary on the New Testament. Grand Rapids: Baker Academic, 2003.

———. *2 Corinthians*. The New American Commentary. Nashville: Broadman & Holman, 1999.

Garrett, Duane A. *Hosea, Joel*. The New American Commentary. Nashville: Broadman & Holman, 1997.

———. *Proverbs, Ecclesiastes, Song of Songs*. The New American Commentary. Nashville: Broadman & Holman, 1993.

———. "Veiled Hearts: The Translation and Interpretation of 2 Corinthians 3." *Journal of the Evangelical Theological Society* 53, no. 4 (2010) 729–72.

Gathercole, Simon. *The Preexistent Son: Recovering the Christologies of Matthew, Mark, and Luke*. Grand Rapids: Eerdmans, 2006.

———. "The Trinity in the Synoptic Gospels and Acts." In *The Oxford Handbook of the Trinity*, edited by Gilles Emery and Matthew Levering, 55–68. Oxford: Oxford University Press, 2011.

Geis, Francis. "The Trinity and the Eternal Subordination of the Son." *Priscilla Papers* 27, no. 4 (2013) 23–28.

Gentry, Peter John, and Stephen J. Wellum. *Kingdom through Covenant: A Biblical-Theological Understanding of the Covenants*. Wheaton, IL: Crossway, 2012.

George, Timothy. *Galatians*. The New American Commentary. Nashville: Broadman & Holman, 1994.

———. *God the Holy Trinity: Reflections on Christian Faith and Practice*. Grand Rapids: Baker Academic, 2006.

Gerhardsson, Birger. *The Shema in the New Testament: Deut 6:4–5 in Significant Passages*. Lund, Sweden: Novapress, 1996.

Gieschen, Charles A. "The Death of Jesus in the Gospel of John: Atonement for Sin?" *Concordia Theological Quarterly* 72, no. 3 (2008) 243–61.

———. "The Real Presence of the Son before Christ: Revisiting an Old Approach to Old Testament Christology." *Concordia Theological Quarterly* 68, no. 2 (2004) 105–26.

Giles, Kevin. "Barth and Subordinationism." *Scottish Journal of Theology* 64, no. 3 (2011) 327–46.

———. "The Doctrine of the Trinity and Subordinationism." *Evangelical Review of Theology*, 28, no. 3 (2004) 270–84.

———. *The Eternal Generation of the Son: Maintaining Orthodoxy in Trinitarian Theology*. Downers Grove, IL: IVP Academic, 2012.

———. "The Evangelical Theological Society and the Doctrine of the Trinity." *Evangelical Quarterly* 80, no. 4 (2008) 323–38.
———. *Jesus and the Father: Modern Evangelicals Reinvent the Doctrine of the Trinity*. Grand Rapids: Zondervan, 2006.
———. "A Personal Response to Stephen R. Holmes." *Evangelical Quarterly* 86, no. 1 (2014) 55–62.
———. "Rejoinder to Robert Letham." *Evangelical Quarterly* 80, no. 4 (2008) 347–48.
———. "Response to Michael Bird and Robert Shillaker: The Son Is Not Eternally Subordinated in Authority to the Father." *Trinity Journal* 30, no. 2 (2009) 237–56.
———. "The Trinity and Subordinationism." *St Mark's Review*, no. 198 (2005) 19–24.
———. "The Trinity without the Tiers." *St Mark's Review*, no. 215 (2011) 39–62.
Gogarten, Friedrich. "God, the Father of Jesus Christ." *Perkins School of Theology Journal* 20, nos. 1–2 (1967) 31–44.
Goldingay, John. *Daniel*. Word Biblical Commentary. Nashville: Thomas Nelson, 1989.
———. *Psalms*. Vol. 1. Baker Commentary on the Old Testament. Grand Rapids: Baker Academic, 2006.
———. *Psalms*. Vol. 2. Baker Commentary on the Old Testament. Grand Rapids: Baker Academic, 2006.
———. *Psalms*. Vol. 3. Baker Commentary on the Old Testament. Grand Rapids: Baker Academic, 2008.
———. *Ezekiel 21–37*. Anchor Yale Bible Commentary. New Haven, CT: Yale University Press, 1995.
Green, Gene L. *Jude and 2 Peter*. Baker Exegetical Commentary on the New Testament. Grand Rapids: Baker Academic, 2008.
———. *The Letters to the Thessalonians*. Pillar New Testament Commentary. Grand Rapids: Eerdmans, 2002.
Green, Joel B. *The Gospel of Luke*. The New International Commentary on the New Testament. Grand Rapids: Eerdmans, 1997.
Greef, Wulfert de, and Lyle D. Bierman. *The Writings of John Calvin: An Introductory Guide*. Exp. ed. Louisville: Westminster John Knox, 2008.
Greenberg, Moshe. *Ezekiel 1–20*. Anchor Yale Bible Commentary. New Haven, CT: Yale University Press, 1995.
Gregory Nazianzen. "Oration 29.3." In *NPNF2*.
———. "Oration 31.14." In *NPNF2*.
Gregory of Nyssa. *Against Eunomius*. In *NPNF2*.
Grosheide, Frederik Willem. *Commentary on the First Epistle to the Corinthians*. The New International Commentary on the New Testament. Grand Rapids: Eerdmans, 1953.
Grundmann, Walter. "ἵστημι." In *TDNT*, 7:638–53.
Grudem, Wayne A. "Biblical Evidence for the Eternal Submission of the Son to the Father." In *The New Evangelical Subordinationism*, edited by Dennis Jowers and Paul House, 223–61. Eugene, OR: Pickwick, 2012.
———. "Doctrinal Deviations in Evangelical-Feminist Arguments about the Trinity." In *One God in Three Persons*, edited by Bruce Ware and John Starke, 17–46. Wheaton, IL: Crossway, 2015.
———. *Systematic Theology: An Introduction to Biblical Doctrine*. Grand Rapids: Zondervan, 1994.

Gruenler, Royce Gordon. *The Trinity in the Gospel of John: A Thematic Commentary on the Fourth Gospel*. Grand Rapids: Baker, 1986.

Gunton, Colin E. *Christ and Creation*. Carlisle, UK: Paternoster, 1992.

———. *Father, Son, and Holy Spirit: Essays toward a Fully Trinitarian Theology*. London: T. & T. Clark, 2003.

———. *The One, the Three, and the Many: God, Creation, and the Culture of Modernity*. Cambridge: Cambridge University Press, 1993.

———. *The Promise of Trinitarian Theology*. 2nd ed. London: T. & T. Clark, 2006.

———. *The Triune Creator: A Historical and Systematic Study*. Grand Rapids: Eerdmans, 1998.

———. *The Doctrine of Creation Essays in Dogmatics, History and Philosophy*. London: T. & T. Clark, 2004.

Guthrie, Donald. *New Testament Theology*. Leicester, UK: IVP, 1981.

Hagner, Donald A. *Matthew 1–13*. Word Biblical Commentary. Nashville: Thomas Nelson, 1993.

———. *Matthew 14–28*. Word Biblical Commentary. Nashville: Thomas Nelson, 1993.

Hamilton, James M. *God's Glory in Salvation through Judgment: A Biblical Theology*. Wheaton, IL: Crossway, 2010.

———. *God's Indwelling Presence: The Holy Spirit in the Old & New Testaments*. Nashville: Broadman & Holman, 2006.

———. "That God May Be All in All." In *One God in Three Persons*, edited by Bruce Ware and John Starke, 95–108. Wheaton, IL: Crossway, 2015.

———. *With the Clouds of Heaven: The Book of Daniel in Biblical Theology*. Downers Grove, IL: IVP, 2014.

Hamilton, Victor P. *The Book of Genesis*. Vol. 1. Grand Rapids: Eerdmans, 1990.

———. *The Book of Genesis*. Vol. 2. Grand Rapids: Eerdmans, 1995.

Hanson, R. P. C. *The Search for the Christian Doctrine of God*. Edinburgh: T. & T. Clark, 1998.

Harriman, James Earl. "Our Father in Heaven: The Dimensions of Divine Paternity in Deuteronomy." PhD diss., The Southern Baptist Theological Seminary, 2005.

Harris, Murray J. *Colossians & Philemon*, Exegetical Guide to the Greek New Testament. Grand Rapids: Eerdmans, 1991.

———. *Jesus as God: The New Testament Use of* Theos *in Reference to Jesus*. Grand Rapids: Baker, 1992.

———. *The Second Epistle to the Corinthians: A Commentary on the Greek Text*. The New International Greek Testament Commentary. Grand Rapids: Eerdmans, 2005.

Hartley, John E. *The Book of Job*. The New International Commentary on the Old Testament. Grand Rapids: Eerdmans, 1988.

———. *Leviticus*. Word Biblical Commentary. Dallas: Word, 1992.

Hawthorne, Gerald F. *Philippians*. Word Biblical Commentary. Waco, TX: Word, 1983.

Haykin, Michael A. G. *The Reformers and Puritans as Spiritual Mentors: Hope Is Kindled*. Kitchener, ON: Joshua, 2012.

Haykin, Michael A. G., Jeremy Pierre, Christopher Cowan, Robert A. Vogel, and Rob Lister. "The SBJT Forum [God the Father]." *Southern Baptist Journal of Theology* 16, no. 1 (2012) 62–70.

Heine, Ronald E. "The Christology of Callistus." *Journal of Theological Studies* 49, no. 1 (1998) 56–91.

Helm, Paul. *John Calvin's Ideas*. Oxford: Oxford University Press, 2004.
Henry, Carl F. H. *God, Revelation, and Authority*. Wheaton, IL: Crossway, 1999.
———. *The Providence of God*. Downers Grove, IL: IVP, 1994.
Hiebert, D. Edmond. *The Thessalonian Epistles: A Call to Readiness*. Chicago: Moody, 1971.
Hill, Wesley. *Paul and the Trinity: Persons, Relations, and the Pauline Letters*. Grand Rapids: Eerdmans, 2015.
Hodge, Archibald Alexander. *Outlines of Theology*. London: Banner of Truth Trust, 1972.
Hodge, Charles. *1 Corinthians*. Crossway Classic Commentaries. Wheaton, IL: Crossway, 1995.
———. *Systematic Theology*. Grand Rapids: Eerdmans, 1965.
Hoehner, Harold W. *Ephesians*. Carol Stream, IL: Tyndale House, 2008.
Hoekema, Anthony A. *Saved by Grace*. Grand Rapids: Eerdmans, 1994.
Hofer, Andrew. "Who Is God in the Old Testament? Retrieving Aquinas after Rahner's Answer." *International Journal of Systematic Theology* 14, no. 4 (2012) 439–58.
Holladay, William Lee. *Jeremiah*. Hermeneia. Minneapolis: Fortress, 1986.
Holmes, Stephen R. *The Holy Trinity: Understanding God's Life*. Milton Keynes, UK: Paternoster, 2012.
———. *The Quest for the Trinity: The Doctrine of God in Scripture, History, and Modernity*. Downers Grove, IL: IVP Academic, 2012.
Hooker, Morna D. *The Gospel according to Saint Mark*. Black's New Testament Commentary. London: Continuum, 1991.
Horrell, David. "Whose Faith(fulness) Is It in I Peter 1:5." *Journal of Theological Studies* 48, no. 1 (1997) 110–15.
Horrell, J. Scott. "Complementarian Trinitarianism: Divine Revelation Is Finally True to the Eternal Personal Relations." In *The New Evangelical Subordinationism*, edited by Dennis Jowers and Paul House, 339–74. Eugene, OR: Pickwick, 2012.
———. "Who's Tampering with the Trinity? An Assessment of the Subordination Debate." *Bibliotheca sacra* 167, no. 668 (2010) 486–88.
Horton, Michael Scott. *The Christian Faith: A Systematic Theology for Pilgrims on the Way*. Grand Rapids: Zondervan, 2011.
Hoskyns, Edwyn Clement, and Francis Noel Davey. *The Fourth Gospel*. London: Faber and Faber, 1947.
House, H. Wayne. "The Eternal Relational Subordination of the Son to the Father in Patristic Thought." In *The New Evangelical Subordinationism*, edited by Dennis Jowers and Paul House, 133–81. Eugene, OR: Pickwick, 2012.
House, Paul R. *1, 2 Kings*. The New American Commentary. Nashville: Broadman & Holman, 1995.
Howard, David M. *Joshua*. The New American Commentary. Nashville: Broadman & Holman, 1998.
Hubbard, Robert L. *The Book of Ruth*. The New International Commentary on the Old Testament. Grand Rapids: Eerdmans, 1988.
Huey, F. B. *Jeremiah, Lamentations*. The New American Commentary. Nashville: Broadman & Holman, 1993.
Huijgen, Arnold. "Divine Accommodation and Divine Transcendence in John Calvin's Theology." In *Calvinus Sacrarum Literarum Interpres*, edited by H. J. Selderhuis, 119–30. Göttingen: Vandenhoeck & Ruprecht, 2008.

Humphrey, Edith M. "The Gift of the Father: Looking at Salvation History Upside Down." In *Trinitarian Theology for the Church: Scripture, Community Worship*, edited by Daniel J. Treier and David Lauber, 79–102. Downers Grove, IL: IVP Academic, 2009.

Hurtado, Larry W. "First-Century Jewish Monotheism." *Journal for the Study of the New Testament* 71 (1998) 3–26.

Hustad, Donald P. *True Worship: Reclaiming the Wonder & Majesty*. Carol Stream, IL: Hope, 1998.

Hurtado, Larry W. *Lord Jesus Christ: Devotion to Jesus in Earliest Christianity*. Grand Rapids: Eerdmans, 2003.

Hyde, Clark. "The Remembrance of the Exodus in the Psalms." *Worship* 62, no. 5 (1988) 404–14.

Japhet, Sara. *I and II Chronicles*. Old Testament Library. Richmond, VA: Westminster John Knox, 1993.

Jeffery, Steve, Michael Ovey, and Andrew Sach. *Pierced for Our Transgressions: Rediscovering the Glory of Penal Substitution*. Wheaton, IL: Crossway, 2007.

Jenni, Ernst. "אָדוֹן *adon* lord." In *TLOT*, 23–29.

Jenson, Robert W. "The Hidden and Triune God." *International Journal of Systematic Theology* 2, no. 1 (2000) 5–12.

———. *Systematic Theology*. New York: Oxford University Press, 1997.

———. *The Triune Identity: God according to the Gospel*. Philadelphia: Fortress, 1982.

Jeremias, Joachim. *Abba: Studien zur neutestamentlichen Theologie und Zeitgeschichte*. Göttingen: Vandenhoeck & Ruprecht, 1966.

———. *The Central Message of the New Testament*. New York: Scribner's Sons, 1965.

———. *Neutestamentliche Theologie: Erster Teil: Die Verkündigung Jesu*. Gütersloh: Mohn, 1988.

Jewett, Paul King. *Man as Male and Female: A Study in Sexual Relationships from a Theological Point of View*. Grand Rapids: Eerdmans, 1975.

Jobes, Karen H. *1 Peter*. Baker Exegetical Commentary on the New Testament. Grand Rapids: Baker Academic, 2005.

Johnson, Keith. "Trinitarian Agency and the Eternal Subordination of the Son: An Augustinian Perspective." In *The New Evangelical Subordinationism*, edited by Dennis Jowers and Paul House, 108–32. Eugene, OR: Pickwick, 2012.

Johnson, Luke Timothy. *Hebrews: A Commentary*. New Testament Library. Louisville: Westminster John Knox, 2006.

———. *The Letter of James*. Anchor Yale Bible Commentary. New Haven, CT: Yale University Press, 2005.

Jowers, Dennis W., and H. Wayne House. *The New Evangelical Subordinationism? Perspectives on the Equality of God the Father and God the Son*. Eugene, OR: Pickwick, 2012.

Justin Martyr. *The First and Second Apologies*. Translated by L. W. Barnard. New York: Paulist, 1997.

Kaiser, Walter C. "עָבַד" In *TWOT*, 639–40.

Kapic, Kelly M. *Communion with God: The Divine and the Human in the Theology of John Owen*. Grand Rapids: Baker Academic, 2007.

Kapic, Kelly M., and Randall G. Gleason. *The Devoted Life*. Downers Grove, IL: IVP, 2004.

Kapic, Kelly M., and Mark Jones, eds. *The Ashgate Research Companion to John Owen's Theology*. Farnham, UK: Ashgate, 2012.

Kauflin, Bob. *Worship Matters: Leading Others to Encounter the Greatness of God*. Wheaton, IL: Crossway, 2008.

Kay, Brian. *Trinitarian Spirituality: John Owen and the Doctrine of God in Western Devotion*. Studies in Christian History and Thought. Milton Keynes, UK: Paternoster, 2007.

Keener, Craig S. *1–2 Corinthians*. Cambridge: Cambridge University Press, 2005.

———. *The Gospel of John: A Commentary*. Peabody, MA: Hendrickson, 2003.

———. "Is Subordination within the Trinity Really Heresy? A Study of John 5:18 in Context." *Trinity Journal* 20, no. 1 (1999) 39–51.

———. *Matthew*. IVP New Testament Commentary. Downers Grove, IL: IVP, 1997.

———. "Subordination within the Trinity: John 5:18 and 1 Cor 15:28." In *The New Evangelical Subordinationism*, edited by Dennis Jowers and Paul House, 39–58. Eugene, OR: Pickwick, 2012.

Kelly, J. N. D. *Early Christian Creeds*. London; New York: Continuum, 2006.

———. *The Epistles of Peter and of Jude*, Black's New Testament Commentary. London: Continuum, 1969.

———. *The Pastoral Epistles*. Black's New Testament Commentary. London: Continuum, 1963.

Kidner, Derek. *Genesis: An Introduction and Commentary*. Downers Grove, IL: IVP, 1967.

Kim, E. C. "The Necessity of Rediscovering Patrology: Why Is the Father Forgotten?" *Asia Journal of Theology* 19, no. 1 (2005) 14–29.

Kim, Sung-Sup. "Engrafting: The Image of Union in Calvin's Commentary on John's Gospel." *Journal of Reformed Theology* 4, no. 2 (2010) 112–28.

Kimel, Alvin F., ed. *Speaking the Christian God: The Holy Trinity and the Challenge of Feminism*. Grand Rapids: Eerdmans, 1992.

Kittel, Gerhard. "εἰκών." In *TDNT*, 2:381–97.

Klein, George L. *Zechariah*. The New American Commentary. Nashville: Broadman & Holman, 2008.

Knight, George W. *The Pastoral Epistles: A Commentary on the Greek Text*. The New International Greek Testament Commentary. Grand Rapids: Eerdmans, 1992.

Knobnya, Svetlana. "God the Father in the Old Testament." *European Journal of Theology* 20, no. 2 (2011) 139–48.

Knoppers, Gary. *I Chronicles 1–9*. Anchor Yale Bible Commentary. New Haven, CT: Yale University Press, 2004.

———. *I Chronicles 10–29*. Anchor Yale Bible Commentary. New Haven, CT: Yale University Press, 2004.

Koessler, John. *God Our Father*. Chicago: Moody, 1999.

Kooi, Cornelis van der, and Donald H. Mader. *As in a Mirror: John Calvin and Karl Barth on Knowing God: A Diptych*. Studies in the History of Christian Traditions. Leiden: Brill, 2005.

Köstenberger, Andreas J. *John*. Baker Exegetical Commentary on the New Testament. Grand Rapids: Baker Academic, 2004.

Köstenberger, Andreas J., and Scott R. Swain. *Father, Son, and Spirit: The Trinity and John's Gospel*. Downers Grove, IL: IVP Academic, 2008.

Kovach, Stephen D., and Peter R. Schemm. "A Defense of the Doctrine of the Eternal Subordination of the Son." *Journal of the Evangelical Theological Society* 42, no. 3 (1999) 461–76.

Kruse, Colin G. *The Letters of John*. Pillar New Testament Commentary. Grand Rapids: Eerdmans, 2000.

Ku, John Baptist. *God the Father in the Theology of St. Thomas Aquinas*. New York: Lang, 2013.

Kuehn, Evan F. "The Johannine Logic of Augustine's Trinity: A Dogmatic Sketch." *Theological Studies* 68, no. 3 (2007) 572–94.

Ladd, George Eldon. *A Commentary on the Revelation of John*. Grand Rapids: Eerdmans, 1972.

———. *The Gospel of the Kingdom; Scriptural Studies in the Kingdom of God*. Grand Rapids: Eerdmans, 1959.

LaCugna, Catherine Mowry. "The Baptismal Formula, Feminist Objections, and Trinitarian Theology." *Journal of Ecumenical Studies* 26, no. 2 (1989) 235–50.

Lane, William L. *The Gospel of Mark*. New International Commentary on the New Testament. Grand Rapids: Eerdmans, 1974.

———. *Hebrews 1–8*. Word Biblical Commentary. Nashville: Thomas Nelson, 1991.

———. *Hebrews 9–13*. Word Biblical Commentary. Nashville: Thomas Nelson, 1991.

Leith, John H. *John Calvin's Doctrine of the Christian Life*. Louisville: Westminster/John Knox, 1989.

Leivestad, R. "μνημονεύω." In *EDNT*, 2:430.

Lenski, R. C. H. *The Interpretation of St. Luke's Gospel*. Minneapolis: Augsburg Fortress, 1961.

———. *The Interpretation of St. Paul's Epistle to the Romans*. Minneapolis: Augsburg Fortress, 1936.

———. *The Interpretation of St. Paul's Epistles to the Colossians, to the Thessalonians, to Timothy, to Titus and to Philemon*. Minneapolis: Augsburg Fortress, 1937.

———. *The Interpretation of St. Paul's Epistles to the Galatians, to the Ephesians and to the Philippians*. Minneapolis: Augsburg Fortress, 1937.

———. *The Interpretation of St. Paul's First and Second Epistle to the Corinthians*. Minneapolis: Augsburg Fortress, 1963.

———. *The Interpretation of the Acts of the Apostles*. Minneapolis: Augsburg, 1961.

Letham, Robert. "Eternal Generation in the Church Fathers." In *One God in Three Persons*, edited by Bruce Ware and John Starke, 109–26. Wheaton, IL: Crossway, 2015.

———. "John Owen's Doctrine of the Trinity in Its Catholic Context and Its Significance for Today." In *The Ashgate Research Companion to John Owen's Theology*, edited by Kelly M. Kapic and Mark Jones, 185–98. Farnham, UK: Ashgate, 2012.

———. *The Holy Trinity: In Scripture, History, Theology, and Worship*. Phillipsburg, NJ: P & R, 2004.

———. "The Man-Woman Debate: Theological Comment." *Westminster Theological Journal* 52, no. 1 (1990) 65–78.

———. "Reply to Kevin Giles." *Evangelical Quarterly* 80, no. 4 (2008) 339–45.

———. "Surrejoinder to Kevin Giles." *Evangelical Quarterly* 80, no. 4 (2008) 348–48.

———. "The Trinity and Subordinationism: The Doctrine of God and the Contemporary Gender Debate." *Westminster Theological Journal* 65, no. 2 (2003) 383–87.

———. *Union with Christ: In Scripture, History, and Theology*. Phillipsburg, NJ: P & R, 2011.
Letham, Robert, and Kevin Giles. "Is the Son Eternally Submissive to the Father?" *Christian Research Journal 2008* (2008) 11–21.
Lewis, Peter. *The Glory of Christ*. Chicago: Moody, 1997.
Lierman, J. *Challenging Perspectives on the Gospel of John*. Wissenschaftliche Untersuchungen zum Neuen Testament, 2. Reihe 219. Tübingen: Mohr Siebeck, 2006.
Lim, Paul. "The Trinity, Adiaphora, Ecclesiology, and Reformation: John Owen's Theory of Religious Toleration in Context." *Westminster Theological Journal* 67, no. 2 (2005) 281–300.
Lincoln, Andrew T. *Ephesians*. Word Biblical Commentary. Dallas: Word, 1990.
———. *The Gospel according to Saint John*. Black's New Testament Commentary. London: Continuum, 2005.
Lister, John Ryan. *The Presence of God: Its Place in the Storyline of Scripture and the Story of Our Lives*. Wheaton, IL: Crossway, 2015.
Longenecker, Richard N. *Galatians*. Word Biblical Commentary. Dallas: Word, 1990.
Longenecker, Richard N., Walter L. Liefeld, David W. Pao, and Robert H. Mounce. *Luke-Acts*. Revised Expositor's Bible Commentary. Grand Rapids: Zondervan, 2005.
Longman, Tremper. *The Book of Ecclesiastes*. New International Commentary on the Old Testament. Grand Rapids: Eerdmans, 1998.
———. *Song of Songs*. New International Commentary on the Old Testament. Grand Rapids: Eerdmans, 2001.
Louw, J. P., and Eugene A. Nida. *Greek-English Lexicon of the New Testament: Based on Semantic Domains*. 2nd ed. New York: United Bible Societies, 1989.
Lowery, David K. "God as Father: With Special Reference to Matthew's Gospel." PhD, University of Aberdeen, 1987.
Macaskill, Grant. *Union with Christ in the New Testament*. Oxford: Oxford University Press, 2013.
Malone, Andrew S. "John Owen and Old Testament Christophanies." *Reformed Theological Review* 63, no. 3 (2004) 138–54.
Marshall, I. Howard. *The Epistles of John*. New International Commentary on the New Testament. Grand Rapids: Eerdmans, 1978.
Martin, Michael D. *1, 2 Thessalonians*, New American Commentary. Nashville: Broadman & Holman, 1995.
Mathews, K. A. *Genesis*. New American Commentary. Nashville: Broadman & Holman, 1996.
McCall, Thomas H. "Relational Trinity: Creedal Perspective." In *Two Views on the Doctrine of the Trinity*, edited by Jason S. Sexton, 113–37. Grand Rapids: Zondervan, 2014.
———. *Which Trinity? Whose Monotheism? Philosophical and Systematic Theologians on the Metaphysics of Trinitarian Theology*. Grand Rapids: Eerdmans, 2010.
McCall, Thomas H., and Keith E. Yandell. "On Trinitarian Subordinationism." *Philosophia Christi* 11, no. 2 (2009) 339–58.
McCarter, P. Kyle. *I Samuel*. Anchor Yale Bible Commentary. New Haven, CT: Yale University Press, 1984.

———. *II Samuel*. Anchor Yale Bible Commentary. New Haven, CT: Yale University Press, 1995.
McClean, John. "Perichoresis, Theosis and Union with Christ in the Thought of John Calvin." *Reformed Theological Review* 68, no. 2 (2009) 130–41.
McClendon, Philip Adam. "Galatians 2:20 as a Corrective to Selected Contemporary Views of Christian Spirituality." PhD diss., Southern Seminary, 2012.
McConville, J. G. *Deuteronomy*. Apollos Old Testament Commentary. Leicester, UK: Apollos, 2002.
McDonald, Suzanne. "The Pneumatology of the 'Lost' Image in John Owen." *Westminster Theological Journal* 71, no. 2 (2009) 323–35.
McDonough, Sean M. *Christ as Creator Origins of a New Testament Doctrine*. New York: Oxford University Press, 2009.
McGrath, Alister E. *Christian Theology: An Introduction*. Oxford: Blackwell, 1994.
McKim, Donald K. *The Cambridge Companion to John Calvin*. Cambridge: Cambridge University Press, 2004.
Mengestu, Abera Mitiku. *God as Father in Paul Kinship Language and Identity Formation in Early Christianity*. Eugene, OR: Pickwick, 2013.
Merrigan, T., and B. Lemmelijn. "From the God of the Fathers to God the Father: Trinity and Its Old Testament Background." *Louvain studies*. 31, nos. 3/4 (2006) 175–95.
Merrill, Eugene H. *Deuteronomy*. The New American Commentary. Nashville: Broadman & Holman, 1994.
———. "Remembering: A Central Theme in Biblical Worship." *Journal of the Evangelical Theological Society* 43, no. 1 (2000) 27–36.
Metzger, Bruce Manning, and United Bible Societies. *A Textual Commentary on the Greek New Testament, Second Edition, a Companion Volume to the United Bible Societies' Greek New Testament*. 4th rev. ed. Stuttgart: United Bible Societies, 1994.
Meyer, Paul W. "'The Father': The Presentation of God in the Fourth Gospel." In *Exploring the Gospel of John: In Honor of D. Moody Smith*, edited by D. Moody Smith, R. Alan Culpepper, and C. Clifton Black, 255–73. Louisville: Westminster John Knox, 1996.
Meyers, Richard J. "The Meaning and Significance of the Messianic Epithets in Isaiah 9:6." ThM thesis, Dallas Theological Seminary, 1992.
Michaels, J. Ramsey. *1 Peter*. Word Biblical Commentary. Nashville: Thomas Nelson, 1988.
Michel, Otto. "μιμνήσκομαι." In *TDNT*, 4:675–83.
Miley, John. *Systematic Theology*, Vol 1. New York: Hunt & Eaton, 1892.
Milgrom, Jacob. *Numbers: The Traditional Hebrew Text with the New JPS Translation*. JPS Torah/Bible Commentary. Philadelphia: Jewish Publication Society of America, 1990.
Miller, J. W. *Calling God "Father": Essays on the Bible, Fatherhood and Culture*. 2nd ed. Mahwah, NJ: Paulist, 1999.
Miller, Stephen R. *Daniel*. The New American Commentary. Nashville: Broadman & Holman, 1994.
Moffatt, James. *The First Epistle of Paul to the Corinthians*. Moffatt New Testament Commentary. London: Hodder and Stoughton, 1938.
Moltmann, Jürgen. *God in Creation: A New Theology of Creation and the Spirit of God*. Minneapolis: Fortress, 1993.

———. *History and the Triune God: Contributions to Trinitarian Theology*. New York: Crossroad, 1992.
Montagu, Jeremy. *Musical Instruments of the Bible*. Lanham, MD: Scarecrow, 2002.
Montefiore, H. A. *A Commentary on the Epistle to the Hebrews*. London: Black, 1964.
———. "God as Father in the Synoptic Gospels." *New Testament Studies* 3, no. 1 (1956) 31–46.
Moo, Douglas J. *The Epistle to the Romans*. The New International Commentary on the New Testament. Grand Rapids: Eerdmans, 1996.
———. *The Letter of James*. Pillar New Testament Commentary. Grand Rapids: Eerdmans, 2000.
———. *2 Peter, Jude*. NIV Application Commentary. Grand Rapids: Zondervan, 1997.
Morris, Leon. *The Epistle to the Romans*. Pillar New Testament Commentary. Grand Rapids: Eerdmans, 1988.
———. *The Gospel according to John*. The New International Commentary on the New Testament. Grand Rapids: Eerdmans, 1995.
Motyer, J. A. *Isaiah: An Introduction and Commentary*. Downers Grove, IL: IVP, 1999.
Moulton, James Hope. *A Grammar of New Testament Greek*. Vol. 1. Edinburgh: T. & T. Clark, 1998.
Mounce, Robert H. *Romans*. The New American Commentary. Nashville: Broadman & Holman, 1995.
Mowery, Robert L. "The Activity of God in the Gospel of Matthew." *Society of Biblical Literature Seminar Papers*, no. 28 (1989) 400–411.
———. "God, Lord and Father: The Theology of the Gospel of Matthew." *Biblical Research* 33 (1988) 24–36.
———. "God the Father in Luke-Acts." In *New Views on Luke and Acts*, edited by Earl Richard, 124–32. Collegeville, MN: Liturgical, 1990.
Müller, Jacobus Johannes. *The Epistles of Paul to the Philippians and to Philemon*. The New International Commentary on the New Testament. Grand Rapids: Eerdmans, 1955.
Muller, Richard A. *Post-Reformation Reformed Dogmatics: The Rise and Development of Reformed Orthodoxy, Ca. 1520 to Ca. 1725*. Grand Rapids: Baker Academics, 2003.
———. "Toward the *Pactum Salutis*: Locating the Origins of a Concept." *Mid-America Journal of Theology* 18 (2007) 11–65.
Murray, John. *The Epistle to the Romans: The English Text with Introduction, Exposition, and Notes*. The New International Commentary on the New Testament. Grand Rapids: Eerdmans, 1968.
———. *Redemption, Accomplished and Applied*. Grand Rapids: Eerdmans, 1975.
Nagel, Norman E. "The Lord Is One." *Concordia Journal* 29, no. 3 (2003) 294–301.
Nah, David S. "Who's Tampering with the Trinity? An Assessment of the Subordination Debate—by Millard J. Erickson." *Religious Studies Review* 36, no. 4 (2010) 274.
Natan, Yoel. *The Jewish Trinity: When Rabbis Believed in the Father, Son, and Holy Spirit*. Chula Vista, CA: Aventine, 2003.
Ng, E. Y. L. "Father-God Language and Old Testament Allusions in James." *Tyndale Bulletin* 54, no. 2 (2003) 41–54.
Ngien, Dennis. *Gifted Response: The Triune God as the Causative Agency of Our Responsive Worship*. Milton Keynes, UK: Paternoster, 2008.
———. "The Trinitarian Dynamic of Worship in John Calvin's Institutes (1559)." *Ephemerides theologicae Lovanienses* 83, no. 1 (2007) 23–51.

Nichols, James Albert, Caroleen Hillriegel, Lois Jones, and Freeman Barton. *Alpha and Omega: Essays on the Trinity in Honor of James A. Nichols, Jr.* Lenox, MA: Henceforth, 1980.

Niskanen, Paul. "YHWH as Father, Redeemer, and Potter in Isaiah 63:7—64:11." *Catholic Biblical Quarterly* 68, no. 3 (2006) 397–407.

Noble, T. A. "Our Knowledge of God according to John Calvin." *Evangelical Quarterly* 54 (1982) 2–13.

———. "Paradox in Gregory Nazianzen's Doctrine of the Trinity." In *Studia Patristica* 27, edited by Elizabeth A. Livingstone, 94–9. Louvain: Peeters, 1993.

Nolland, John. *The Gospel of Matthew: A Commentary on the Greek Text.* The New International Greek Testament Commentary. Grand Rapids: Eerdmans, 2005.

———. *Luke 1—9:20.* Word Biblical Commentary. Dallas: Word, 1989.

Nutzel, J. M. "προσκυνέω." In *EDNT*, 3:173.

O'Brien, Peter Thomas. *Colossians, Philemon.* Word Biblical Commentary. Waco, TX: Word, 1982.

———. *The Epistle to the Philippians: A Commentary on the Greek Text.* The New International Greek Testament Commentary. Grand Rapids: Eerdmans, 1991.

———. *The Letter to the Ephesians.* Pillar New Testament Commentary. Grand Rapids: Eerdmans, 1999.

O'Day, Gail R. "'Show Us the Father, and We Will Be Satisfied' (John 14:8)." *Semeia* 85 (1999) 11–18.

Oden, Thomas C. *The Living God: Systematic Theology.* San Francisco: HarperSanFrancisco, 1992.

Oh, Changlok. "Beholding the Glory of God in Christ: Communion with God in the Theology of John Owen (1616–83)." PhD diss., Westminster Theological Seminary, 2006.

Oliver, Richard S. "The Development and Evaluation of a Seminary Course in Worship Theology." DMin project, Dallas Theological Seminary, 2007.

Oliver, Robert W. *John Owen: The Man and His Theology.* Phillipsburg, NJ: Presbyterian & Reformed, 2002.

Ollerton, Andrew J. "*Quasi Deificari*: Deification in the Theology of John Calvin." *Westminster Theological Journal* 73, no. 2 (2011) 237–54.

Origen. *Commentary on the Gospel of John.* In *ANF*.

———. *On First Principles.* In *ANF*.

Osborne, Grant R. *Matthew.* Zondervan Exegetical Commentary on the New Testament. Grand Rapids: Zondervan, 2010.

———. *Revelation.* Baker Exegetical Commentary on the New Testament. Grand Rapids: Baker Academic, 2002.

Oswalt, John. *The Book of Isaiah.* Grand Rapids: Eerdmans, 1996.

Ovey, Michael J. *Your Will Be Done: Exploring Eternal Subordination, Divine Monarchy and Divine Humility* London: Latimer Trust, 2016.

Owen, John. *Biblical Theology, Or, the Nature, Origin, Development, and Study of Theological Truth, in Six Books: In Which Are Examined the Origins and Progress of Both True and False Religious Worship, and the Most Notable Declensions and Revivals of the Church, from the Very Beginning of the World.* Morgan, PA: Soli Deo Gloria, 1994.

———. *The Works of John Owen.* Edited by William H. Goold. 24 vols. London: T. & T. Clark, 2009.

Owen, John, Kelly M. Kapic, and Justin Taylor. *Overcoming Sin & Temptation*. Wheaton, IL: Crossway, 2006.
Owen, John, and Peter Toon. *The Correspondence of John Owen (1616-1683): With an Account of His Life and Work;* Cambridge: James Clarke, 1970.
Owen, Paul. "Calvin and Catholic Trinitarianism: An Examination of Robert Reymond's Understanding of the Trinity and His Appeal to John Calvin." *Calvin Theological Journal* 35, no. 2 (2000) 262–81.
Packer, J. I. *A Quest for Godliness: The Puritan Vision of the Christian Life*. Wheaton, IL: Crossway, 1990.
Parker, T. H. L. *Calvin's Doctrine of the Knowledge of God*. Rev. ed. Grand Rapids: Eerdmans, 1959.
———. *The Doctrine of the Knowledge of God: A Study in the Theology of John Calvin*. New York: Allenson, 1952.
Parry, Robin A. *Worshipping Trinity: Coming Back to the Heart of Worship*. 2nd ed. Eugene, OR: Cascade, 2012.
Parsons, Burk, ed. *John Calvin: A Heart for Devotion, Doctrine & Doxology*. Lake Mary, FL: Reformation Trust, 2008.
Partee, Charles. *The Theology of John Calvin*. Louisville: Westminster John Knox, 2008.
Peeler, Amy L. B. "'You Are My Son': The Family of God in the Epistle to the Hebrews." PhD diss., Princeton Theological Seminary, 2011.
Pelikan, Jaroslav. *The Christian Tradition: A History of the Development of Doctrine*. Chicago: University of Chicago Press, 1971.
Peterson, David. *Engaging with God: A Biblical Theology of Worship*. Grand Rapids: Eerdmans, 1993.
———. *Possessed by God: A New Testament Theology of Sanctification and Holiness*. Downers Grove, IL: IVP, 1995.
Peterson, Robert A. "Union with Christ in the Gospel of John." *Presbyterion* 39, no. 1 (2013) 9–29.
Petuchowski, Jakob Josef. "'Do This in Remembrance of Me' (1 Cor 11:24)." *Journal of Biblical Literature* 76, no. 4 (1957) 293–98.
Pierce, Timothy M., and E. Ray Clendenen. *Enthroned on Our Praise: An Old Testament Theology of Worship*. Nashville: B & H Academic, 2008.
Piper, John. "Are There Two Wills in God?" In *Still Sovereign: Contemporary Perspectives on Election, Foreknowledge, and Grace,* edited by Thomas R. Schreiner and Bruce A. Ware, 107–31. Grand Rapids: Baker, 2000.
———. "Prolegomena to Understanding Romans 9:14–15: An Interpretation of Exodus 33:19." *Journal of the Evangelical Theological Society* 22, no. 3 (1979) 203–16.
Piper, John, and Jonathan Edwards. *God's Passion for His Glory: Living the Vision of Jonathan Edwards, with the Complete Text of the End for Which God Created the World*. Wheaton, IL: Crossway, 1998.
Piper, John, Justin Taylor, and Paul Kjoss Helseth, eds. *Beyond the Bounds: Open Theism and the Undermining of Biblical Christianity*. Wheaton, IL: Crossway, 2003.
Polhill, John B. *Acts*. The New American Commentary. Nashville: Broadman & Holman, 1995.
Rahner, Karl. *The Trinity*. Translated by Catherine Mowry La Cugna. New York: Crossroad, 2005.
Rainbow, Paul Andrew. "Monotheism and Christology in I Corinthians 8.4–6." PhD diss., University of Oxford, 1987.

Rakestraw, Robert V. "Becoming Like God: An Evangelical Doctrine of Theosis." *Journal of the Evangelical Theological Society* 40, no. 2 (1997) 257–69.

Ralston, Tim. "'Remember' and Worship." *Reformation and Revival* 9, no. 3 (2000) 77–89.

Rehnman, Sebastian. *Divine Discourse: The Theological Methodology of John Owen*. Texts and Studies in Reformation and Post-Reformation Thought. Grand Rapids: Baker Academic, 2002.

Reid, J. K. S. *Calvin: Theological Treatises*. Louisville: Westminster John Knox, 1954.

Reinhartz, Adele. "'And the Word Was Begotten': Divine Epigenesis in the Gospel of John." *Semeia* no. 85 (1999) 83–103.

———. "Introduction: 'Father' as Metaphor in the Fourth Gospel." *Semeia* no. 85 (1999) 1–10.

Reymond, Robert L. *A New Systematic Theology of the Christian Faith*. Nashville: Thomas Nelson, 1998.

Rheaume, Randall. "Equality and Hierarchy within the God of John's Gospel." PhD diss., University of Wales, Lampeter, 2010.

———. "John's Jesus on Life Support: His Filial Relationship in John 5:26 and 6:57." *Trinity Journal* 33, no. 1 (2012) 49–75.

Richardson, Kurt A. "Calvin on the Trinity." In *John Calvin and Evangelical Theology: Legacy and Prospect: In Celebration of the Quincentenary of John Calvin*, edited by Sung Wook Chung, 32–42. Louisville: Westminster John Knox, 2009.

Richardson, Neil. *Paul's Language about God*. Sheffield, UK: Sheffield Academic, 1994.

———. *James*. New American Commentary. Nashville: Broadman & Holman, 1997.

Rico, Samuel Lewis. "Thirsting for God: The Levitical Inheritance Motif in the Apocalypse." *Westminster Theological Journal* 74, no. 2 (2012) 417–33.

Ringe, Sharon H. "Reading Back, Reading Forward." *Semeia* 85 (1999) 189–94.

Robertson, S. "Sonship in John's Gospel." *Asia Journal of Theology* 25, no. 2 (2011) 315–33.

Rooker, Mark F. *Leviticus*. The New American Commentary. Nashville: Broadman & Holman, 2000.

Rösel, Martin. "The Reading and Translation of the Divine Name in the Masoretic Tradition and the Greek Pentateuch." *Journal for the Study of the Old Testament* 31, no. 4 (2007) 411–28.

Ross, Allen P. *Creation and Blessing: A Guide to the Study and Exposition of Genesis*. Grand Rapids: Baker, 1996.

———. "Did the Patriarchs Know the Name of the LORD?" In *Giving the Sense: Understanding and Using Old Testament Historical Texts*, edited by David M. Howard, Jr. and Michael A. Grisanti, 323–39. Grand Rapids: Kregel, 2003.

———. *Recalling the Hope of Glory: Biblical Worship from the Garden to the New Creation*. Grand Rapids: Kregel, 2006.

Rowe, C. Kavin. "Biblical Pressure and Trinitarian Hermeneutics." *Pro Ecclesia* 11, no. 3 (2002) 295–312.

Rowe, John Nigel. "Origen's Doctrine of Subordination." PhD diss., University of Leeds, 1982.

Sailhamer, John. *The Pentateuch as Narrative: A Biblical-Theological Commentary*. Grand Rapids: Zondervan, 1992.

Sanders, Fred. *The Image of the Immanent Trinity: Rahner's Rule and the Theological Interpretation of Scripture*. New York: Lang, 2005.

Sanders, John. *The God Who Risks: A Theology of Divine Providence.* Downers Grove, IL: IVP Academic, 2007.

Sanders, Matthew Lee. "Subordinate But Equal: The Intra-Trinitarian Subordination of the Son to the Father in the Theologies of P. T. Forsyth and Jürgen Moltmann." PhD diss., University of St Andrews, 2010.

Saville, Andy. "The Old Testament Is Explicitly Christian." *Churchman* 127, no. 1 (2013) 9–28.

Schelbert, Georg. *Abba Vater: Der Literarische Befund Vom Altaramäischen Bis Zu Den Späten Midrasch- Und Haggada-Werken in Auseinandersetzung Mit Den Thesen Von Joachim Jeremias.* Göttingen: Vandenhoeck & Ruprecht, 2011.

Schemm, Peter R. "Taxis or Praxis? Why Trinitarians Do Not Make Good Feminists." *Faith and Mission* 22, no. 1 (2004) 23–40.

Schmidt, W. H. "אֱלֹהִים *elohim* God." In *TLOT*, 115–26.

Schreiner, Thomas R. *1, 2 Peter, Jude.* The New American Commentary. Nashville: Broadman & Holman, 2003.

———. "Head Coverings, Prophecies, and the Trinity: 1 Corinthians 11:2–16." In *Recovering Biblical Manhood and Womanhood: A Response to Evangelical Feminism*, edited by John Piper and Wayne Grudem, 124–39. Wheaton, IL: Crossway, 1991.

———. *The King in His Beauty: A Biblical Theology of the Old and New Testaments.* Grand Rapids: Baker Academic, 2013.

———. *Romans.* Baker Exegetical Commentary on the New Testament. Grand Rapids: Baker, 1998.

Schreiner, Thomas R., and Matthew R. Crawford. *The Lord's Supper: Remembering and Proclaiming Christ Until He Comes.* Nashville: B & H Academic, 2010.

Scott, Julius J. "Archegos: The Salvation History of the Epistle to the Hebrews." *Journal of the Evangelical Theological Society* 29, no. 1 (1986) 47–54.

Selderhuis, H. J. *Calvin's Theology of the Psalms.* Texts and Studies in Reformation and Post-Reformation Thought. Grand Rapids: Baker Academic, 2007.

Sexton, Jason Scott. "The State of the Evangelical Trinitarian Resurgence." *Journal of the Evangelical Theological Society* 54, no. 4 (2011) 787–807.

Smalley, Stephen S. *The Revelation to John: A Commentary on the Greek Text of the Apocalypse.* Downers Grove, IL: IVP Academic, 2005.

Shedd, William G. T. *Dogmatic Theology.* Minneapolis: Klock & Klock, 1979.

Slotemaker, John Thomas. "John Calvin's Trinitarian Theology in the 1536 Institutes: The Distinction of Persons as a Key to His Theological Sources." In *Philosophy and Theology in the Long Middle Ages*, edited by Kent Emery et al., 781–810. Leiden: Brill, 2011.

Smail, Thomas Allan. *The Forgotten Father.* London: Hodder and Stoughton, 1980.

Smith, Billy K., and Franklin S. Page. *Amos, Obadiah, Jonah.* The New American Commentary. Nashville: Broadman & Holman, 1995.

Smith, Gary V. *Isaiah 1–39.* The New American Commentary. Nashville: Broadman & Holman, 2007.

———. *Isaiah 40–66.* The New American Commentary. Nashville: Broadman & Holman, 2009.

Smith, Gordon T. "The Sacraments and the Embodiment of Our Trinitarian Faith." In *Trinitarian Theology for the Church: Scripture, Community, Worship*, edited by

Daniel J. Treier and David Lauber, 185–203. Downers Grove, IL: IVP Academic, 2009.

Smith, Morton H. *Systematic Theology*. Greenville, SC: Greenville Seminary Press, 1994.

Soulen, R. Kendall. *The Divine Name(s) and the Holy Trinity*. Louisville: Westminster John Knox, 2011.

Spence, Alan. "John Owen and Trinitarian Agency." *Scottish Journal of Theology* 43, no. 2 (1990) 157–73.

Spencer, William David. "An Evangelical Statement on the Trinity." In *The New Evangelical Subordinatio*nism, edited by Dennis Jowers and Paul House, 213–22. Eugene, OR: Pickwick, 2012.

Spinks, Bryan D. "Trinitarian Belief and Worship." In *God's Life in Trinity*, edited by Miroslav Volf and Michael Welker, 211–22. Minneapolis: Fortress, 2006.

Starr, James M. *Sharers in Divine Nature: 2 Peter 1:4 in Its Hellenistic Context*. Stockholm: Almqvist & Wiksell, 2000.

Stein, Robert H. *Mark*. Baker Exegetical Commentary on the New Testament. Grand Rapids: Baker Academic, 2008.

Stibbe, M. W. G. "Telling the Father's Story: The Gospel of John as Narrative Theology." In *Challenging Perspectives on the Gospel of John*, edited by J. Lierman, 170–93. Tübingen: Mohr-Siebeck.

Storms, C. Samuel. *Chosen for Life: The Case for Divine Election*. Wheaton, IL: Crossway, 2007.

Strong, Augustus Hopkins. *Systematic Theology*. Philadelphia: American Baptist Publication Society, 1907.

Stover, Dale A. "The Pneumatology of John Owen: A Study of the Role of the Holy Spirit in Relation to the Shape of Theology." PhD diss., McGill University, Montreal, 1967.

Stuart, Douglas. *Exodus*. The New American Commentary. Nashville: Broadman & Holman, 2006.

———. *Hosea–Jonah*. Word Biblical Commentary. Waco, TX: Word, 1987.

Sweeney, Marvin A. *I & II Kings*. Old Testament Library. Richmond, VA: Westminster John Knox, 2007.

Swinburnson, Benjamin W. "John Calvin, Eternal Generation, a Communication of Essence: A Reexamination of His Views." *Kerux* 25, no. 1 (2010) 26–49.

Tan, Kim Huat. "The Shema and Early Christianity." *Tyndale Bulletin* 59, no. 2 (2008) 181–206.

Tasker, David. *Ancient Near Eastern Literature and the Hebrew Scriptures about the Fatherhood of God*. New York: Lang, 2004.

Taylor, Richard A., and E. Ray Clendenen. *Haggai, Malachi*. The New American Commentary. Nashville: Broadman & Holman, 2004.

Tertullien. "*Q. Septimii Florentis Tertulliani Adversus Praxean Liber*," *Tertullian's Treatise Against Praxeas*. Translated by Ernest Evans. London: SPCK, 1948.

Thayer, Joseph Henry. *Thayer's Greek-English Lexicon of the New Testament: Coded with the Numbering System from Strong's Exhaustive Concordance of the Bible*. Peabody, MA: Hendrickson, 1996.

Thiessen, Henry Clarence. *Introductory Lectures in Systematic Theology*. Grand Rapids: Eerdmans, 1949.

Thiessen, M. "'The Rock Was Christ': The Fluidity of Christ's Body in 1 Corinthians 10.4." *Journal for the Study of the New Testament* 36, no. 2 (2013) 103–26.

Thiselton, Anthony C. *The First Epistle to the Corinthians: A Commentary on the Greek Text*. The New International Greek Testament Commentary. Grand Rapids: Eerdmans, 2000.

Thomas, Robert L., and W. Wilkins. *Exhaustive Concordance of the Bible: Hebrew, Aramaic and Greek Dictionaries*. Anaheim, CA: Foundation, 1998.

Thompson, J. A. *The Book of Jeremiah*. New International Commentary on the Old Testament. Grand Rapids: Eerdmans, 1980.

———. *1, 2 Chronicles*. The New American Commentary. Nashville: Broadman & Holman, 1994.

Thompson, Marianne Meye. *The God of the Gospel of John*. Grand Rapids: Eerdmans, 2001.

———. *The Promise of the Father: Jesus and God in the New Testament*. Louisville: Westminster/John Knox, 2000.

Tigay, Jeffrey H. *Deuteronomy: The Traditional Hebrew Text with the New JPS Translation*. JPS Torah/Bible Commentary. Philadelphia: Jewish Publication Society of America, 1996.

Tillich, Paul. *Systematic Theology*. Chicago: University of Chicago Press, 1951.

Tolmie, D. Francois. "The Characterization of God in the Fourth Gospel." *Journal for the Study of the New Testament* 20, no. 69 (1998) 57–75.

Toon, Peter. *God's Statesman: The Life and Work of John Owen*. Grand Rapids: Zondervan, 1973.

———. *Our Triune God: A Biblical Portrayal of the Trinity*. Wheaton, IL: Victor, 1996.

Toorn, K. van der, Bob Becking, and Pieter Willem van der Horst. *Dictionary of Deities and Demons in the Bible*. Grand Rapids: Eerdmans, 1999.

Torrance, James B. *Worship, Community, and the Triune God of Grace*. Carlisle, UK: Paternoster, 1996.

Torrance, Thomas F. "Calvin's Doctrine of the Trinity." *Calvin Theological Journal* 25, no. 2 (1990) 165–93.

———. "The Christian Apprehension of God the Father." In *Speaking the Christian God: The Holy Trinity and the Challenge of Feminism*, edited by Alvin Kimel, 120–43. Grand Rapids: Eerdmans, 1992.

———. *The Christian Doctrine of God: One Being Three Persons*. Edinburgh: T. & T. Clark, 1996.

———. *Trinitarian Perspectives: Toward Doctrinal Agreement*. Edinburgh: T. & T. Clark, 1994.

Torrance, Thomas F., and Richard W. A. McKinney. *Creation, Christ, and Culture: Studies in Honour of T. F. Torrance*. Edinburgh: T. & T. Clark, 1976.

Treier, Daniel J., and David Lauber. *Trinitarian Theology for the Church: Scripture, Community, Worship*. Downers Grove, IL: IVP Academic, 2009.

Trueman, Carl R. *The Claims of Truth: John Owen's Trinitarian Theology*. Carlisle, UK: Paternoster, 1998.

———. "John Owen and Andrew Fuller." *Eusebia: The Bulletin of the Andrew Fuller Center for Baptist Studies* 9 (2008) 71–95.

———. *John Owen: Reformed Catholic, Renaissance Man*. Great Theologians Series. Aldershot, UK: Ashgate, 2007.

Tsumura, David Toshio. *The First Book of Samuel*. New International Commentary on the Old Testament. Grand Rapids: Eerdmans, 2007.

Underhill, Evelyn. *Worship*. New York: Harper, 1937.

VanGemeren, Willem A. "ABBA in the Old Testament?" *Journal of the Evangelical Theological Society* 31, no. 4 (1988) 385-98.

Van der Toorn, K. "God (I)." In *Dictionary of Deities and Demons in the Bible*, edited by. Bob Becking and Pieter W. van der Horst, 352-53. Grand Rapids: Eerdmans, 1999.

Van Eerden, Brad Lee. "John's Depiction of God the Father: An Analysis of the God Language in the Fourth Gospel." PhD diss., Dallas Theological Seminary, 2003.

Van Groningen, Gerard. "God, Names of." In *Baker Encyclopedia of the Bible*, edited by Walter A. Elwell and Barry J. Beitzel, 881-82. Grand Rapids: Baker, 1988.

Van Wijk-Bos, Johanna W. H. *Reimagining God: The Case for Scriptural Diversity*. Louisville: Westminster John Knox, 1995.

Verhoef, Pieter A. *The Books of Haggai and Malachi*. New International Commentary on the Old Testament. Grand Rapids: Eerdmans, 1987.

Vickers, Brian J. "The Lord's Supper: Celebrating the Past and Future in the Present." In *The Lord's Supper: Remembering and Proclaiming Christ Until He Comes*, edited by Thomas R. Schreiner and Matthew R. Crawford, 313-40. Nashville: B & H Academic, 2010.

Waaler, Erik. *The Shema and the First Commandment in First Corinthians: An Intertextual Approach to Paul's Re-Reading of Deuteronomy*. Tübingen: Mohr Siebeck, 2008.

Wainwright, Arthur William. *The Trinity in the New Testament*. London: SPCK, 1962.

Wainwright, Geoffrey. "Trinitarian Worship." In *Speaking the Christian God*, edited by Alvin Kimel, 209-21. Grand Rapids: Eerdmans, 1992.

Wallace, Daniel B. *Greek Grammar beyond the Basics: An Exegetical Syntax of the New Testament*. Grand Rapids: Zondervan, 1996.

Waltke, Bruce K. *The Book of Proverbs: Chapters 1-15*. New International Commentary on the Old Testament. Grand Rapids: Eerdmans, 2004.

———. *The Book of Proverbs: Chapters 15-31*. New International Commentary on the Old Testament. Grand Rapids: Eerdmans, 2005.

———. *A Commentary on Micah*. Grand Rapids: Eerdmans, 2007.

Wanamaker, Charles A. *The Epistles to the Thessalonians: A Commentary on the Greek Text*. The New International Greek Testament Commentary. Grand Rapids: Eerdmans, 1990.

Ware, Bruce A. "Christian Worship and Taxis within the Trinity." *Southern Baptist Journal of Theology* 16, no. 1 (2012) 28-42.

———. *Father, Son, and Holy Spirit: Relationships, Roles, and Relevance*. Wheaton, IL: Crossway, 2005.

———. *God's Greater Glory: The Exalted God of Scripture and the Christian Faith*. Wheaton, IL: Crossway, 2004.

———. *God's Lesser Glory: The Diminished God of Open Theism*. Wheaton, IL: Crossway, 2000.

———. *The Man Christ Jesus: Theological Reflections on the Humanity of Christ*. Wheaton, IL: Crossway, 2012.

———. "A Modified Calvinist Doctrine of God." In *Perspectives on the Doctrine of God: Four Views*, 76-120. Nashville: B & H Academic, 2008.

———. "Tampering with the Trinity: Does the Son Submit to His Father?" *Journal for Biblical Manhood and Womanhood* 6, no. 1 (2001) 1-17.

Ware, Bruce A., and John Starke, eds. *One God in Three Persons: Unity of Essence, Distinction of Persons, Implications for Life*. Wheaton, IL: Crossway, 2015.

Ware, Bruce A., Paul Helm, Roger E. Olson, and John Sanders. *Perspectives on the Doctrine of God: 4 Views*. Nashville: B & H Academic, 2008.

Warfield, Benjamin Breckinridge, and Ethelbert Dudley Warfield. *Calvin and Calvinism*. London: Oxford University Press, 1931.

Watts, Thomas A. "Two Wills in Christ? Contemporary Objections Considered in the Light of a Critical Examination of Maximus the Confessor's Disputation with Pyrrhus." *The Westminster Theological Journal* 71, no. 2 (2009) 455–87.

Webber, Robert E. *Ancient-Future Worship (Ancient-Future): Proclaiming and Enacting God's Narrative*. Grand Rapids: Baker, 2008.

Weedman, Mark. "Augustine's *De Trinitate* 5 and the Problem of the Divine Names 'Father' and 'Son.'" *Theological Studies* 72, no. 4 (2011) 768–86.

Wellum, Stephen J. "Irenic and Unpersuasive." *Journal for Biblical Manhood & Womanhood* 15, no. 2 (2010) 37–47.

Wenham, Gordon J. *The Book of Leviticus*. Grand Rapids: Eerdmans, 1979.

———. *Genesis. 1–15*. Word Biblical Commentary. Waco, TX: Word, 1987.

———. *Genesis. 16–50*. Dallas: Word, 1994.

———. *Numbers: An Introduction and Commentary*. Tyndale Old Testament Commentaries. Leicester, UK: IVP, 1981.

———. *The Psalter Reclaimed: Praying and Praising with the Psalms*. Wheaton, IL: Crossway, 2013.

Westminster Assembly. *The Westminster Confession of Faith: Edinburgh Edition*. Philadelphia: Young, 1851.

Whitman, Tyler R. "The End of the Incarnation: John Owen, Trinitarian Agency and Christology." *International Journal of Systematic Theology* 15, no. 3 (2013) 284–300.

Widdicombe, Peter. "Fatherhood and the Conception of God in Early Greek Christian Literature." *Anglican Theological Review* 82, no. 3 (2000) 519–36.

———. *The Fatherhood of God from Origen to Athanasius*. Oxford Theological Monographs. Oxford: Oxford University Press, 1994.

———. "The Fathers on the Father in the Gospel of John." *Semeia* no. 85 (1999) 105–25.

Wilterdink, Garret A. "Fatherhood of God in Calvin's Thought." *Reformed Review* 30, no. 1 (1976) 9–22.

Witherington, Ben, III. *The Acts of the Apostles: A Socio-Rhetorical Commentary*. Socio-Rhetorical Commentary. Grand Rapids: Eerdmans, 1997.

———. "Spirited Discourse about God Language in the New Testament." *Biblical Archaeology Review* 38, no. 3 (2012) 28.

Witherington, Ben, and Laura Michaels Ice. *The Shadow of the Almighty: Father, Son and Spirit in Biblical Perspective*. Grand Rapids: Eerdmans, 2002.

Won, Jonathan Jong-Chun. "Communion with Christ: An Exposition and Comparison of the Doctrine of Union and Communion with Christ in Calvin and the English Puritans." PhD diss., Westminster Theological Seminary, 1989.

Wood, Donald. "Maker of Heaven and Earth." *International Journal of Systematic Theology* 14, no. 4 (2012) 381–95.

Woudstra, Marten H. *The Book of Joshua*. New International Commentary on the Old Testament. Grand Rapids: Eerdmans, 1981.

Wright, Christopher J. H. *Knowing God the Father through the Old Testament*. Downers Grove, IL: IVP Academic, 2007.

———. *Knowing the Holy Spirit through the Old Testament*. Downers Grove, IL: IVP Academic, 2006.

Wright, N. T. "One God, One Lord." *The Christian Century* 130, no. 24 (2013) 22–27.

Wyatt, Peter. *Jesus Christ and Creation in the Theology of John Calvin*. Princeton Theological Monographs. Allison Park, PA: Pickwick, 1996.

Yamauchi, Edwin. "זָכַר" In *TWOT*, 241–43.

———. "חוה" In *TWOT*, 267–69.

Yarbrough, Robert W. *1–3 John*. Baker Exegetical Commentary on the New Testament. Grand Rapids: Baker Academic, 2008.

———. "Divine Election in the Gospel of John." In *Still Sovereign: Contemporary Perspectives on Election, Foreknowledge, and Grace*, edited by Thomas R. Schreiner and Bruce A. Ware, 47–62. Grand Rapids: Baker, 2000.

Yarnell, Malcolm B. *God the Trinity: Biblical Portraits*. Nashville: B & H Academic, 2016.

Young, Edward J. *The Book of Isaiah: The English Text, with Introduction, Exposition, and Notes*. Grand Rapids: Eerdmans, 1965.

Young, Pamela Dickey. "The Fatherhood of God at the Turn of Another Millennium." *Semeia* no. 85 (1999) 195–202.

Zemek, George J. "Grandeur and Grace: God's Transcendence and Immanence in Psalm 113." *Master's Seminary Journal* 1, no. 2 (1990) 129–48.

Author Index

Akin, Daniel L., 82n100
Alexander, T. Desmond, 160, 160n28
Alford, Henry, 37
Allen, David L., 111
Aloisi, John, 136n11
Aquinas, Thomas, 9, 10, 11, 46n102
Arnold, Clinton E., 72n48, 75n65
Athanasius, 5, 6, 6n20, 143
Augustine, 8, 9, 11n44, 118, 165, 167, 167n53
Ayres, Lewis, 6n20, 8
Azurdia, Arturo G., 198n69

Baars, Arie, 11n45, 12n47
Barackman, Floyd, 14
Barrett, Charles, 167
Barrick, William D., 35n48
Barth, Karl, 11n43, 84
Basil of Caesarea, 6, 96, 109, 176
Bauckham, Richard J., 29n22, 33, 41, 89, 128, 135n6
Bavinck, Herman, 22, 96
Beale, G. K., 92n36, 94n46, 101, 115n18, 130n77, 162n38, 170, 190n52
Beeley, Christopher A., 7
Belleville, Linda L., 39
Berkhof, Louis, 14, 22, 70n42, 72, 88
Bilezikian, Gilbert, 15, 164
Bird, Michael F., 100, 144
Block, Daniel I., 35n48
Boxall, Ian, 94
Bray, Gerald L., 2, 4, 5n17, 9, 9n36, 46, 200
Burk, Denny, 121n41
Burton, Ernest, 145n44
Butin, Philip W., 64

Butin, Philip W., 85n3

Calvin, John, 11, 12, 55, 46n102, 56, 64, 65, 65n25, 65n26, 66n26, 85, 85n3, 86, 86n11, 167
Campbell, Constantine, 137n15, 138n18
Carey, George L., 126n59
Carson, D. A., 50n116, 51n122, 67, 67n29, 115n18, 120n40, 124n53, 129n74, 136n12, 174n3, 181
Chafer, Lewis S., 62n11
Chambers, Talbot W., 43n95
Chapell, Bryan, 182n29
Chen, Diane G., 15n57, 43n92
Ciampa, Roy E., 138, 169
Clarke, Rosalind, 99n60
Claunch, Kyle, 11n45, 143n38
Cocceius, Johannes, 77n76
Cowan, Christopher, 52, 122n47, 123, 134, 158
Cranfield, C. E. B., 196n67
Culver, Robert D., 61, 63n15

Dahl, Nils, 1, 193n59
Dahms, J. V., 55n140, 167
Davis, Barry C., 36n57
De Vries, Simon J., 185n38
Doyle, Robert C., 12n47, 57n149
Duhm, Bernard, 63n13
Durand, Emmanuel, 11n40, 49, 200

Edwards, Jonathan, 174n1
Ellingworth, Paul, 111n1116
Enns, Paul, 70
Erickson, Millard J., 15, 16, 43n94, 59, 64n16, 118, 165n45

Feinberg, John S., 55n140, 62, 63n14, 69, 71n43
Ferguson, Sinclair B., 95
Fisher, Matthew, 1, 15, 44n96, 57, 122n45
Frame, John M., 64n17, 72n49, 90, 100n63, 101n72, 170
France, R. T., 159
Fuller, Andrew, 182

Garrett, Duane, 35
Gathercole, Simon, 33n38, 118
Gentry, Peter, 103, 104
Gerhardsson, Birger, 35n48
Gieschen, Charles A., 34n46, 126n59
Giles, Kevin, 15, 16, 45, 45n100, 55, 55n142
Gregory of Nazianzus, 7, 11n44, 136
Gregory of Nyssa, 6
Grudem, Wayne, 15, 44n97, 45n101, 61, 76
Grundmann, Walter, 80
Gunton, Colin, 11n45, 87, 96, 97
Guthrie, Donald, 89

Hamilton, James M., 103n76, 135n8, 154, 168, 169, 172
Harriman, James, 43n92
Harris, Murray J., 26, 29, 30, 37, 38, 52n129, 94n44, 96, 168n56
Helm, Paul, 11n44, 12n46, 98n59
Hill, Wesley, 153
Hodge, Charles, 64n16, 168
Hoehner, Harold W., 75n63, 94n45
Hoekema, Anthony, 148
Hofer, Andrew, 28n20
Holmes, Stephen R., 5n14, 33n39
Horrell, J. Scott, 15, 44, 55n140, 148n54
Horton, Michael, 90, 91, 101, 108
House, H. Wayne, 17, 49n115
Hurtado, Larry, 33
Hustad, Donald P., 177

Ice, Laura M., 15n57

Jeffery, Steve, 126n59
Johnson, Keith, 9
Jowers, Dennis W., 17

Justin Martyr, 3

Kapic, Kelly M., 13n50
Kauflin, Bob, 198, 198n70
Keener, Craig, 164
Knight, George W., 74n58
Koessler, John, 2
Köstenberger, Andreas, 1, 15, 56n147, 68, 116n20, 123, 127n65, 198
Kruse, Colin, 67n34, 138n16, 139
Ku, John, 10n38

Ladd, George E., 125n55, 155, 170
Leivestad, R., 184n34
Lenski, R. C. H., 39, 92n37, 167
Letham, Robert, 5, 9n37, 12, 13n50, 15, 46n105, 56n146, 88, 89n21, 176, 198
Lewis, Peter, 106
Lincoln, Andrew T., 92n35
Lister, Ryan, 91

Macaskill, Grant, 137n15
Marcellus of Ancyra, 167
Marshall, I. Howard, 148n52, 154n8
McCall, Thomas H., 15, 17, 49n115, 119n32
McClendon, Philip A., 177n12
Mengestu, Abera, 15n57, 43n92
Merrill, Eugene H., 178
Meyer, Paul W., 53
Meyers, Richard J., 43n95
Moltmann, Jürgen, 84
Moo, Douglas J., 35n49, 66n27, 76n72, 81, 81n94, 134n5, 192n57
Morris, Leon, 94, 95n50, 124n52, 127n61
Muller, Richard A., 77n76
Müller, Jacobus J., 140n26
Murray, John, 66, 127n63, 196

Noble, Thomas, 7
Nützel, J. M., 191

O'Brien, Peter, 75n62, 75n66, 107, 140
Oden, Thomas, 108
Origen, 5, 5n17, 10, 11, 55, 153n1
Osborne, Grant, 53n131, 73, 159

Oswalt, John, 161n34
Ovey, Michael J., 17, 51, 119, 126n59, 165, 166
Owen, John, 12, 13, 13n51, 14, 77, 77n77, 77n79, 78, 78n82, 79, 127n64, 186, 187n42

Parry, Robin A., 109n92, 187
Partee, Charles, 85n5
Peeler, Amy, 43n92
Peterson, David, 147, 147n49, 150n63, 189
Peterson, Robert, 137
Piper, John, 82n98

Rahner, Karl, 28, 28n19, 31, 37
Rainbow, Paul, 93
Rakestraw, Robert V., 149
Ralston, Tim, 179
Rheaume, Randy, 51n122
Richardson, Kurt A., 79
Rico, Samuel, 163, 163n42
Rosner, Brian, 138, 169
Ross, Allen P., 23n8, 188
Rowe, C. Kavin, 28n20, 28n21

Sach, Andrew, 126n59
Sanders, Fred, 136n10
Saville, Andy, 34n43
Schreiner, Thomas, 30n27, 74n59, 102, 127n61, 157
Shillaker, Robert, 144
Smail, Thomas, 1, 2n4, 15n57, 45, 176
Smalley, Stephen, 71

Smith, Gordon T., 195
Soulen, R. Kendall, 22
Spencer, William David, 21
Starke, John, 17
Stein, Robert H., 34n44, 81n95
Storms, C. Samuel, 75n61
Swain, Scott R., 1, 56n147, 68, 116n20, 123, 198

Tertullian, 4
Thiselton, Anthony, 142, 143
Thompson, Marianne Meye, 15n57, 122, 123
Toon, Peter, 29n22
Torrance, James B., 177
Torrance, T. F., 11n44, 43, 87, 98
Trueman, Carl, 79

Wainwright, Arthur, 106, 109n92, 187
Ware, Bruce A., 15, 16, 17, 49n115, 54n139, 60n2, 70, 84n1, 90, 91, 98, 105, 143, 176n6, 183n31,
Warfield, B. B., 11n44, 85n5
Wellum, Stephen, 103, 104, 119
Widdicombe, Peter, 5, 15n57, 44n98
Witherington, Ben, 15n57
Wright, Christopher, 29n22, 33, 99

Yarbrough, Robert W., 68n35
Yarnell, Malcolm, 55n140
Young, Edward J., 72n46, 160n31

Zemek, George J., 90n27

Subject Index

adoption, 144, 192

biblical spirituality, 177n12

Christocentric Trinitarianism, 19, 20, 109, 129, 181, 198, 200
Christomonism, 177, 200
compatibilism, 71, 71n43
consummation, 20, 58, 154
covenant of redemption, 68, 77, 77n76, 78
creation, 19, 57, 71, 84
creation by the Spirit, 95
creation through the Son, 87
creation, *ex nihilo*, 87, 91, 97

decree, 19, 57, 82
decree, characteristics of, 62, 63, 64
decree, determinations and allowances, 70
distinct appropriations, see Trinity, distinct appropriations of

Ecclesiology, Trinitarian shape of, 142
election, 64, 65, 74, 75, 76, 127
eternal generation, see God the Son, eternal generation of
eternal procession, see God the Holy Spirit, eternal procession of
eternal rewards, 158

filioque, 8, 141n27
foreknowledge, 66, 66n27, 76
forgiveness, 139

giving of the Holy Spirit, 19

God the Father, as *aitia*, 7, 8, 52, 165
God the Father, as *autotheos*, 5, 11
God the Father, as fountain of deity, 5, 8, 13n51, 28, 52, 54
God the Father, as initiator, 12, 14, 17, 22, 54, 57, 58, 86, 110, 119, 133, 152, 169, 179
God the Father, as *principium*, 8, 9, 52, 165
God the Father, authority of, 15, 17, 45, 125, 164, 166
God the Father, eternal name, 6, 43
God the Father, metaphor of, 1, 15, 15n57, 42, 201
God the Father, neglect of, 1, 9, 14, 200
God the Father, person of, 5
God the Father, priority of, 21
God the Father, unbegottenness of, 3, 5, 10n38, 58
God the Father, will of, 134
God the Holy Spirit, as "living water," 135, 135n7, 163, 171, 190n53
God the Holy Spirit, as *Adonai*, 36
God the Holy Spirit, as *kurios*, 41
God the Holy Spirit, as *theos*, 39
God the Holy Spirit, as *Yahweh*, 34
God the Holy Spirit, eternal name, 55
God the Holy Spirit, eternal procession of, 6, 8, 54, 58
God the Son, as "Eternal Father," 43n95
God the Son, as *Adonai*, 36
God the Son, as *Elohim*, 31
God the Son, as ideal worshipper, 183
God the Son, as *kurios*, 41
God the Son, as *monogenes*, 54–55n140
God the Son, as *theos*, 38

God the Son, as *Yahweh*, 33
God the Son, eternal generation of, 5, 11, 54, 58
God the Son, eternal name, 55

indwelling, 135
inseparable operations, see Trinity, inseparable operations of

judgment, 80, 81, 156
justification, 127n64, 138

miracles, 100, 101
modern subordination controversy, 15, 16, 17, 49n115, 143

Nicene Creed, 3n7, 7, 11n45, 17, 55n140
Nicene-Constantinople Creed, 11n44, 55, 87, 109

pactum salutis, see covenant of redemption
Paterology, definition of, x, 1n3, 17
penal, substitutionary atonement, 126, 126n59, 160
predestination, 64, 767
pro-Nicene Fathers, 6, 9, 11, 11n45, 47
providence, 19, 71, 84
providence by the Spirit, 97, 107
providence through the Son, 97, 106

reconciliation, 139
redemption, 57, 74, 139
regeneration, 141
resurrection, Trinitarian shape of, 154
revelation, 111
revelation by the Spirit, 112
revelation through the Son, 111

sanctification, 20, 146
Savoy Declaration, 77
sending of Son, 19, 117
servant songs of Isaiah, 63n13, 160
shema, 35

theodicy, 72n49
taxis, see Trinity *taxis* of
Trinity, differing roles, 53
Trinity, distinct appropriations of, 3, 12, 14, 57, 58, 118

Trinity, divine monarchy of, 7, 8, 17, 165, 166, 171, 172
Trinity, divine nature, 49. 50, 51, 52
Trinity, divine will of, 17
Trinity, immanence of, 90, 175
Trinity, incomprehensibility, 47
Trinity, inseparable operations of, 3, 8, 9, 11, 14, 56, 57, 58, 69, 79, 118, 151, 169
Trinity, mutual indwelling, 6, 56, 87
Trinity, personal names of, 22, 58
Trinity, proper names of, 22, 27, 58
Trinity, *taxis* of, 6, 14, 18, 19, 20, 22, 30, 46, 57, 58, 85, 152
Trinity, transcendence of, 90, 175
Trinity, unity of, 8, 17, 21, 58

unbegotten, see God the Father, unbegottenness of
unbelief, Trinitarian shape of, 150, 156
union with Christ, 19, 137

Westminster Confession of Faith, 77n78
Westminster Larger Catechism, 60
worship, church as New Covenant priesthood, 193
worship, church as New Covenant temple, 191
worship, definition of, 20, 177, 178
worship, evangelism as, 195
worship, God the Son the direct object, 125, 173, 181
worship, Holy Spirit worthy of, 109, 163n41, 173, 187
worship, Lord's supper, 184, 198
worship, prayer as, 192, 198
worship, preaching as, 198
worship, remembrance as, 178
worship, service as, 193
worship, singing as, 198
worship, spiritual fruit, 197
worship, spiritual gifts, 197
worship, spiritual sacrifices, 196
worship, submission as, 188
worship, terminates with the Father, 46, 135, 163, 179, 186
worship, Trinitarian shape of, 58, 109, 173, 176, 178

Scripture Index

Genesis

1–2	30, 113n9
1:1–3	88
1:1	19, 23
1:2	19, 31, 57, 95, 109
1:3	30
1:4	92
1:6–9	30
1:10	92
1:11	30
1:12	92
1:18	92
1:21	92
1:25	92
1:26–27	31, 100
1:26–28	160
1:26	31
1:31	92
2	23, 32
2:2	31
2:4	24n9, 89
2:5	24n9
2:7–9	24n9, 32
2:7	19, 25, 95, 109
2:15	24n9, 193
2:18	32
2:21–23	24n9, 32
3:1	24n9
3:8–9	24n9
3:13–14	24n9
3:15	113
3:22	24n9, 31
4:26	25n10
6:8	100
7:16	24n9
9:15–16	24n9
9:26	23n9
11:7	31
12	113n13
12:1–3	110
12:1–4	32n35
12:7–8	25n10, 32n35
13:4	25n10
14:19	89
14:22	89
15	26, 113n13
15:1–10	32n35
15:2	26n14, 35
15:8	26n14, 35
15:13–14	32n35
16:7–14	34, 114n15, 119n36
16:13	25n10
17:1	23n7
18	34n43
21:17–19	34, 114n15, 119n36
21:33	25n10
22:11–18	34, 119n36
22:12	114n15
22:16–18	32n35
24:3	23n9
24:7	23n9
24:12	23n9, 26n13
24:27	23n9, 26n13
24:42	23n9, 26n13
24:48	23n9, 26n13
26:24	24n9
26:25	25n10
27:20	24n9
28:13	23n9
28:21	24n9

Genesis (continued)

31:11–13	34, 114n15, 119n36
32:9	24n9
32:24–30	34, 119n36
41:38	108
48:15–16	34, 119n36
50:20	63

Exodus

2:14	108
2:24	179
3:1—4:17	114
3:2–6	34, 119n36
3:4–7	32n35
3:4	24n9
3:12	194
3:14	25, 86
3:15–16	24n9
3:15	32n35
3:18	24n9
4:5	24n9
4:10	26n14
4:23	194
5:1	24n9
5:3	24n9
5:22	26n14
6:2	24n9
6:3	23n8
6:5	179
6:7	24n9, 25
7:16	24n9, 194
8:10	24n9
8:26–28	24n9
9:1	24n9
9:13	24n9
9:16	32n35
9:28	24n9
9:30	24n9
10:3	24n9
10:7–8	24n9
10:16–17	24n9
10:25–26	24n9
10:26	194
12:14	179
13:3	179
13:9	179
13:21	108
14:19–22	34, 119n36
15:11	174
15:17	26n14
15:18	164
15:26	24n9
16:12	24n9, 25
18:1	24n9
19:3	24n9
19:5–6	194
20:2	24n9
20:5	24n9
20:7	24n9
20:8	179
20:10	24n9
20:12	24n9, 45
20:24	179, 185
23:17	26n14
23:19	24n9
23:20	32n35
23:25	24n9
24:8	32n35
25:1—26:30	188
26:31—31:18	188
29:42–46	189
29:45–46	25
29:46	24n9
31:3	107n86
32:11	24n9
32:27	24n9
33–34	48n109, 120
33:12—34:9	26n14
33:18	28
33:19	27–28, 134
34:6–7	28, 120
34:23	26n14, 27n16
34:24	24n9
34:26	24n9
34:34	34
35:31	107n86
40:34–38	114n16

Leviticus

4:22	24n9

11:44–45	24n9, 32n35
18:2	24n9
18:4	24n9
18:21	24n9
18:30	24n9
19:2–4	24n9
19:2	32n35
19:10	24n9
19:12	24n9, 32n35
19:14	24n9
19:18	197
19:25	24n9
19:31	24n9
19:34	24n9
19:36	24n9
20:7–8	32n35
20:7	24n9
20:24	24n9
20:26	32n35
21:6	24n9
21:8	24n9
21:12	24n9
21:21	24n9
22:33	24n9
23:22	24n9
23:28	24n9
23:40	24n9
23:43	24n9
24:22	24n9
25:17	24n9
25:38	24n9
25:55	24n9
26:1	24n9
26:13	24n9
26:42	179
26:44	24n9
26:45	24n9, 179

Numbers

1:53	194
3:7–8	194
4:23–24	194
4:26	194
10:9–10	24n9
11:25–29	108
11:29	161n35
15:41	24n9
22:18	24n9
23:21	24n9
27:16	24n9

Deuteronomy

1:6	24n9
1:10	24n9
1:11	24n9
1:19–21	24n9
1:25–26	24n9
1:30–32	24n9
1:41	24n9
2:7	24n9
2:29–30	24n9
2:33	24n9
2:36–37	24n9
3:3	24n9
3:18	24n9
3:20–22	24n9
3:24	26n14, 101
4:1–5	24n9
4:7	24n9
4:10	24n9
4:19	24n9
4:21	24n9
4:23–25	24n9
4:28	89
4:29–31	24n9
4:31	179
4:34–35	24n9
4:39–40	24n9
5:2	24n9
5:6	24n9
5:9	24n9
5:11–12	24n9
5:14–16	24n9
5:24–27	24n9
5:32–33	24n9
6:1–5	24n9
6:3	24n9
6:4–5	32n35
6:4–9	35n48
6:5	197
6:10	24n9
6:13	24n9, 32n35

Deuteronomy *(continued)*

6:15–17	24n9, 32n35
6:20	24n9
6:24–25	24n9
7:1–2	24n9
7:6	24n9
7:9	24n9, 117
7:12	24n9
7:16	24n9, 160, 194
7:18–25	24n9
8:2	24n9
8:3	32n35
8:5–7	24n9
8:10–11	24n9
8:14	24n9
8:18–20	24n9
9:3–7	24n9
9:16	24n9
9:23	24n9
9:26	26n14
10:9	24n9
10:12–13	194
10:12	24n9
10:14	24n9
10:17	27n16
10:20	24n9
10:22	24n9
11:1–2	24n9
11:12–13	24n9
11:13–21	35n48
11:22	24n9
11:25	24n9
11:27–31	24n9
12:1	24n9
12:4–12	24n9
12:5	189
12:15	24n9
12:18	24n9
12:20–21	24n9
12:27–31	24n9
13:3–5	24n9
13:10	24n9
13:12	24n9
13:16	24n9
13:18	24n9
14:1–2	24n9
14:21	24n9
14:23–26	24n9
14:29	24n9
15:4–7	24n9
15:10	24n9
15:14–15	24n9
15:18–21	24n9
15:37–41	35n48
16:1–2	24n9
16:5–11	24n9
16:15–22	24n9
17:1–2	24n9
17:8	24n9
17:12	24n9
17:14–15	24n9
17:19	24n9
18:5	24n9
18:7	24n9
18:9	24n9
18:12–16	24n9
18:15–22	32n35, 115
18:15	124, 161n35
19:1–3	24n9
19:8–10	24n9
19:14	24n9
20:1	24n9
20:4	24n9
20:13–18	24n9
21:1	24n9
21:5	24n9
21:10	24n9
21:23	24n9
22:5	24n9
23:5	24n9
23:14	24n9
23:18	24n9
23:20	24n9
23:23	25n9
24:4	25n9
24:9	25n9
24:13	25n9
24:18–19	25n9
25:15–16	25n9
25:19	25n9
26:1–5	25n9
26:5	24n9
26:10–16	25n9
26:17	24n9
26:19	25n9

27:2–10	25n9	2:11	25n9
28:1–2	25n9	3:3	25n9
28:8	25n9	3:9	25n9
28:13	25n9	3:13	26n14
28:15	25n9	4:1–9	180
28:45	25n9	4:5	25n9
28:47	25n9	4:23–24	25n9
28:52–53	25n9	5:13–16	34, 119n36
28:58	25n9	7:7	26n14
28:62	25n9	7:13	24n9
29:2	185	7:19–20	24n9
29:4	32n35, 185	8:7	25n9
29:6	25n9, 185	8:30–35	180
29:10	25n9	8:30	24n9
29:12	25n9	9:9	25n9
29:15	25n9	9:18–19	24n9
29:18	25n9	9:24	25n9
29:24–28	185	10:19	25n9
29:25	24n9	10:40	24n9
29:29	25n9, 185	10:42	24n9
30:1–10	25n9	13:14	24n9
30:6	185, 186n39	13:33	24n9
30:10–14	185	14:8–9	25n9
30:16	25n9	14:14	24n9
30:20	25n9	18:3	24n9
31:3	25n9	18:6	25n9
31:6	25n9, 32n35	22:3–5	25n9
31:11–13	25n9	22:5	194
31:26	25n9	22:16	24n9
32	33n40	22:19	25n9
32:3	24n9	22:22	24n9
32:4	33, 101n70, 117	22:24	24n9
32:15	23n7	22:29	25n9
32:21	32n35	22:34	24n9, 180
32:35	32n35, 103	23:3	25n9
32:39	103	23:5	25n9
32:43	32n35	23:8	25n9
33	180	23:10–11	25n9
34:10–12	115	23:1–16	180
		23:13–16	25n9
		24:2	24n9
Joshua		24:17	25n9
		24:18–19	24n9
1:9	25n9	24:24	25n9
1:11	25n9	24:27	24n9
1:13	25n9		
1:15	25n9		
1:17	25n9		

Judges

2:1–5	34, 119n36
2:12	24n9
3:7	25n9
4:6	24n9
5:3	24n9
6:10	25n9
6:11–14	34, 119n36
6:11–27	114n15
6:22	26n14
6:26	25n9
8:34	25n9
9:2	179n18
10:10	24n9
11:21	24n9
11:23	24n9
11:24	25n9
13:2–23	34, 119n36
13:8	26n14
16:28	26n14, 27n16, 179n18
20:18	24n9
21:3	24n9
24:2	24n9

Ruth

2:12	24n9

1 Samuel

1:11	179n18
2:2	24n9
2:25	24n9
3:3	24n9
4:1	180
4:4	24n9
6:20	24n9
7:8	25n9
7:12	180
10:19	24n9
12:6–18	180
12:9	25n9
12:12	25n9
12:14	25n9
12:19	25n9
13:13	25n9
13:14	32n35
14:41	24n9
14:45	24n9
15:15	25n9
15:21	25n9
15:30	25n9
17:45	24n9
20:12	24n9
23:10–11	24n9
25:29	25n9
25:32	24n9
25:34	24n9
30:6	25n9

2 Samuel

3:9	24n9
5:10	24n9
6:2	24n9
6:7	24n9
7:12–16	32n35
7:18–20	26n14
7:22	27n16
7:24	24n9
7:25	25n9
7:26–27	24n9
7:28	27n16
7:29	26n14
10:12	24n9
12:7	24n9
14:11	25n9
14:17	25n9
18:28	25n9
22:7	24n9
22:22	24n9
22:32	24n9
22:47	24n9
24:3	25n9
24:23–24	25n9

1 Kings

1:17	25n9
1:30	24n9
1:36	24n9
1:48	24n9

2:3	25n9	\multicolumn{2}{c}{2 Kings}
2:23	24n9		
2:26	26n14	2:14	24n9
3:5	24n9	5:11	25n9
3:7	25n9	9:6	24n9
5:3–5	25n9	10:18–18	160, 194
8:1–65	180	10:21–23	160, 194
8:15	24n9	10:31	24n9
8:17	24n9	14:25	24n9
8:20	24n9	16:2	25n9
8:23	24n9	17:7	25n9
8:25	24n9	17:9	25n9
8:28	25n9	17:14	25n9
8:53	26n14	17:16	25n9
8:57	25n9	17:19	25n9
8:59	25n9	17:39	25n9
8:60	24n9	18:5	24n9
8:61	25n9	18:12	25n9
8:65	25n9	18:22	25n9
9:9	25n9	19:4	25n9
10:9	25n9	19:19	25n9
11:4	25n9	19:15	24n9, 89
11:9	24n9	19:16	24n9
11:31	24n9	19:19–20	24n9
13:6	25n9	20:3	179n18
13:21	25n9	20:5	24n9
14:7	24n9	21:12	24n9
14:13	24n9	21:22	24n9
15:3–4	25n9	22:15	24n9
15:30	24n9	22:18	24n9
16:13	24n9	23:21	25n9
16:26	24n9		
16:33	24n9	\multicolumn{2}{c}{1 Chronicles}
17:1	24n9		
17:12	25n9	11:2	25n9
17:14	24n9	13:2	25n9
17:20–21	25n9	13:10	25n9
18:10	25n9	14:10	25n9
18:21	24n9	15:12	24n9
18:24	24n9	15:13	25n9
18:36–37	24n9	15:14	24n9
18:39	24n9	15:26	24n9
19:10	24n9	16:4	24n9, 180
19:14	24n9	16:14	25n9
22:53	24n9	16:26	89
		16:36	24n9
		17:16–17	25n9

1 Chronicles (continued)

17:20	24n9
17:22	24n9
17:24	24n9
17:26	24n9
19:13	24n9
21:15	24n9
21:17	24n9, 25n9
22:12	5n9
22:6	24n9
22:7	25n9
22:11–12	25n9
22:18–19	25n9
23:25	24n9
24:19	25n9
28:2	24n9
28:4	24n9
28:8	25n9
28:9	24n9
28:12	24n9
28:20	25n9
29:1	25n9
29:10	24n9
29:16	25n9
29:18	24n9
29:20	24n9, 25n9

2 Chronicles

1:1	25n9
1:9	25n9
2:4	25n9
5:1	24n9
6:4	24n9
6:7	24n9
6:10	24n9
6:14	24n9
6:16–17	24n9
6:19	25n9
6:41–42	25n9
6:42	179n18
7:22	24n9
9:8	25n9
10:15	24n9
11:16	24n9
13:5	24n9
13:10	24n9
13:11	25n9
13:12	24n9
13:18	24n9
14:2	25n9
14:4	24n9
14:7	25n9
14:11	25n9
15:4	24n9
15:9	25n9
15:12–13	24n9
16:7	25n9
18:13	24n9
18:31	24n9
19:4	24n9
19:7	25n9
20:6	24n9
20:15	24n9
20:19	24n9
20:20	25n9
20:29	24n9
21:10	24n9
21:12	24n9
22:7	24n9
24:7	24n9
24:9	24n9
24:18	24n9
24:24	24n9
26:5	24n9
26:16	25n9
26:18	25n9
27:6	25n9
28:5	25n9
28:6	24n9
28:9	24n9
28:10	25n9
28:24–25	24n9
29:5	24n9
29:6	25n9
29:10	24n9
30:1	24n9
30:5–7	24n9
30:8–9	25n9
30:19	24n9
30:22	24n9
31:6	25n9
31:20	24n9
32:8	25n9

32:11	25n9	9:3–5	25n9
32:16	25n9	9:6–7	99
32:17	24n9	9:6	19, 89
33:12	25n9	9:7	24n9
33:13	24n9	10:29	27n14, 27n16
33:16	24n9	10:34	25n9
33:17	25n9	13:14	179n18
33:18	24n9	13:31	179n18
34:8	25n9		
34:23	24n9		
34:26–27	24n9	## Job	
34:33	24n9, 25n9	1:8–9	24n9
35:3	25n9	2:3	24n9
36:5	25n9	5:10	100
36:12	25n9	5:13	30n24
36:13	24n9	14:5	72
36:15	24n9	33:4	19, 89, 95, 109
36:18	24n9	34:14–15	99
36:23	24n9	38–39	89
		42:2	63

Ezra

Psalms

1:2–3	24n9	2:1–12	32n35
1:5	24n9	2:6–9	157
2:68	24n9	2:7–9	14
3:8	24n9	2:7	54–55, 55n140
4:1	24n9	3:7	24n9
4:3	24n9	5:7	189
6:21–22	24n9	7:1	25n9
7:6	24n9	7:3	25n9
7:27	24n9	8:1	25, 27n14
7:28	25n9	8:2	32n35
8:28	24n9	8:4–6	32n35, 100
8:35	24n9	8:9	25, 27n14
9:5	25n9	13:3	25n9
9:8	25n9	14:1–7	32n35
9:15	24n9	14:2	24n9
10:11	24n9	16:2	26n14
		16:8–11	32n35
		18:6	24n9

Nehemiah

1:5	24n9	18:21	24n9
5:13	24n9	18:28	25n9
5:19	179n18	18:31	24n9
8:6	24n9	18:46	24n9
8:9	25n9	18:49	32n35
8:10	26n14	19:1	174

Psalms (continued)

20:7	25n9
22:1–8	32n35
22:1	78n82
22:22	32n35
22:27–28	180
22:30	194
24:1	32n35
24:5	24n9
25:6	179n18
29:2	25
29:10	102
30:2	25n9
30:8	26n14
30:12	25n9
31:5	32n35
31:14	24n9
33:6	19, 89, 95, 109
33:9	89
33:10–11	62
33:11	60
33:12	24n9
34:8	32n35
34:15–16	32n35
34:20	32n35
35:22	26n14
35:23	26n13
35:24	25n9
36:1	32n35
38:15	24n9, 26n14
38:21	24n9
39:4	72
40:3	24n9
40:5	25n9
40:6–8	14, 32n35, 120
40:7–8	78n82
40:8	76, 78n82
40:17	26n13
41:13	24n9
44:22	32n35
45:6	18, 31
45:7	78n82
46:7	24n9
46:11	24n9
47:1–9	102
47:5	24n9
48:1	24n9
48:8	24n9
50:1	25n9
51:11	108
53:1–6	32n35
54:4	26n13
55:16	24n9
56:10	24n9
58:6	24n9
59:5	24n9
68:2	26n14
68:3–4	23
68:8	23
68:16	24n9
68:17–19	36
68:17	26n13
68:26	24n9
68:32–35	23
68:32	26n13
69:6	27n16
69:9	32n35, 191n56
69:13	24n9
70:1	24n9
70:5	24n9
71:5	26n14
71:16	26n14
72:18	24n9
73:28	26n14, 27n16
74:17	72
75:8	127n62
76:11	25n9
78	33n40
78:23–24	32n35
80:4	24n9
80:19	24n9
81:10	25n9
82:6	32n35
84:3	24n9
84:8	24n9
84:11	25n9
86:12	26n13
88:1	24n9
89:8	24n9
89:26	78n82
89:27–28	32n35
89:50	179n18
90:2	89

90:17	26n13	115:1	174
91:2	24n9	115:3	64
91:11–12	32n35	115:4	89
92:13	24n9	115:12	179
93:1	102	116:5	24n9
94:11	32n35	118:6	32n35
94:22	24n9	118:22–23	32n35
94:23	25n9	118:26	32n35
95	33n40, 102	119:49	179n18
95:3–5	103	119:55	180
95:6–7	189	119:89–91	72
95:7–11	32n35	121:2	89
96:5	89	122:9	25n9
96:8	25	123:2	25n9
97:5	26n14	124:8	89
98:3	179	132:1	179n18
99:5	25n9	132:11	32n35
99:8–9	25n9	134:3	89
100:3	24n9	135:5	26n14
101:26	89	135:6	63
102:25–27	18, 33	135:7	100
102:25	89	135:13	25n9
103:17–18	180	135:15	89
103:19	102	139:16	72–73
104:1	25n9	140:7	27n14
104:4	32n35	144:15	24n9
104:24	62, 89	145:3	47
104:29–30	99	145:4	180
104:30	19, 95, 108	145:13	117
104:33	24n9	146:2	24n9
105	180	146:5	25n9
105:7	25n9	146:10	24n9, 164
105:8	179	147:7	24n9
106:4	179n18	147:12	24n9
106:45	179		
106:47	25n9		
106:48	24n9	Proverbs	
109:21	27n14		
109:26	25n9	2:5	24n9
110	36, 40, 168	3:19	89
110:1–7	32n35	3:34	32n35
111:4	185	8:25	55, 55n140
111:5	179	16:4	72
113:1–4	90, 175	16:33	72
113:4–9	91	8:22–30	78n82
113:5–9	90, 175	8:22–31	31
113:5	25n9		

Isaiah

1:9	32n35
1:10	24n9
1:24	26n14
2:8	89
3:1	26n14
3:15	26n14
3:17	26n14
6	115n19
6:1–12	34, 36
6:3	115n19, 198
6:8	31
6:10	115n19
7:7	26n14
7:11	25n9
7:14	31, 116
8:8	31
8:10	31
8:17–18	32n35
9:2	31
9:6–7	43n95
9:6	31
9:7	32n35, 164
10:16	26n14
10:22–23	32n35
10:23–24	26n14
10:33	26n14
11:2–3	32n35
11:4–5	159
13:6	155n14
13:9	155n14
14:26–27	72
14:27	63
17:6	24n9
19:4	26n14
21:10	24n9
21:17	24n9
22:5	26n14
22:12	26n14
22:14–15	26n14
24:15	24n9
25:1	24n9
25:8	26n14
25:9	24n9
26:13	25n9
28:11–12	32n35
28:16	26n14, 32n35, 35, 72
28:22	26n14
29:13	36, 150, 181
30:15	26n14
32:15	108
35:2	24n9
36:7	25n9
37:4	25n9
37:16–17	24n9
37:16	89
37:20	25n9
37:21	24n9
38:3	179n18
38:5	24n9
40:3	24n9, 34
40:8	32n35
40:10	26n14
40:12–28	64
40:12–31	89
40:13	29n22, 32n35
40:27–28	24n9
40:28	24n9, 47
41:4	94
41:8–9	194
41:13	25n9
41:17	24n9
41:29	194
42:1–9	32n35, 63n13, 160
42:1	78n82, 159, 160n30
42:6	78n82
42:8	25, 89
42:18–24	194
43:3	25n9
43:7	174
43:21	74n59, 174
44:1–8	185
44:2	72
44:6	94
44:22–23	185
45:3	24n9
45:5	24n9
45:18	24n9, 70–71
45:23–24	33
45:23	32n35
46:8–9	180
46:9–10	63

48:9–11	174	63:11	185
46:11	72	64:4	32n35
48:1–2	24n9	65:1–2	32n35
48:11	64	65:13	26n14
48:12	95	65:15	26n14
48:16	26n14	66:1–2	32n35
48:17	25n9	66:9	24n9
49:1–13	63n13, 160	66:19–21	198
49:4–5	24n9	66:19	180
49:5–6	63n13, 194		
49:6	32n35		
49:9	78n82	## Jeremiah	
49:14	26n14	1:6	26n14
49:22	26n14	2:17	25n9
50:4–9	26n14, 63n13, 160	2:19	26n14, 27n16
50:10	24n9	2:20	160, 194
51:15	25n9	2:22	26n14
51:17	127n62	3:13	25n9
51:20	24n9	3:21–23	25n9
51:22	27n16	3:25	25n9
52:4	26n14	4:10	26n14
52:10	24n9	5:4–5	24n9
52:12	24n9	5:14	24n9
52:13—53:12	32n35, 63n13, 160	5:19	25n9
53	78n82	5:24	25n9
53:1	31	7:3	24n9
53:10	14, 77	7:11	32n35
54:5	23	7:20	26n14
54:5–6	24n9	7:21	25n9
55:3	32n35, 115n18	7:28	25n9
55:5	25n9	8:14	25n9
55:7	24n9	9:15	25n9
56:7	32n35	9:24	34
56:8	26n14	10:10	24n9
57:15	91	10:12	89
59:13	24n9	11:3	25n9
59:20–21	32n35	13:12	25n9
60:9	25n9	13:16	25n9
60:19	24n9	14:13	26n14
61:1–3	32n35	14:21	179n18
61:1	26n14, 36	14:22	25n9
61:2	24n9	15:16	25n9
61:6	24n9	16:9	25n9
61:10	24n9	16:10	25n9
61:11	26n14	19:3	25n9
62:3	24n9	19:15	25n9
63:2–3	155n16	21:4	25n9
63:7	180		

Jeremiah (continued)

22:9	25n9
23:2	25n9
23:36	24n9
24:5	25n9
24:7	25n9
25:15	25n9, 127n62
25:27	25n9
26:13	25n9
26:16	25n9
27:4	25n9
27:21	25n9
28:2	25n9
28:14	25n9
29:4	25n9
29:8	25n9
29:21	25n9
29:25	25n9
30:2	25n9
30:9	25n9
31:1	24n9
31:6	25n9
31:18	25n9
31:23	25n9
31:31–34	33n35, 116, 185
31:33	24n9
31:35–37	72
32:14–15	25n9
32:17	26n14
32:25	26n14
32:27	24n9
32:36	25n9
33:4	25n9
33:25	100
34:2	25n9
34:13	25n9
35:13	25n9
35:17–19	25n9
37:3	25n9
37:7	25n9
38:17	25n9
39:16	25n9
40:2	25n9
42:3–6	25n9
42:9	24n9
42:13	25n9
42:15	24n9
42:18	24n9
42:20–21	25n9
43:1–2	25n9
43:10	24n9
44:2	24n9
44:7	24n9
44:11	24n9
44:25	24n9
44:26	26n14
45:2	24n9
46:10	26n14, 155n14
46:25	24n9
48:1	24n9
49:5	26n14
50:4	25n9
50:18	24n9
50:25	26n14
50:28	25n9
50:31	26n14
50:40	24n9
51:5	24n9
51:10	25n9
51:12	72
51:15	89
51:33	24n9

Lamentations

2:7	26n14
2:20	26n14
5:1	179n18

Ezekiel

2:4	26n14
3:11	26n14
3:27	26n14
4:14	26n14
5:5	26n14
5:7–8	26n14
5:11	26n14
6:3	26n14
6:11	26n14
7:2	26n14
7:5	26n14
8:1	26n14
9:8	26n14

SCRIPTURE INDEX

11:7–8	26n14	20:5	26n14, 27n16
11:13	26n14	20:7	25n9
11:16–17	26n14	20:9	64
11:21	26n14	20:19–20	25n9
12:10	26n14	20:27	26n14
12:19	26n14	20:30–31	26n14
12:23	26n14	20:33	26n14
12:25	26n14	20:36	26n14
12:28	26n14	20:39–40	26n14
13:3	26n14	20:44	26n14
13:8–9	26n14	20:47	26n14
13:13	26n14	20:49	26n14
13:16	26n14	21:7	26n14
13:18	26n14	21:13	26n14
13:20	26n14	21:24	26n14
14:4	26n14	21:26	26n14
14:6	26n14	21:28	26n14
14:11	26n14, 27n16	22:3	26n14
14:14	26n14	22:12	26n14
14:16	26n14	22:19	26n14
14:18	26n14	22:28	26n14
14:20–21	26n14	22:31	26n14
14:23	26n14	23:22	26n14
15:6	26n14	23:28	26n14
15:8	26n14	23:31–33	127n62
16:3	26n14	23:32	26n14
16:8	26n14	23:34–35	26n14
16:14	26n14	23:46	26n14
16:19	26n14	23:49	26n14
16:23	26n14	24:3	26n14
16:30	26n14	24:6	26n14
16:36	26n14	24:9	26n14
16:43	26n14	24:14	26n14
16:48	26n14	24:21	26n14
16:59	26n14	24:24	26n14
16:60	179	25:3	26n14
16:63	26n14	25:6	26n14
17:3	26n14	25:8	26n14
17:9	26n14	25:12–16	26n14
17:16	26n14	26:3	26n14
17:19	26n14	26:5	26n14
17:22	26n14	26:7	26n14
18:3	26n14	26:14–15	26n14
18:9	26n14	26:19	26n14
18:23	26n14	26:21	26n14
18:30	26n14	27:3	26n14
18:32	26n14	28:2	26n14
20:3	26n14	28:6	26n14

Ezekiel *(continued)*

28:10	26n14
28:12	26n14
28:22	26n14
28:24–25	26n14
28:26	25n9
29:3	26n14
29:8	26n14
29:13	26n14
29:16	26n14
29:19–20	26n14
30:2	26n14
30:3	155n14
30:6	26n14
30:10	26n14
30:13	26n14
30:22	26n14
31:10	26n14
31:15	26n14
31:18	26n14
32:3	26n14
32:8	26n14
32:11	26n14
32:14	26n14
32:16	26n14
32:31–32	26n14
33:11	26n14
33:25	26n14
33:27	26n14
34:2	26n14
34:8	26n14
34:10–11	26n14
34:15	26n14
34:17	26n14
34:20	26n14
34:24	24n9
34:30–31	26n14, 27n16
34:30	25n9
35:3	26n14
35:6	26n14
35:11	26n14
35:14	26n14
36:2–7	26n14
36:13–15	26n14
36:20–23	174
36:22–23	26n14, 185
36:22	72
36:23–32	36
36:25–32	33n35, 171, 185
36:31	185
36:32–33	26n14
36:37	26n14
37:3	26n14
37:5	26n14
37:9	26n14
37:12	26n14
37:19	26n14
37:21	26n14
38:3	26n14
38:10	26n14
38:14	26n14
38:17–18	26n14
38:21	26n14
39:1	26n14
39:5	26n14
39:8	26n14
39:10	26n14
39:13	26n14
39:17	26n14
39:20	26n14
39:22	25n9
39:25	26n14
39:28	25n9
39:29	26n14
40:1—47:12	34, 119n36
43:18–19	26n14
43:27	26n14
44:2	24n9
44:6	26n14
44:9	26n14
44:12	26n14
44:15	26n14
44:27	26n14
45:9	26n14
45:15	26n14
45:18	26n14
46:1	26n14
46:16	26n14
47:13	26n14
47:23	26n14
48:29	26n14

Daniel

2:21	70, 72–73
2:23	73n50
2:44	103, 160
4:3	103, 160
4:8–9	108
4:34–35	103, 160
4:35	70
6:26–27	160
7:9	86n11
7:13–14	33n35
7:14	103, 160, 164
7:18	103
7:27	103
9:3	26n13
9:4	27n16
9:9	26n13
9:10	25n9
9:13–14	25n9
9:15	26n13
9:17	26n13
9:19	26n13
9:20	25n9

Hosea

1:7	25n9
1:10	33n35
2:23	33n35
3:5	25n9
4:1	24n9
5:4	24n9
6:6	33n35
7:10	25n9
11:1	33n35
12:9	25n9
12:15	24n9
13:4	25n9
14:1	25n9

Joel

1:14	25n9
1:15	155n14
2:1	155n14
2:11	155n14
2:13–14	25n9
2:17	24n9
2:23	25n9
2:26–27	25n9
2:28–29	33n35, 161n35
2:31	155n14
3:13	155n16
3:14	155n14
3:17	25n9

Amos

1:8	26n14
3:7–8	26n14
3:7	112
3:11	26n14
3:13	27n16
4:2	26n14
4:5	26n14
4:11	24n9
4:13	24n9, 89
5:3	26n14
5:14–16	24n9
5:16	27n16
5:18	155n14
5:20	155n14
5:24–27	33n35
5:27	24n9
6:8	24n9, 27n16
6:14	24n9
7:1–2	26n14
7:4–6	26n14
7:8	26n14
8:1	26n14
8:3	26n14
8:9	26n14
8:11	26n14
9:5	26n14
9:8	26n14
9:15	25n9

Obadiah

1	26n14
15	155n14

Jonah

1:9	24n9
2:1	25n9
2:6	25n9
2:7	180
4:6	25n9

Micah

1:2	26n14
4:2	24n9
4:5	25n9
4:7	164
4:13	26n14
5:2–5	33n35
5:4	25n9, 78n82
6:6	24n9
6:8	24n9
7:7	24n9
7:10	5n9
7:17	25n9

Habakkuk

1:5	33n35
1:12	25n9
2:14	174
3:18	24n9
3:19	26n14

Zephaniah

1:7–8	155n14
1:7	27n14
1:14	155n14
2:7	25n9
2:9	24n9
3:2	24n9
3:17	25n9

Haggai

1:12	25n9
1:14	24n9
2:6	33n35, 72

Zechariah

1:1—6:8	34, 119n36
2:5	108
4	53n131
4:6	33n35
6:13	78n82
6:15	25n9
8:7	78n82
8:23	24n9
9:14	27n14
9:16	25n9
10	180
10:1	100
10:6	25n9
11:4	25n9
12:5	24n9
13:7	33n35
13:9	24n9
14:5	25n9
14:9	35n48

Malachi

1:2–3	33n35
1:11	25
1:14	26n14
2:10	35n48
2:16	24n9
2:17	24n9
3:1	26n14, 33n35, 78n82
3:2	80
3:3	108
3:14	24n9
4:5	155n14

Matthew

1:20	57
1:22–23	116
1:23	189
1:24	40n83
2:2	161
2:6	33n35
2:13	40n83
2:15	33n35

SCRIPTURE INDEX

2:19	40n83	12:4	142
3:2	125	12:6	190
3:3	34	12:7	33n35
3:11	159	12:8	122
3:16–17	122	12:9	183
3:16	141	12:18–21	32n35
3:17	32n35, 124	12:28	125, 141
4:3–10	124	12:31–32	159
4:4	32n35	12:32	14
4:6–7	32n35	13:11	125
4:10	32n35, 183	13:43	163
4:13–16	31	13:54	183
4:17	125	14:23	183
4:23	183	14:33	190
5:12	158	15:3	181
5:16	183	15:6	150
5:33	32n35, 195	15:7–9	36, 181
5:45	100, 104	15:8	150
5:48	32n35	15:13	36n53
6:1	158	15:19	141
6:4	158	15:31	125
6:6	158, 192	16:16	51n121, 89n24, 104n78
6:9–10	125		
6:9–13	198	16:27	158
6:9	192	17:5	32n35, 124, 184
6:10	103	18:5	124
6:18	158	18:14	148
6:24	195	18:19	192
6:26	104	19:4	31, 92
6:30–32	104	19:6	31
7:21–22	42	19:17	49–50
8:9	141	19:26	135
8:12	158	20:19	50
8:14	141	20:23	164
9:8	124–25, 183	20:28	161, 183
9:13	33n35	21–25	183
9:35	183	21:12	183
9:38	41, 192	21:13	32n35
10:7	125	21:16	32n35
10:28	157	21:42	32n35
10:29–30	63, 72	22:13	158
10:29	73, 104	22:16	124
10:40	124, 137	22:21	195
11:10	32n35, 33n35, 116	22:31–32	154
11:25–26	47, 125, 134	22:32	32n35, 99, 179n17
11:25	13, 41	22:37–39	197
11:27	31, 60–61, 118, 125	22:37	32n35, 35n48
		22:44	32n35, 36, 129

Matthew (continued)

23:39	154
23:47	184
24:22	81
24:29	33n35
24:30	33n35
24:31	152
24:36	154
25:30	158
25:31–46	158
25:34	62, 82, 158, 163
25:41	158
25:46	133, 152, 158
26:17–19	183
26:28	33n35
26:31	33n35
26:36	183
26:39	77
26:42	77
26:56	33n35
26:63	51n121, 89n24, 104n78
26:64	31, 32n35, 33n35, 36
27:11	161
27:39	32n35
27:43	32n35
27:46	32n35
28:2	40n83
28:9	190
28:17	190
28:18	31, 33n35, 118, 129, 164
28:19	42, 46, 50, 118

Mark

1:2	32n35, 33n35, 116
1:3	34
1:11	32n35, 124
1:14–15	124
1:21	183
1:24	120
1:35	118, 183
1:39	183
2:7	124
2:10	124
2:11–12	125, 183
2:28	32n44
3:1	183
3:29	159
4:11	125
5:19–20	34n44
5:19	41, 124
6:2	183
7:6–7	36, 181
7:6	150
7:8	130
7:13	150
7:28	34n44
8:38	154
9:7	32n35, 124, 184
9:12	32n35
9:29	183
9:37	124
9:43	158
9:47	192
9:48	158
10:6	31, 92
10:18	50
10:27	135
10:40	164
10:45	161, 183
11:3	34n44
11:9	32n35, 40n82
11:15	183
11:17	32n35
12:10–11	32n35
12:11	40n82
12:14	124
12:17	195
11:25	192
12:26	32n35, 99, 179n17
12:26–27	154
12:28–34	35n48
12:29–30	32n35, 40n82
12:29	42
12:30–33	197
12:32–33	32n35
12:33	33n35
12:35–37	34n44
12:36	32n35, 36, 40n82, 129
13:19–20	154

13:20	41, 81	2:15	41
13:26	33n35	2:20	184
13:27	152	2:22–23	120
13:32	154	2:22	40n84
13:35	34n44	2:23–24	40n82
14:12–16	183	2:26	40n84
14:27	33n35	2:27–32	183
14:36	77	2:29	41
14:50	33n35	2:32	32n35
14:62	32n35, 33n35 36	2:36–38	183
15:29	32n35	2:39	40n84
15:34	32n35	2:42–50	183
16:19	32n35, 36	3:4–6	34
		3:16	159
		3:21	183
	Luke	3:22	32n35, 122
1–2	114n17	4:3–12	124
1:6	40n84, 114	4:4	32n35
1:8–17	114	4:8	32n35, 40n82, 183
1:9	40n84	4:10–12	32n35
1:11	40n83	4:12	40n82
1:15–17	41, 116	4:15–16	183
1:17	33n35	4:18–19	32n35, 36, 40n82, 122
1:24–25	41	4:34	120
1:28	41	4:43	124
1:32–33	32n35, 164	4:44	183
1:32	41	5:16	183
1:34–35	57	5:17	40n84, 124
1:35	50, 121	5:21	124
1:37	121	5:24–26	125, 183
1:38	41	5:24	124
1:43	114n17	6:6	183
1:46–55	112	6:12	183
1:46–47	183	6:23	158
1:46	41	6:25	158
1:54	183	7:15–16	125, 183
1:55	32n35, 99	7:27	32n35, 33n35, 116
1:58	40n84	8:10	125
1:66	40n84	9:18	183
1:68–78	112	9:26	154
1:68–69	183	9:35	32n35, 74n60, 123, 184
1:68	41	9:42–43	125, 183
1:73	32n35, 99	9:48	124
1:76	33n35, 34, 41	10:2	41
2:9	40n83	10:9	125
2:11	114n17	10:10	118
2:14	183		

Luke (continued)

10:11	125
10:16	124
10:20	125
10:21–22	47, 125
10:21	41, 134
10:22	60–61
10:27	32n35, 40n82, 197
11:2	192
11:9	192
11:13	192
12:5	157
12:6	104
12:10	33n39
12:12	159
12:24	104
12:28	104
12:32	192
13:10	183
13:12–13	125, 183
13:29	163
13:35	40n82, 154
13:48–49	41n84
14:15	163
15:11–24	201
15:25–30	202
15:35–36	41n84
15:40	41n84
16:13	195
16:14	41n84
16:15	149
16:22–28	158
16:32	41n84
17:14–16	125, 183
17:32	184n34
18:7–8	154
18:19	50
18:25	41n84
18:27	135
19:10	41n84
19:20	41n84
19:38	40n82
18:42–43	125, 183
19:37	125, 183
19:46	32n35
19:47	183
20:1	183
20:17	32n35
20:25	195
20:37–38	154
20:37	32n35, 99, 179n17
20:42–43	32n35, 36, 129
20:42	40n82
21:26–27	33n35
21:37	183
22:7–15	183
22:19	184
22:20	33n35
22:22	77
22:28–30	164
22:34–35	36
22:42	77
23:46	32n35, 127
23:47	125, 183
24:49	79, 131
24:51–53	125, 183
24:52	189–90
22:69	129
23:35–36	32n35

John

1:1–2	52
1:1–3	50
1:1	33n39, 38, 43, 85
1:3–4	42
1:3	19, 30, 30n27, 85n3, 89, 93
1:6	116
1:10	93
1:12–13	19, 66
1:12	133, 145
1:13	80, 133, 141
1:14	17, 43, 44n96, 48, 57, 120, 161, 181, 189
1:17	48n109, 114, 120
1:18	34, 38, 44, 48, 50, 119, 161, 161n35, 175, 182, 189, 198
1:21	116
1:23	34
1:29–30	116
1:29	126

SCRIPTURE INDEX

1:31	116n21	5:7–8	171
1:32	52	5:17	85
1:33–34	116	5:18	53, 122
1:33	56n148, 116n21	5:19–20	45, 61, 123
1:36	126	5:20–29	50
1:45	32n35, 115	5:21	56, 60, 154
1:49	129	5:22	31, 158
1:51	129	5:23–24	117n28
2:1–11	123	5:23	56, 124–25, 150, 181, 183
2:13	183		
2:14–17	112on38, 83	5:25	154
2:17	32n35, 191n56	5:26	51, 51n122, 56, 82n97
2:19	128		
2:22	128, 184	5:27	158
2:23	183	5:28–29	113n10
3:2	100n63, 124n52	5:30	61, 77, 117n28, 183
3:3–8	80		
3:3	129	5:36–38	117n28, 124n52
3:5–8	95	5:42	150
3:5–6	141	5:43	48n109, 120
3:5	129, 171	5:44	149
3:8	141	5:46	19, 114
3:13	122	6:1–14	123
3:14	114n14	6:4	183
3:16–17	19, 119	6:14	32n35
3:16	44n97, 54, 54n140, 67, 78, 78n82	6:16–21	123
		6:27	48n109, 120
		6:29	117n28
3:17	51n122	6:31	32n35, 114n14
3:19	149	6:32–33	48, 121
3:27	136	6:32	101
3:28	116	6:35	34
3:31–35	122	6:37–44	49, 82n97
3:34	117n28, 125	6:37–38	14
3:35	45, 65n25	6:37	61, 66–67, 136
3:36	20, 133, 151	6:38–40	67, 81
4:10–24	171	6:38–39	117n28
4:10	135	6:38	77, 123–24, 183
4:14	51, 107	6:39	154
4:20–24	190, 195	6:40	141
4:23	135, 175, 179, 190, 198	6:44–65	175
		6:44–45	19
4:24	49, 76–77	6:44	117n28, 133, 136
4:34	117n28, 123–24, 183	6:45	137
		6:46	44
4:35–38	198	6:48	34
4:46–54	123	6:51	34
5:1–18	123		

John (continued)

6:57	51, 51n122, 56, 117n28
6:59	183
6:63	51
6:63	52n130
6:63	95, 107, 109, 120, 136, 155, 159
6:69	48, 48n109
7:1–10	183
7:16	117n28, 124
7:17	123
7:28–29	117n28
7:28	48, 121
7:33	117n28, 129
7:37–39	47n106, 171
7:38–39	51, 107, 135n7, 190n53
7:42	33n35
8:12	32n35, 34
8:16	117n28, 158
8:18	117n28
8:26–27	48, 121
8:26	117n28
8:28–29	45
8:28	56, 127, 161n35
8:29	117n28, 122, 124
8:38	45, 124
8:40	124
8:42	57, 117n28, 119, 150
8:47	150
8:49–50	125
8:49	45
8:54–55	125
8:55	45
8:56	34n43
8:58	34, 50
9:1–41	123
9:3–4	57
9:3	124n52
9:4	117n28, 123
9:5	34
9:16	48n110, 121
9:28	34
9:29	48n110, 114, 121
9:31	123
9:39–41	115n19
10:11	34
10:14–15	127n65
10:14	34
10:15	56
10:16	33n35, 184
10:17–18	126, 128
10:18	122
10:22	183
10:25	124n52
10:27–28	141
10:27	67, 137n13
10:28–29	20, 67, 147
10:29	53n135, 66, 133, 141
10:30	35n48, 53
10:32–33	123
10:32	57
10:34	32n35
10:36	67, 117n28
10:37–38	100n63, 124n52
10:37	57
10:38	19, 56–57
11:1–44	123
11:4	125
11:21–22	124n52
11:25	34, 129
11:27	48n109, 120
11:41–42	124n52
11:42	117n28
11:52	145
11:55	183
12:13	32n35, 40n82, 48n109, 120
12:27–28	126
12:32	137n13
12:38	32n35, 40n82
12:40	115n19, 151
12:41	19, 34, 36, 115
12:44–45	117n28, 124
12:49–50	124
12:49	117n28, 161n35
12:50	56
13:3	122, 129
13:16	53n135

13:20	117n28, 124	17:1–5	44
13:31–32	126	17:1	21, 68, 126
14:2	163	17:2	66–67, 127
14:6	34, 50	17:3	5, 39n74, 48, 117n28, 121, 133, 142
14:10	19, 56–57		
14:12	54		
14:16–17	52n130, 133–34	17:4–5	14, 50n116, 174n3
14:16	50, 151	17:4	125
14:17	137, 147n49	17:5	52, 68, 130
14:20	19, 56, 134–35, 191	17:6	66–67, 198
		17:8	117n28
14:21	50	17:9	66
14:23–24	150	17:7–14	50
14:24	117n28	17:11	53, 129, 147, 198
14:26	56n148, 124n53, 134, 136, 151, 186n39	17:13	129
		17:14	124
		17:15	147
14:27	31	17:17–18	20
14:28	45, 53	17:17	133, 146
14:31	124, 183	17:18	117n28, 147
15:1–2	147, 151	17:21–22	137
15:1	34	17:21	19, 21, 56
15:5	34	17:21, 23, 25; 20:21	
15:8	147		118n28
15:9	50, 124n53	17:22–24	50
15:10	124	17:22	53
15:15	124	17:23–24	21
15:16	60	17:23	50, 137, 147
15:19	60	17:24	50, 52, 54, 60, 66–67
15:21	117n28		
15:23–24	133, 150	17:25	48n110, 121
15:26	8, 50, 54, 112n8, 133–35, 136, 136n10, 141, 147n49, 151, 191	17:26	50, 137
		18:9	66
		18:11	127
		18:20	183
16:2–3	150	18:36	31, 129
16:5	117n28, 129	18:37	184
16:8–11	136	19:36	32n35
16:12–15	124n53	20:17	44, 129
16:13	136n9, 147n49	20:22	56n148
16:15	53, 136	20:28	33n39, 34, 38, 50, 181
16:17	129		
16:28	129	20:31	142
16:32	122	21:22	60
16:33	31		
17	50, 183		

Acts

1:4	79, 131
1:6–7	103
1:7	81
1:24	41
2:1–4	134
2:3	108
2:14–39	112
2:16–21	33n35, 161n35
2:19	100n63
2:20–21	40n82, 41n85
2:20	155n14
2:22	57, 100n63, 124
2:23	63–64, 72, 81, 126
2:24	128
2:25–28	32n35
2:25	40n82
2:30–31	32n35, 112
2:30	29, 115
2:32	128
2:33–36	129
2:33	29, 79, 131, 160n33
2:34	40n82
2:36	89
2:39	41, 134
2:47	40n84
3:12–26	112
3:13	29, 32n35, 99, 179n17
3:15	93, 128
3:18	29, 63, 112
3:20	41, 81
3:22–23	161n35
3:22	32n35, 40n82, 115
3:25–26	29
3:25	32n35, 99
4:10	128
4:11	32n35
4:23	77
4:24	41, 92
4:25–26	32n35
4:25	92n33, 112
4:26–27	115
4:26	40n82
4:27–28	63, 72
4:27	92n33
4:28	77, 126
4:29	41
4:30	100n63
5:3–4	39
5:9	41
5:14	41n85
5:19	40n83
5:30	29, 128
5:31	129
7:2–53	112
7:2	99
7:3–7	32n35
7:8	99
7:9–43	112
7:17	99
7:24	154n6
7:30–35	32n35
7:31–36	101
7:31–35	114
7:31	41
7:32	99, 179n17
7:33	41
7:37	115
7:42–43	33n35
7:44–50	112
7:44	114
7:49–50	32n35
7:51–53	112
7:53	114n15
7:55–56	101n67, 129
7:55	112
7:59–60	187n45, 192n58
8:22	41
8:24	41
8:25–26	40n84
8:25	41n85
8:39	40n84
9:2	34n44
9:31	40n84
10:36	31
10:38	122
10:40	128
10:42	80, 152, 156
10:44	133
11:16	41n85
11:18	184
12:7	40n83
12:10	41

12:17	40n84	26:18	32n35
13:2	41n85, 187n45, 192n58	26:23	32n35
		27:24	157
13:10	34n44		
13:17	101		

Romans

13:22–23	32n35, 115		
13:23	40n83, 101n68	1:1–2	47n108
13:30	128	1:2	19
13:32	112	1:2–3	58, 111
13:33–35	128	1:4	50, 89, 128, 128n70
13:33–34	32n35		
13:34	115	1:7	47n108, 135, 140
13:41	33n35	1:16	129
13:44	40n84, 41n85	1:17	117
13:47	32n35, 40n82, 81	1:18	133, 149
13:48–49	41n85	1:19–20	47
13:48	80, 185	1:21	149
14:15	51n121, 89n24, 92, 104n78	1:24	151
		1:25	92, 149–50
14:17	104	1:26	151
14:31	105	1:28	149, 151
15:12	100n63	1:30	149
15:17	40n82	2:4	149
15:35–36	41n85	2:5	151, 155n14
16:7	141n27	2:6–11	157
16:15	41	2:16	157
16:17	34n44	2:29	186n39
16:26	184	3:2	112
16:32	41n85	3:3	113
17:24–25	92	3:6	157
17:26–28	105	3:10–12	32n35
17:26	63, 72–73, 100	3:18	32n35
17:29	31	3:19	157
17:31	80, 128, 152, 156	3:23	150
18:25–26	34n44	3:24	127, 138–39
19:9	34n44	3:25	127
19:10	41n85	3:26	117, 139
19:11	100n63	3:29–30	35n48
19:20	41n85	3:30	32n35
19:23	34n44	4:2	113
20:28	39	4:3	32n35, 35, 99, 113
20:31	184n34	4:5	138
20:32	147	4:8	40n82
22:4	34n44	4:9	32n35, 35
24:14	34n44	4:13	32n35
24:15	113n10, 152	4:17	35n49, 113, 141
24:22	34n44	4:18	32n35, 35
26:6	112		

Romans *(continued)*

4:20	113, 180
4:21	113
4:22	32n35
4:24	35n49
5:1	31, 133
5:2	127, 195
5:5	141, 145, 191
5:8	78, 127
5:9–10	127
5:9	138–39, 158
5:10–11	139
5:11	195
5:12–21	161
6	196
6:4	128
6:10	128
6:17	192n56
6:22	146, 196
7:4	195
7:25	149n57, 192n56
8:3	117, 126
8:4	138n19
8:7	149
8:8–9	151
8:8	150
8:9	19, 50, 56n148, 141, 141n27
8:11	13, 128n70, 155
8:13	145, 192
8:14–18	20
8:14–17	146, 192
8:15–17	192
8:20–23	163
8:23	140
8:26–28	108
8:26	50
8:28–29	81n93
8:28	19, 105, 135, 145
8:29–30	75n64
8:29	66, 76, 81n94, 133
8:30	81, 134
8:31–132	145
8:32	126
8:33	76, 139
8:34	32n35, 36, 129
8:36	32n35
8:37	145
8:39	145
9–11	62
9:5	33n39, 38, 50, 76n73, 134n4
9:6	111
9:8	144
9:11	66, 75
9:13	33n35
9:14–15	60
9:15	134
9:17–18	81
9:17	181
9:18	60, 134
9:20–21	92
9:22–23	60
9:22	81, 151
9:23	58, 76, 81, 163
9:25–26	33n35
9:26	51n121, 89n24, 105n78
9:27–29	32n35
9:29	40n82
9:33	32n35, 35
10:2	181
10:9	128
10:11	32n35, 35
10:16	32n35, 40n82
10:19	32n35
10:21	32n35
11:2	66
11:3	40n82
11:8	32n35
11:11	32n35
11:26–27	32n35
11:27	33n35
11:33–36	47
11:33–35	64
11:33–34	62
11:33	60, 76, 190
11:34	29n22, 32n35, 40n82
11:36	13n51, 76, 109, 167, 190, 199
12:1–2	142
12:1	193, 196
12:11	41
12:19	32n35, 40n82, 103

13:1–4	142	2:9	32n35, 76
13:1	72–73	2:11–12	49
14:10	20, 152, 157	2:11	141n27
14:11	32n35	2:12	138, 141
14:12	20	2:14	141n27, 175
14:17	138n19	2:16	29n22, 32n35, 40n82
15:6–7	195		
15:6	184	3:5	41
15:8	117	3:6–7	129
15:9–10	32n35	3:9	142
15:9	184	3:10	140
15:11	40n82	3:14	158
15:13	145	3:16–17	142
15:14	161n35	3:16	30n24, 141
15:16	46, 111	3:19	30n24
15:30	46, 192	3:20	32n35, 40n82
15:33	140	3:23	30n24, 93
16:16	142	4:1	195
16:20	140, 187n45	5:5	155n14
16:25–27	182	5:17	94
16:25	145	5:19	94
16:26	19, 111	6:9–10	158
16:27	149n57, 190	6:9	58, 163
		6:11	138–39
1 Corinthians		6:13–14	142
		6:19–20	187
1	34	6:19–20	138
1:2	89	6:19	141
1:3	140	6:20	195
1:4–7	138	7	142
1:8	155n14	7:15	135
1:9	117	7:17	195
1:9	135	7:24	72, 195
1:18	129	7:40	141n27
1:21	175	8:4–6	35n48
1:24	129	8:4	32n35
1:27–28	66	8:6	14, 19, 30, 42, 85, 89, 93–94, 106, 142
1:30	31, 58, 129, 133, 140		
1:31	34, 41n85	10:4	33, 101, 101n70
2:1	117	10:26	32n35, 40n82
2:3–5	33n35	10:31	174, 195–96
2:4–5	138	11:3	93, 127n65, 143–44
2:5	145		
2:6–16	47	11:7	31
2:7	57, 75n64, 76, 111	11:8–9	32
2:9–11	146	11:16	142
		11:22	142

1 Corinthians (continued)

11:24	184, 33n35
12:3	141n27
12:4–6	142, 197
12:6	61
12:7	144
12:8–19	197
12:11	50, 60–61
12:13	144
12:18	20, 81, 142
12:20–30	197
12:24	20, 142
12:28	81, 100n63, 142
12:31	197
13:1–3	197
13:12	146, 161n35
14:21	32n35, 40n82
14:36	111
14:37	41
15:4	32n35
15:9	142
15:10	140
15:20–28	166
15:21–23	40
15:22–28	159
15:22	113, 161
15:24–28	20, 13, 166, 170
15:24	58, 153, 172, 176
15:25	32n35, 36, 40
15:27	32n35, 40, 58, 106
15:28	39–40, 58, 89, 93, 152–53, 172, 177
15:28	127n65
15:38	31
15:42–44	96
15:45	32, 161
15:47	32
15:50	58, 163
15:54–57	167
15:57	145
16:23	187n45

2 Corinthians

1:1	142
1:2–3	145
1:2	140
1:9–10	181, 192n56
1:10	145
1:18	113
1:20	117, 149n57, 195
1:21–22	46, 58, 133, 138
1:21	141
1:22	140
1:27–28	75
2:14	145
2:17	111, 195
3:3	33n35, 36, 46, 51n121, 89n24, 105n78
3:6	33n35, 95, 109, 155, 186n39, 195
3:16–18	34
3:17–18	42
3:17	33n39, 41, 108
3:18	133, 146
4:1	195
4:2	111
4:3–4	175
4:4	117
4:6–7	145
4:6	30, 30n26, 142
4:14	20, 128, 154
5:5	140
5:10	152, 157
5:11	20, 145
5:19	127
5:18–20	139
5:20	181, 195
5:21	19, 110, 126
6:1	181
6:16	51n121, 89n24, 105n78, 142, 144
6:18	40n82, 144
7:6	145
9:8	140
9:13	195
9:14	192
10–11	34
10:13	195
10:17	34
11:7	111
11:31	190
12:8	187n45, 192n58

13:4	20, 128, 154	**Ephesians**	
13:11	140		
13:13–14	21	1	68
13:13	42	1:2	140
13:14	21, 46, 50, 65	1:3–14	75, 109, 176
		1:3–6	14, 78
Galatians		1:3–5	76
		1:3	ix, 190
		1:4	x, 54, 60, 62–63, 68–69, 72, 82n97
1:1–4	113n11		
1:1	128	1:5–6	174
1:4–5	66	1:5	69, 144
1:5	190	1:7–9	ix
1:6	134	1:7–8	139
1:13	142	1:8–9	x
1:16	134	1:9–10	19, 68, 103, 108
1:22	142	1:10	x, 109, 129
1:24	190	1:11	57, 60, 62, 64, 69, 104–5
2:17	138		
2:20	177n12	1:12	174, 190
2:21	134	1:13	133
3:5	100n63, 141	1:14	140, 174, 190
3:6	32n35, 99, 139	1:17	32n35, 141
3:8	19, 32n35, 99, 113, 139	1:18–19	192
		1:19–20	13, 146
3:11	139	1:20	32n35, 36
3:16	32n35, 114n15	1:22	19, 32n35, 106, 110, 129, 143
3:17–21	19, 113		
3:18	99	2:4–5	141
3:20	35n48	2:6	161
3:26	144	2:7	20, 58, 152, 173
4:4	19, 44, 117	2:8	13, 134
4:5	144	2:9	14, 141
4:6	44, 46, 57n148	2:10–11	72
4:7	145	2:10	195
4:9	20, 133, 145, 192	2:16	127, 139
5:8	135	2:18	46, 49, 109, 127, 176, 186, 192
5:16	150		
5:18	150	2:19–21	191n55
5:21	58, 163	2:19	133, 142
5:22–23	197	2:20	32n35, 35
5:22	150	2:22	114, 191
5:25	150, 195	3:9–11	75n68
6:8	155	3:9	92, 111
6:18	187n45	3:10–11	129
		3:10	174
		3:11	62 68, 77
		3:12	127, 192

Ephesians (continued)

3:14–16	46
3:15	92, 110
3:19	133, 192
3:20	140n26, 145
3:21	152, 190
4:1	195
4:4–6	35n48
4:6	110
4:8	36
4:12	198
4:15	143
4:24	31, 146
4:30	140, 141n27
5:2	161
5:5	58, 163
5:6	158
5:18–20	193
5:19	184, 185n36
5:20	192n56
5:22	192n56
5:23	143–44
5:27	176
6:10–11	161

Philippians

1:2	140
1:6	154, 155n14
1:10	155n14
1:11	195
1:19	57n148, 141n27
1:27	195
1:29	13
2:6–11	128
2:6–8	57, 110
2:6	38, 53, 117, 120
2:9–11	109, 160n33, 176
2:9–10	181
2:9	19, 42, 129
2:10–11	19, 32n35, 110, 190
2:10	33
2:11	89, 113n8, 176
2:12–13	195
2:13	58, 72
2:15	144
2:16	155n14
3:3	49n112, 109, 141n27, 176, 186–87
3:14	155, 195
3:21	50
4:6	192
4:7	140
4:9	140
4:18	197
4:18–19	145
4:20	190
4:23	187n45

Colossians

1:2	140
1:3	106
1:6	140
1:9–11	192
1:12	139, 192n56
1:14	140
1:15–20	104
1:15	50, 53, 117, 146, 161, 189
1:16–17	19
1:16	30, 43n95, 57, 89, 94
1:17	13n51, 106
1:18	143
1:19	117
1:20–22	139
1:20	127
1:22	127
1:25	111
1:26–27	68
1:27	19, 133
1:29	192
2:2	68, 192
2:3	50
2:9	53, 181
2:10	143
2:12–13	141
2:12	128

2:13–14	127, 139	**2 Thessalonians**	
2:13	186		
2:15	129	1:1	142
2:19	143–44	1:2	140
3:1	19, 32n35, 36, 129	1:3	192n56
3:5–6	158	1:4	142, 158
3:10	31, 146	1:5	58, 157–58, 163
3:16–17	192n56	1:6–7	20, 154
3:16	161n35, 185, 185n36	1:10	155n14
		1:11–12	65n26
3:17	149n57	1:11	135
3:24	158	2:2–3	155n14
4:3	192	2:13	63, 66, 72–73, 76, 192n56
6:63	106		
		2:14	133, 133 135
		2:16–17	187n45, 192n58
1 Thessalonians		2:16	145
		3:5	145, 187n45, 192n58
1:1	142		
1:2	192n56	3:16	140, 187n45, 192n58
1:4	66, 145		
1:5	136	3:18	187n45
1:8	181		
1:10	128	**1 Timothy**	
2:2	111		
2:8–9	111	1:2	140
2:9	184n34	1:11	111
2:12	135, 195	1:12	187n45, 192n58
2:13	111, 181, 192n56	1:15	78n82
2:14	142	2:5	19, 35n48, 117, 161
3:9	192n56		
3:11–13	187n45, 192n58	2:7	81
4:1	195	2:13	31n30
4:3	142	3:5	142
4:7	135	3:15	51n121, 89n24, 105n78, 142
4:8	141		
4:14	20, 154	3:16	95
5:2	155n14	4:3–4	92
5:4	155n14	4:10	51n121, 89n24, 105n78, 192n56
5:9	76, 81, 146		
5:16–18	192	5:4	195
5:23	20, 140, 146	6:13	92
5:24	146	6:15–16	172
5:28	187n45	6:15	41
		6:16	47, 110
		6:17	192n56

2 Timothy

1:1	82
1:2	140
1:8–10	74
1:9	54, 62, 146
1:12	155n14, 192n56
1:16–18	187n45, 192n58
1:18	155n14
2:9	112
2:19	40n83
3:16	112
4:1	158
4:8	155n14
4:22	187n45, 192n58

Titus

1:1	74
1:2	74, 82
1:3	111
1:4	82n99, 140
1:16	133, 150
2:5	111
2:10	19, 112
2:13	33n39, 38, 50
2:14	32n35
3:4–7	139
3:4–6	141
3:4	117
4:5	112

Philemon

3	140
25	187n45

Hebrews

1:1–2	44n97, 85, 111
1:1	29, 43n95, 110
1:2–3	106
1:2	30, 30n27, 42, 57, 94
1:3	13n51, 19, 32n35, 36, 50, 53, 129, 146, 161, 189
1:5–6	55n140
1:5	32n35, 54, 78n82
1:6–7	32n35
1:8–9	31, 33n39, 131
1:8	18, 38
1:10–12	18, 33, 89
1:13	32n35, 36, 129
2:2	114n15
2:4	100n63
2:5–8	161
2:5	89
2:6–8	32n35
2:8	89
2:9	126
2:12–13	32n35, 131, 184
2:17	131
3:1–6	124
3:4	92
3:6	142
3:7–4:7	102
3:7	31n29, 112
3:12	51n121, 89n24, 105n78
3:13	161n35
3:14	31n29
3:15	32n35
3:18	151
4:3–5	151
4:3	32n35
4:4	31
4:5	32n35
4:10	31
4:14–16	184
4:14	132
4:16	49, 145, 193
5:1	114, 197
5:4	114
5:5–6	55n140
5:5	32n35, 54, 132
5:6	32n35, 36
5:7	128
5:10	32n35, 36, 132
6:4	105
6:6–7	105
6:13–14	32n35
6:13	99, 113
6:17	113
6:20	32n35, 36, 161

7:3	32n35, 36	10:37–38	181
7:17	32n35, 36	11:3	30, 111
7:19	145	11:4–7	181
7:21	32n35, 36, 40n82	11:6	158
7:25	132, 145, 184	11:7	100
8:1–2	129	11:8	32n35
8:1	32n35, 36, 184	11:10–11	181
8:2	41, 184	11:12	32n35
8:5	114	11:19	181
8:6	116	11:25	181
8:8–12	33n35, 116	11:27	181
8:8–11	40n82	12:2	32n35, 36, 100n64, 129
8:8	116		
8:9	101	12:5–7	145
9:11	161	12:5–6	40n82
9:14	51n121, 89n24, 105n78, 126, 146	12:9–10	145
		12:14	41
9:15	82	12:22	51n121, 89n24, 105n78
9:20	32n35, 114		
9:26–27	161	12:26	33n35
9:26	110	12:28–29	192n56
10:3	184	13:5	32n35
10:5–9	121	13:6	40n82
10:5–8	32n35	13:8	50
10:7	77, 183	13:13	193n59
10:8–10	78n82	13:15–16	197
10:9	77, 183	13:15	193
10:10	184	13:20	33n35, 128
10:12–13	32n35, 36	13:21	146
10:12	110, 129, 161		
10:14	184		
10:15–17	116		
10:15	112		
10:16–17	33n35	**James**	
10:16	40n82	1:1	105n79
10:18	184	1:5	192
10:19	49, 161, 193	1:7	41, 192
10:20–22	193	1:12	82, 162
10:20	49n113	1:13	64, 72
10:21–22	145	1:17	49, 105, 141n30, 145
10:22	33n35, 36, 49n113, 161		
		1:18	79, 141–42
10:23	116, 181	1:27	197
10:29–31	156	2:1	73n55, 105n79
10:30	32n35, 103	2:5	75, 82, 161
10:31	51n121, 89n24, 105n78	2:19	ix, 35n48, 150
		2:23	32n35, 99, 113, 179n17
10:36	192n56	2:26	150

James *(continued)*

3:9	31, 41, 73n55
3:12	79
4:4	73n55
4:5	141
4:6–8	73n55
4:6	32n35
4:7	161
4:9	41
4:12	157
4:13–15	72–73
4:15	41
5:4	40n82, 151
5:7–8	73n55
5:10–11	40n82
5:19	79

1 Peter

1:1–2	95
1:2	63, 140
1:3	133, 141
1:5	148
1:6–7	108
1:7–9	148n54
1:10–12	124n53
1:11	57n148, 141n27
1:15	49, 135, 149
1:16	32n35
1:19–20	54
1:20	62
1:21	128, 181
1:23	142
1:24–25	32n35
2:3–4	32n35
2:4–5	196
2:4	35, 74
2:5–7	32n35
2:5–6	142
2:5	114, 191
2:6	35, 74
2:7–8	81
2:9–10	175
2:9	32n35, 69, 74, 149, 161, 196
2:10	33n35
3:10–12	32n35
3:12	40n82, 145, 151
3:18	100n65, 127
3:20	100
3:21	100n65
3:22	110, 129
4:1	100n65
4:11	113n8, 149n57, 174
4:13	185
5:5	32n35
5:9	161
5:6–7	192
5:10–11	172
5:10	149

2 Peter

1:1–2	100n66
1:1	38
1:2	140, 149
1:3–4	148
1:4	82, 137
1:11	38n72
1:12–13	184
1:17–18	124
1:17	100n66
1:21	100n66, 112
2:4	100n66
2:5	100
2:9	41
2:11	41
2:21	154n9
3:1–2	184
3:2	154n9
3:5–6	100
3:5	30, 100n66
3:8–10	41
3:9	82, 154
3:10	155n14
3:12	82n103, 100n66, 155n14
3:13	82, 162
3:15	41
3:18	38n72, 154n9

1 John

1:1–2	48n111, 122
1:2	51
1:5	51n121
2:2	127
2:15–16	149
2:15	150
2:17	123
2:20	161n35
2:22–23	150
2:25	82
2:27	33n35, 161n35
3:1	67
3:2	20, 145–46, 155
3:8	127
3:9–10	147
3:10	150
3:20	148
3:24	135, 191
4:1	136
4:2–3	135, 191
4:2	56n148, 141n27
4:4	161
4:7–8	147
4:7	50, 133
4:8	49–50, 133, 150
4:9–13	50n117
4:9–10	44n97, 78, 122n43
4:9	119
4:10	68, 127
4:12	119
4:14	122n43, 126
4:13	135, 191
4:16	50
4:19	68
4:20	150
5:1	147
5:4	147–48
5:9–11	82n100
5:11–12	141
5:11	122n43
5:13	142
5:18	55n142, 147
5:20	39, 48, 50, 121, 133

2 John

3	140
8	158
9	150

3 John

11	150

Jude

1	135
3	195
4	150
5	101
9	40n82
24–25	149, 173, 202
24	80, 133, 151
25	152

Revelation

1:1	136n9
1:4–5	141
1:4	50n116, 53, 174n3
1:5	19, 129
1:6	32n35, 161, 171
1:7	33n35
1:8	49, 92, 92n37, 158, 171
1:9–10	136n9
1:9	171
1:13–18	130
1:13	33n35
1:17	94
2:7	32, 131n79, 162
2:8	94
2:10–11	162
2:11	131n79
2:17	131n79, 161
2:18	136n9
2:26	162
2:29	131n79
3:1	53n131, 56n148, 131n79, 136n9, 141n27

Revelation (continued)

Ref	Pages
3:5	162
3:6	131n79
3:12	78n82, 162
3:13	131n79
3:14	94–95, 136n9
3:21	162, 164
3:22	131n79
4:2–5	130
4:5	53n131, 56n148, 141n27
4:6	131
4:8	41, 92n37, 158, 171
4:10	191
4:11	19, 41, 71, 92, 104
5:1	130
5:5	71, 131
5:6–14	191
5:6	50n116, 53n131, 56n148, 141n27, 163n41, 174n3
5:7	71
5:9	66, 127
5:10	32n35, 171
5:13–14	131
5:13	128, 161, 163n41, 189
5:14	191
6:9–11	73
6:10	41
6:16–17	155
6:16	71
6:17	80
7:2–3	147
7:2	51n121, 89n24, 105n78
7:10	71, 161
7:11	191
7:14–17	163
7:15	58
7:16	162n36
7:17	171
8:4	147
9:20	156, 191
10:6	92
10:7	73, 136n9
10:10	191
11:4	40n82
11:15–19	170
11:15	33n35, 40n82
11:16	191
11:17–18	158
11:17	41, 92n37, 158n22, 171
11:18	152
12:5	129
12:10	171
13:1–8	191
13:4	156
13:8	54, 62, 82, 156
13:12	156, 191
13:15	156, 191
14:1	147
14:7	92, 191
14:9	191
14:10	127n62, 158
14:11	156, 191
14:12	148
14:14	33n35
14:19	155
15:1	155
15:3–4	184
15:3	41, 92n37, 158n22, 171
15:4	191
15:7–8	155
16:1	155
16:2	156, 191
16:5–7	156
16:6	41
16:7	92n37, 158n22, 171
16:9	156
16:11	156
16:14	155, 155n14
16:19	127n62, 156
16:21	156
17:1	73
17:2	156
17:8	62, 82
17:14	73n56
7:15–17	162
17:17	72–73
18:3	156

18:8	40n82, 92n37, 158n22, 156, 171
18:20	156
19:1–2	156
19:4	191
19:5	32n35
19:6–8	162
19:6	33n35, 41, 49, 171
19:7	185
19:11	161
19:14	161
19:15	156
19:16	130
19:17	156
19:19–21	191
19:20	156
20:4–5	152
20:4	171, 191
20:6	32n35, 155, 162
20:10–11	158
20:11	152
20:14	158
21:1–3	20
21:1–2	162
21:1–2	189n50
21:3	33n35, 92n38, 152, 163
21:4	162n36
21:5	93n38, 152, 162
21:6	92, 95
21:7	93n38, 163
21:8	158
21:10–11	162, 189n50
21:22	40n82, 92n37, 158n22, 161–62, 171, 189n50
21:23	50n116
21:27	82
22:1–5	171, 189n50, 199
22:1–3	20, 162
22:1	47, 163
22:2	32
22:3–5	174
22:3–4	161–63, 198
22:3	58, 94
22:4	147, 152
22:5–6	40n82
22:5	92n37, 152, 158n22, 161–62, 171
22:6	136n9
22:8	191
22:12–13	50
22:13	94, 130
22:14	32, 162
22:17	163, 171
22:19	32

www.ingramcontent.com/pod-product-compliance
Lightning Source LLC
Chambersburg PA
CBHW071933240426
43668CB00038B/1524